Innovations in Education

Innovations in Education

Reformers and Their Critics

Fifth Edition

John Martin Rich
The University of Texas at Austin

Allyn and Bacon, Inc.
Boston London Sydney Toronto

To Audrey

Copyright © 1988, 1985, 1981, 1978, 1975 by Allyn and Bacon, Inc.
A Division of Simon & Schuster
7 Wells Avenue
Newton, Massachusetts 02159

Innovations in education: reformers and their critics/ [compiled by]
   John Martin Rich.—5th ed.
      p. cm.
   Includes bibliographies and index.
   ISBN 0-205-11104-1 (pbk.)
   1. Educational innovations—United States. 2. Education—United
States—Philosophy. I. Rich, John Martin.
LB1027.3.I55 1987
370′.1—dc19   87-19861
                                                           CIP

Series editor: Susanne F. Canavan
Cover administrator: Linda K. Dickinson
Production coordinator: Helyn Pultz
Editorial-production service: TKM Productions
Cover designer: Susan Slovinsky

Printed in the United States of America

10 9 8 7 6 5 4 3 2 1 92 91 90 89 88 87

Contents

Preface

Education today is in a state of ferment. We hear about the loss of confidence in public education, the enrollment growth in private schools, the excellence movement, widespread changes in education at the state level, the reform of teacher education, merit raises, and the impending technological revolution in education. In light of these and other significant developments, a number of reformers have offered ideas for extricating education from the morass in which it finds itself. These writers are distinguished by their ability to break with tradition and the conventional modes of perceiving educational problems and situations. They have advanced some bold and imaginative proposals for transforming education.

All too frequently the proposals of these reformers are either accepted so uncritically that their ideas become dogmas rather than possible ways of liberating thought and action, or else they are rejected out of hand. In this book, selections by reformers are followed by those of their critics to overcome this problem. In this way readers can gain a balance of viewpoints, weigh reformers' strengths and weaknesses, and use the material to help develop their own positions.

There is considerable interest today in promising innovations and alternatives in education. They exhibit possibilities for new curricular and instructional patterns as well as a break with traditional forms of school organization and financial support. Both the pros and cons of these innovations and alternatives are presented here.

Thus the book consists of two parts. Part I contains representative selections by today's leading educational reformers. Part II is composed of selections, both pro and con, on the latest and most prominent educational innovations. The innovations presented may include but are not restricted to those advocated by the specific reformers in Part I. Introductions precede the main parts, laying the background for the ideas that follow. Readers may find it useful to read over the discussion questions and activities before reading the selections.

The fifth edition features changes in both parts of the book. In Part I, some new reformers and critics are introduced, more representative or up-to-date selections by earlier reformers are provided whenever appropriate, and some reformers who once were prominent but have faded have been deleted. New innovations and alternatives in Part II include the excellence movement, financial reform, teacher education programs, merit pay, and sex education. Other features include new selections for some of the innovations and alternatives retained from the fourth edition; updated suggested readings, biographies, and appendix; and new introductions, discussion questions, and activities wherever needed. The numerous teaching methodologies currently in use have not been included but have been left for methods courses.

I wish to thank the following reviewers for their useful ideas: Robert Beck, University of Minnesota; Arthur Brown, Wayne State University; Richard L. Hopkins, University of Maryland; Jim Rooney, Pennsylvania State University; and Paul Schumann, Loyola Marymount University. I am grateful to Philip J. Schwartz for valuable computer searches and bibliographic assistance, to Deborah C. Clark for her very helpful and efficient secretarial assistance, and to Susanne F. Canavan of Allyn and Bacon for her confidence in the project. I have also been encouraged to undertake this edition by favorable informal feedback by the many who successfully used the book in their classes and by the reactions of my own students.

While preparing this edition I have been impressed by the great ferment in education. I hope the reader, too, will be caught up in the intellectual excitement of contrasting ideas and vigorous search for solutions to today's most pressing educational problems.

Part I

Educational Reformers and Their Critics

Education today is under criticism. Many citizens believe that discipline in schools is far too lax; others believe that schools should return to the basics and fundamentals. Some students are concerned that schools and colleges do not adequately prepare them for the world of work; others find schools to be basically alienating institutions that deny them the freedom to learn as they choose. A number of reformers have joined this criticism with a more penetrating analysis of greater scope that seeks to locate the roots of the malaise. These reformers view many educational practices as anachronistic and dehumanizing and attempt to show how these conditions can be overcome and new ways of educating can be initiated.

Enrollments have declined in some school districts and funding has been shifted to other needed community services. Many agree that taxes are too high, with some communities even defeating school bond issues. Citizens are demanding that schools become more accountable and that both teachers and students demonstrate requisite competencies.

How should the dissatisfaction toward public education be handled? Reformers have addressed themselves to a wide range of problems and have offered a number of startling recommendations for reconceptualizing, restructuring, and revitalizing education. The essays in this anthology provide viewpoints that should inform, stimulate thought, and encourage readers to reason carefully in order to clarify their own thinking about the topics addressed. If, in fact, readers are able to accept neither the reformers' nor the critics' positions, then it is their task to explore beyond what is provided here. (The suggested readings and discussion questions and activities should help).

1

THE TASKS OF EDUCATIONAL
REFORM

Generally one thinks the purpose of reform is to amend what is defective, vicious, corrupt, or depraved. It also aims to remove an abuse, a wrong, or errors, and to make changes for the better. Reform, which means to correct, rectify, amend, and remedy by making something right which is wrong, also implies changing something to eliminate imperfections or effect a new form of character, as in changing a policy within an institution.

The two characteristic types of reform are programmatic and systemic. *Programmatic reform* refers to curricula and programs that are used in or influence organized instruction; it also is associated with innovation. An *innovation* is any new idea, method, or device that, in contrast to change, is deliberately introduced for some purpose. One could be an innovator but not a reformer, but every programmatic reformer is an innovator and much more, since he or she goes beyond merely introducing one or more innovations by developing an organized plan for change that may embody various innovations organized to achieve new goals. Thus both the scope and intent of programmatic reform differs from innovation.

Systemic reform pertains to authority relationships and the distribution and allocation of power and resources that control the educational system as a whole. It is often carried out beyond the school, drawing upon social and political forces with which reformers need to be aligned; it calls for a redistribution of power and resources. There has been considerable programmatic reform during this century but a dearth of systemic reform—which is generally understandable because of its threat to the educational power structure.

To perceive what is needed, reformers must be highly sensitive to abuses and imperfections and be dissatisfied and restless once they are uncovered; then they must develop a broad view and a bold vision of what is possible and seek to disseminate new ideas widely in hopes that the proposed reform will be implemented. While it is heartening to have strong organizational support, access to the media, and generous financial backing, few reformers can initially boast of such advantages. Some reformers may feel that their task has been completed once they write and speak to the widest possible audience. Others may go further by setting up learning experiments (Skinner), teaching in public or private schools (Holt), counseling students (Rogers), working with prospective teachers (Adler), raising funds to support reform programs (Jackson), teaching adults literacy skills (Freire), or setting up a free school (Neill).

THE CONTINUITY OF
EDUCATIONAL REFORM

Today's educational reform is part of a process that began many years ago. Of course current reform has some distinctive features, but it is indebted to a long and colorful history that can only be ignored at our peril. While today's reformers may wear flashy new shoes, they still stand on the shoulders of great thinkers of the past. Many of the earliest reformers' ideas were associated with a movement or an educational philosophy; therefore it may be helpful to see how each reformer relates to these broader patterns. Our survey will selectively focus on twentieth-century American educators but will relate them to European antecedents.

Sense Realism

Early European educational philosophy had an affect on twentieth-century American education by its opposition to formalism and abstraction in instruction, its deductive approach, its emphasis on rote learning, and its reliance upon the teacher's authority and the written word. In opposition to this prevailing system were Wolfang Ratich (1571–1635), John Amos Comenius (1592–1670), and Johann Heinrich Pestalozzi (1746–1827), who developed different principles of instruction sometimes known as *sense realism.*

Things should be studied before words because words and language itself are more abstract, according to the sense realism theory. For example, in a science demonstration, a thing or experiment would be shown first and then an explanation would follow. Everything was to be learned by an inductive process that Francis Bacon (1561–1626) had advocated. The young, said Comenius, should see real and useful things that can make an impression on the senses and the imagination. If the thing is not available, a representation should be used. Books should have pictures, diagrams, charts; and many pictures should be hung in the classroom. Too often students in traditional schools were required to learn by rote and therefore would not have necessarily understood the material committed to memory; thus rote learning was discouraged by sense realists.

Nature, said Pestalozzi, makes no sudden leaps but unfolds gradually. Consequently, every instructional act should be a small, scarcely perceptible addition to what the learner already knows. Material should become more complex only as the learner's intellectual abilities mature. Each step must be well mastered before the next step is taken. Objects are indispensable, Pestalozzi believed, and must precede pictures. The picture comes later and aids the child in making the transition to drawing, reading, and writing. The child does not just wait passively to receive objects of nature but takes an active role in analyzing and abstracting the qualities of the object. Instruction should proceed from the known to the unknown, from the concrete to the abstract, or from the particular to the general.

Twentieth-century progressives in Europe and America took up the principles of sense realism and combined them with their own ideas. Sense realism, however, was far more suited to elementary than to advanced instruction. It did not develop a sophisticated theory of how the mind works or explain the operations of higher cognitive processes. Nevertheless it was a salutary corrective and an important advance over the inflexible and authoritarian instructional practices of the period.

Romanticism

Sweeping across Western Europe and Russia in the late eighteenth and early nineteenth centuries, *romanticism* became a broad movement that greatly influenced poetry, prose, painting, architecture, music, education, and the tenor of thought. It sought a simpler life, elevated feelings and emotions over intellect, empathized and identified with the poor and downtrodden, deified the child, expressed a love of animals and the beauties of nature, and contrasted these charms to the corruptions and cruelties of urban life. Jean Jacques Rousseau (1712–1778), the leading French romantic, was a highly influential figure in political and educational thought, whose ideas also influenced literary sensibility. Rousseau believed that man is born free yet everywhere he is in the chains of corrupt institutions. One approach to removing these chains was to educate the child close to nature by removing him from organized social life. Thus Emile, Rousseau's imaginary pupil, would grow up naturally by letting the laws of nature unfold and not having to perform tasks before readiness was evident. Rousseau attacked the notion of original sin and depravity by declaring that the child is born good. He recognized different stages of growth, explaining how the tutor would relate to Emile at each stage, and the different materials and activities that would be appropriate to introduce in light of the child's naturally unfolding inner development. The program would emphasize activities and experiences, deemphasize book learning, seek to avoid bad habits and instill good ones, and restrict desires so that they are in proportion to the ability to fulfill them. By late adolescence, Emile would have acquired the requisite abilities to return to the larger society, learn from it, but not be corrupted by it.

Child-Centered Progressivism

Progressivism was both a movement and a philosophy for educating the child that developed in America and Western Europe during the early part of this century. It was based on placing the child centerstage in the educational process, emphasizing the child's needs and interests, striving to develop "the whole child"—not just the child's mind but the emotional, moral, social, and physical characteristics as well. Such educators as Francis W. Parker (1837–1902) adapted curriculum to the needs of individual learners and emphasized more active learning and less dependence on textbooks. William Heard Kilpatrick (1871–1965) opposed a curriculum composed of disparate subjects and instead promoted the use of student projects. For child-centered progressives, the teacher was no longer a taskmaster or authority figure but one who helped guide meaningful learning activities. The subject matter curriculum, which represents the way scholars organize knowledge, is not consonant with the way the child learns; consequently, programs were based more on the student's needs and interests and on valuable experiences and activities.

The child-centered progressives were influenced by sense realism and romanticism. Learning activities were usually approached inductively and were based upon concrete experiences before any generalizations were drawn. Progressive classrooms usually had many sensory objects—children's drawings, photographs of historical figures, bulletin boards, science displays, with live animals in some instances. Progressives believed in firsthand experiences that included frequent field trips.

As for romanticism, child-centered progressives held that the child was born basically good and therefore there is no need to place many restrictions on the child's self-expression. Although they did not educate the child away from society, they did believe in nature study and readiness for learning. Some progressives were more permissive with children than Rousseau advocated, and the teacher was more of an organizer of learning activities than a fount of knowledge. Pupil-teacher planning was promoted as not only a democratic procedure but one that would improve learning outcomes.

Child-centered progressivism was criticized by essentialists and other groups. *Essentialism* believes that the goals of education are to develop the mind and prepare people for citizenship responsibilities by having them study essential knowledge embodied in a subject curriculum that is taught by a knowledgeable teacher who expects students to respect authority and exhibit disciplined behavior. Essentialists charged progressives with neglecting basic knowledge, failing to discipline students properly, insufficiently developing their minds, and not preparing them adequately for citizenship responsibilities. Essentialism also rejected romanticism and the romantic view of the child.

Dewey's Pragmatism

Although John Dewey (1859–1952) was also considered a progressive as well as a pragmatist, he was not child-centered and criticized this branch of the movement for alleged excesses. Dewey claimed that one cannot develop a philosophy merely by doing just the opposite of what one is against. In other words, since the traditional teacher was usually authoritarian, the child-centered educator became permissive and laissez-faire; in opposition to subject matter developed in advance and neatly laid out in compartments, were substituted the techniques of teacher-pupil planning and reliance on firsthand experience; and in opposition to external discipline free activity was used.

Dewey sought the relationship between organized bodies of knowledge and the emerging interests and curiosities of the children. He agreed with child-centered educators that one should begin with children's interests, but differed from these educators by stating that one should connect these interests to what they ought to become interested in. The generic method of education, for Dewey, was the scientific method, which he believed could be applied to all areas of human inquiry by teaching problem solving. Reflective thinking or problem solving begins with an indeterminate situation where puzzlement arises, the problem is then defined, and an hypothesis is advanced to guide observation and the collection of data. The hypothesis is then elaborated and sometimes transformed to deal with the problem more expeditiously and effectively, and finally the hypothesis is tested by overt and imaginative action and is either accepted or rejected. If accepted, an indeterminate situation has been made more determinate; whereas if rejected, a new hypothesis will need to be introduced, elaborated, and tested.

Dewey's pragmatism related to his reflective thinking process. Rather than *truth,* Dewey preferred the term, *warranted assertibility* to refer to the end result of having hypotheses successfully tested. Once one reaches the final stage of the reflective thinking process and accepts the original hypothesis as fulfilling the conditions of the situation, and once it has been subject to public verification, one is warranted in asserting the statement. *Pragmatism,* in other words, holds that ideas must be referred to their consequences for their truth and meaning. Ideas become instruments for solving problems, attaining goals, and anticipating future experiences.

For Dewey, life is development and development is growth. Because the characteristics of life are growth, education is one with growth. Additionally, since growth is relative to nothing but further growth, education is not subordinate to anything except more education. Education, Dewey says, is a continuous reorganization, reconstruction, and transformation or experience that adds to the meaning of experience and improves the ability to deal with subsequent experience.

Although Dewey achieved a wide following, his ideas were criticized by many different groups and divergent philosophies. Most prominent were those who rejected his pragmatism because it renounced absolute truths and values. Some held that there are some truths that remain true for all times and places, and these are the truths that should constitute the curriculum. And one cannot be considered an educated person until having wrestled with these ideas. Moreover, in contrast to Dewey's emphasis on the educative process, critics insisted on concentrating more on assuring specific learning outcomes that are measurable. More recently, a group of reformers, referred to as romantic naturalists (though they may have had some affinities with progressivism), rejected Dewey's conviction that schools can be sufficiently improved to become fully educative institutions.

Romantic Naturalists

The *romantic naturalists* of the late 1960s and early 1970s shared some beliefs with the early progressives. Like the progressives, they believed that the child rather than the subject matter should be the focal point—the child's needs, interests, and concerns. They also objected to practices that stifled initiative, creativity, and freedom to develop, and sought to make the classroom a place where children were free to move about, question, and explore their interests.

But whereas the progressives believed that enlightenment and human progress could be provided by extending the benefits of a more responsive public education to all youth, such romantic naturalists as John Holt, Herbert Kohl,

Jonathan Kozol, and the early writings of Neil Postman and Charles Wein-gartner generally held that school systems have become highly bureaucratic institutions that establish unwarranted constraints over youth, stifling their creativity and alienating them from schools. Some urged open classrooms and free schools; others offered different alternatives.

Paul Goodman, for instance, while seeing a need for compulsory education in the primary grades, opposed its extension to the high school. He recommends that the funds for compulsory secondary education be turned over to youth to establish their own learning communities and enable them to be free to ex-periment with their own life styles and seek their self-identity. The funds could also be used to promote apprenticeship programs. Ivan Illich goes further by recommending that compulsory schooling be abolished, the whole system be dismantled, and society be deschooled. He proposes instead informal learning arrangements in the larger society that would be based on natural interest and curiosity and entered into voluntarily. Thus the faith that Dewey and the progressives had in innovative organized schooling was, from Illich's viewpoint, seriously misguided.

Although the romantic naturalists have concentrated on how the student can overcome alienating learning conditions, they have made less of a contri bution to curriculum theory. How the organizational and administrative struc-ture can be transformed so that their ideas could be effectively implemented is seldom discussed. Thus they have rarely concentrated on the power struc-ture and how it can be changed. Even Illich's deschooled society offers no as-surance that the kinds of learning networks envisioned will be successful be-cause the larger society itself remains essentially unchanged. Romantic naturalists also fall into Rousseau's trap in their belief in the basic goodness and natural curiosity of the child who, once freed from restrictions, will blos-som naturally. But what is known about child development today suggests that far more structure and guidance are needed than the romantic naturalists would provide, if the child is to develop healthily and become an educated person.

Humanistic Education

Humanistic education was a movement of the 1970s that had more in com-mon with early progressive education than did the views of the romantic naturalists. Humanistic education advocated the principles of treating the stu-dent as a person and integrating cognitive learning and affective experience.

Rational beings are people and must not be treated merely as means but also as ends in themselves. Thus the teacher would endeavor to gain an em-pathetic understanding of the students' feelings and values, and an understand-ing of how students perceive their schooling. Teachers should become more con-cerned with the personal development of each student than with acquiring bodies of knowledge. Teachers should seek to understand students as whole persons and avoid labeling them, since those who use labels apply a label to a behavior pattern and then posit the label as the cause of the behavior. Moreover labeling may legitimize mistreatment and set children apart from one another. Thus such labels as *slow learner, delinquent, troublemaker,* and others may prove self-defeating.

Humanistic educators agree that the affective side of education has been generally neglected by schools, more emphasis should be placed on it, and it should be more fully integrated with cognitive learning. The affective domain includes values, attitudes, feelings, and emotions. Many programs in values education have been instituted to enable students to develop greater awareness of their values and to think more critically and constructively about them so that their decisions will be better informed (see Part II on cognitive moral development and values clarification).

Numerous objections, however, have been raised against humanistic education. It is charged that such programs are likely to neglect the study of organized subject matter and the basics. There is concern by some parents that their children may be indoctrinated or inculcated with a set of values different from their own, and they insist that such matters should be the responsibility of the parents. Some educators claim that most teachers are not adequately prepared to handle affective education programs. Moreover, it is suggested that such programs are difficult to evaluate. Even some of the basic concepts in humanistic education are difficult to agree upon and are extremely complex. Nevertheless, despite these criticisms, the ideals of the early progressives of educating the "whole child" were carried forward effectively by some exceptional humanistic educators such as Carl Rogers.

Freudianism

Sigmund Freud (1856–1939), Austrian neurologist and father of psychoanalysis, had a vast influence on modern thought with his theory of psychoneurosis and his stress on the role of sexuality in human development. Freud believed that there are basic sex and aggressive drives and stated a hard determinism in which early childhood greatly influenced the structure of personality in adulthood. His psychoanalysis sought the roots of neuroses by unearthing from the unconscious repressed wishes and desires of childhood.

Freud's influence on education, though important, was indirect and diffuse. Psychoanalytic theory offered the notion of *sublimation,* which held that the gratification of instinctual impulses, usually of a sexual or aggressive nature, could be achieved by substituting socially accepted behavior for expression of the prohibited drives. Teachers were to recognize unconscious motivation and seek to sublimate the child's repressed desires into socially useful channels. Teachers must also understand their own unconscious in order to improve the way they relate to students.

One example of Freud's ideas in education was Margaret Naumberg's Children's School in New York City in 1915. She thought the child should be weaned from egocentrism but found the task of doing so much more complex than most educators had imagined. Conventional education, she believed, only dealt with symptoms of the basic drives and therefore frequently led to further repression. Thus she sought to bring the child's unconscious to consciousness by permitting greater freedom, especially in the arts, which she thought would bring out the child's inner life. Children would also have to relinquish their dependence on textbooks and teachers and begin to develop independence of thought and action. Other examples of Freudian ideas in education are A. S. Neill's Summerhill.

Freud's theory has been criticized as not being scientific: it is not falsifiable and is unamenable to other canons of scientific experimentation and testing. Although Freud believed that his stages of psychosexual development and other findings were universal, they appear to be not only culturally relative but relative to certain social classes within a culture. Psychoanalysis itself has proven to be an extremely costly, time-consuming process that has a rather poor record of overcoming patients' psychoneuroses. Moreover, hardly any teachers have the technical preparation to apply Freudian techniques properly. Even if more teachers or guidance counselors developed such skills, one could still seriously question whether the application of psychotherapy is a purpose of schooling.

Reconstructionism

A new educational philosophy emerged during the 1930s under the leadership of George S. Counts and Harold Rugg, and was later brought to fruition by Theodore Brameld. *Reconstructionism* recognized that progressivism had made certain advances over traditional education in teacher-pupil relations and teaching methodology, but it charged that progressivism had become fixated on the child and thereby had failed to develop long-range, compelling goals for a society undergoing great social, political, and economic transformations. The crises that gave reconstructionism its urgency were the Great Depression of the 1930s and the earliest dangers of nuclear annihilation in the 1950s. The reconstructionists urged that a new social order be built that would fulfill basic democratic values and harmonize the underlying forces of the modern world. They put forth such ideas as that working people should control institutions and resources if the world is to become democratic. The aim should be the development of an international democracy or world government in which all nations will participate.

An education for a reconstructed society must recognize the interdependence of the world's population (as in cases of ecological and economic problems). Thus students need to study the realities of the modern world and recognize that they live in a global village. The teacher, therefore, critically examines the cultural heritage, explores controversial issues, provides a vision of a new and better world, and enlists students' efforts to promote programs of cultural renewal. The teacher attempts to convince students of the validity of reconstructionist beliefs but employs democratic procedures in doing so.

Although reconstructionism undergirds its beliefs and proposals by drawing upon findings from the social and behavioral sciences, the established empirical conclusions from these disciplines may well be insufficient to use in developing a planned international world order. Thus many of their assertions lack sufficient scientific backing. Reconstructionists have also been accused of indoctrinating students. While Brameld denied the charge, Counts insisted that it is not whether "imposition" will take place but the source from which it will come. Rather than have ruling groups or classes impose ideas on society, teachers, according to Counts, should take the lead in helping to build a new social order. But, one can ask, is this an appropriate goal for education? Reconstructionism does demand a commitment of the educator who in turn tries to bring about strong student commitment. It therefore assumes—probably erroneously—that a consensus can be reached on guiding ideals, goals, and values. In contrast, followers of Dewey would claim that students should be taught to use the scientific method but be free to arrive at their own conclusions.

TYPES OF REFORMERS

As an analogy, let us imagine a situation where five experts are called in to examine a complex machine that fails to operate properly. After examining the machine *A* and *B* think the breakdown is minor, whereas *C, D,* and *E* consider it serious and of major proportions. *A* says that the machine is a good one and all that is needed is a workable part, which he promptly installs. *B* agrees with *A* that it is a good machine and that the breakdown stems from a defective part; however, *B* believes that the part itself is obsolescent and therefore invents a new type of part that she claims will work more efficiently. *C, D,* and *E* agree with one another that the entire machine is obsolescent; they disagree, however, over what should be done about it. *C* points out extensive changes in the machine that will make it more effective; whereas *D* argues that the machine should be replaced by one that is different and much better. *E,* on the other hand, contends that all such machines can be abolished and society instead can have individuals and voluntary groups design a device that is not a machine but will provide genuine benefits.

Applying these five types to innovators and reformers, we can distinguish two types of establishment educators: a conventional and an innovative one. They share the view that the system should be both maintained and improved, but established educators place greater emphasis on maintenance. In the previous illustration, Individual *A* is a *conventional establishment educator* who believes that schools are basically good and when things go wrong they can be rectified by rearranging and reorganizing some aspect of the system. *B* shares with *A* a belief in the value of the system; however, *B* is an *innovative establishment educator* who believes that when problems arise innovations should be introduced and effectively implemented. Critics of the reformers would most likely be conventional establishment educators or innovative establishment educators. Some critics, however, may be neither educators nor key establishment members; but they are supportive of the establishment and essentially endorse the same position as *A* or *B*. They could be called *conventional critic* (Type A) or *innovative critic* (Type B). A number of the authors in Part II are innovative establishment educators or innovative critics.

Types *C*, *D*, and *E* are reformers. They all believe that drastic changes are needed and they seek to correct abuses; however, they disagree as to what should be done. Type *C* could be called a *system reformer*, one who believes that the school system is salvageable but that extensive and drastic changes may need to be made before it can truly provide quality education. *D* believes that public schools are too defective to offer a quality education and are unlikely to overcome their endemic weaknesses in the near future. *D* is an *options reformer;* he has left the public school to develop options, such as free schools, outside public education. Finally, reformer *E* is a *deschooler,* who usually argues that compulsory schooling should be abolished, support for formal systems be withdrawn, and learning should take place in informal networks within the community.

You may wish to keep these different types in mind while reading the selections in Part I to see whether doing so promotes better understanding of reformers and critics.

REFORM RATIONALES

Reformers may appeal to one or more of the following rationales to justify their arguments: (1) quality, (2) quantity, (3) equity, (4) rights, (5) decision making, and (6) restoration. Reforms that appeal to quality refer either to the outcomes of education or the process. An outcome criterion would focus on desirable outcomes amenable to behavioral formulation and measurement (competency testing, for instance). On the other hand, some reformers appeal to the worthwhileness of the educational process itself and the excitement and stimulation students find in learning (Summerhill and open education).

An appeal to quantity calls for larger appropriations, greater and more extensive facilities, and more specialists. Such appeals were made during the post–World War II period of high birth rates and the later Sputnik era that appropriated more funds for training scientists and engineers in order to surpass the Russians in the space race. It is also seen today in the demand for higher teacher salaries.

Appeals to equity argue for reform on grounds that fairer and more equal distribution of educational resources and more equal access are needed. Such arguments are characteristic of the school desegregation movement and recent school financial reform proposals (such as the *Serrano* case in California).

A rationale that appeals to rights usually claims that certain fundamental rights have been denied and a need exists to rectify injustices and protect rights.

Examples are arguments to eliminate corporal punishment, enact school dress codes, and protect children's rights.

Those arguments appealing to decision making allege that certain community groups have been denied a voice in decisions about public education, consequently, reforms are demanded to make decision making more widely shared. The community control movement, in which minorities seek power to make key decisions in neighborhood schools, is a case in point.

Finally, an appeal to restoration is based on the conviction that present standards and programs are inferior to those of the past. This argument is similar to the quality appeal except that it primarily seeks to restore neglected standards rather than invent new ones. The back-to-basics movement is an example.

Thus, depending on the case, reformers appeal to a rationale of quality, quantity, equity, rights, decision making, or restoration. Deliberations about educational reform are likely to be improved by greater attention to the concept of reform and the rationale of reform arguments.

1

Goals and Curricular Connections

Under the sponsorship of the Carnegie Foundation, Ernest L. Boyer has recently made a study of the American high school in which fifteen varied schools from all sections of the country were investigated. He found that "high schools lack a clear and vital mission. They are unable to find common purpose or establish educational priorities that are widely shared." As a consequence, he recommended that every high school develop clearly stated goals that can be supported by students, and he suggested four goals to guide curriculum development.

Boyer's proposed core curriculum would be structured around those ideas, experiences, and traditions that were significant at a particular time in history. These shared experiences include our history, use of symbols, group and institutional membership, need for well-being, relation to nature, and our dependence on technology. Elective clusters would be introduced in the last two years of high school.

In the selection by Boyer, he explains why he believes general education needs to be reemphasized, and he offers six themes for structuring the curriculum. Rich compares the Boyer Report with two earlier national studies and three more recent studies. He finds that the report's goals lack a sufficient rationale and the proposed core curriculum, among other things, is deficient in providing coherence and integration.

Seeing the Connectedness of Things

Ernest L. Boyer

Ernest L. Boyer (b. 1928) studied at Greenville College (A.B.) and the Unversity of Southern California (M.A., Ph.D., LL.D.). He has served as Chancellor of SUNY, U.S. Commissioner of Education, and is currently President of the Carnegie Foundation for Advancement of Teaching. He is the recipient of a number of awards and honorary degrees.

In his book, *The Mountain People,* anthropologist Colin Turnbull describes a once-thriving North African tribal community in which, through adversity, relationships have broken down. Common values have deteriorated; traditions have lost their evocative power. The social cement holding the tribe together—its heritage, values, and mutual relationships—has crumbled. The result, says Turnbull, is the breakdown of community.

On a different scale, such a decline threatens our society. Today's young people have grown up in a fractured, atomized world in which the call for individual gratification booms forth on every side while social claims are weak. Students are educationally more competitive, geared toward training for jobs, and more committed to getting higher grades. They are optimistic about their own futures, believing they will get good jobs, good money, and good things, but they are pessimistic about the future of the nation and the world. Consequently, students are more committed to their personal futures than to the future we face together.

Sadly, most schools exacerbate this tendency toward self-preoccupation and social isolation. Electives, with their emphasis on individual interests, continue to increase while general education is in shambles. Among educators there is no agreement about the purposes of schooling; we are more confident about the length of education than we are about its substance.

As a global society, we simply cannot afford a generation that fails to see or care about connections. To deny our relationship with one another and with our common home, Earth, is to deny the realities of existence. Clearly, the time has come for educators to focus on the aims of common learning.

To reaffirm general education in no way diminishes the significance of diversity in education. The uniqueness of each individual is a fact to be cherished, not deplored. To recognize that this nation is not one culture but many; to defend the rights of minorities; to preserve the right to dissent, even to disobey, are to acknowledge the essentials of a free society. Schools must respond to the special needs of students.

But while affirming diversity, the school curriculum also must acknowledge the claims of the larger society that give meaning to students' lives. General education is not a sentimental tradition; our future well-being, and perhaps even our survival, may depend on students' understanding the reality of interdependence.

Therefore, the mission of general education is to help students understand that they are not only autonomous individuals, but also members of a human community to which they are accountable. In calling for a reaffirmation of general education, the aim is to help restore the balance. By focusing on those experiences that knit isolated individuals into a community, general education can have a central purpose of its own.

Which human experiences should be the focus of a common curriculum for the schools? Obviously, many different lists could be drawn up. For purposes of discussion, I suggest six themes that may provide an appropriate structure for the nation's schools.

SHARED USE OF SYMBOLS

Use of symbols separates human beings from all other forms of life. Language gives individuals their identities, makes transition possible, and binds society together. All students, from the first years of formal schooling, should learn not only to read and write, but to read with understanding, write with clarity, and listen and speak effectively. In addition, they should become proficient in the use of numbers, which constitute an essential and universally accepted symbol system,

too. Mastery of these skills is the foundation of common learning. Without them, the goals of general education will be fatally undermined.

But developing language skills, as important as this may be, is not enough. Students should also come to understand why and how language has evolved, how messages reveal the values of a culture, how words and thoughts interact, and how feelings and ideas are conveyed through literature.

Students should explore, as well, how we communicate nonverbally through music, dance, and the visual arts. They should understand how these forms of expression permit us to convey subtle meanings, express intense emotions; and how, uniquely, nonverbal symbols can stir a deep response in others.

The impact of mass communication should also be examined. In the United States, children watch television 6,000 hours before they spend a single hour in the classroom. Students urgently need what might be called "tube literacy," to help them see how visual and auditory signals reinforce each other, how ideas can be distorted, how thoughts and feelings can be subliminally conveyed, and how the accuracy and reliability of messages can be tested.

The language of computers merits study, too. Every generally-educated student should learn about this pervasive signal system that increasingly controls our day-to-day transactions.

The goals just proposed are ambitious but essential if students are to survive in a world where symbols hold the community together.

SHARED MEMBERSHIP IN GROUPS AND INSTITUTIONS

Institutions are a fact of life. They touch almost every aspect of our being—economic, educational, familial, political, and religious. Because we pass so much of our lives in institutions, the general education curriculum should look at their origin; how they evolve, grow strong, become oppressive or weak, and sometimes die. It should examine, as well, how institutions work, explore the interaction between institutions and individuals, and show how such interaction both facilitates and complicates our existence.

In addition to this broad-gauge approach, I suggest a more inductive study, one that looks more penetratingly at a *single* institution—the Peace Corps, the AFL-CIO, the American Rifle Association, the city council—or one related, perhaps, to a student's special field of interest. How did the institution begin? What were its initial purposes? What new missions has it assumed? To whom is it accountable? Is the institution still vital, or is it being maintained because of ceremony and tradition?

The goal should be to help students see that everyone shares membership in the "common institutions" of our culture—those social structures that shape our lives, impose obligations, restrict choices, and provide services that we could not obtain in isolation.

SHARED PRODUCING AND CONSUMING

Students should understand that everyone produces and that, through this process, we are dependent on each other. This is an essential part of common learning.

General education should explore the significance of work, a form of both consumption and production, in the lives of individuals and examine how work patterns reflect the values and shape the social climate of a culture. Such a curriculum would ask: What have been the historical, philosophical, religious,

and social attitudes toward work around the world? How are notions about work related to social status and human dignity? What determines the different status and rewards we grant to different forms of work? Why is some work highly rewarded and other work relatively unrewarded? In addition, general education should help students discover that work, at its very best, can be life-fulfilling. As Eugene Delacroix wrote, through work "We seek not only to produce but to give value to time."

This is not to suggest that the nation's schools become vocational institutions. But production and consumption are central to our common experience. They are the ways we define ourselves. Their study can be a legitimate, demanding part of general education.

SHARED RELATIONSHIP WITH NATURE

All life forms on our planet are inextricably interlocked and no education is complete without an understanding of the ordered, interdependent nature of the universe. General education should introduce students, not just to the "facts" of science—the basic concepts, theories, and relationships—but to the methodology of science, too. All students should come to understand how science is a process of trial and error; how, through observation and testing, theories are defined, sometimes discarded, and often give rise to other theories. Students should learn about the applications of science and see how scientific discoveries have led to a flood of inventions and new technologies that bring with them both benefits and risks.

Finally, there is the matter of science and citizenship. If students are intelligently to evaluate the pros and cons of nuclear power, space exploration, food additives, and pollution standards, they must become more knowledgeable about underlying facts and principles behind the headlines.

Becoming a responsible human being in the last quarter of the 20th century means learning about the great power of science, its pervasive influence in all aspects of our lives, and our own shared relationship with nature. This is an essential part of common learning.

SHARED SENSE OF TIME

An understanding of our shared heritage—past and future—should be expected of all students. General education should focus on the seminal ideas and events that have decisively shaped the course of history. More than a collection of facts, this approach would emphasize the convergence of social, religious, political, economic, and intellectual forces in the study of a few carefully chosen themes. Students should learn that the chronicle of humanity is by no means a swift and straight march in the direction of progress. It is an endlessly varied struggle to resolve tensions over freedom and authority, conformity and rebellion, war and peace, rights and responsibilities, equality and exploitation. At bottom, an inquiry into the roots of our civilization should be seen as a study of continuity and change, with leaps forward and spills backward.

It is not enough for students to be told that events have taken place; ideas have been expressed, and societies have risen, flourished, and declined. The approach we envision would emphasize the *interrelationship* between ideas and culture. It would explore, not just governments and leaders, but "ordinary" people, not just politics and diplomacy, but also literature, and religion, and the family.

The fundamental question must be: What has the past to do with us? How does it shape our world today? In looking to the past, we gain a new perspective on the present.

In addition to this look backward, common learning must also gaze forward. General education should help all students understand how past visions of the future have shaped the course of history. They should be asked to think about the "options for the future" we confront today. Above all, students should begin to understand that much of what we call "the future" has, in fact, been predetermined by political, economic, social, and scientific decisions of the past.

The kind of air we breathe, the way we travel, the nature of the social order, patterns of global relationships, the jobs we can and cannot choose: these matters and most others are not totally open to chance. Decisions of the past have shaped *our* world, and tomorrow's world is being shaped today. Exploring our shared sense of time is a central part of common learning.

SHARED VALUES AND BELIEFS

A study of the personal and social significance of shared values should be the capstone to common learning. Through general education, all students examine the distinctions we make between beliefs and "facts," and how values are formed, transmitted, and revised. They should examine, too, the values currently held in our society, looking at the ways such values are socially enforced, and how societies react to unpopular beliefs. General education should introduce all students to the powerful role political ideologies, and particularly religion, have played in shaping, throughout history, the convictions of individuals and societies.

Each student should be able to identify

the premises inherent in his or her own beliefs, learn how to make responsible decisions, and engage in a frank and searching discussion of some of the ethical and moral choices that confront us all. Such a study relates directly to the general education themes we have just discussed. In every one of these shared experiences, moral and ethical choices must be made. How, for example, can messages be conveyed honestly and effectively? How can institutions serve the needs of both the individual *and* the group? On what basis is a vocation selected or rejected? Where can the line be drawn between conservation and exploitation of natural resources? These are the sorts of consequential ethical and moral issues that a common learning curriculum must confront.

In the end, we must recognize that general education is not a single set of courses.

It is a program with a clear objective, one that can be achieved in a variety of ways. And while there may be great flexibility in the process, it is the clarity of purpose that is crucial.

Nearly 40 years ago in *Liberal Education,* Mark Van Doren wrote:

> The connectedness of things is what the educator contemplates to the limit of his capacity. No human capacity is great enough to permit a vision of the world as simple, but if the educator does not aim at the vision no one else will and the consequences are dire when no one else does. . . . The student who can begin early in life to think of things as connected, even if he revises his view with every succeeding year, has begun the life of learning.

Seeing "the connectedness of things" is the goal of common learning.

Educational Goals and Curricular Decisions in the New Carnegie Report

John Martin Rich

The Carnegie Foundation has recently issued another important survey and assessment of American public education (hereafter referred to as the Boyer Report), this time devoted to secondary education and authored by Ernest L. Boyer, president of the Carnegie Foundation and former U.S. Commissioner of Education (Boyer, 1983).

The purpose of this paper is to examine and evaluate two vital areas of the Boyer Report: educational goals and curricular decisions. First, some comparisons will be made with two earlier Carnegie reports; next, goals and curriculum in the Boyer Report will be evaluated; finally, the Boyer Report will be briefly compared to other contemporary national surveys.

A COMPARISION OF CARNEGIE REPORTS

A two-year study completed in 1959 that attracted national attention was James B. Conant's study of 50 comprehensive high schools in 17 states (Conant, 1959). Conant found that the comprehensive high school could provide adequate programs of citizenship education, vocational education, and challenging studies for the more able student. Conant identified the more gifted students as about 15 percent of the high school population; he recommended that each of these students study three or four years in the basic disciplines, take at least five subjects each year with homework of 15 hours or more each week. Placement tests would determine the appropriate sections for the academically talented, and effective guidance programs would be needed to assist this group and the rest of the student population, who would take a more limited number of advanced courses in the basic disciplines.

The Conant Report was likely influenced by the Cold War, the launching of Sputnik, and the National Defense Education Act; its publication aroused a greater national consciousness about the status of American education. Tying in to the space race with the Soviet Union, it called attention to: the need for more academically able girls to enter science and mathematics programs, the ne-

From John Martin Rich, "Educational Goals and Curricular Decisions in the New Carnegie Report," The High School Journal 69 (February–March 1986):222–227. Reprinted with permission from The University of North Carolina Press.

Note: This paper was presented at the American Educational Studies Association in San Francisco, Nov. 9, 1984. The author wishes to thank Joseph L. DeVitis for organizing and chairing the session and suggesting the topic of this paper.

glect of foreign languages, and a more complete education for all students in the comprehensive high school.

In sharp contrast, Charles Silberman's Carnegie-sponsored study, published in 1970, emerged during the upheavals of the civil rights movement, the Vietnam War, and student militancy on campuses. Not surprisingly, the tone and content differed markedly from the Conant Report.

Silberman (1970) deplored the school's preoccupation with order and control. This preoccupation could be found in a focus on time and the clock (although time frequently was not used productively) and on the demand for silence. The repressiveness he observed was reinforced by parental attitudes that viewed discipline as more important than student self-inquiry. At the root of the problem is "mindlessness," the failure "to think seriously or deeply about the purposes or consequences of education" (Silberman, 1970). Silberman's curricular solution was to promote the growth of open classrooms.

In many respects, the Boyer Report is more similar to the Conant Report, both stylistically and substantively, than to Silberman's. Both in style and tone Boyer and Conant express themselves in an objective, detached, and straightforward manner. In contrast, Silberman is idiosyncratic, digressive, fond of injecting items and case studies, and is given to waxing passionately about his favorite nostrums. Substantively, both Boyer and Conant exhibit essentialist elements, while Silberman is more of a neoprogressive. Conant does not deviate from the subject curriculum, and the Boyer Report largely adheres to it as well.

GOALS AND THE CURRICULUM

The Boyer Report studied 15 high schools in all sections of the country that varied considerably, including small rural schools, alternative schools, magnet schools, big-city schools, suburban schools, and other types. Educational goals were found to be only of marginal concern at the district level; whereas high schools' written goals were often vaguely stated and generally ignored. Boyer found that "high schools lack a clear and vital mission. They are unable to find common purpose or establish educational priorities that are widely shared" (1983). He recommended that every high school develop clearly stated goals that were understood and supported by students. Here Silberman would heartily agree.

Boyer advocated four essential goals and stated how they could be achieved. First was that of learning to think critically and communicate effectively through a mastery of language. Second, students should learn about themselves, their human heritage, and the world in which they live through a core curriculum. Third, students should be prepared for the world of work and further education through electives. Finally, all students should fulfill their civic and social responsibilities through school and community service.

As for the curriculum, Boyer found that many high schools offered a wide range of electives. He did not object to the numerous electives as long as an academic core was provided. Guidance for students in planning their programs, however, was usually found to be inadequate. The curriculum, moreover, was not discussed by faculty in terms of what should be the content of a high school education and what it means to be an educated person.

The proposed core curriculum would be structured around those ideas, experiences, and traditions that were significant at a particular time in history. These shared experiences include our history, use of symbols, group and institutional membership, need for well-being, relation to nature, and our dependence on technology. This curriculum, Boyer believes, is appropriate for all students.

Boyer believes that the mastery of English is the first and most essential goal of education, because literacy is the most important tool for learning. Thought and language, he holds, are inextricably connected; and with greater proficiency in self-expression, the quality of thinking will improve. Moreover, those not proficient in the primary language of their culture are greatly disadvantaged in school and the larger society. It is recommended that language proficiency be assessed one year prior to entering high school; that teachers of English be limited to 20 students in each class, and that no more than two basic English classes be included within the teacher's load; and that a one-semester speech course be included in the program.

In terms of the core curriculum, all students should begin to develop "cultural literacy." Included in a cultural literacy program would be a one-year course in literature (although not a great books program), some study in the fine arts, and two years of foreign language study. To supply the shared experiences that include our history, Boyer recommended a one-year study of United States history that would provide an understanding at a deeper level, a one-year Western civilization course, and a one-semester required course that studies a single non-Western nation. The shared experiences of group and institutional membership would consist of a one-year course in American government that explores traditions of democratic thought, government structures, and current political and social issues.

Shared experiences in our relations with nature and technology would include a two-year sequence in the biological and physical sciences, two years of mathematics and additional courses for those qualified to take them, a one-semester course in technology,

and a course in health and lifetime fitness.

Vocational education is complicated by a rapidly changing job market and the inability of most schools to offer a sufficient range of courses. Job prospects for vocational students, it was found, are not much better than for those in nonspecified programs, with the exception of secretarial positions. High school vocational programs are caught between the prospects of a job market featuring many low-paying, dead-end jobs for which formal education is not required and high-tech jobs that require more training than most high schools can supply. Boyer recommends that as part of the core, a seminar on work be offered that examines its importance in the lives of everyone; that tracking be abolished and replaced with a single-track program; and that only vocational courses be offered that have intellectual substance rather than narrow "marketable" skills.

The required courses of the core would constitute two-thirds of the total units needed for graduation. The last two years of high school would be considered a "transition school" where half the time is devoted to the core and the other half to elective clusters. These clusters would be a carefully planned program for each student consisting of five or six courses that would permit further study of selected academic subjects or explorations of career options, or a combination of both. In order to offer these courses, schools will have to draw more on the resources of the larger society and expect students to assume greater responsibility for their own education. The transition school can include work with mentors, and early college study or apprenticeship outside of school.

In assessing the Boyer Report, one is first struck by the clearly stated goals and the exceptional balance of the curriculum as a whole. Many glaring weaknesses in most high school curriculums have been overcome by requiring a study of vital but neglected areas: fine arts, non-Western cultures, foreign languages, technology, and the world of work and vocations in the lives of people. Moreover, by eliminating the tracking system, invidious discrimination is reduced. And by mixing in a coherent plan of electives with the core curriculum during the last two years, student choice and individual differences are recognized. The reason that the curriculum appears to be exceptionally balanced lies with the broad range of studies in the core, from the fine arts to the sciences; the inclusion of significant but commonly neglected studies; and the opportunity to pursue a meaningful program of electives.

Despite these genuine achievements, real problems remain with both the goals and the curriculum. The emphasis on clearly stated goals is commendable, but it is unclear why this set of goals should be accepted. The goals are baldly stated as though their worth is self-evident; however, no rationale or justification is given other than indirectly through the curriculum as a fulfillment of the goals. But the curriculum should not determine the goals or render the goals a mere curriculum appendage; rather, the goals should help give direction to curriculum decisions. Since innumerable goals are available, why choose these four? Even those readers who find these goals worth adopting will have to search elsewhere for a rationale to support their decision. Thus the Boyer Report, in contrast to its greater attention in providing a curriculum rationale, appeals to authority or intuition rather than reasoned grounds for goal acceptance.

Problems of coherence and integration arise in a varied and complex curriculum. The Boyer Report has made an attempt to handle this problem, but it appears to be insufficient. The report states that teachers must view the curriculum coherently and work together cooperatively. Students will try to make connections by participating in a Senior Independent Project—a written report that deals with a contemporary issue that requires drawing upon various disciplines. But no attention is given to constructing the curriculum around broad themes or major questions that everyone will face. Such themes could include: the individual's relation to the environment; the individual's relations to others and institutions; or the individual and social reform. Some examples of the major questions: What is human nature? Does the universe have a purpose? What is the good life?

Another problem with the curriculum is that it is a subject curriculum, which fails to acknowledge much that has been done in curriculum experimentation over the past 50 years. The early progressive education movement broke sharply with the subject curriculum and offered a wide range of new forms, from broad fields to the experience curriculum. Nor does the Boyer Report recognize the structure of the disciplines approach. Even though some emphasis is placed on an inquiry approach in social studies and other fields, a consistent and systematic inquiry approach is not utilized, and the structure of the disciplines model is essentially ignored.

Boyer generally argues convincingly for each discipline introduced in the core, but much less convincingly for the relative weight accorded to each discipline in the overall curriculum: Why, for instance, two years of science and two years of mathematics rather than one year or three years?

An even more serious criticism is the justification of a core or required curriculum. In order to justify such a curriculum, several questions should be answered in the affirmative. Can all students learn and become proficient in the same subjects? Does the core curriculum recognize different learning styles? And does the core curriculum place more emphasis on *what* one learns rather than learning *how* to learn? The Boyer Report does not address these questions. But it does appear that, in light of previous results with required curriculums for all students, insufficient attention is being given to individual differences, varied learning styles, and too much emphasis is placed on what must be learned rather than how to learn more effectively. By providing an elective cluster and a Senior Independent Project, the Boyer Report copes with these problems better than some required curricula but does not do enough within the required courses themselves to offset these problems.

COMPARISON OF CURRENT REPORTS

Among many national commission reports published in the last year or so, the Boyer Report will be briefly compared with three other widely recognized, nationally sponsored reports. These reports include *A Nation at Risk,* under a commission created by Secretary of Education T. H. Bell (1983); Mortimer Adler's *The Paideia Proposal* (1982); and Theodore Sizer's study of high schools titled *Horace's Compromise* (1984).

Although each of the three reports refers, either directly or indirectly, to goals, none of them provides a sufficiently adequate justification for the goals chosen; therefore, our attention will be given to brief comparisons of their curricular proposals with the Boyer Report. An adequate justification of goals should include relating goal choices to a value theory or an educational philosophy, a conceptual analysis of the goal statements, and a delineation of the linkage between the goals and the curriculum.

A Nation at Risk is written in a strident, urgent style employing military metaphors reminiscent of the Sputnik era. Warning that the nation stands on the verge of losing its prominence as a world leader in industry and commerce because of its education failures, the Commission recommends a high school curriculum for all students consisting of three years each of English, mathematics, science, and social studies, and one-half year of computer science. The college-bound student would be required to take two years of a foreign language. The Commission generally believes that more is better—more homework, a longer school day and school year—although research supporting this claim is not presented.

In comparison, the Boyer Report does not fall into the "more is better" trap, and it offers a broader, better balanced curriculum by recognizing important, neglected subjects and the need for meaningful elective clusters.

The Paideia Proposal attempts to provide a liberal and general education for every student and is a required curriculum that provides no electives or specialized courses. Electives, Adler holds, are appropriate for different forms of preparation for the professions or technical careers at the post-high school level. Adler's curriculum is subject not only to all the criticisms made earlier about required curriculums but is probably also inconsistent with Adler's goal of preparation for good citizens by learning to make intelligent choices, in proportion to their maturity and judgment, about critical decisions that affect their lives, which would include some responsibility for curricular choice.

Theodore Sizer visited more than 40 American secondary schools, some extensively, some briefly, and relates his intensely personal observations, which stylistically are not unlike Silberman's case study approach. Sizer (1984) asserts that the essential claims in education are literacy, numeracy, and civic understanding; and he believes that the students' work should be focused on using their minds. He would organize a high school into four areas or large departments: inquiry and expression; mathematics and science; literature and the arts; philosophy and history. Sizer attempts to avoid a fragmented view of knowledge, to teach less but to engage students in a few more important ideas more deeply; he is also opposed to master plans that standardize instruction because no one set of procedures, he believes, can serve all students well.

Of the four current national reports, Sizer's plan has the virtues of simplicity and adaptability to divergent school populations. Yet even those who are generally sympathetic with a broad fields approach and interdisciplinary programs, will likely find Sizer's plan too amorphous and underdeveloped to become a functional curriculum design.

Despite the difficulties noted earlier that the Boyer Report does not adequately address, it is still better balanced, more carefully supported in terms of the choice of curriculum content, and the clearest and most incisively designed of the recent national reports considered here. It deserves a wide audience, vigorous discussion, and ample testing in numerous secondary schools.

REFERENCES

Adler, M. J. (1982). *The Paideia Proposal: An Educational Manifesto.* New York: Macmillan.

Boyer, E. L. (1983). *High School: A Report on Secondary Education in America.* New York: Harper & Row.

Conant, J. B. (1959). *The American High School Today.* New York: McGraw-Hill.

National Commission on Excellence in Education. (1983). *A Nation at Risk: The Imperative for Educational Reform.* Washington, D.C.: U.S. Government Printing Office.

Silberman, C. E. (1970). *Crisis in the Classroom.* New York: Random House.

Sizer, T. R. (1984). *Horace's Compromise: The Dilemma of the American High School.* Boston: Houghton Mifflin.

DISCUSSION QUESTIONS AND ACTIVITIES

1. What are the grounds Boyer provides for a reemphasis on general education?
2. Will this emphasis conflict with or deny human diversity and individuality?
3. What are the six themes enunciated by Boyer that are designed to provide an appropriate curricular structure?
4. Identify the goals and rationales used to support these themes and determine their ability to do so.
5. Why does Boyer stress "the connectedness of things" rather than a single set of courses?
6. Compare and contrast the Boyer Report with earlier studies made by Conant and Silberman.
7. What should be the relation of the core to elective clusters? How can the elective cluster be handled effectively?
8. Has Boyer provided an adequate rationale for the goals of his program?
9. Have the problems of coherence and integration been adequately handled?
10. What are the dangers, if any, of a required curriculum?
11. Compare the Boyer Report with other recent national studies in terms of their curricular proposals.
12. Visit local secondary schools and gather data on their general education program. Compare the findings to the recommendations in the Boyer Report.
13. Trace the changes in general education programs at the secondary level during

the past twenty-five years. Present your findings in class.

SUGGESTED READINGS

Books By Ernest L. Boyer

The Book and Education. Washington, D.C.: Library of Congress, 1980.

Educating for Survival. New Rochelle, N.Y.: Change Magazine Press, 1977. (with Martin Kaplan)

High School: A Report on Secondary Education in America. New York: Harper & Row, 1983.

High School/College Partnerships. Washington, D.C.: American Association for Higher Education, 1981.

Higher Learning in the Nation's Service. Washington, D.C.: Carnegie Foundation for the Advancement of Teaching, 1981. (with Fred M. Hechinger)

A Quest for Common Learning: The Aims of General Education. Washington, D.C.: Carnegie Foundation for the Advancement of Teaching, 1981. (with Arthur Levine)

2

Restructuring Secondary Schools

Over the past decade Sizer visited over one hundred schools; and during his two years of field work, he visited over forty American secondary schools. Sizer found that public school teachers are overworked and cannot devote sufficient attention to each student; moreover, they are unable to control their destiny because of a bureaucratic maze.

Sizer states four goals, three of which are essential for responsible citizenship and government. He then divides the curriculum into four areas or large departments and thereby disavows the traditional subject curriculum and its problem of fragmentation. Sizer endorses Whitehead's dictum not to teach too many subjects and that whatever you teach, teach thoroughly. Thus students would learn more while being taught less. Compulsory schooling should end upon demonstration of a "mastery of the minimal"; and since most students can do so before senior high school, schooling at that level would be voluntary. Diplomas would be awarded upon demonstrated mastery rather than after four years of study or the collection of a set number of credits. Students are also likely to be motivated in good schools—schools that have standards and are challenging rather than threatening, stable, clear about their mission, fair, and decent places that deserve loyalty.

In Sizer's selection, he argues against compartmentalization, indicates four areas around which the curriculum can be clustered, and presents a plan for reducing the total number of students for which each teacher has responsibility. Finn, however, warns that in Sizer's plan the "entire heritage of Western civilization is merely an educational option."

Essential Schools:
A First Look

Theodore R. Sizer

Theodore R. Sizer (b. 1932) was educated at Yale University (B.A.) and Harvard University (M.A., Ph.D.). He is a former Dean of Faculty of Education at Harvard and a former Headmaster of Phillips Academy. He is the recipient of honorary degrees and is author of Horace's Compromise *and other books about education.*

A Study of High Schools, cosponsored by NASSP and the Commission on Educational Issues[1] of the National Association of Independent Schools is in its fourth of five years, the conclusions are beginning to take form, and three books outlining findings and recommendations will be published.[2]

My volume, *Horace's Compromise: The Dilemma of the American High School Today,* will be issued in January 1984. It focuses on teaching and learning—on the excessive compromises that serious school people are all too often forced to make. A history of the American high school since 1940 by Robert Hampel will be published in the spring. And an analysis of schools arising from close observation of 15 secondary schools across the country during the 1981–82 academic year will appear in the fall, written by Arthur G. Powell, David K. Cohen, and Eleanor Farrar.

No reader of the *Bulletin* will be surprised to hear that we found high schools to be very complicated, rich institutions (far more complicated, and thus fragile, than many policy makers today seem to realize, alas). To reduce our findings and recommendations to a few brief pages, therefore, is difficult, and carries the great risk of glibness, oversimplification, and overgeneralization. However, I will take that risk, at least for my own volume, in order to give NASSP members a first glimpse of what we have found.

At the start, I must emphasize that the focus of our study has been narrow, primarily on the "insides" of schools—on the critical triangle of student, teacher, and subject and on the climate of the school in which this triangle functions. There are, of course, many important problems "outside" of schools—the forms of governmental control, finance, and teacher education, to mention but a few. Consequential though these are, our study has

From Theodore R. Sizer, "Essential Schools: A First Look," NASSP Bulletin 67 (October 1983): 33–38. Reprinted with permission.

[1] The Commission on Education Issues is a programmatically autonomous unit within NAIS devoted to policy studies affecting American education. Scott Thomson, executive director of NASSP and John Esty, president of NAIS, are commissioners, as are 10 other educators from public and private schools and universities, and journalism.

[2] Houghton Mifflin will publish these volumes in 1984.

not directly addressed them. We choose to concentrate closely on what we believe is the heart of the matter.

SOME OBSERVATIONS

First, some impressions arising from our visits in the field:

• The extent of free high school education in this country is astonishing. The crusade for universal secondary education, envisioned almost 100 years ago, is now a reality. The American high school may be this century's most far-reaching and generous social invention. Unfortunately, and despite well-intentioned, sincere efforts, many schools are not uniformly productive and serve some of their students poorly.

• While community values and populations vary widely across the country, the basic structure of the high school is strikingly common, and it is markedly similar to its 1890 founding model. Students are grouped by age; the substance of learning is organized by academic departments largely akin to those of the 1890s; the primary pedagogy is lecturing in one form or another, in separate blocks of time each of something under an hour; school is in session from Labor Day to mid-June; and student accomplishment is measured in the coinage of credits earned and time spent ("four years of English"). Even the rituals of going to school—proms, athletic events, student organizations—are remarkably consistent across all kinds of schools and across time. Given the size and demographic diversity of this country and changes in American society and in scholarship during the last 50 years, this stubbornly persistent common structure is extraordinary.

• Unfortunately, this structure does not serve its purpose well and is the root cause of the schools' weak productivity.

• While not structural, some key differences among schools are significant and usually follow the income group of the particular students served. Schools for poor youngsters are, on the whole, more troubled and more neglected by the society than those for children of wealthier families. This sad finding should surprise no one and should shame everyone.

• Some groups of students—the honors track, or the athletes, or the special education group or, even, the persistently troublesome kids—get relatively intensive individual attention. They are "known" in schools, and their programs often serve them very effectively. The unspecial majority, however, often remains anonymous and relatively unchallenged.

• Just as Charles Silberman found in the late 1960s, our principal conclusion after observing students is their docility in classrooms. While there are, of course, many exceptions, most high school students go along in an unchallenging way with their school's routines. They expect to be entertained as well. Too many are not intellectually engaged, and their ultimate performance, particularly in complex reasoning skills, shows it. However, given the structure of high schools and the loads which most teachers carry, "engaging" students in the academic realm is often very difficult to accomplish. Many students, however, colorfully engage in extracurricular and social realms. The contrast between their behavior in class and outside of it is marked.

• The high school curriculum is overloaded and unwisely values mere coverage more than mastery of intellectual skills. Its division into academic subjects, while hallowed by age and tradition, functions poorly.

- The quality of professional staff is higher than today's media would have us believe, but many teachers and principals are angry and frustrated. Many are also seriously underpaid.
- The current trend toward more centralized direction of schools increases staff demoralization and even lessens the opportunities for principals and teachers to adapt their programs to real and pressing local needs.
- Schools are largely judged on the basis of data which happens to be easy to collect and to manipulate statistically. Taken alone, such data can produce strikingly misleading assessments.

SOME RECOMMENDATIONS

Where does this lead us?

I ask that we consider a substantial restructuring of the high school. Big and politically risky though that task is, it is about time that we tackle it.

The current high school structure dates back to, and arises from, the beliefs of the 1890's. We've learned much and changed much since then, and we can do better than continuing to operate a school designed when Henry Ford's Model T was new.

First must come some changes in the ways that we look at the school and its mission. The metaphors we live by professionally are both subtle and deeply rooted. Altering them will take courage. For example, high school should not primarily be a place where adults "deliver a service" to adolescents. The key workers must be the students; only they can do the learning. We must stop thinking

of ways to "give" or "present" material to kids and explore how we can *inspire* them to get it for themselves. The difference between "giving" and "inspiring" is crucial.

Another example is the dependence on "time spent" as the criterion for learning— "four credit hours of science," "two years of mathematics," "at least 180 days a year," "52,000 minutes per year." "Time spent" is but one factor in learning, and there are others, such as motivation and learning style, which are more important.

A further example is age grading. When we meet a youngster, the first question many of us ask him or her is what grade he or she is in. However, we all learn at different rates at different times; to assume all of us at 15 are essentially two years from completing secondary education is a serious oversimplification. On the contrary, we must take students where they are, not where somebody else's age-related norm says they should be.

Finally, we must be ready to look across the existing subjects of the curriculum and to find ways of reconstructing knowledge to most aptly conform to current scholarship, the way people learn, and the adolescents' world. Compartmentalization by English-mathematics-science-social studies-foreign language-physical education-et al. is not the most productive way of organizing a high school program. It will take an heroic leap for each of us to escape the entrapment of this manner of organization and the hold on us of our own disciplines.

In a word, we must get our minds open and make sure that the metaphors and constructs by which we live professionally can stand honest criticism.

Given such a frame of mind, what of the structure? There is no one detailed answer. It is no contradiction to say that each school should have its own ethos and individuality and that the structure of all schools should reflect a common set of essential principles. Common ends are desirable and so are appropriately differentiated means.

We should start defining these essentials, the principles by which new high schools can be structured:

1. *No one should enter high school-level studies who has not clearly mastered the basic educational requirements of a citizen in a democracy—literacy, numeracy, and civic understanding.*

These elementary studies should be provided free until each young person masters them. Attendance at school until that mastery is attained must be compulsory. Secondary school studies should focus on more advanced work. No citizen should be compelled to pursue these studies, but all citizens should be guaranteed free access to them for six years, to be taken at any point during their lives. (The practical effects of this will be that no student who does not want to attend will be in high school and that a student whose behavior unmistakably signals that he does not want to work at school can be expelled— with the clear understanding that he can return when he later gets his act together. The momentum of tradition, however, guarantees that most adolescents will attend school.)

2. *The high school should focus on helping adolescents to learn to use their minds.*

It should not attempt to be "comprehensive," but it can properly assist students in learning how to make decisions that arise in their private and work lives. (Technical, vocational, and career education for all Americans should be concentrated for citizens of all ages in special institutions, such as community colleges or existing, but expanded vocational technical high schools. A cross-age mix of students will benefit all. Part-time enrollment should be encouraged.)

3. *The tone of the high school should be one of unanxious expectation.*

School should be a purposeful place, safe and focused on the tasks at hand. The primary burden for learning should be squarely on the students, and they and their families should be unequivocally clear about this. The school should consciously promote the virtues of *decency*; it should go to lengths to insist on fair, generous, and empathetic behavior.

4. *The diploma should be awarded only upon a student's exhibition of mastery of the high school's program.*

"Time served" and "credits earned" would disappear as criteria for performance. So would age-related promotion. An exhibition should be more than one paper-and-pencil test; there must be a variety of ways and times whereby each student can exhibit his or her mastery. (No practical task will be more difficult for school staff than designing and administering these exhibitions; none will be more important, as the exhibition will be a specific representation of the goals of the school. An excellent point of departure for construction of an exhibition can be the College Board's recent report, "Academic Preparation for College: What Students Need To Know and Be Able To Do." While prepared for the college bound, it can readily be adapted for all students.)

5. *The primary pedagogy of the high school should be "coaching,"* as defined by Mortimer Adler in his recent *Paideia Proposal.*

The critical intellectual skills that shape effective reasoning depend on this technique, and on sustained questioning. (One cannot *tell* a student to think deeply and inquire wisely, he or she has to learn it personally, albeit assisted by a critic-teacher.) Students should be helped to teach themselves (the practical effect of this policy will be to limit "coverage" of material. The resulting tradeoff of breadth to depth is worthwhile: less is more.)

6. *The program of study must be simple and universal.*

The complexity and confusion of the existing curriculum must be eased, in order to provide a setting where students can learn a few things well and learn how to learn. All students would be enrolled at all times in all areas, but the obvious need for variety and student choice would be accommodated *within* each of those areas. (A practical example of a simplified course of study is to cluster the curriculum, and its teachers, into but four areas: inquiry and expression; mathematics and science; literature and the arts; philosophy and history.)

7. *Teaching and learning must be personalized to the greatest extent possible.*

No high school teacher should have responsibility for more than 80 pupils. (The practical implications of this are radical, as most teachers today work with almost twice as many students. There are a variety of steps one can take to reduce the student-teacher ratio, such as increasing the percentage of adults in a school who are actively teaching, and expecting cross-subject instruction—one teacher working with 80 students in English and social studies rather than 160 in just one of these fields. There are extra benefits to be found in cross-subject teaching, and the risks can be minimized by team arrangements. The shift toward expecting students to teach themselves more—homework or independent study—can free class time now spent in lecturing, at least to some degree.)

Personalization is the only way to take advantage of our new understanding of differing learning styles. Again, the short-term cost may be to "coverage": the student may have to know fewer dates in history and fewer phyla in biology than heretofore. The long-term gains—in students' confidence, effectiveness, and ability to teach themselves—clearly outweigh the cost, however.

8. *Control of the detailed school program must be given to the principal and teachers at the level of each school.*

While the standards and shape of the culminating exhibitions may properly be largely in the hands of state or school district authorities, the design of the means to reach them must rest with those who best know each particular group of students. Centralized, standardized practice almost always leads to low standards; decentralized authority provokes commitment from school people on the firing line and increases the chances of wise response to the special needs and opportunities that each student has.

CONCLUSION

These eight principles represent a beginning. Many will find them genteel, elitist, and unrealistic. Visiting dozens of schools across this country, however, has convinced me that they need be none of these things. The greatest insult to young citizens is to assign them to their "appropriate track" early in life (say at age 14). To give everyone a chance to learn to use her or his mind well is not gentility, but democracy. A focus on the mind is not elitism, but a necessity in a complex, turbulent culture and economy. It lies at the core of all careers.

An education in how to think rigorously and imaginatively is the ultimate modern vocational education. It is not unrealistic to find some students reacting poorly to academic teaching—because it is poor teaching. It is realistic to assert that there is an academic approach to every adolescent's motivation and learning style. As long as we give some things up in the existing school program, it is realistically possible to get faculty-student ratios down and to improve teacher salaries.

However, it may be unrealistic to think that many educators, students, parents, and school board members will accept our analysis to the degree necessary to attempt to create newly-structured high schools along these principles, ones which can be called Essential Schools. However, and at the same time, an honestly realistic person knows that some other commonly-accepted remedies—a few more dollars added to teachers' salaries, a year or two of this subject or that added to the diploma requirements, and competency tests for teachers—are not going to ignite the fire necessary to make our schools significantly more productive and effective.

Perhaps a middle ground can be found, with school boards and state authorities encouraging a number of communities to establish experimental Essential Schools and run them long enough to test them thoroughly. The best can ultimately serve as models.

America created in the 1890s the design for a secondary school which now is accepted worldwide. Do we have the courage, imagination, and idealism to shape a fresh design, one powerfully attuned to the 1990s?

Teaching and Learning: The Dilemma of the American High School

Chester E. Finn, Jr.

Chester E. Finn, Jr., formerly Professor of Education and Public Policy at Vanderbilt University, is Assistant Secretary for Educational Research and Improvement and Counselor to the Secretary in the U.S. Department of Education.

Besieged and benumbed as we already are by proliferating studies of American education, we might fairly wonder what could possibly justify another one. Yet even after nearly two years of commission reports, task forces, presidential hoopla, gubernatorial activism, and a thousand solemn conferences, Theodore Sizer's book is, initially, a refreshing addition to the literature.

For one thing, it acknowledges and cele-

From Chester E. Finn, Jr., "Teaching and Learning: The Dilemma of the American High School." Reprinted from Commentary *77 (May 1984):64, 66, 68, 70, by permission; all rights reserved.*

brates the existence of private schools, institutions which educate more than four million children but which were banished from the pages of all the recent reports on education. For another thing, it is written primarily from the standpoint of the teacher and the student, rather than from atop some public-policy pinnacle, and its glimpses into actual schools and classrooms are far more realistic—and sympathetic—than those offered by the competition. What is more, the prose is brisk, clean, and nearly free of "educationese."

Unfortunately, it is also nearly free of educational content. As with a fizzy drink made from chemical sweeteners, the initial refreshment is not accompanied by much nutrition. The compromising Horace of the title turns out not to be the great Roman poet and satirist so well-remembered by veterans of fourth-year Latin, but one Horace Smith, a fifty-three-year-old suburban high-school English teacher who moonlights at a liquor store. His compromise—a real and painful one skillfully drawn by Sizer—is the balance he has struck between the bottomless instructional needs of his too numerous students and what he is able to supply within the constraints of fifty-minute periods and twenty-four-hour days. Horace is no loafer: as Sizer makes clear, he is in fact an exemplary teacher, severely limited in his pedagogical effectiveness by the circumstances within which he must function.

Such problems are real enough and deeply frustrating to the dedicated teacher. Five classes a day of thirty or so youngsters each; students who function at many different levels of ability, preparation, and motivation; short class periods punctuated by announcements, messengers, and record-keeping—this can be pretty discouraging to the person who became an English instructor because he loved literature and wanted to initiate children into its joys.

We instinctively empathize with Horace and want to alter his school both so that he will be able to accomplish more and so that he and others like him will want to continue teaching, mindful as we are that the alternative is a cadre of practitioners entering the classroom not because they love their subjects but because they weren't smart enough, ambitious enough, or well-enough educated to get better jobs.

But empathy is not enough. The book's troubles begin with the matter of exactly what Horace's students are supposed to end up knowing. What should be the content of a good secondary education? This is never a trivial question, and especially not at the present time, when the intense interest being paid to school reform by governors, legislators, boards of regents, business leaders, even university presidents, has created a rare opportunity to turn the smorgasbord of elective courses in family living and revolutionary movements into some semblance of an orderly curriculum.

Yet Sizer declines to prescribe content. Worse, he comes very close to arguing that the choice of content does not really much matter, that any book or fact or problem or event is as suitable as any other—at least in the hands of a gifted teacher—for coaching an eager pupil in the necessary intellectual plays.

Horace's Compromise is indeed splendid on "cognitive skills," both the simple ones (decoding words on a page, handling number problems) and the important advanced ones like abstract reasoning, clear exposition, and analysis. It borrows heavily from Mortimer Adler's *The Paideia Proposal* and displays comparable sophistication about the nature of various intellectual processes and the pedagogical approaches most apt to develop them. Anyone successfully completing the required part of a secondary education designed by

Theodore Sizer would have gained a lot more skills than most high-school students acquire today, and would in that sense be better prepared to cope with the challenges of further education and of modern life.

But he would know very little about the society he was entering, about its heritage, its works of art, its internal tensions or its external threats. He would have acquired little or none of what E. D. Hirsch, Jr., has termed "cultural literacy."

This bobtailed education results from an insidious combination: Sizer's beatification of pedagogy itself—the act of teaching—together with a relative indifference to curriculum content, and his minimalist view of "the essential claims of the state" with respect to education. Those claims, he insists, are precisely three: literacy, numeracy, and "civic understanding," the last a welcome addition here defined as "a grasp of the basis for consensual democratic government, a respect for its processes, and acceptance of the restraints and obligations incumbent on a citizen." But that is as far as Sizer goes, at least in compulsory education. "Once those minima are demonstrably reached," he says, "the state has no right whatsoever to compel a citizen to attend school" or "to compel her or him to learn anything else." All subsequent education would thus be voluntary—available, even enticing, but optional.

This vision is as audaciously attractive as it is outrageously inadequate. It may be possible to shrink most of the problems that beset American secondary education by eliminating all youngsters who meet Sizer's "minima" and thereupon decide they have had enough of schooling. And there is no denying that too many people today—working in offices, wandering the streets, and sitting in college classrooms, as well as those still in school—never do attain minimum lev-

els of much of anything. But do the "claims" of society upon its children really stop short of Shakespeare, Emerson, and Frost, of Plato, Locke, and Marx, of Jefferson, Lincoln, and Roosevelt? Leaving aside entirely the demands of technological literacy and scientific competency, are we really prepared to conclude, with Sizer, that history, literature, and philosophy are, strictly speaking, electives, and that the entire heritage of Western civilization is merely an educational option, lying outside the domain of that which the society may reasonably oblige its youngest members to learn? Is it really an "abuse of state power," as Sizer suggests, to require teenagers not only to ponder the implications of the Bill of Rights (which he sensibly advises as a basic text for "civic understanding") but also to read a bit of Melville, a little Conrad, a smidgen of Longfellow, to examine the conceptions of justice and morality in *To Kill a Mockingbird* or the wellsprings of character in *Abe Lincoln Grows Up*?

To be sure, Sizer does not rule out the possibility of such study. He merely excludes it from the compulsory part of education. In truth, his idealized high school, trimmed down to four departments, with far fewer students per teacher, and with the day vastly more flexible than at present, is a beguiling notion, as are his suggestions for the virtual exclusion of vocational training and the deemphasis on athletics and other extracurricular activities. Himself a historian, teacher, and former high-school headmaster (as well as one-time dean of the Harvard Graduate School of Education), Sizer depicts a school that would be far more intellectually challenging than most are today. It would be a school populated by outstanding teachers free from the harassments of meddlesome administrators, and by motivated, spontaneously well-behaved students who have already acquired the essential skills and are continuing their studies because they want to.

Some critics have suggested that this imaginary school looks awfully like Phillips Academy, the superb private school that Sizer previously headed. The implication is that *Horace's Compromise* suffers from an advanced case of educational elitism. In fact, I believe, the opposite may be more true: the book reflects an extraordinarily optimistic, even romantic, neoprogressivism that is slightly reminiscent of A.S. Neill and Summerhill. Sizer appears to believe both that youngsters will only learn that which they want to learn when they are motivated to learn it *and* that, given the right institutional circumstances, practically all youngsters will eventually want to learn practically everything that adults might want them to.

Sizer's feeling for adolescents is deep and sensitive, and his portraits of them as individuals are vivid and affectionate. He correctly points out that a number of schools, blindly following regulations specifying what must be "covered" in which courses, engage in the utter folly—and unintentional cruelty—of handing an eight-hundred-page world history textbook to "Dennis," a tenth grader who has never really learned to read; that many a "Miss Romagna" never engages the intellectual participation of "Melissa"; and that it is far too common for "Mr. Brody," slightly intimidated by his students, to enter into a "Conspiracy for the Least" with them, whereby the teacher makes practically no demands and in return the youngsters refrain from hassling him. But the assumption that seems to underlie the entire book is that (except for those pupils with chronic discipline problems, whom Sizer rightly insists be sent out of school) the institutional arrangements of the high school should accom-

modate themselves to the impulses and anxieties of the teenage population rather than the knowledge and priorities of the adults who presumably have something to teach. Sizer is ostentatiously nonjudgmental about the students, reporting calmly on his observation of drug deals, libidinous displays, even some ugly peer behavior, in the schools he has visited. The only adolescent trait he explicitly condemns is "docility."

Since the dawn of the 20th century, American education has been riven by two competing approaches: molding the child to the standards and expectation of the school, or shaping the school to the interest and enthusiasms of the student. *Horace's Compromise* does not fall completely into the latter camp; indeed, one suspects that Horace Smith himself would be uncomfortable there. But it is there that the author's sincere reformist zeal appears to focus, and it is in this crucial respect that Sizer differs from the National Commission on Excellence in Education, from most other contemporary school critics, and certainly from the lay boards and elected officials who are now striving to strengthen the educational systems of their states and communities.

Sizer, too, will have a chance to put his ideas into practice. He is moving to Brown University (an institution whose undergraduate curriculum is celebrated for its lack of requirements) to head the education department and, from that perch, to organize a network of public and private high schools that will voluntarily transform themselves into places where Horace will have to make fewer and less painful compromises. We should wish Sizer and Horace Smith well. We should even consider sending our children to their schools, for the teaching there will be superb and the students will all be eager. But will any of them be motivated to read the poems written two millennia ago by the other Horace? And if not, will any of them be obliged to do so, on the grounds that there are some things every educated person ought to know?

DISCUSSION QUESTIONS AND ACTIVITIES

1. According to Sizer, what common structures are found in American high schools? How well do these structures serve their purposes?
2. Why is compartmentalization not the most productive way of organizing a high school program, and what can be done to change it?
3. Why does Sizer believe that the secondary school should focus on advanced work, and that no student should be compelled to attend? Explain why you agree or disagree.
4. Sizer says that "school should be a purposeful place, safe and focused on tasks at hand." Is this not a description of most schools?
5. Do you believe that the curriculum can be successfully clustered into the four areas Sizer enumerates?
6. Does Sizer offer a realistic plan for reducing the total number of students for which each high school teacher has responsibility?
7. Does Sizer fail to prescribe the content of a good secondary education?
8. Finn, while applauding Sizer's curriculum for teaching valuable skills, warns that, in Sizer's plan, the "entire heritage of Western civilization is merely an educational option." Is Finn's statement accurate?
9. More surprisingly, Finn claims that Sizer's plan is not elitist (as some critics have suggested), but is in the romantic, neoprogressive vein reminiscent of Summerhill. Is this an accurate interpretation?
10. Finn believes that there are some things that every educated person ought to know. Does Sizer? Do you?
11. Compare Sizer's plans with those of Boyer (Chapter 1) and Adler (Chapter 3).
12. See if you can locate schools that have adopted Sizer's plan and develop a report on your findings.

SUGGESTED READINGS

Books by Theodore R. Sizer

The Age of the Academies (editor). New York: Bureau of Publications, Teachers College, Columbia University, 1964.

Horace's Compromise: The Dilemma of the American High School. Boston: Houghton Mifflin, 1984.

Places for Learning, Places for Joy. Cambridge, Mass.: Harvard University Press, 1973.

Religion and Public Education (editor). Boston: Houghton Mifflin, 1967.

A Review and Comment on National Reports: Perspectives. Reston, Va.: National Association of Secondary School Principals, 1983.

Secondary Schools at the Turn of the Century. New Haven, Conn.: Yale University Press, 1964.

3

The Paideia Proposal

Since the philosophy of perennialism underlies Adler's educational proposals, a word about that philosophy is in order. Adler holds that there are absolute truths and values that are knowable, many of which are expressed in the *Great Books of the Western World*. The ultimate ends of education are the same for all persons at all times and everywhere; these ends are absolute and universal principles. The ultimate ends are the first principles, and the means in general are the secondary principles.

The problems of education are both theoretical and practical. A theoretical question is one that inquires about the nature of things, as in educational science and history. A practical question asks what should be done. Practical questions have three levels: the first and most specific is practice that deals with particular cases; the second is policy that pertains to a class of cases in which rules can be formulated; and the third is the principles that deal with universals or all cases (the realm of educational philosophy).

Education, for Adler, is a process by which the abilities of humans are perfected through artistically developed good habits. Education is a cooperative enterprise and no person can completely educate himself or herself. In other words, the infant is dependent upon adults—learning skills are initially acquired from others.

Adler envisions the goals of schooling to be the same for all students. This rests on his view of human nature: human beings are essentially rational creatures and rationality is not only a distinguishing trait (from animals) but also one of their best traits. Rationality needs systematic attention and cultivation; this can best be done under a plan of systematic schooling.

Adler's Paideia Proposal provides a more tangible grounding for his educational thought in a specific curriculum. His curriculum consists of three divisions: the first is devoted to acquiring knowledge in three subject areas; the second is designed to develop intellectual skills of learning; and the third is devoted to enlarging the understanding of ideas and values. Different methods of instruction are employed in each division.

The Paideia Proposal: Rediscovering the Essence of Education

Mortimer Adler

Mortimer Jerome Adler (b. 1902) was awarded the Ph.D. by Columbia University and taught at that institution, the University of Chicago, and was a visiting lecturer at St. John's College. It was at the University of Chicago, in conjunction with Robert Maynard Hutchins, that he developed the Great Books program. Professor Adler has been Director of the Institute of Philosophical Research since 1952. Since 1966 he has served as Director of Editorial Planning of the 15th edition of Encyclopedia Britannica *and has been Chairman of the Board of Editors since 1974. Since 1945 he has been Associate Editor of the* Great Books of the Western World *and in 1952 developed its Syntopicon. Professor Adler is author and co-author of more than thirty books, ranging from religious to scientific studies. Philosophically, he is one of the leading perennialists.*

In the first 80 years of this century, we have met the obligation imposed on us by the principle of equal educational opportunity, but only in a quantitative sense. Now, as we approach the end of the century, we must achieve equality in qualitative terms.

This means a completely one-track system of schooling. It means, at the basic level, giving all the young the same kind of schooling, whether or not they are college bound.

We are aware that children, although equal in their common humanity and fundamental human rights, are unequal as individuals, differing in their capacity to learn. In addition, the homes and environments from which they come to school are unequal —either predisposing the child for schooling or doing the opposite.

Consequently, the Paideia Proposal, faithful to the principle of equal educational opportunity, includes the suggestion that inequalities due to environmental factors must be overcome by some form of preschool preparation—at least one year for all and two or even three for some. [See definition and list of participants on page 45.] We know that to make such preschool tutelage compulsory at the public expense would be tantamount to increasing the duration of compulsory schooling from 12 years to 13, 14, or 15 years. Nevertheless, we think that this preschool adjunct to the 12 years of compulsory basic schooling is so important that some way must

be found to make it available for all and to see that all use it to advantage.

THE ESSENTIALS OF BASIC SCHOOLING

The objectives of basic schooling should be the same for the whole school population. In our current two-track or multitrack system, the learning objectives are not the same for all. And even when the objectives aimed at those on the upper track are correct, the course of study now provided does not adequately realize these correct objectives. On all tracks in our current system, we fail to cultivate proficiency in the common tasks of learning, and we especially fail to develop sufficiently the indispensable skills of learning.

The uniform objectives of basic schooling should be threefold. They should correspond to three aspects of the common future to which all the children are destined: (1) Our society provides all children ample opportunity for personal development. Given such opportunity, each individual is under a moral obligation to make the most of himself and his life. Basic schooling must facilitate this accomplishment. (2) All the children will become, when of age, full-fledged citizens with suffrage and other political responsibilities. Basic schooling must do everything it can to make them good citizens, able to perform the duties of citizenship with all the trained intelligence that each is able to achieve. (3) When they are grown, all (or certainly most) of the children will engage in some form of work to earn a living. Basic schooling must prepare them for this or that specific job while they are still in school.

To achieve these three objectives, the character of basic schooling must be general and liberal. It should have a single, required, 12-year course of study for all, with no electives except one—an elective choice with regard to a second language, to be selected from such modern languages as French, German, Italian, Spanish, Russian, and Chinese. The elimination of all electives, with this one exception, excludes what *should* be excluded—all forms of specialization, including particularized job training.

In its final form, the Paideia Proposal will detail this required course of study, but I will summarize the curriculum here in its bare outline. It consists of three main columns of teaching and learning, running through the 12 years and progressing, of course, from the simple to the more complex, from the less difficult to the more difficult, as the students grow older. Understand: The three columns (see chart below) represent three distinct modes of teaching and learning. They do not represent a series of courses. A specific course or class may employ more than one mode of teaching and learning, but all three modes are essential to the overall course of study.

The first column is devoted to acquiring knowledge in three subject areas: (A) language, literature, and the fine arts; (B) mathematics and natural science; (C) history, geography, and social studies.

The second column is devoted to developing the intellectual skills of learning. These include all the language skills necessary for thought and communication—the skills of reading, writing, speaking, listening. They also include mathematical and scientific skills; the skills of observing, measuring, estimating, and calculating; and skills in the use of the computer and of other scientific instruments. Together, these skills make it possible to think clearly and critically. They once were called the liberal arts—the intellectual skills indispensable to being competent as a learner.

The third column is devoted to enlarging the understanding of ideas and values. The materials of the third column are books (*not*

The Paideia Curriculum

	Column One	Column Two	Column Three
Goals	Acquisition of Organized Knowledge	Development of Intellectual Skills and Skills of Learning	Improved Understanding of Ideas and Values
	by means of	by means of	by means of
Means	Didactic Instruction, Lecturing, and Textbooks	Coaching, Exercises, and Supervised Practice	Maieutic or Socratic Questioning and Active Participation
	in these three subject areas	in these operations	in these activities
Subject Areas, Operations, and Activities	Language, Literature, and Fine Arts	Reading, Writing, Speaking, Listening, Calculating, Problem Solving, Observing, Measuring, Estimating, Exercising Critical Judgment	Discussion of Books (Not Textbooks) and Other Works of Art
	Mathematics and Natural Science		Involvement in Music, Drama, and Visual Arts
	History, Geography, and Social Studies		

The three columns do not correspond to separate courses, nor is one kind of teaching and learning necessarily confined to any one class.

textbooks), and other products of human artistry. These materials include books of every variety—historical, scientific, and philosophical as well as poems, stories, and essays—and also individual pieces of music, visual art, dramatic productions, dance productions, film or television productions. Music and works of visual art can be used in seminars in which ideas are discussed; but as with poetry and fiction, they also are to be experienced aesthetically, to be enjoyed and admired for their excellence. In this connection, exercises in the composition of poetry, music, and visual works and in the production of dramatic works should be used to develop the appreciation of excellence.

The three columns represent three different kinds of learning on the part of the student and three different kinds of instruction on the part of teachers.

In the first column, the students are engaged in acquiring information and organized knowledge about nature, man, and human society. The method of instruction here, using textbooks and manuals, is didactic. The teacher lectures, invites responses from the students, monitors the acquisition of knowl-

edge, and tests that acquisition in various ways.

In the second column, the students are engaged in developing habits of performance, which is all that is involved in the development of an art or skill. Art, skill, or technique is nothing more that a cultivated, habitual ability to do a certain kind of thing well, whether that is swimming and dancing, or reading and writing. Here, students are acquiring linguistic, mathematical, scientific, and historical *know-how* in contrast to what they acquire in the first column, which is *know-that* with respect to language, literature, and the fine arts, mathematics and science, history, geography, and social studies. Here, the method of instruction cannot be didactic or monitorial; it cannot be dependent on textbooks. It must be coaching, the same kind used in the gym to develop bodily skills; only here it is used by a different kind of coach in the classroom to develop intellectual skills.

In the third column, students are engaged in a process of enlightenment, the process whereby they develop their understanding of the basic and controlling ideas in all fields of subject matter and come to appreciate better all the human values embodied in works of art. Here, students move progressively from understanding less to understanding more— understanding better what they already know and appreciating more what they already have experienced. Here, the method of instruction cannot be either didactic or coaching. It must be the Socratic, or maieutic, method of questioning and discussing. It should not occur in an ordinary classroom with the students sitting in rows and the teacher in front of the class, but in a seminar room, with the students sitting around a table and the teacher sitting with them as an equal, even though a little older and wiser.

Of these three main elements in the re-quired curriculum, the third column is completely innovative. Nothing like this is done in our schools, and because it is completely absent from the ordinary curriculum of basic schooling, the students never have the experience of having their minds addressed in a challenging way or of being asked to think about important ideas, to express their thoughts to defend their opinions in a reasonable fashion.

The only thing that is innovative about the second column is the insistence that the method of instruction here must be coaching carried on either with one student at a time or with very small groups of students. Nothing else can be effective in the development of a skill, be it bodily or intellectual. The absence of such individualized coaching in our schools explains why most of the students cannot read well, write well, speak well, listen well, or perform well any of the other basic intellectual operations.

The three columns are closely interconnected and integrated, but the middle column—the one concerned with linguistic, mathematical, and scientific skills—is central. It both supports and is supported by the other two columns. All the intellectual skills with which it is concerned must be exercised in the study of the three basic subject-matters and in acquiring knowledge about them, and these intellectual skills must be exercised in the seminars devoted to the discussion of books and other things.

In addition to the three main columns in the curriculum ascending through the 12 years of basic schooling, there are three adjuncts: One is 12 years of physical training, accompanied by instruction in bodily care and hygiene. The second, running through something less than 12 years, is the development of basic manual skills, such as cooking, sewing, carpentry, and the operation of all kinds of machines. The third, reserved for the last year or two, is an introduction to the whole world of work—the range of occupations in which human beings earn their livings. This is not particularized job training. It is the very opposite. It aims at a broad understanding of what is involved in working for a living and of the various ways in which that can be done. If, at the end of 12 years, students wish training for specific jobs, they should get that in two-year community or junior colleges, or on the job itself, or in technical institutes of one sort or another.

Everything that has not been specifically mentioned as occupying the time of the school day should be reserved for after-hours and have the status of extracurricular activities.

Please note: The required course of study just described is as important for what it *displaces* as for what it introduces. It displaces a multitude of elective courses, especially those offered in our secondary schools, most of which make little or no contribution to general, liberal education. It eliminates all narrowly specialized job training, which now abounds in our schools. It throws out of the curriculum and into the category of optional extracurricular activities a variety of things that have little or no educational value.

If it did not call for all these displacements, there would not be enough time in the school day or year to accomplish everything that is essential to the general, liberal learning that must be the content of basic schooling.

THE QUINTESSENTIAL ELEMENT

So far, I have set forth the bare essentials of the Paideia Proposal with regard to basic schooling. I have not yet mentioned the quintessential element—the *sine qua non*—without which nothing else can possibly come to frui-

tion, no matter how sound it might be in principle. The heart of the matter is the quality of learning and the quality of teaching that occupies the school day, not to mention the quality of the homework after school.

First, the learning must be active. It must use the whole mind, not just the memory. It must be learning by discovery, in which the student, never the teacher, is the primary agent. Learning by discovery, which is the only genuine learning, may be either unaided or aided. It is unaided only for geniuses. For most students, discovery must be aided.

Here is where the teachers come in—as aids in the process of learning by discovery not as knowers who attempt to put the knowledge they have into the minds of their students. The quality of the teaching, in short, depends crucially upon how the teacher conceives his role in the process of learning, and that must be as an aid to the student's process of discovery.

I am prepared for the questions that must be agitating you by now: How and where will we get the teachers who can perform as teachers should? How will we be able to staff the program with teachers so trained that they will be competent to provide the quality of instruction required for the quality of learning desired?

The first part of our answer to these questions is negative: We *cannot* get the teachers we need for the Paideia program from schools of education *as they are now constituted*. As teachers are now trained for teaching, they simply will not do. The ideal—an impracticable ideal—would be to ask for teachers who are, themselves, truly educated human beings. But truly educated human beings are too rare. Even if we could draft all who are now alive, there still would be far too few to staff our schools.

Well, then, what can we look for? Look

for teachers who are actively engaged in the process of *becoming* educated human beings, who are themselves deeply motivated to develop their own minds. Assuming this is not too much to ask for the present, how should teachers be schooled and trained in the future? First, they should have the same kind of basic schooling that is recommended in the Paideia Proposal. Second, they should have additional schooling, at the college and even the university level, in which the same kind of general, liberal learning is carried on at advanced levels—more deeply, broadly, and intensively than it can be done in the first 12 years of schooling. Third, they must be given something analogous to the clinical experience in the training of physicians. They must engage in practice-teaching under supervision, which is another way of saying that they must be *coached* in the arts of teaching, not just given didactic instruction in educational psychology and in pedagogy. Finally, and most important of all, they must learn how to teach well by being exposed to the performances of those who are masters of the arts involved in teaching.

It is by watching a good teacher at work that they will be able to perceive what is involved in the process of assisting others to learn by discovery. Perceiving it, they must then try to emulate what they observe, and through this process, they slowly will become good teachers themselves.

The Paideia Proposal recognizes the need for three different kinds of institutions at the collegiate level: The two-year community or junior college should offer a wide choice of electives that give students some training in one or another specialized field, mainly those fields of study that have something to do with earning a living. The four-year college also should offer a wide variety of electives, to be chosen by students who aim at the various professional or technical occupations that require advanced study. Those elective majors chosen by students should be accompanied, for all students, by one required minor, in which the kind of general and liberal learning that was begun at the level of basic schooling is continued at a higher level in the four years of college. And we should have still a third type of collegiate institution—a four-year college in which general, liberal learning at a higher level constitutes a required course of study that is to be taken by all students. *It is this third type of college, by the way, that should be attended by all who plan to become teachers in our basic schools.*

At the university level, there should be a continuation of general, liberal learning at a still higher level to accompany intensive specialization in this or that field of science or scholarship, this or that learned profession. Our insistence on the continuation of general, liberal learning at all the higher levels of schooling stems from our concern with the worst cultural disease that is rampant in our society—*the barbarism of specialization.*

There is no question that our technologically advanced industrial society needs specialists of all sorts. There is no question that the advancement of knowledge in all fields of science and scholarship, and in all the learned professions, needs intense specialization. But for the sake of preserving and enhancing our cultural traditions, as well as for the health of science and scholarship, we need specialists who also are generalists—generally cultivated human beings, not just good plumbers. We need truly educated human beings who can perform their special tasks better precisely because they have general cultivation as well as intensely specialized training.

Changes indeed are needed in higher education, but those improvements cannot reasonably be expected unless improvement in basic schooling makes that possible.

THE FUTURE OF OUR FREE INSTITUTIONS

I already have declared as emphatically as I know how that the quality of human life in our society depends on the quality of the schooling we give our young people, both basic and advanced. But a marked elevation in the quality of human life is not the only reason improving the quality of schooling is so necessary—not the only reason we must move heaven and earth to stop the deterioration of our schools and turn them in the opposite direction. The other reason is to safeguard the future of our free institutions.

They cannot prosper, they may not even survive, unless we do something to rescue our schools from their current deplorable deterioration. Democracy, in the full sense of that term, came into existence only in this century and only in a few countries on earth, among which the United States is an outstanding example. But democracy came into existence in this century only in its initial conditions, all of which hold out promises for the future that remain to be fulfilled. Unless we do something about improving the quality of basic schooling for all and the quality of advanced schooling for some, there is little chance that those promises ever will be fulfilled. And if they are not, our free institutions are doomed to decay and wither away.

We face many insistently urgent problems. Our prosperity and even our survival depend on the solution of those problems— the threat of nuclear war, the exhaustion of essential resources and of supplies of energy, the pollution or spoilage of the environment, the spiraling of inflation accompanied by the spread of unemployment.

To solve these problems, we need resourceful and innovative leadership. For that to arise and be effective, an educated populace is needed. Trained intelligence—not only on the part of leaders, but also on the part of followers—holds the key to the solution of the problems our society faces. Achieving peace, prosperity, and plenty could put us on the threshold of an early paradise. But a much better education system than now exists also is needed, for that alone can carry us across the threshold. Without it, a poorly schooled population will not be able to put to good use the opportunities afforded by the achievement of the general welfare. Those who are not schooled to enjoy society can only despoil its institutions and corrupt themselves.

HERE'S WHAT PAIDEIA MEANS

The Greek word Paideia (pronounced PIE-day-uh) means general, humnistic learning—the learning that should be the common possession of all human beings. That is why we adopted *paideia* as the name for our project and our proposals.

The Paideia group has spent more than two years thinking about what must be done to rescue our schools from the anything-but-innocuous desuetude into which they have fallen. My summary of the Paideia Proposal in the accompanying article must necessarily omit many details. But I have tried to describe the essentials of our proposals for the reform of basic schooling.

The other participants in the Paideia Project include the following:

Jacques Barzun, formerly provost of Columbia University, currently literary advisor of Charles Scribner's Sons;

Otto Bird, formerly head of the program of general studies, University of Notre Dame;

Leon Botstein, president of Bard College, Annandale-on-Hudson, N.Y.;

Ernest Boyer, president of the Carnegie Foundation for the Advancement of Teaching, Washington, D.C.;

Nicholas Caputi, principal of Skyline High School, Oakland, Calif.;

Douglass Cater, senior fellow of the Aspen (Colorado) Institute for Humanistic Studies;

Donald Cowan, formerly president of University of Dallas, and currently fellow of the Dallas Institute for Humanities and Culture;

Alonzo Crim, superintendent of schools, Atlanta;

Clifton Fadiman, director of the Council for Basic Education, Washington, D.C.;

Richard Hunt, director of program, Andrew W. Mellon Faculty Fellowships in the Humanities, Harvard University;

Ruth Love, superintendent of schools, Chicago;

James Nelson, director of the Wye Institute, Queenstown, Md.;

James O'Toole, professor of management in the Graduate School of Business Administration University of Southern California, Los Angeles;

Theodore Puck, president of the Eleanor Roosevelt Institute for Cancer Research, Denver;

Adolph Schmidt, member of the Board of Visitors and Governors of St. John's College, Annapolis, Md.;

Adele Simmons, president of Hampshire College, Amherst, Mass.;

Theodore Sizer, formerly headmaster of Phillips Academy-Andover;

and finally, my close associates at the Institute for Philosophical Research in Chicago, **Charles Van Doren, John Van Doren** and **Geraldine Van Doren.**—M.A.

The Paideia Proposal: Noble Ambitions, False Leads, and Symbolic Politics

Willis D. Hawley

Willis D. Hawley is Dean and Professor of Political Science at George Peabody College for Teachers, Vanderbilt University. His articles have appeared in a number of education journals.

Any idea that has the support of both Mortimer Adler and Albert Shanker is an idea worth engaging and, some would say, worrying about. *The Paideia Proposal* enjoys the endorsement not only of these two luminaries but of people as diverse in background and commitments as Benjamin Mays, William Friday, Theodore Sizer, Ruth Love, Jacques Barzun, Alonzo Crim, Ernest Boyer, Clifton Fadiman, and Gus Tyler.* It has been the focus of national news magazines and TV talk shows. Bookstores in many parts of the country report that the attractive 84-page "manifesto" is already sold out.

Interest in the Paideia group's proposal seems traceable to the growing national concern that our schools are not preparing our young people for the challenges of what Daniel J. Boorstin calls "the technological republic" and that this failure, especially when compared to the achievements of other nations, threatens our economic prosperity and even our national security.

The Paideia proposal eloquently urges on us a single-track core curriculum for elementary and secondary schools and certain strategies for teaching those subjects. There is much to admire in the proposal. There is no question that we need to change the curriculum of American schools to make it more rigorous and to ensure attention to more advanced mathematics, science, and language competencies. And, it is surely time that we ask more of youngsters than we are asking

From Willis D. Hawley, "The Paideia Proposal: Noble Ambitions, False Leads, and Symbolic Politics." Reprinted with permission from EDUCATION WEEK, Volume II, Number 12 (November 24, 1982).

*Benjamin Mays, president emeritus, Atlanta Board of Education; William Friday, president, University of North Carolina; Theodore R. Sizer, chairman, "A Study of High Schools" and former headmaster, Phillips Academy, Andover; Ruth B. Love, superintendent of schools, Chicago; Jacques Barzun, former provost of Columbia University, author, and critic; Alonzo Crim, superintendent, Atlantic Public Schools; Ernest L. Boyer, president, Carnegie Foundation for the Advancement of Teaching; Clifton Fadiman, author and critic; Gus Taylor, assistant president, International Ladies Garment Workers Union.

and that we insist that the gaps in achievement among and within most schools be reduced dramatically. It is easy to identify with Mr. Adler and his colleagues in the Paideia group when they assert that we should insist on education of superior quality for all Americans, regardless of their social background.

As a call to renewed interest in the quality of our schools, as a stimulant to reexamine what is being taught, and as a challenge to expect more of our schools and of our young people, the Paideia proposal contributes much to the growing demand for educational change. But as a guide to action, which it purports to be, the proposal leads us down primrose paths and away from the main roads we need to travel if we are to secure, as almost all now agree we must, higher quality education for all the nation's youngsters.

The Paideia Proposal is not a blueprint for a new structure within which we can bring about meaningful change in the effectiveness of our schools. Rather, it is an artist's rendering that pays little attention either to the terrain upon which the new structure will be built or to the practical problems of financing and construction.

Mr. Adler is impatient with those who charge that the proposal is impractical. He has been quoted as saying ". . . I don't see why our group, having come up with the proposal, should solve all the practical problems." Nice work, if you can get it. But one reason one might want to engage practicalities is that they often suggest important shortcomings of an idea. Educational reformers are well acquainted with windmills, and the lesson of past reform efforts is that the search for "a solution" or "an approach" is futile. If only it were as simple as deciding what it would be nice for everyone to know (which is, according to the Paideia proposal, *everything* except vocation skills).

But the key to improving our schools is not curriculum reform. Americans have always sought a quick and simple fix to what they have perceived to be the problems of schools. However, meaningful changes will require that we undertake the complicated jobs of improving teaching, dealing with diversity, and ensuring effective management of resources. Better curricula will help, to be sure, but they are not *the* answer.

The inadequacies of our schools mirror the characteristics of our society. Dramatic inequalities of income, racial and social class discrimination, chronic unemployment in some sectors, and the historically low status of education are the causes, not the products, of schools' shortcomings.

The Paideia group's proposal fails us for at least three reasons: the idea of a core curriculum is not only impractical but educationally unsound; its attention to evidence about learning and school effectiveness seems nonexistent; and its emphasis on curriculum as the vehicle for change puts the cart before the horse and seems likely to direct attention away from more promising but more complicated solutions.

The single-track core curriculum proposed by Mr. Adler and his colleagues insists that all children learn the same things in schools. For example, all children are expected to know calculus. The first question is: Can all children learn—and become proficient in—the same subjects? It is one thing to say, as many scholars and educators now do, that almost all children can be expected to acquire certain knowledge and skills and to demonstrate reasonably high levels of achievement. It's quite another to neglect the reality that successful efforts to do this require heavy emphasis on a limited number of subjects and the adaptation of the pace and content of learning to the capabilities of students. Never mind that teachers do not know many of the things that the Paideia proposal says students need to learn. Let me assert that a majority of the nation's brightest college students—or philosophers—could not employ calculus to solve a problem if their lives depended on it. Fortunately, few of us are in such mortal danger or ever will be. The Paideia group wants everyone to learn everything—our language, a foreign language, literature, fine arts, mathematics, natural science, history, geography, and social studies. On top of this, students will take 12 years of physical education as well as industrial arts; they will be involved in drama, music, and the visual arts; and they'll learn how to exercise critical and moral judgments. Let him or her among us . . . cast the first stone.

The second problem with the idea of a core curriculum is that it assumes that all students learn in the same way. What people can learn—even if they have the same capabilities—is related to what they want to learn and to differences in the ways they acquire, process, and integrate information. These differences in interest and "learning style" are affected not only by what goes on in schools, but by differences in genes and in home and community environments.

Third, the Paideia group's heavy emphasis on a core curriculum ascribes more importance to *what* one learns than to the acquisition of an ability to learn and a love of learning. In a society where the average person may change occupations five times and where the ability to use new information may be the most important determinant of success, our concept of what it means to be an educated person will need to change. It will be more important to be a learner than to be learned.

In dealing with the teaching and learning process, the Paideia proposal imagines that one can divide the things to be learned into three classes and for each of these a par-

ticular pedagogical approach is most appropriate. No evidence is offered to support this important assertion. Research on effective teaching suggests that good teachers have a broad repertoire of teaching skills and that while teaching a given subject the teachers easily move from one to another in meeting the needs of their students.

Those who study how children learn will be surprised to find that lectures and description are strongly recommended teaching styles and that the group advocates "coaching" as the major way to ensure that children develop their intellectual skills.

To accept fully the argument of the Paideia group, educators would need to overlook much of the recent research on effective teaching and effective schools because that research directs the quest of better education to concerns largely unaddressed in the proposal.

The history of American education is replete with efforts to find, as the Stanford University scholar David Tyack has put it, the "one best system." We want desperately to make the big play that will, in itself, turn the game around. Whether it is desegregation, open classrooms, technology, or curriculum reform, we persist in searching for *the* solution. In many ways, curriculum reform is the most attractive strategy for change. It is easily explained, can be imposed from above (seemingly), is hard to argue against, and, if properly articulated, holds out hopes for great change. Everyone knows that a better cake can be had through a better recipe. But experience indicates that curriculum reform is illusory. The distance between mandating a curriculum and student learning is great indeed. The "new math," for example, stumbled on teacher incapacity and parental ignorance. The results of the more recent legislatively imposed requirements that economics (especially free enterprise) be taught in schools should provide no sense of security to those who worry about the collapse of our economy or the triumph of democratic socialism.

Curriculum reform is not only difficult to achieve at the classroom level, but the imposition of new structures lulls us into a sense of false security. As Soviet educators know, if people see everyone taking physics courses, they are less likely to ask whether students are learning about physics. And, as university professors know, if the curriculum is rigorous, the blame for student failure can be assigned to students.

The point here is the argument of Murry Edleman (professor of political science at the University of Wisconsin) that many public changes in structures can be thought of as symbolic politics. They create the illusion of real change, which, in turn, dampens the fires of reform and induces quiescence. The Paideia proposal is patent medicine in this sense. Unfortunately, the formula that will improve the health of the body education is more complicated and, probably, more difficult to sell.

At best, this critique may seem like overkill to many. The goals of the Paideia group are noble ones, after all, and the proposal will surely encourage us to rethink what we are doing. Isn't it all right to set high goals and let others worry about whether it can really work? No, it is not.

First, to pursue the holy grail with no certainty of its powers and without a reasonably good map is not likely to be productive. Such a quest, instead, is likely to be frustrating and to engage energies that could be better spent on the pursuit of more promising ways to improve American education.

Second, we have substantially increased our knowledge about effective teaching and effective schools, and it seems important to pursue the directions suggested by this relatively recent research. Some school systems are now engaging successfully in such pursuits though they are certainly less dramatic than the steps the Paideia group would have us take.

Third, a major obstacle to securing an educational system that produces high academic achievement among all youngsters is the social and economic inequality that distinguishes the United States from most other industrialized nations. The relationship between family income and academic performance is powerful. The Paideia proposal takes note of this fact by urging a system of preschool education, but it does not emphasize this strategy nor does it recognize that persistent efforts to expand publicly supported, early-childhood programs, which now serve less than one-third of the children who are legally eligible for (much less need) such services, have been unsuccessful. Nor does the Paideia proposal grapple with the fact that differences in the wealth of the haves and the have nots is growing and that the proportion of school children from families *below* the median income is rising. It is not enough to hold high hopes.

A growing body of knowledge about teaching and learning suggests directions for change that can increase the academic achievement of students from different backgrounds. A strategy for change must be of many parts. A core curriculum, much less one taught in specified ways, does not emerge from the accumulated knowledge as a strategy that has worked or is likely to work in the United States.

Instead, the research tells us, among other things, that student learning is fostered by engaging students in intensive success-bringing learning experiences, by using interactive teaching strategies, by refocusing the principal's efforts on instructional support, by restructuring decision making at the school level, by adapting the curriculum to student needs while insisting on high performance and steady progress, by creating school climates that emphasize academic achievement, by promoting change from the bottom up, and by encouraging stability in interpersonal contacts and curricula.

This is not an exhaustive list of promising strategies for school improvement. And, to be sure, we need to know more. But now that we are beginning both to understand systematically how to meet effectively the very diverse needs of students and to have the ability to learn more, it is time to put that knowledge and capacity to work.

There is in the land a sense that the improvement of our schools is not only necessary but possible. But failure to recognize that low achievement is critically related to poverty, to racial, class, and ethnic discrimination, and to the prospect of unemployment upon graduation is a form of national self-delusion. Changes in our educational system could improve the education of almost all children. But even if we make substantial progress in what and how we teach, the fundamental inequalities of income, status, and opportunities created by our economic, political, and social systems make it very unlikely that we will achieve equal outcomes for all.

DISCUSSION QUESTIONS AND ACTIVITIES

1. Does quality education require a one-track system of schooling?
2. How would some of the larger environmental inequalities be overcome in the Paideia Proposal?
3. What is the rationale for a single, required, twelve-year course of study for all?
4. Examine the three broad divisions of the curriculum. What features do you consider necessary? What needs to be added?
5. Adler's curriculum displaces many elective courses presently found in schools, specialized job training, and optional extracurricular activities. Explain why you agree or disagree with him over this decision.
6. Is Adler's plan adequate for selecting and preparing qualified teachers to staff his program?
7. In contrast to Adler, Hawley claims that the key to school improvement is not curriculum reform. What, then, is the key?
8. Can all students learn and become proficient in the same subject?
9. Does the Paideia Proposal assume that all students learn in the same way? Does it also emphasize what one learns more than acquiring an ability to learn and developing a love of learning?
10. What recent findings from research about teaching and learning does the Paideia Proposal neglect?
11. Make a survey of present school systems for programs similar to the Paideia Proposal and evaluate their success.
12. Explain the recent history of American education for similar programs. Trace and appraise their progress.
13. Organize a classroom debate of the Paideia Proposal and the perennialist philosophy on which it rests.

SUGGESTED READINGS

Principal Educational Works of Mortimer J. Adler

Adler has written more than thirty books and numerous articles. Listed below are his more important publications about education. See *Books in Print* for his other works.

A General Introduction to the Great Books and to a Liberal Education. Chicago: Encyclopedia Britannica, 1954. (with Peter Wolff)

"In Defense of the Philosophy of Education." In *Forty-first Yearbook of the National Society for the Study of Education,* Part I, ed. Nelson B. Henry. Chicago: University of Chicago Press, 1942, pp. 197–249.

How to Read a Book, rev. ed. New York: Simon & Schuster, 1972. (with Charles van Doren)

Paideia Problems and Possibilities. New York: Macmillan, 1983.

The Paideia Program: An Educational Syllabus. New York: Macmillan, 1984.

The Paideia Proposal. New York: Macmillan, 1982.

Philosopher at Large: An Intellectual Autobiography. New York: Macmillan, 1977.

Reforming Education in America. Boulder, Col.: Westview Press, 1977.

The Revolution in Education. Chicago: University of Chicago Press, 1958.

Works About the Paideia Proposal and Mortimer J. Adler's Educational Philosophy

Aubrey, R. F. "Reform in Schooling: Four proposals on an Educational Quest." *Journal of Counseling and Development* 63 (December 1984):204–213.

Childs, John L. *Education and Morals.* New York: Appleton-Century-Crofts, 1950, ch. 5.

Delattre, E. J. "The Paideia Proposal and American Education." 83rd Yearbook, Part II, National Social Studies Education, 1984, pp. 143–153.

Gilli, A. C. "The Role of Vocational Studies and Training in General-Liberal School." *Journal of Industrial Teacher Education* 21 (Spring 1984):13–24.

Gregory, M. W. "A Response to Mortimer Adler's Paideia Proposal." *Journal of General Education* 36, no. 2 (1984):70–78.

Hook, Sidney. *Education for Modern Man,* enlarged ed. New York: Knopf, 1963, ch. 3.

Johnson, T. W. "Classicists versus Experimentalists: Reexamining the Great Debate." *Journal of General Education* 36, no. 4 (1985):280–279.

Spear, K. "The Paideia Proposal. The Problems of Means and Ends in General Education." *Journal of General Education* 36, no. 2 (1984):79–86.

4

Beyond Freedom and Dignity

B. F. Skinner's behaviorism avoids deductive theories and relies on an inductive approach in his experimentation. His investigations start with empirical data and proceed tentatively to limited-range generalizations. Skinner rejects any method of inquiry that does not depend on sensory observation. He limits his system to description rather than the customary goal of explanation. His system attempts to avoid reductionism by defining concepts in terms of observables rather than reducing them to physiological states.

The simple unit of behavior is the reflex, which consists of "any observed correlation of stimulus and response." There are two types of behavior: respondent and operant. Behavior is called *respondent* when it is correlated to "specific eliciting stimuli"; behavior is *operant* when no stimuli are present. *Stimulus* means any modification of the environment, and a *response* is a correlated part of the behavior.

Conditioning in the form of respondent behavior is used by Skinner in his experiments with pigeons. Reinforcement (reward) is dependent on the response. Whenever the pigeon exhibits the desired response as a result of stimuli, the response is reinforced by providing food. On the other hand, with operant conditioning the response comes first and then it becomes reinforced. It is through operant conditioning that the efficiency of behavior is improved. This form of conditioning builds a repertoire by which we handle such processes as walking, playing games, using tools, and other activities.

In Skinner's selection, he opposes both humanistic and cognitive psychology. He explains the role of programmed materials in fostering greater learning and cites four principles to improve teaching.

Peters accuses Skinner of holding musty nineteenth-century views and attacking straw men. Skinner exhibits a form of utilitarianism that pushes the instrumental approach to life to its limits and poses the danger, according to Peters, of some people using their freedom to deny others their dignity.

The Shame of
American Education

B. F. Skinner

B. F. Skinner (b. 1904) is an internationally known behaviorist recognized for his system of operant conditioning, contributions to programmed learning, and his utopian system of controls based on positive reinforcement. He was educated at Hamilton College (A.B.) and Harvard University (M.A., Ph.D.). He has taught at a number of universities, served as Edgar Pierce Professor at Harvard, and is now a professor emeritus there. A prolific author of influential studies, Skinner is the recipient of numerous awards and honorary degrees from American and foreign universities.

On a morning in October 1957, Americans were awakened by the beeping of a satellite. It was a Russian satellite, Sputnik. Why was it not American? Was something wrong with American education? Evidently so, and money was quickly voted to improve American schools. Now we are being awakened by the beepings of Japanese cars, Japanese radios, phonographs, and television sets, and Japanese wristwatch alarms, and again questions are being asked about American education, especially in science and mathematics.

Something does seem to be wrong. According to a recent report of the National Commission on Excellence in Education (1983), for example, the average achievement of our high-school students on standardized tests is now lower than it was a quarter of a century ago, and students in American schools compare poorly with those in other nations in many fields. As the commission put it, America is threatened by "a rising tide of mediocrity."

The first wave of reform is usually rhetorical. To improve education we are said to need "imaginative innovations," a "broad national effort" leading to a "deep and lasting change," and a "commitment to excellence." More specific suggestions have been made, however. To get better teachers we should pay them more, possibly according to merit. They should be certified to teach the subjects they teach. To get better students, scholarship standards should be raised. The school day should be extended from 6 to 7 hours, more time should be spent on homework, and the school year should be lengthened from 180 to 200, or even 220, days. We should change what we are teaching. Social studies are all very well, but they should not take time away from basics, especially mathematics.

As many of us have learned to expect, there is a curious omission in that list: It contains no suggestion that teaching be improved. There is a conspiracy of silence about teaching as a skill. The *New York Times* publishes a quarterly survey of education. Three recent issues (Fisk, 1982, 1983a, 1983b) contained 18 articles about the kinds of things being taught in schools; 11 articles about the financial problems of students and schools; 10 articles about the needs of special students, from the gifted to the disadvantaged; and smaller numbers of articles about the selection of students, professional problems of teachers, and sports and other extracurricular activities. Of about 70 articles, only 2 had anything to do with how students are taught or how they could be taught better. Pedagogy is a dirty word.

In January 1981, Frederick Mosteller, president of the American Association for the Advancement of Science, gave an address called "Innovation and Evaluation" (Mosteller, 1981). He began with an example of the time which can pass between a scientific discovery and its practical use. The fact that lemon juice cures scurvy was discovered in 1601, but more than 190 years passed before the British navy began to use citrus juice on a regular basis and another 70 before scurvy was wiped out in the mercantile marine—a lag of 264 years. Lags have grown shorter but, as Mosteller pointed out, are often still too long. Perhaps unwittingly he gave another example. He called for initiatives in science and engineering education and said that a major theme of the 1982 meeting of the association would be a "national commitment to educational excellence in science and engineering for all Americans" (p. 886).

When Mosteller's address was published in *Science,* I wrote a letter to the editor (Skinner, 1981) calling attention to an experiment in teaching algebra in a school in Roanoke, Virginia (Rushton, 1965). In this experiment an eighth-grade class using simple teaching machines and hastily composed instructional programs went through *all* of ninth-grade algebra in *half* a year. Their grades met ninth-grade norms, and when tested a year later the students remembered rather more than usual. Had American educators decided that that was the way to teach algebra? They had not. The experiment was done in 1960, but education had not yet made any use of it. The lag was already 21 years long.

A month or so later I ran into Mosteller. "Did you see my letter in *Science* about teaching machines?" I asked. "Teaching machines?" he said, puzzled. "Oh, you mean *computers*—teaching machines to *you*." And, of course, he was right. Computer is the current word. But is it the right one? Computers are now badly misnamed. They were designed to compute, but they are not computing when they are processing words, or displaying Pac-Man, or aiding instruction (unless the instruction is in computing). "Computer" has all the respectability of the white-collar executive, whereas "machine" is definitely blue-collar, but let us call things by their right names. Instruction may be "computer aided," and all good instruction must be "interactive," but machines that teach are teaching machines.

I liked the Roanoke experiment because it confirmed something I had said a few years earlier to the effect that with teaching machines and programmed instruction one could teach what is now taught in American schools in half the time with half the effort. I shall not review other evidence that that is true. Instead, I shall demonstrate my faith in a technology of teaching by going out on a limb. I claim that the school system of any large American city could be so redesigned, at little or no additional cost, that students would come to school and apply themselves to their work with a minimum of punitive coercion and, with very rare exceptions, learn to read with reasonable ease, express themselves well in speech and writing, and solve a fair range of mathematical problems. I want to talk about why this has not been done.

The teaching machines of 25 years ago were crude, of course, but that is scarcely an explanation. The calculating machines were crude, too, yet they were used until they could be replaced by something better. The hardware problem has now been solved, but resistance to a technology of teaching survives. The rank commercialism which quickly engulfed the field of teaching machines is another possible explanation. Too many people rushed in to write bad programs and make promises that could not be kept. But that should not have concealed the value of programmed instruction for so many years. There is more than that to be said for the marketplace in the selection of a better mousetrap.

PSYCHOLOGICAL ROADBLOCKS

I shall argue that educators have not seized this chance to solve their problems because the solution conflicts with deeply entrenched views of human behavior, and that these views are too strongly supported by current psychology. Humanistic psychologists, for example, tend to feel threatened by any kind of scientific analysis of human behavior, particularly if it leads to a "technology" that can be used to intervene in people's lives. A technology of teaching is especially threatening. Carl Rogers has said that teaching is vastly overrated, and Ivan Illich has called for the de-schooling of society. I dealt with the problem in *Beyond Freedom and Dignity* (Skinner, 1971). To give a single example, we do not like to be told something we already know, for we can then no longer claim credit for having known it.

To solve that problem, Plato tried to show that students already possess knowledge and have only to be shown that they possess it. But the famous scene in Plato's *Meno* in which Socrates shows that the slaveboy already knows Pythagoras's theorem for doubling the square is one of the great intellectual hoaxes of all time. The slaveboy agrees

with everything Socrates says, but there is no evidence whatsoever that he could then go through the proof by himself. Indeed, Socrates says that the boy would need to be taken through it many times before he could do so.

Cognitive psychology is causing much more trouble, but in a different way. It is hard to be precise because the field is usually presented in what we may call a cognitive style. For example, a pamphlet of the National Institute of Education (1980) quotes with approval the contention that "at the present time, modern cognitive psychology is the dominant theoretical force in psychological science as opposed to the first half of the century when behavioristic, anti-mentalistic stimulus-response theories of learning were in the ascendance" (p. 391). (The writer means "ascendant.") The pamphlet tells us that cognitive science studies learning, but not in quite those words. Instead, cognitive science is said to be "characterized by a concern with understanding the mechanisms by which human beings carry out complex intellectual activities including learning" (p. 391). The pamphlet also says that cognitive science can help construct tests that will tell us more about what a student has learned and hence how to teach better, but here is the way it says this: "Attention will be placed on two specific topics: Applications of cognitive models of the knowledge structure of various subject matters and of learning and problem solving to construction of tests that identify processes underlying test answers, analyze errors, and provide information about what students know and don't know, and strategies for integrating testing information with instructional decisions" (p. 393). Notice especially the cognitive style in the last phrase—the question is not "whether test results can suggest better ways of teaching" but "whether there are strategies for integrating testing information with instructional decisions."

The Commission on Behavioral and Social Sciences and Education of the National Research Council (1984) provides a more recent example in its announcement of a biennial program plan covering the period 1 May 1983 to 30 April 1985. The commission will take advantage of "significant advances . . . in the cognitive sciences" (p. 41). Will it study learning? Well, not exactly. The members will "direct their attention to studies of fundamental processes underlying the nature and development of learning" (p. 41). Why do cognitive psychologists not tell us frankly what they are up to? Is it possible that they themselves do not really know?

Cognitive psychology is certainly in the ascendant. The word *cognitive* is sprinkled through the psychological literature like salt—and, like salt, not so much for any flavor of its own but to bring out the flavor of other things, things which a quarter of a century ago would have been called by other names. The heading of an article in a recent issue of the APA *Monitor* (Turkington, 1983) tells us that "cognitive deficits" are important in understanding alcoholism. In the text we learn simply that alcoholics show losses in perception and motor skills. Perception and motor skills used to be fields of psychology; now they are fields of cognitive science. Nothing has been changed except the name, and the change has been made for suspicious reasons. There is a sense of profundity about "cognitive deficits," but it does not take us any deeper into the subject.

Much of the vogue of cognitive science is due to advances in computer technology. The computer offers an appealing simplification of some old psychological problems. Sensation and perception are reduced to input; learning and memory to the processing, storage, and retrieval of information; and action to output. It is very much like the old stimulus-response formula patched up with interven-

ing variables. To say that students process information is to use a doubtful metaphor, and how they process information is still the old question of how they learn.

Cognitive psychology also gains prestige from its alignment with brain research. Interesting things are certainly being discovered about the biochemistry and circuitry of the brain, but we are still a long way from knowing what is happening in the brain as behavior is shaped and maintained by contingencies of reinforcement, and that means that we are a long way from help in designing useful instructional practices.

Cognitive science is also said to be supported by modern linguistics, a topic to which I am particularly sensitive. Programmed instruction emerged from my analysis of verbal behavior (Skinner, 1957), which linguists, particularly generative grammarians, have, of course, attacked. So far as I know they have offered no equally effective practices. One might expect them to have improved the teaching of languages, but almost all language laboratories still work in particularly outmoded ways, and language instruction is one of the principal failures of precollege education.

Psycholinguistics moves in essentially the same direction in its hopeless commitment to development. Behavior is said to change in ways determined by its structure. The change may be a function of age, but age is not a variable that one can manipulate. The extent to which developmentalism has encouraged a neglect of more useful ways of changing behavior is shown by a recent report (Siegler, 1983) in which the number of studies concerned with the development of behavior in children was found to have skyrocketed, whereas the number concerned will how children learn has dropped to a point at which the researcher could scarcely find any examples at all.

There are many fine cognitive psychologists who are doing fine research, but they are not the cognitive psychologists who for 25 years have been promising great advances in education. A short paper published in *Science* last April (Resnick, 1983) asserts that "recent findings in cognitive science suggest new approaches to teaching in science and mathematics" (p. 477), but the examples given, when expressed in noncognitive style, are simply these: (a) Students learn about the world in "naive" ways before they study science; (b) naive theories interfere with learning scientific theories, (c) we should therefore teach science as early as possible; (d) many problems are not solved exclusively with mathematics; qualitative experience is important; (e) students learn more than isolated facts; they learn how facts are related to each other; and (f) students relate what they are learning to what they already know. If these are *recent* findings, where has cognitive science been?

Cognitive psychology is frequently presented as a revolt against behaviorism, but it is not a revolt; it is a retreat. Everyday English is full of terms derived from ancient explanations of human behavior. We spoke that language when we were young. When we went out into the world and became psychologists, we learned to speak in other ways but made mistakes for which we were punished. But now we can relax. Cognitive psychology is Old Home Week. We are back among friends speaking the language we spoke when we were growing up. We can talk about love and will and ideas and memories and feelings and states of mind, and no one will ask us what we mean; no one will raise an eyebrow.

SCHOOLS OF EDUCATION

Psychological theories come into the hands of teachers through schools of education and teachers' colleges, and it is there, I think, that we must lay the major blame for what is happening in American education. In a recent article in the *New York Times* (Botstein, 1983), President Leon Botstein of Bard College proposed that schools of education, teachers' colleges, and departments of education simply be disbanded. But he gave a different reason. He said that schools of that sort "placed too great an emphasis on pedagogical techniques and psychological studies" (p. 64), when they should be teaching the subjects the teachers will eventually teach. But disbanding such schools is certainly a move in the wrong direction. It has long been said that college teaching is the only profession for which there is no professional training. Would-be doctors go to medical schools, would-be lawyers go to law schools, and would-be engineers go to institutes of technology, but would-be college teachers just start teaching. Fortunately it is recognized that grade- and high-school teachers need to learn to teach. The trouble is, they are not being taught in effective ways. The commitment to humanistic and cognitive psychology is only part of the problem.

Equally damaging is the assumption that teaching can be adequately discussed in everyday English. The appeal to laymanship is attractive. At the "Convocation on Science and Mathematics, in the Schools" called by the National Academies of Sciences and Engineering, one member said that "what we need are bright, energetic, dedicated young people, trained in mathematics . . . science . . . or technology, mixing it up with 6- to 13-year-old kids in the classroom" (Raizen, 1983, p. 19). The problem is too grave to be solved in any such way. The first page of the report notes with approval that "if there is one American enterprise that is local in its design and control it is education" (p. 1). That is held to be a virtue. But certainly the commission would not approve similar statements about medicine, law, or science and technology. Why should the community decide how children are to be taught? The commission is actually pointing to one explanation of why education is failing.

We must beware of the fallacy of the good teacher and the good student. There are many good teachers who have not needed to learn to teach. They would be good at almost anything they tried. There are many good students who scarcely need to be taught. Put a good teacher and a good student together and you have what seems to be an ideal instructional setting. But it is disastrous to take it as a model to be followed in our schools, where hundreds of thousands of teachers must teach millions of students. Teachers must learn how to teach, and they must be taught by schools of education. They need only to be taught more effective ways of teaching.

A SOLUTION

We could solve our major problems in education if students learned more during each day in school. That does not mean a longer day or year or more homework. It simply means using time more efficiently. Such a solution is not considered in any of the reports I have mentioned—whether from the National Institute of Education, the American Association for the Advancement of Science, the National Research Council, or the National Academies of Sciences and Engineering. Nevertheless, it is within easy reach. Here is all that needs to be done.

1. Be clear about what is to be taught. When I once explained to a group of grade-school teachers how I would teach children to spell words, one of them said, "Yes, but can you teach spelling?" For him, students spelled

words correctly not because they had learned to do so but because they had acquired a special ability. When I told a physicist colleague about the Roanoke experiment in teaching algebra, he said, "Yes, but did they learn algebra?" For him, algebra was more than solving certain kinds of problems; it was a mental faculty. No doubt the more words you learn to spell the easier it is to spell new words, and the more problems you solve in algebra the easier it is to solve new problems. What eventually emerges is often called *intuition*. We do not know what it is, but we can certainly say that no teacher has ever taught it directly, nor has any student ever displayed it without first learning to do the kinds of things it supposedly replaces.

2. Teach first things first. It is tempting to move too quickly to final products. I once asked a leader of the "new math" what he wanted students to be able to do. He was rather puzzled and then said, "I suppose I just want them to be able to follow a logical line of reasoning." That does not tell a teacher where to start or, indeed, how to proceed at any point. I once asked a colleague what he wanted his students to do as a result of having taken his introductory course in physics. "Well," he said, "I guess I've never thought about it that way." I'm afraid he spoke for most of the profession.

Among the ultimate but useless goals of education is "excellence." A candidate for president recently said that he would let local communities decide what that meant. "I am not going to try to define excellence for them," he said, and wisely so. Another useless ultimate goal is "creativity." It is said that students should do more than what they have been taught to do. They should be creative. But does it help to say that they must acquire creativity? More than 300 years ago, Molière wrote a famous line: "I am asked by the learned doctors for the cause and reason why opium puts one to sleep, to which I reply that there is in it a soporific virtue, the nature of which is to lull the senses." Two or three years ago an article in *Science* pointed out that 90% of scientific innovations were accomplished by fewer than 10% of scientists. The explanation, it was said, was that only a few scientists possess creativity. Molière's audiences laughed. Eventually some students behave in creative ways, but they must have something to be creative with and that must be taught first. Then they can be taught to multiply the variations which give rise to new and interesting forms of behavior. (Creativity, incidentally, is often said to be beyond a science of behavior, and it would be if that science were a matter of stimulus and response. By emphasizing the selective action of consequences, however, the experimental analysis of behavior deals with the creation of behavior precisely as Darwin dealt with the creation of species.)

3. Stop making all students advance at essentially the same rate. The phalanx was a great military invention, but it has long been out of date, and it should be out of date in American schools. Students are still expected to move from kindergarten through high school in 12 years, and we all know what is wrong: Those who could move faster are held back, and those who need more time fall farther and farther behind. We could double the efficiency of education with one change alone—by letting each student move at his or her own pace. (I wish I could blame this costly mistake on developmental psychology, because it is such a beautiful example of its major principle, but the timing is out of joint.)

No teacher can teach a class of 30 or 40 students and allow each to progress at an optimal speed. Tracking is too feeble a remedy. We must turn to individual instruments for part of the school curriculum. The report of the convocation held by the National Acade-

mies of Sciences and Engineering refers to "new technologies" which "can be used to extend the educational process, to supplement the teacher's role in new and imaginative ways" (Raizen, 1983, p. 15), but no great enthusiasm is shown. Thirty years ago educational television was promising, but the promise has not been kept. The report alludes to "computer-aided instruction" but calls it the latest "rage of education" and insists that "the primary use of the computer is for drill" (p. 15). (Properly programmed instruction is *never* drill if that means going over material again and again until it is learned.) The report also contains a timid allusion to "low-cost teaching stations that can be controlled by the learner" (p. 15), but evidently these stations are merely to give the student access to video material rather than to programs.

4. Program the subject matter. The heart of the teaching machine, call it what you will, is the programming of instruction—an advance not mentioned in any of the reports I have cited. Standard texts are designed to be read by the student, who will then discuss what they say with a teacher or take a test to see how much has been learned. Material prepared for individual study is different. It first induces students to say or do the things they are to learn to say or do. Their behavior is thus "primed" in the sense of being brought out for the first time. Until the behavior has acquired more strength, it may need to be prompted. Primes and prompts must then be carefully "vanished" until the behavior occurs without help. At that point the reinforcing consequences of being right are most effective in building and sustaining an enduring repertoire.

Working through a program is really a process of discovery, but not in the sense in which that word is currently used in education. We discover many things in the world around us, and that is usually better than being told about them, but as individuals we can discover only a very small part of the world. Mathematics has been discovered very slowly and painfully over thousands of years. Students discover it as they go through a program, but not in the sense of doing something for the first time in history. Trying to teach mathematics or science as if the students themselves were discovering things for the first time is not an efficient way of teaching the very skills with which, in the long run, a student may, with luck, actually make a genuine discovery.

When students move through well-constructed programs at their own pace, the so-called problem of motivation is automatically solved. For thousands of years students have studied to avoid the consequences of not studying. Punitive sanctions still survive, disguised in various ways, but the world is changing, and they are no longer easily imposed. The great mistake of progressive education was to try to replace them with natural curiosity. Teachers were to bring the real world into the classroom to arouse the students' interest. The inevitable result was a neglect of subjects in which children were seldom naturally interested—in particular, the so-called basics. One solution is to make some of the natural reinforcers—goods or privileges—artificially contingent upon basic behavior, as in a token economy. Such contingencies can be justified if they correct a lethargic or disordered classroom, but there should be no lethargy or disorder. It is characteristic of the human species that successful action is automatically reinforced. The fascination of video games is adequate proof. What would industrialists not give to see their workers as absorbed in their work as young people in a video arcade? What would teachers not give to see their students applying themselves with the same eagerness? (For that matter, what would any of us not give

to see ourselves as much in love with our work?) But there is no mystery; it is all a matter of the scheduling of reinforcements.

A good program of instruction guarantees a great deal of successful action. Students do not need to have a natural interest in what they are doing, and subject matters do not need to be dressed up to attract attention. No one really cares whether Pac-Man gobbles up all those little spots on the screen. Indeed, as soon as the screen is cleared, the player covers it again with little spots to be gobbled up. What is reinforcing is successful play, and in a well-designed instructional program students gobble up their assignments. I saw them doing that when I visited the project in Roanoke with its director, Allen Calvin. We entered a room in which 30 or 40 eighth-grade students were at their desks working on rather crude teaching machines. When I said I was surprised that they paid no attention to us, Calvin proposed a better demonstration. He asked me to keep my eye on the students and then went up on the teacher's platform. He jumped in the air and came down with a loud bang. Not a single student looked up. Students do not have to be made to study. Abundant reinforcement is enough, and good programming provides it.

THE TEACHER

Individually programmed instruction has much to offer teachers. It makes very few demands upon them. Paraprofessionals may take over some of their chores. That is not a reflection on teachers or a threat to their profession. There is much that only teachers can do, and they can do it as soon as they have been freed of unnecessary tasks.

Some things they can do are to talk to and listen to students and read what students write. A recent study (Goodlad, 1983) found that teachers are responding to things that students say during only 5% of the school day. If that is so, it is not surprising that one of the strongest complaints against our schools is that students do not learn to express themselves.

If given a chance, teachers can also be interesting and sympathetic companions. It is a difficult assignment in a classroom in which order is maintained by punitive sanctions. The word *discipline* has come a long way from its association with *disciple* as one who understands.

Success and progress are the very stuff on which programmed instruction feeds. They should also be the stuff that makes teaching worthwhile as a profession. Just as students must not only learn but know that they are learning, so teachers must not only teach but know that they are teaching. Burnout is usually regarded as the result of abusive treatment by students, but it can be as much the result of looking back upon a day in the classroom and wondering what one has accomplished. Along with a sense of satisfaction goes a place in the community. One proposed remedy for American education is to give teachers greater respect, but that is putting it the wrong way around. Let them teach twice as much in the same time and with the same effort, and they will be held in greater respect.

THE ESTABLISHMENT

The effect on the educational establishment may be much more disturbing. Almost 60 years ago Sidney Pressey invented a simple teaching machine and predicted the coming "industrial revolution" in education. In 1960 he wrote to me, "Before long the question will need to be faced as to what the student is to do with the time which automation will save him. More education in the same place or earlier completion of full-time education?" (Sidney Pressey, personal communication, 1960). Earlier completion is a problem. If what is now taught in the first and second grades can be taught in the first (and I am sure that it can), what will the second-grade teacher do? What is now done by the third- or fourth-grade teacher? At what age will the average student reach high school and at what age will he or she graduate? Certainly a better solution is to teach what is now taught more effectively and to teach many other things as well. Even so, students will probably reach college younger in years, but they will be far more mature. That change will more than pay for the inconvenience of making sweeping administrative changes.

The report of the National Commission on Excellence in Education (1983) repeatedly mistakes causes for effects. It says that "the educational foundations of our society are being eroded by a rising tide of mediocrity," but is the mediocrity causing the erosion? Should we say that the foundations of our automobile industry are being eroded by a rising tide of mediocre cars? Mediocrity is an effect, not a cause. Our educational foundations are being eroded by a commitment to laymanship and to theories of human behavior which simply do not lead to effective teaching. The report of the Convocation on Science and Mathematics in the Schools quotes President Reagan as saying that "this country was built on American respect for education. . . . Our challenge now is to create a resurgence of that thirst for education that typifies our nation's history" (Raizen, 1983, p. 1). But is education in trouble because it is no longer held in respect, or is it not held in respect because it is in trouble? Is it in trouble because people do not thirst for education, or do they not thirst for what is being offered?

Everyone is unhappy about education, but what is wrong? Let us look at a series of questions and answers rather like the series of propositions that logicians call a *sorites*:

1. Are students at fault when they do not learn? No, they have not been well taught.
2. Are teachers then at fault? No, they have not been properly taught to teach.
3. Are schools of education and teachers' colleges then at fault? No, they have not been given a theory of behavior that leads to effective teaching.
4. Are behavioral scientists then at fault? No, a culture too strongly committed to the view that a technology of behavior is a threat to freedom and dignity is not supporting the right behavioral science.
5. Is our culture then at fault? But what is the next step?

Let us review the sorites again and ask what can be done. Shall we:

1. Punish students who do not learn by flunking them?
2. Punish teachers who do not teach well by discharging them?
3. Punish schools of education which do not teach teaching well by disbanding them?
4. Punish behavioral science by refusing to support it?
5. Punish the culture that refuses to support behavioral science?

But you cannot punish a culture. A culture is punished by its failure or by other cultures which take its place in a continually evolving process. There could scarcely be a better example of the point of my book *Beyond Freedom and Dignity*. A culture that is not willing to accept scientific advances in the understanding of human behavior, together with the technology which emerges from these advances, will eventually be replaced by a culture that is.

When the National Commission on Excellence in Education (1983) said that "the essential raw materials needed to reform our education system are waiting to be mobilized" it spoke more truly than it knew, but to mobilize them the commission called for "leadership." That is as vague a word as excellence. Who, indeed, will make the changes that must be made if education is to play its proper role in American life? It is reasonable to turn to those who suffer most from the present situation.

1. Those who pay for education—primarily taxpayers and the parents of children in private schools—can simply demand their money's worth.
2. Those who use the products of grade- and high-school education—colleges and universities on the one hand and business and industry on the other—cannot refuse to buy, but they can be more discriminating.
3. Those who teach may simply withdraw from the profession, and too many are already exercising their right to do so. The organized withdrawal of a strike is usually a demand for higher wages, but it could also be a demand for better instructional facilities and administrative changes that would improve classroom practices.

But why must we always speak of higher standards for students, merit pay for teachers, and other versions of punitive sanctions? These are the things one thinks of first, and they will no doubt make teachers and students work harder, but they will not necessarily have a better effect. They are more likely to lead to further defection. There is a better way: Give students and teachers better reasons for learning and teaching. That is where the behavioral sciences can make a contribution. They can develop instructional practices so effective and so attractive in other ways that no one—student, teacher, or administrator—will need to be coerced into using them.

Young people are by far the most important natural resource of a nation, and the development of that resource is assigned to education. Each of us is born needing to learn what others have learned before us, and much of it needs to be taught. We would all be better off if education played a far more important part in transmitting our culture. Not only would that make for a stronger America (remember Sputnik), but we might also look forward to the day when the same issues could be discussed about the world as a whole—when, for example, all peoples produce the goods they consume and behave well toward each other, not because they are forced to do so but because they have been taught something of the ultimate advantages of a rich and peaceful world.

REFERENCES

Botstein, L. (1983, June 5). Nine proposals to improve our schools. *New York Times Magazine*, p. 59.

Fisk, E. B. (Ed.). (1982, November, 14). Fall survey of education [Supplement]. *New York Times*.

Fisk, E. B. (Ed.). (1983a, January 9). Winter survey of education [Supplement]. *New York Times*.

Fisk, E. B. (Ed.). (1983b, April 24). Spring survey of education [Supplement]. *New York Times*.

Goodlad, J. L. (1983). *A place called school.* New York: McGraw-Hill.

Mosteller, F. (1981). Innovation and evaluation. *Science, 211,* 881–886.

National Commission on Excellence in Education. (1983, April). *A nation at risk: The imperative for educational reform.* Washington, DC: U.S. Department of Education.

National Institute of Education. (1980). Science and technology and education. In *The five-year outlook: Problems, opportunities and constraints in science and technology* (Vol. 2, 391–399). Washington, DC: National Science Foundation.

National Research Council, Commission on Behavioral and Social Sciences and Education. (1984). Biennial program plan, May 1, 1983–April 30, 1985. Washington, DC: National Academy Press.

Raizen, S. (1983). *Science and mathematics in the schools: Report of a convocation.* Washington, DC: National Academy Press.

Resnick, L. B. (1983). Mathematics and science learning: A new conception. *Science, 220,* 477–478.

Rushton, E. W. (1965). *The Roanoke experiment.* Chicago: Encyclopedia Britannica Press.

Siegler, R. S. (1983). Five generalizations about cognitive development. *American Psychologist, 38,* 263–277.

Skinner, B. F. (1957). *Verbal behavior.* New York: Appleton-Century-Crofts.

Skinner, B. F. (1971). *Beyond freedom and dignity.* New York: Alfred A. Knopf.

Skinner, B. F. (1981). Innovation in science teaching. *Science, 212,* 283.

Turkington, C. (1983, June). Cognitive deficits hold promise for prediction of alcoholism. *APA Monitor,* p. 16.

Survival, The Soul or Personal Relationships

R. S. Peters

R. S. Peters (b. 1919) is one of today's leading educational philosophers. Formerly a dean and department chairman of the Faculty of Education at University of London's Institute of Education, he is now a professor emeritus. He is a member of the National Academy of Education and has contributed to various encyclopedias, philosophy journals, periodicals, and newspapers in the areas of psychology, political thought, philosophy, and philosophy of education.

This book [*Beyond Freedom and Dignity*] was proclaimed in *Science News* as 'one of the most important happenings in twentieth-century psychology', which is perhaps a revealing verdict on the history of psychology in this century. For Skinner's attitudes and ideas belong to the nineteenth century. Basically he is a Utilitarian who values happiness and who thinks that it is attainable if the environment can be more systematically controlled. Things can be fixed up all right for human benefit by the employment of a technology of human behaviour. This technology embodies the old inductivist view of science that generalisations are gradually built up out of systematic experimentation. The principles employed are the old principles of the association of ideas dressed up in their modern guise of the conditioning of responses which subserve the survival of the individual and the species.

Survival, of course, now seems a more urgent question than it did to nineteenth-century perfectibilists. In this respect Skinner's attitudes are less confident, less infected by a belief in the inevitability of progress. For he is very much a contemporary American as well, a member of a nation that has lost its nerve and shed some of its old arrogance. There is the Vietnam war, pollution, the blacks, the student drop-out, drugs and the threat of over-population. These are beginning to look like predicaments, not like problems that can be solved or fixed up—at least not until men are more persuaded of the possibilities opened up by Skinner's technology of behaviour.

Skinner passionately wants to persuade his contemporaries that salvation lies in submitting to control of the environment for their own good; but he is thwarted by their obstinate attachment to their freedom and dignity as human beings. Hence his book. And here again his adversary comes straight out of the nineteenth century. For he claims that their attachment is due to their belief in "autonomous man," which he interprets as implying a belief in a little man within a man. The old Behaviourists, like J. B. Watson, were of course scared stiff of the soul. Hence their onslaught on the immaterial stuff of consciousness of which it was alleged to

From Review of B. F. Skinner's "Beyond Freedom and Dignity," by R. S. Peters. Times Educational Supplement *(March 3, 1972). Reprinted with permission.*

be composed. Skinner, somewhat quaintly, ascribes similar beliefs to those who nowadays believe in the autonomy of the individual. He sets up straw men to attack who are musty with the smell of Victorian haylofts. I do not think that he wilfully or wickedly misrepresents his adversaries; he is not that sort of man. Basically he is a simple fellow who is too unsophisticated in these matters to understand what they say nowadays.

Skinner admits that the 'literature of freedom' has done much to eliminate aversive practices. But it has placed too much emphasis on changing states of mind instead of the circumstances on which they depend. And, more importantly, escape is sought from all controllers—even from those who control the environment for people's good. Such squeamishness spells race suicide and is based on the superstition of the little man within who is subject to no constraints. These pre-scientific hang-ups are now a luxury that men must do without if they are to survive, though historically they have done some good. Belief in freedom, for instance, has led to opposition to punishment, which is an ineffective form of control; for it induces people not to behave in certain ways but does not shape their behaviour in a positive direction. The individual has to find his own path—and gets credit for it to boot because of the mysterious workings of conscience, another stronghold of autonomous man.

But the alternatives to punishment proposed by freedom-lovers are also ineffective because they are tied to the superstition of autonomy. Permissiveness, for instance, exonerates the teacher or parent from responsibility for control and simply leaves the child to be controlled by other features of the environment. Socratic midwifery gives the teacher more power and the individual credit. So both are satisfied, but at the cost of more precise knowledge about factors in the environment which are the real determinants of learning. Guidance relies on horticultural metaphors. There is control all right; but is is cloaked by the pretence that the shaping is brought about by inner growth. Dependence on things, as advocated by Rousseau and Dewey, is more effective and saves a lot of time and energy. People, too, can be used as things for shaping others. But the teacher must be careful to arrange such things. Finally there is the more high-minded policy of changing people's minds by urging or persuading them. This is ineffective; for it is really only the changing of behaviour that counts. Mind manipulators overlook past contingencies that are in fact operative and attribute efficacy to the man within.

Skinner sees that hard-headed shaping of behaviour presupposes some view of value; for when is a man in good shape? His answer is Bentham's translated into behaviouristic jargon. Pleasure is positive reinforcement and this becomes both the standard of right and wrong and the throne to which the chain of causes and effects is fastened. Good things are positive reinforcers; so behavioural science is the science of values. Men are guided by their concern for happiness—i.e. by personal reinforcers, that have survival value. They reinforce their fellows who act 'for the good of others'—i.e. who do things that reinforce others. Practices develop that have long-term reinforcing effects. Morals are therefore basically a matter of good husbandry, of fixing things up for human benefit. People tell the truth because they are reinforced for so doing. The scientist does not cook his results because others will check them. This is how men in fact behave and, presumably, how they should—though Skinner, like Bentham, is not altogether clear about the difference.

In the evolution of culture the most important criterion of 'progress' is thus the emergence of enhanced sensitivity to the consequences of behaviour, and increasing ability to predict them. Culture must now be more consciously designed so that long-term goods are promoted. The ingenuity that has produced cars and space-crafts must be turned to fixing up the ghettos, pollution and the use of leisure. Man must accept the view of himself that behavioural science has revealed. It is indeed more appropriate, when contemplating him, to exclaim 'How like a dog' rather than 'How like a god.' God is not dead; for he was never alive. But man will exterminate himself if he does not pay attention to providing the reinforcement contingencies which will shape his survival and turn his back on all the superstitions associated with his own autonomy.

Obviously those who believe in freedom will not take kindly to this paternalistic paean. Neither will their hackles subside when Skinner assures them that controllers are themselves controlled—the master by the slave, the parent by the child, and that a system can be worked out in which controllers have to submit to their own controls. But between their snarls of fitting indignation they can reflect that Skinner's hard-headed *naïveté* performs a useful service. I do not mean just that his uninhibited approach leads him to draw attention to matters that the tender-minded are apt to gloss over—e.g. the amount of manipulation involved in progressive methods, the inescapability of some form of social control, the ham-handed character of much reform inspired by a hatred of control and injustice. I mean rather that he pushes an instrumental approach to life to its limits and thus reveals a vision of life that is the logical outcome of presuppositions that many seem to share with him.

The Utilitarians, in the main, were not prepared to be completely consistent. They worried about the implication that justice and truth-telling had to be defended instrumentally by reference to their alleged consequences in terms of human happiness. J. S. Mill stood fast on liberty and was half-hearted in his attempt to provide a Utilitarian underpinning for it. He saw its connection with the pursuit of truth, whose connection with the pursuit of happiness he did not explore. Skinner, however, is quite uninhibited. He was nurtured in a cultural *milieu* which enabled William James to proclaim that truth is that which enables the individual to glide happily from one experience to another, and John Dewey to assert that truth is that which works. Happiness becomes the criterion both of what is right and of what is true. Man, the fixer, is the measure of all things. The good life is a smooth flow of positive reinforcement.

But Skinner has pushed this ancient arrogance even further. For, because of his quaint sensitivities about the soul, descriptions as well as justifications are couched in instrumental terms. He thinks states of mind causally inoperative; so he tends to describe them in terms of their overtly observable antecedents and consequences. The result is that, on occasions, one does not literally know what he is talking about. This comes out very clearly in his treatment of human dignity. Understandably he can give no account of this value; for it is connected with the view that we have of a man as having a point of view, as a person who is not to be used or manipulated for his own or anyone else's good. Skinner is reduced to just jibbering about it and to scattering reinforcements around like bird-seed. For it not only starkly confronts his whole instrumental outlook; it also activates his horror of consciousness.

Skinner's set of descriptions are really an attempt to discourse with kings of science whilst retaining the common touch of ordinary speech which is founded on quite different presuppositions. He even fudges things with the use of that blessed term 'the environment.' For what effects people generally are not just the physical properties of things or people but how they view them. 'Responses,' too, save at the level of very simple movements, cannot be distinguished without reference to the individual's view of his situation. When he waves his arm, for instance, is he signaling, expressing irritation, or performing a ritual? The basic trouble with Behaviourists is that they have never had an adequate concept of 'behaviour.' Presumably, too, in writing his book Skinner is trying to change people's beliefs about themselves. But he thinks attempts to change people's minds an ineffective way of trying to influence them. How, then, can he justify what he is doing in writing his book, or even give an account of it in terms of his own theory?

Those who believe in 'the autonomous man' do not necessarily subscribe to a belief in the soul. They agree with Skinner that behaviour has 'causes' but they wish to distinguish those that involve the individual's understanding and decisions from those that do not. They also, like Piaget, probably want to distinguish between levels of behaviour—between the level when people (especially children) are induced to act for the sake of reward or approval from the level when they can also act because of genuine reasons connected with the situation itself. Some people, for instance, go to concerts because they genuinely enjoy listening to music, though others may go because of wanting to keep up with their neighbours. Because, in their past, they too may have gone for such extrinsic reasons, it does not follow that they are still just under the influence of that type of 'reinforcement.' Skinner, of course, would probably call all this 'reinforcement'; but that is because,

in the face of the refutation of his theory, he has extended the meaning of 'reinforcement' so that it includes every possible form of motivation. So like many other psychological concepts (e.g. 'drive') it ends up by explaining nothing.

In morals, too, it may be the case that, at a certain stage of development, people learn to tell the truth or to keep their promises by being positively reinforced. But they also have to understand what it is to tell the truth and what a promise is. Eventually they may come to see that they should tell the truth because, unless this were the general rule, what is true could not be discovered and communicated. And truth matters—whatever its consequences for survival. For it is one of the values that define a tolerable form of survival. The autonomous man is the person who attempts to be 'authentic' or genuine in his attitudes and beliefs, who tries to free himself from sole dependence on the extrinsic reinforcers so beloved by Skinner. So he values truth and subjects what he is told to constant criticism. He abhors a society, like Skinner's Utopia, in which people believe what it pays them to believe and gladly submit to Pavlovian paternalism.

The value, therefore, of Skinner's naïve fanaticism is to have pushed instrumentalism to its logical limits. He has really no interest in how things are or in people's perspectives on the world. He is concerned only about how things and people will be and in their past as a guide to future manipulations. For him, as for the Puritans whom he despises, salvation lies always ahead, even though it is now downgraded to survival. At the end of his book he says that 'no theory changes what it is about; man remains what he has always been.' But this ignores one of the most important truths about man which is that he alone of creatures lives in the light of theories about himself and behaves differently because of them. The danger is that men may come to believe what Skinner says. They may use their freedom to deny others their dignity.

DISCUSSION QUESTIONS AND ACTIVITIES

1. Skinner believes that with teaching machines and programmed materials one could teach in half the time with half the effort what is now being taught. Has he made a sound case?
2. What grounds are cited for the opposition to Skinner's technology of teaching by both humanistic and cognitive psychology?
3. Why would disbanding schools of education not solve the problem of improving teaching?
4. Explain Skinner's four principles to improve teaching.
5. Peters accuses Skinner of holding nineteenth-century views. What are these views, and why should it be wrong to hold them?
6. Is Peters correct in stating that Skinner's position is a form of utilitarianism?
7. Why is Skinner unable to deal effectively with the concept of "human dignity"?
8. Explain what Peters means by his claim that behaviorists lack an adequate concept of "behavior" and, as a consequence, Skinner cannot give an account, in terms of his own theory, of what he is doing by writing a book.
9. Why is Skinner's treatment of "reinforcement" inadequate for explaining behavior?
10. Observe classrooms where positive reinforcement and programmed materials are used. Interview teachers as to the effectiveness of Skinnerian methods and materials.
11. Read Skinner's *The Technology of Teaching* and make a book report to the class.
12. Organize a classroom debate comparing the relative merits of Skinner's behaviorism with cognitive psychology.

SUGGESTED READINGS

Works by B. F. Skinner

About Behaviorism. New York: Knopf, 1974.

The Analysis of Behavior. New York: McGraw-Hill, 1961. (with James G. Holland)

The Behavior of Organisms. New York: Appleton-Century-Crofts, 1938.

Beyond Freedom and Dignity. New York: Knopf, 1971.

Contingencies of Reinforcement. New York: Appleton-Century-Crofts, 1969.

Cummulative Record. New York: Appleton-Century-Crofts, 1972.

Enjoy Old Age. New York: Warner Books, 1985. (with M. E. Vaughan)

A Matter of Consequences. New York: New York University Press, 1985.

Particulars of My Life. New York: Knopf, 1979.

Reflections on Behaviorism and Society. Englewood Cliffs, N.J.: Prentice-Hall, 1978.

Schedules of Reinforcement. New York: Appleton-Century-Crofts, 1957.

Science and Human Behavior. New York: Macmillan, 1953.

The Shaping of a Behaviorist. New York: Knopf, 1979.

"Some Issues Concerning the Control of Human Behavior: A Symposium," *Science* 124 (November 30, 1956):1057. (with Carl R. Rogers)

The Technology of Teaching. New York: Appleton-Century-Crofts, 1968.

Verbal Behavior. Englewood Cliffs, N.J.: Prentice-Hall, 1957.

Walden Two. New York: Macmillan, 1948.

Cassettes

"A Dialogue on Education and the Control of Human Behavior," 6 cassettes. New York: Norton, 1976. (with B. F. Skinner)

"Interview with B. F. Skinner." 1 cassette, mono 2-track. Los Altos, Calif.: Sound Ed Rpts, 1969.

Works About B. F. Skinner

Carpenter, Finley. *The Skinner Primer.* New York: Free Press, 1974.

Dews, P. B., ed. *Festschrift for B. F. Skinner.* New York: Appleton-Century-Crofts, 1970.

Evans, Richard Isadore. *B. F. Skinner: The man and His Ideas.* New York: Dutton, 1968.

Freedman, Anne E. *The Planned Society: An Analysis of Skinner's Proposals.* Kalamazoo, Mich.: Behaviordelia, 1972.

Geiser, Robert L. *Behavior Mod and the Managed Society.* Boston: Beacon Press, 1976.

Karen, Robert L. *An Introduction to Behavior Theory and Its Applications.* New York: Harper & Row, 1974.

Machan, Tibor R. *The Psuedo-Science of B. F. Skinner.* New Rochelle, N.Y.: Arlington House, 1974.

Milhollan, Frank. *From Skinner to Rogers: Contrasting Approaches to Education.* Lincoln, Neb.: Professional Educators Publications, 1972.

Nye, Robert D. *Three Psychologies: Perspectives from Freud, Skinner, and Rogers,* 2nd ed. Monterey, Calif.: Brooks/Cole, 1981.

———. *What is B. F. Skinner Really Saying?* Englewood Cliffs, N.J.: Prentice-Hall, 1979.

Puligandla, R. *Fact and Fiction in B. F. Skinner's Science and Utopia.* St. Louis: W. H. Green, 1974.

Wheeler, John Harvey, ed. *Beyond the Primitive Society.* San Francisco: W. H. Freeman, 1973.

Articles About B. F. Skinner

Bordin, E. S. "Two Views of Human Nature." *New York University Education Quarterly* 12 (Winter 1981): 29–32.

Burton, G. M. "Skinner, Piaget, Maslow, and the Teachers of Mathematics: Strange Companions?" *Arithmetic Teacher* 24 (March 1977): 246–250.

Elias, J. L. "B. F. Skinner and Religious Education." *Religious Education* 69 (September 1974): 558–567.

Gates, L. "Piaget's Model is Superior in Fostering Learning." *Reading Improvement* 15 (Summer 1978): 127–129. Discussion: 17 (Spring 1980): 14–17; 17 (Summer 1980): 97–99.

Harris, D. "Discipline of the Structure, Meaning and Acquisition of Learning, with Special References to Noam Chomsky and B. F. Skinner. *Cambridge Journal of Education* 7, no. 2 (1977): 114–123.

Kitchener, R. F. "Critique of Skinnerian Ethical Principles." *Counseling and Values* 23 (April 1979): 138–147.

Kneller, G. F., and S. L. Hackbarth. "Analysis of Programmed Instruction." *The Educational Forum* 41 (January 1977): 180–187.

Krantz, D. L. "Relation of Reflection and Action: The Intellectual and Clinical Impact of B. F. Skinner and R. D. Laing." *American Journal of Orthopsychiatry* 48 (April 1978): 214–227.

Mowrer, V. M. "Present State of Behaviorism." *Education* 97 (Fall 1976): 4–23. Reply: T. T. Jackson 98 (Fall 1977): 56.

Price, G. "Is Science a Servant or Master? *Times Higher Education Supplement* 485 (February 19, 1982): 10.

Roper, V. "Influence of Learning Theory on the Behavior of the Teacher in the Classroom." *Educational Theory* 24 (Spring 1974): 155–160.

Royzyck, E. G. "Functional Analysis of Behavior." *Educational Theory* 25 (Summer 1975): 278–302.

Silva, D. "From Skinner to Instruction." *Educational Technology* 19 (May 1979): 51–52.

Teller, G. D. "Is Behaviorism a Form of Humanism?" *Educational Leadership* 34 (May 1977): 637–638.

5

Illiterate America

In his book, *Illiterate America*, Kozol estimates that 25 million Americans cannot read at fifth-grade level, and 35 million more read at less than ninth-grade level. He argues that this illiteracy costs $20 billion a year, and that the cost in lost jobs and political and economic disenfranchisement is inestimable.

Kozol told members of Congress that the federal government needs to earmark at least $1 billion a year over the next three years for literacy. But it would probably take $10 billion to "turn the tide," he said. Kozol criticized the Reagan administration for having a "myopic" policy on the issue. Presently, state and local governments along with corporate and local volunteers reach only 3 percent of adult illiterates.

He proposes the mobilization of a national campaign sponsored by government leaders and involving mass participation. Kozol plans to reach people through "foot walkers"—volunteers who can circulate in the community, identify needs, and seek help. In a second stage he would mobilize 5 million literacy workers at a cost of $10 billion annually. The third stage would go beyond functional literacy to change the workplace.

The illiterate adult is silent and unseen, lives in fear of being discovered, and is socially withdrawn. The children of illiterate adults tend to become illiterate themselves. Only about 2 million are now being served in adult nonschool programs.

In the selection by Kozol, he outlines the magnitude of the problem and proposes an organizational plan and methodology to help overcome it. Mikulecky asserts that Kozol leaves an erroneous impression that illiteracy is rampant, and that Kozol does not place any responsibility for the problem on the illiterate.

How We Can Win:
A Plan to Reach and
Teach Twenty-Five
Million Illiterate Adults

Jonathan Kozol

Jonathan Kozol (b. 1936) was a leader in the free school movement and is known for his book, Free Schools. *His earlier experiences in the Boston public schools are conveyed in his award-winning* Death at an Early Age. *Illiteracy has become his central concern, which is expressed in his book,* Illiterate America.

The problem is vast. The resolution is known and clearly within reach. The price of our refusal to confront the problem is unspeakable catastrophe.

Already, the dimensions of the problem dwarf the reaches of our comfortable imaginations.

Twenty-five million American adults can neither read nor write nor handle basic mathematical computations. An additional thirty to forty million American adults cannot read or write enough to understand a complicated danger warning on a bottle of medication, fire warnings in a factory, or instructions for operation of a piece of expensive and complex machinery in a warehouse. In few words, these people cannot hold even entry-level jobs.

THE DIMENSIONS OF THE PROBLEM

A racial/ethnic breakdown renders these figures even more disturbing: Sixteen percent of white adults, 44 percent of blacks, 56 percent of those of Spanish surname, cannot read well enough to understand a want ad—or write well enough to fill out a relatively simple application for a job.

The personal price is repetitive humiliation, constant anguish, and the fear of being "caught." The social and economic price can be reduced to hard and measurable numbers. According to one source, the total cost to American taxpayers, solely in the funding of welfare programs and in loss of productivity, is at least six billion dollars yearly. Another six billion dollars are spent each year to maintain seven hundred thousand illiterate men and women in Federal or state prisons. The loss of billions more dollars is attributable to needless accidents that lead to the destruction of sophisticated technological equipment.

A simple example of the latter cost is documented by Senator George McGovern in his speech of September 1978: "An astounding thirty percent of Navy recruits . . . are a danger to themselves and to costly naval equipment because they lack basic educational skills. One illiterate recruit recently caused two hundred fifty thousand dollars in damage because he could not read a repair manual."

The tragedy of the situation of the worker is underscored in these words: "He tried [but] failed to follow the instructions."

A number of earnest efforts have been made to meet this problem at the highest governmental level. Congress first addressed the challenge of adult illiteracy in the Economic Opportunity Act of 1964—and again in the Adult Education Act of 1966. In spite of these two major pieces of legislation, the current Federal allocation amounts to only one dollar for each illiterate adult. The funds available reach only two to four percent of those in need.

In 1972, Congress gave evidence of renewed commitment to end illiteracy with the Right to Read program. The program was downgraded six years later, in 1978, after being labeled a failure by its own director.

The picture is not as bleak as it may seem from the statistics. There is no question that many men and women learned to read and write as a direct result of excellent programs and painstaking efforts carried out by various government-sponsored programs, as well as by independent efforts carried out by earnest and hardworking volunteers trained and organized by Literacy Volunteers of America, Laubach Literacy International, and several other groups that have been working at the grass roots throughout the past two decades.

Hard work has been done. It has been done by good and dedicated people. As we have seen, however, it has reached no more than two to four percent of those in need.

Our task, in these first years of a new decade, is to reach—and teach—those twenty to twenty-five million who have not been reached before. It seems apparent that additional funding of ongoing programs will not significantly alter the numbers of those who learn to read and write. For those who have not yet been reached, it seems apparent that something new is needed. That "something new" is an approach that has never been ventured in this country: an all-out effort, a total mobilization, a national campaign.

"THOSE WHO KNOW, TEACH . . . "

Up to this point in United States history, when we spoke of literacy efforts we were speaking of programs that involved at most two or three hundred thousand volunteers. In a nation of 25 million totally illiterate adults, it is obvious that a "literacy army" of at least five million volunteers will be essential if we are to train as many as five volunteers for every 25 illiterate adults.

How can we find so many potential literacy teachers? What methods will they use? Where will they carry out their work?

We will find them, if we dare to look and to transcend some of our age-old preconceptions, among the student populations of the high schools, colleges, and universities of the United States. Certainly we cannot hope to find five million volunteers among the teachers in the public schools. Those teachers who are already there, in largest numbers, will be obliged to stay. Many, moreover, will not be prepared to join a grass-roots struggle of this kind. Others may *wish* to join and help, but only in a supervisory role, or may be held back by permanent family obligations from the total, personal commitment to a struggle so consuming and so vast. It is not extravagant to suggest, then, that we might begin to look to students who are now in universities and high schools.

According to one scenario I have seen, students would first be formed into effective, tightly organized teams of twenty-five to thirty members each. Team leaders might be found among some of those highly motivated teachers who would otherwise be teaching the same students in schools or universities. In such a case, it would seem to make sense for college instructors to receive their customary salary from the college in which they would ordinarily be teaching. (Whether the colleges will agree to this or not is an entirely different matter; but it would not hurt to ask.)

Apart from all else, it seems to me that there is a high degree of practical and political logic in any plan that can liberate young people, for one full semester of their lives, from traditional courses such as "Problems of Democracy" in order to enable them, instead, to go out into the world and start to *solve* one of those problems.

In speaking of methods and of motivation, it seems to me that at least two issues are immediately at stake. One of them is the attitude of our youthful literacy workers as the energetic, but no longer patronizing, partners of their own illiterate pupils. The effort to transcend a long American tradition of benevolent, but too often condescending, generosity in earlier ventures of this kind may very well prove to be the most ambitious aspect of the struggle. There is a deep well of essential human kindliness and compassion in our nation; but there is at the same time—and in almost the same breath—a disturbing inclination to attempt to remake those who we help in our own image.

The consequence is cultural and psychological invasion of the least defended people in the land. It is, in my belief, for this reason above all others that literacy programs of the past have shown so little progress. The recipients of largesse from an outside party are seldom so eager, or able, to learn as those who work, with a sense of common cause, to win the power of the written word in order to possess and to transform some little portion of the world in which they dwell.

This leads, then, to the question of the methods we shall use. In every nation in which successful literacy campaigns have been carried out, the key to success has been a combination of the choice of teachers and the choice of words. In our own case I am convinced that we must not allow ourselves to choose a word, or a body of words, that come out of a pre-selected list of "appropriate vocabulary" chosen by others (experts, bureaucrats, or far-distant teachers), but rather to elicit—and then to give back again—the words that live already in the rich oral vocabularies of our pupils.

The words I suggest are called by some scholars, "active words," by others, "generative words." I call them "dangerous words"— strong and volatile syllables of passion and elucidation—the clarification, for example, of a complex system of oppressions that may or may not, before that moment, have been visible or vivid in the learner's mind.

What are examples of the kinds of words that we in the United States might logically attempt to use? I would not start with "Dick" and "Jane," but rather with words like "grief" and "pain" and "love" and "lust" and "longing," "lease" and "license," "fever," "fear," "infection," "nation," "doctor," "danger," "fire" and "desire," "prison," "power," "protest," "progress," or "police."

My purpose in suggesting these words is not to encourage a radical's version of cultural invasion by arrogant prescription. The goal is not to try to "plant" these words and concepts in the minds of those who wish to learn to read and write. The purpose, rather, is—first through the process of prior dialogue, later in the day-to-day relationship of teacher and learner—to dig down into the deep soil of those incipient concepts, dreams, longings, and ideals that exist already in the consciousness of even the most broken and seemingly most silent of the poor.

Where, in the most specific physical respect would literacy instruction logically take place?

My suggestion would be to hold classes in the neighborhood, in the area where the people live. Prospective learners and teachers together might work at renovating an old discarded building in order to create a new literacy center for the client population. The center might offer a place of rest and sleep for literacy workers or a quiet place of study for the workers and their pupils during daytime hours. Being a joint venture, the product of the sweat and toil of both, the literacy workers might properly, and symbolically, hand over the building to the neighborhood people once the literacy work has been achieved.

It would remain—a symbol of decency, reminder of struggle—long years after the literacy workers have returned to their own families, to their studies and their homes.

Another View of Illiterate America

Larry Mikulecky

Larry Mikulecky is a faculty member at Indiana University.

Illiterate America is Jonathan Kozol's combination political and scholarly analysis of illiteracy in America. In this book he attempts to "describe the problem and delineate a plan of action." In addition, he promises:

I will do my best to shape a vision and refine a definition of that universal humane literacy which has eluded us so long but which represents a sane, essential, and realistic goal for a society that hopes to govern not by the mechanical and docile aquiescence of the governed but by the informed consent of those who are empowered to participate with the act of governance itself. (p. 12)

The juxtapostion of these goals is a model demonstration of the strengths, ambitions, tensions, and problems inherent to this book. In places, Kozol writes clearly, insightfully, and often accurately about adult illiteracy. In the next paragraph or page, however, the pendulum of Kozol's attention is likely to swing to philosophical or political rhetoric.

From Review of Jonathan Kozol's Illiterate America, *by Larry Mikulecky. Reprinted with permission from* Journal of Reading Behavior *18 (Spring 1986):171–174.*

Kozol switches from objective presenter of information to strident political rhetorician seemingly at will. This requires a certain wariness on the part of the reader who may not be sure when he is being given legitimate information and when he is being manipulated and persuaded.

This tension between book as information provider and book as political persuader exists from the moment the reader first sets eyes on the cover. For example, a somber gray block on the red, white, and blue cover proclaims to the casual browser that "One out of every three adult Americans *cannot* read this book." This is accurate information and may even be conservative given Kozol's tendency to cite James Joyce, W. H. Auden, and to use 66-word sentences like the one quoted above. Less than one third of adults are college educated and this book is written for an educated audience. The cover and much of the book, however, create the inaccurate impression that illiteracy *per se* is rampant. Kozol claims there are 60 million illiterate American adults. This figure is within the range of "functional" and "marginal" illiterates identified in the Adult Performance Level (APL) study of the early 1970s (Northcutt, 1973).

According to most studies, including the APL, only a small fraction of these 60 million adults are "illiterate" in the commonly accepted sense of being unable to read a word. Perhaps 10% read below the World War II draft cut-off of a fourth-grade level. When Kozol highlights case studies to bring data to life and give statistics political reality, he paints poignant portraits of real suffering and real people from the bottom 10% of the 60 million adults. He creates an impression of a nation of virtual illiterates. Yet, most of these 60 million can read somewhere between fourth- and ninth-grade levels—levels that were socially acceptable a few decades ago.

Because difficulty levels of reading materials on the job and throughout daily life have climbed, there is a painful gap between current literacy demands and the education levels of this fourth- to ninth-grade level group of adults. This is a *major* educational and social problem but one somewhat more complex than can be conveyed by a general statistic or blanket label. There are people who can justifiably be called illiterate and they do need basic help. A good many others, however, might better be termed "undereducated," not so much needing basic literacy training as a good deal more education to thrive in the face of higher literacy demands. Volunteer programs and mobilizations aimed at "illiterates" are not going to be appropriate for this larger percentage of the 60 million adults Kozol identifies.

Kozol and the team of researchers who used Guggenheim funding to help gather research for this book have made available to those concerned with literacy some useful information. Much of the book's data documenting the economic and social costs of literacy has been gathered from hard-to-locate government reports, interviews, and out-of-the-way publications not usually cited in educational research. Kozol's history and analysis of literacy data from the national census is extremely useful for anyone wishing to use or interpret census literacy figures. The book contains a particularly strong chapter on the children of non-readers in which Kozol presents and elaborates on some of Thomas Sticht's ideas (1982) about improving literacy of both parents and their children through specially designed adult literacy efforts. Kozol's attempts "to describe the problem" are valuable and worth the purchase of this book.

Much about *Illiterate America*, however, is distracting rhetoric at best and misleadingly inaccurate at worst. Kozol's failure to adequately differentiate between truly illiterate adults and the millions of undereducated adults who have difficulty with increasing literacy demands feeds the mistaken national impression that we are a nation of illiterates. Kozol dismisses as ineffective the efforts of many existing organizations that deal with illiteracy. This dismissal appears to be because the organizations do not mimic his own experiences with literacy training in "freedom schools" which linked literacy instruction to political activities. Literacy networks and coalitions are denigrated by Kozol with the judgement:

> They network nothingness. They form a coalition of historic losers. They "keep in touch"—or so they claim. With what? With one another's failure. (p. 50)

After sarcastically describing military literacy efforts, which even Kozol acknowledges accomplish some degree of literacy success in relation to military goals, Kozol again waxes rhetorical. He notes:

> Benjamin is functionally competent at last. One day he may have his chance to press the button that releases that long, trim, and slender instrument of death that he so much resembles. Is this the kind of literacy we want? (p. 86)

The "plan of action" Kozol proposes in the middle section of the book amounts to a good deal of grass roots political organizing with heavy recruiting of "illiterates" by "illiterates." This is be coupled with a federal literacy program on the order of the WPA of the Roosevelt years along with massive federal funding between now and the year 2000 directed toward other aspects of this problem.

The final section of Kozol's book is entitled "Beyond Utility" and provides a forum for Kozol to air his views on humanistic education, technological obsessions, the role of universities in Kozol's world view, what Kozol sees as the prospects for today's stu-

dents, and what Kozol thinks about bilingual literacy. "Beyond Utility" is vintage Kozol. The attempt in earlier chapters to weave together factual material with opinion and rhetoric is abandoned. Factual and research information presented in the first portion give way to citations from Thoreau, W. H. Auden, James Joyce, and C. P. Snow. All rhetorical restraints are discarded.

Other reviewers, most notably Charles Murray in the *Wall Street Journal* (1985), have noted that Kozol's rhetoric beats relentlessly and that every failing seems to be blamed on the system and none on the individual who didn't learn during 12 years of schooling. I am not suggesting a "blame the victim" stance. I am simply noting that examination of whatever portion of responsibility rests with individuals seems to be missing from Kozol's book. Such a broader, more even-handed examination would potentially detract from the book's political thrust.

Kozol's insistence on linking literacy solutions to a single political stance becomes particularly annoying when one considers that very little literacy work is currently being done by political organizers. It usually takes close to 100 hours of instruction and feedback for an adult to gain the equivalent of one grade level in reading ability. This work is sometimes exciting and occasionally extremely rewarding. Much of it, however, is slow, dull, and repetitious work. It is currently being done by low-paid professionals, volunteers, church groups, and an assortment of other altruistic individuals. Many of these people who contribute large chunks of their lives to make small dents in a massive problem voted for Ronald Reagan and do not subscribe to Kozol's politics or use his rhetoric.

I am concerned that the useful sections of *Illiterate America* will be lost to those concerned with literacy because of the anachronistic stridency of the book's rhetoric. To the extent that today's college students are potential literacy volunteers, Kozol's efforts may even be counter-productive. College students, who in past decades volunteered time for others, are concerned with getting jobs and paying off their own indebtedness for education. They may be convinced to give time for others, but it is not likely to be through the rhetoric in this book. Some of my current students have already responded to Kozol's attempts to raise national consciousness while marketing his book on television talk shows. A student willing to speak out commented, "Oh yeah, I saw him on T.V. He's like that ad I saw in the paper which said 2 out of 3 adults would be illiterate by the year 2000. I don't believe that either."

Illiterate America contains enough useful information to justify its purchase. The reader must, however, be willing to hunt for this information and understand that the price of admission is both the cost of the book and agreeing to be the audience for a rhetorical exercise.

REFERENCES

Murray, C. (1985, September 3). Grading the schools. *The Wall Street Journal* (p. 22).

Northcutt, N. (Ed.). (1973). *Adult performance levels.* Austin, TX: University of Texas.

Sticht, T. (1982). *Literacy and human resource development.* Alexandria, VA: HumRRO.

DISCUSSION QUESTIONS AND ACTIVITIES

1. Describe the magnitude of the illiteracy problem in America by the number and level of illiterates, the cost in lost productivity, and the impact of their disability upon themselves.
2. Why have federal programs and independent efforts so far been unable to greatly reduce illiteracy?
3. Appraise Kozol's scenario for organizing to reduce illiteracy.
4. Certain "dangerous words" must be used. Why employ this approach rather than the more traditional one?
5. Mikulecky claims that Kozol conveys the inaccurate impression that illiteracy is rampant. Reinterpret the figures to determine which author is correct.
6. What is the difference between illiterates and those who are "undereducated"?
7. What portion of responsibility for illiteracy rests with the individual and what part with the system?
8. Investigate adult literacy programs in your local community and report your findings in class.
9. Organize a debate on illiteracy that considers its magnitude, causes, and plans for amelioration.

SUGGESTED READINGS

Books by Jonathan Kozol

Alternative Schools: A Survivor's Guide. New York: Continuum, 1982.

Children of the Revolution: A Yankee Teacher in the Cuban Schools. New York: Dell, 1980.

Death at an Early Age. Boston: Houghton Mifflin, 1967.

Free Schools. Boston: Houghton Mifflin, 1972.

Illiterate America. New York: Doubleday Anchor Press, 1985.

The Night Is Dark and I Am Far from Home. A Political Indictment of U.S. Public Schools. New York: Continuum, 1980.

On Being a Teacher. New York: Continuum, 1981.

Prisoners of Silence: Breaking the Bonds of Adult Illiteracy in the United States. New York: Continuum, 1980.

6

The Emancipation of Teaching

Although heavily influenced by Marxism, Henry A. Giroux is highly critical of deterministic and structural tendencies within contemporary Marxist philosophy and its failure to develop a theory of subjectivity. He seeks to develop a theory for a radical pedagogy. This is undertaken by seeking a depth psychology to understand the mechanism of domination and the process of liberation. Giroux develops a concept of critical discourse within a post-Marxism framework that brings together the Frankfurt School on the one end and Paulo Freire on the other.

He does not see radical teachers as free-floating revolutionaries but as persons within and outside of schools who might develop educative practices outside of established institutions. Giroux wants schools to participate in recreating a new society; he views schools as potent vehicles for social change. Key players in this drama are teachers and students. The school will seek to unite theory and practice as it provides unified cognitive and affective characteristics that will liberate the individual and bring about social reconstruction.

In the selections that follow, Giroux shows the dangers of the technocratic approach in education and proposes that these dangers can be overcome by restructuring the nature of teacher work so that teachers become transformative intellectuals. Colin Lacey offers three serious criticisms of Giroux's ideas.

Teachers as Transformative Intellectuals

Henry A. Giroux

A former high school history teacher, Henry A. Giroux (b. 1943) has taught at Boston University and is currently Associate Professor of Education at Miami University, Oxford, Ohio. Among his books are Ideology, Culture, and the Process of Schooling *and* Theory and Resistance in Education. *He is also a contributor to education and social theory journals. His primary focus is on the roles that schools play in promoting success and failure among different classes and groups of students, especially the way schools mediate values and messages that result in special privileges for some groups.*

The call for educational reform has gained the status of a recurring national event, much like the annual Boston Marathon. There have been more than 30 national reports since the beginning of the 20th century, and more than 300 task forces have been developed by the various states to discover how public schools can improve educational quality in the United States.[1] But unlike many past educational reform movements, the present call for educational change presents *both* a threat and challenge to public school teachers that appears unprecedented in our nation's history. The threat comes in the form of a series of educational reforms that display little confidence in the ability of public school teachers to provide intellectual and moral leadership for our nation's young. For instance, many of the recommendations that have emerged in the current debate either ignore the role teachers play in preparing learners to be active and critical citizens, or they suggest reforms that ignore the intelligence, judgment and experience that teachers might offer in such a debate. Where teachers do enter the debate, they are the object of educational reforms that reduce them to the status of high-level technicians carrying out dictates and objectives decided by "experts" far removed from the everyday realities of classroom life.[2] The message appears to be that teachers do not count when it comes to

From Henry A. Giroux, *"Teachers as Transformative Intellectuals,"* Social Education *49 (May 1985):376–379. Reprinted from* Social Education *with permission of the National Council for the Social Studies.*

[1] K. Patricia Cross, "The Rising Tide of School Reform Reports," *Phi Delta Kappan,* 66:3 (November 1984), p. 167.

[2] For a more detailed critique of the reforms, see my book with Stanley Aronowitz, *Education Under Siege* (South Hadley, MA: Bergin and Garvey Publishers, 1985); also see the incisive comments on the impositional nature of the various reports in Charles A. Tesconi, Jr., "Additive Reforms and the Retreat from Purpose," *Education Studies* 15:1 (Spring 1984), pp. 1–11; Terrence E. Deal, "Search-

critically examining the nature and process of educational reform.

The political and ideological climate does not look favorable for teachers at the moment. But it does offer them the challenge to join in a public debate with their critics as well as the opportunity to engage in a much-needed self-critique regarding the nature and purpose of teacher preparation, inservice teacher programs and the dominant forms of classroom teaching. Similarly, the debate provides teachers with the opportunity to organize collectively so as to struggle to improve the conditions under which they work and to demonstrate to the public the central role that teachers must play in any viable attempt to reform the public schools.

In order for teachers and others to engage in such a debate, it is necessary that a theoretical perspective be developed that redefines the nature of the educational crisis while simultaneously providing the basis for an alternative view of teacher training and work. In short, recognizing that the current crisis in education largely has to do with the developing trend towards the disempowerment of teachers at all levels of education is a necessary theoretical precondition in order for teachers to organize effectively and establish a collective voice in the current debate. Moreover, such a recognition will have to come to grips not only with a growing loss of power among teachers around the basic conditions of their work, but also with a changing public perception of their role as reflective practitioners.

I want to make a small theoretical contribution to this debate and the challenge it

calls forth by examining two major problems that need to be addressed in the interest of improving the quality of "teacher work," which includes all the clerical tasks and extra assignments as well as classroom instruction. First, I think it is imperative to examine the ideological and material forces that have contributed to what I want to call the proletarianization of teacher work; that is, the tendency to reduce teachers to the status of specialized technicians within the school bureaucracy, whose function then becomes one of managing and implementing curricula programs rather than developing or critically appropriating curricula to fit specific pedagogical concerns. Second, there is a need to defend schools as institutions essential to maintaining and developing a critical democracy and also to defending teachers as transformative intellectuals who combine scholarly reflection and practice in the service of educating students to be thoughtful, active citizens. In the remainder of this essay, I will develop these points and conclude by examining their implications for providing an alternative view of teacher work.

TOWARD A DEVALUING AND DESKILLING OF TEACHER WORK

One of the major threats facing prospective and existing teachers within the public schools is the increasing development of instrumental ideologies that emphasize a technocratic approach to both teacher preparation and classroom pedagogy. At the core of the current emphasis on instrumental and pragmatic factors in school life are a number of important pedagogical assumptions. These include: a call for the separation of conception from execution; the standardization of school knowledge in the interest of managing and controlling it; and the devaluation

ing for the Wizard: The Quest for Excellence in Education," *Issues in Education* 2:1 (Summer 1984), pp. 56–67; Svi Shapiro, "Choosing Our Educational Legacy: Disempowerment or Emancipation?" *Issues in Education* 2:1 (Summer 1984), pp. 11–22.

of critical, intellectual work on the part of teachers and students for the primacy of practical considerations.[3]

This type of instrumental rationality finds one of its strongest expressions historically in the training of prospective teachers. That teacher training programs in the United States have long been dominated by a behavioristic orientation and emphasis on mastering subject areas and methods of teaching is well documented.[4] The implications of this approach, made clear by Zeichner, are worth repeating:

> Underlying this orientation to teacher education is a metaphor of "production," a view of teaching as an "applied science" and a view of the teacher as primarily an "executor" of the laws and principles of effective teaching. Prospective teachers may or may not proceed through the curriculum at their own pace and may participate in varied or standardized learning activities, but that which they are to master is limited in scope (e.g., to a body of professional content knowledge and teaching skills) and is fully determined in advance by others often on the basis of research on teacher effectiveness. The prospective teacher is viewed primarily as a passive recipient of this professional knowledge and plays little part in determining the substance and direction of his or her preparation program.[5]

The problems with this approach are evident in John Dewey's argument that teacher training programs that emphasize only technical expertise do a disservice both to the nature of teaching and to their students.[6] Instead of learning to reflect upon the principles that structure classroom life and practice, prospective teachers are taught methodologies that appear to deny the very need for critical thinking. The point is that teacher education programs often lose sight of the need to educate students to examine the underlying nature of school problems. Further, these programs need to substitute for the language of management and efficiency a critical analysis of the less obvious conditions that structure the ideological and material practices of schooling.

Instead of learning to raise questions about the principles underlying different classroom methods, research techniques and theories of education, students are often preoccupied with learning the "how to," with "what works," or with mastering the best way to teach a *given* body of knowledge. For example, the mandatory field-practice seminars often consist of students sharing with each other the techniques they have used in managing and controlling classroom discipline, organizing a day's activities and learning how to work within specific time tables. Examining one such program, Jesse Goodman raises some important questions about the incapacitating silences it embodies. He writes:

> There was no questioning of feelings, assumptions, or definitions in this discussion. For example, the "need" for external rewards and

---

[3] For an exceptional commentary on the need to educate teachers to be intellectuals, see John Dewey, "The Relation of Theory to Practice," in John Dewey, *The Middle Works, 1899–1924,* edited by Jo Ann Boydston (Carbondale, Southern Illinois University Press, 1977), [originally published in 1904]. See also, Israel Scheffler, "University Scholarship and the Education of Teachers," *Teachers College Record,* 70:1 (1968), pp. 1–12; Henry A. Giroux, *Ideology, Culture, and the Process of Schooling* (Philadelphia: Temple University Press, 1981).

[4] "See for instance, Herbert Kliebard, "The Question of Teacher Education," in D. McCarty (ed.) *New Perspectives on Teacher Education* (San Francisco: Jossey-Bass, 1973).

[5] Kenneth M. Zeichner, "Alternative Paradigms on Teacher Education, *Journal of Teacher Education* 34:3 (May-June 1983), p. 4.

[6] Dewey, op. cit.

punishments to "make kids learn" was taken for granted; the educational and ethical implications were not addressed. There was no display of concern for stimulating or nurturing a child's intrinsic desire to learn. Definitions of *good kids* as "quiet kids," *workbook work* as "reading," *on-task time* as "learning," and *getting through the material on time* as "the goal of teaching"—all went unchallenged. Feelings of pressure and possible guilt about not keeping to time schedules also went unexplored. The real concern in this discussion was that everyone "shared."[7]

Technocratic and instrumental rationalities are also at work within the teaching field itself, and they play an increasing role in reducing teacher autonomy with respect to the development and planning of curricula and the judging and implementation of classroom instruction. This is most evident in the proliferation of what has been called "teacher-proof" curriculum packages.[8] The underlying rationale in many of these packages reserves for teachers the role of simply carrying out predetermined content and instructional procedures. The method and aim of such packages is to legitimate what I call management pedagogies. That is, knowledge is broken down into discrete parts, standardized for easier management and consumption, and measured through predefined forms of assessment. Curricula approaches of this sort are management pedagogies because the central questions regarding learning are reduced to the problem of management, i.e., "how to allocate resources (teachers, students and material) to produce the maximum number of certified . . . students within a designated time."[9] The underlying theoretical assumption that guides this type of pedagogy is that the behavior of teachers needs to be controlled and made consistent and predictable across different schools and student populations.

What is clear in this approach is that it organizes school life around curricular, instructional and evaluation experts who do the thinking while teachers are reduced to doing the implementing. The effect is not only to deskill teachers, to remove them from the processes of deliberation and reflection, but also to routinize the nature of learning and classroom pedagogy. Needless to say, the principles underlying management pedagogies are at odds with the premise that teachers should be actively involved in producing curricula materials suited to the cultural and social contexts in which they teach. More specifically, the narrowing of curricula choices to a back-to-basics format, and the introduction of lock-step, time-on-task pedagogies operate from the theoretically erroneous assumption that *all students can* learn from the same materials, classroom instructional techniques and modes of evaluation. The notion that students come from different histories and embody different experiences, linguistic practices, cultures and talents is strategically ignored within the logic and accountability of management pedagogy theory.

TEACHERS AS TRANSFORMATIVE INTELLECTUALS

In what follows, I want to argue that one way to rethink and restructure the nature of teacher work is to view teachers as transfor-

---

[7] Jesse Goodman, "Reflection and Teacher Education: A Case Study and Theoretical Analysis," *Interchange* 15:3 (1984), p. 15.

[8] Michael Apple, *Education and Power* (Boston: Routledge & Kegan Paul, Ltd., 1982).

[9] Patrick Shannon, "Mastery Learning in Reading and the Control of Teachers and Students," *Language Arts* 61:5 (September 1984), p. 488.

mative intellectuals. The category of intellectual is helpful in a number of ways. First, it provides a theoretical basis for examining teacher work as a form of intellectual labor, as opposed to defining it in purely instrumental or technical terms. Second, it clarifies the kinds of ideological and practical conditions necessary for teachers to function as intellectuals. Third, it helps to make clear the role teachers play in producing and legitimating various political, economic and social interests through the pedagogies they endorse and utilize.

By viewing teachers as intellectuals, we can illuminate the important idea that all human activity involves some form of thinking. In other words, no activity, regardless of how routinized it might become, can be abstracted from the functioning of the mind in some capacity. This is a crucial issue, because by arguing that the use of the mind is a general part of all human activity we dignify the human capacity for integrating thinking and practice, and in doing so highlight the core of what it means to view teachers as reflective practitioners. Within this discourse, teachers can be seen not merely as "performers professionally equipped to realize effectively any goals that may be set for them. Rather [they should] be viewed as free men and women with a special dedication to the values of the intellect and the enhancement of the critical powers of the young."[10]

Viewing teachers as intellectuals also provides a strong theoretical critique of technocratic and instrumental ideologies underlying an educational theory that separates the conceptualization, planning and design of curricula from the processes of implementation and execution. It is important to stress that teachers must take active responsibility for raising serious questions about what they

teach, how they are to teach, and what the larger goals are for which they are striving. This means that they must take a responsible role in shaping the purposes and conditions of schooling. Such a task is impossible within a division of labor in which teachers have little influence over the ideological and economic conditions of their work. This point has a normative and political dimension that seems especially relevant for teachers. If we believe that the role of teaching cannot be reduced to merely training in the practical skills, but involves, instead, the education of a class of intellectuals vital to the development of a free society, then the category of intellectual becomes a way of linking the purpose of teacher education, public schooling and inservice training to the very principles necessary for developing a democratic order and society.

I have argued that by viewing teachers as intellectuals those persons concerned with education can begin to rethink and reform the traditions and conditions that have prevented schools and teachers from assuming their full potential as active, reflective scholars and practitioners. It is imperative that I qualify this point and extend it further. I believe that it is important not only to view teachers as intellectuals, but also to contextualize in political and normative terms the concrete social functions that teachers perform. In this way, we can be more specific about the different relations that teachers have both to their work and to the dominant society.

A fundamental starting point for interrogating the social function of teachers as intellectuals is to view schools as economic, cultural and social sites that are inextricably tied to the issues of power and control. This means that schools do more than pass on in an objective fashion a common set of values and knowledge. On the contrary, schools are

----

[10] Israel Scheffler, op, cit., p. 11.

places that represent forms of knowledge, language practices, social relations and values that are representative of a particular selection and exclusion from the wider culture. As such, schools serve to introduce and legitimate *particular* forms of social life. Rather than being objective institutions removed from the dynamics of politics and power, schools actually are contested spheres that embody and express a struggle over what forms of authority, types of knowledge, forms of moral regulation and versions of the past and future should be legitimated and transmitted to students. This struggle is most visible in the demands, for example, of right-wing religious groups currently trying to institute school prayer, remove certain books from the school library, and include certain forms of religious teachings in the science curricula. Of course, different demands are made by feminists, ecologists, minorities and other interest groups who believe that the schools should teach women's studies, courses on the environment, or black history. In short, schools are not neutral sites, and teachers cannot assume the posture of being neutral either.

In the broadest sense, teachers as intellectuals have to be seen in terms of the ideological and political interests that structure the nature of the discourse, classroom social relations and values that they legitimate in their teaching. With this perspective in mind, I want to conclude that teachers should become transformative intellectuals if they are to subscribe to a view of pedagogy that believes in educating students to be active, critical citizens.

Central to the category of transformative intellectual is the necessity of making the pedagogical more political and the political more pedagogical. Making the pedagogical more political means inserting schooling directly into the political sphere by arguing that schooling represents both a struggle to define meaning and a struggle over power relations. Within this perspective, critical reflection and action become part of a fundamental social project to help students develop a deep and abiding faith in the struggle to overcome economic, political, and social injustices, and to further humanize themselves as part of this struggle. In this case, knowledge and power are inextricably linked to the presupposition that to choose life, to recognize the necessity of improving its democratic and qualitative character for all people, is to understand the preconditions necessary to struggle for it.

Making the political more pedagogical means utilizing forms of pedagogy that embody political interests that are emancipatory in nature; that is, using forms of pedagogy that treat students as critical agents; make knowledge problematic; utilize critical and affirming dialogue; and make the case for struggling for a qualitatively better world for all people. In part, this suggests that transformative intellectuals take seriously the need to give students an active voice in their learning experiences. It also means developing a critical vernacular that is attentive to problems experienced at the level of everyday life, particularly as they are related to pedagogical experiences connected to classroom practice. As such, the pedagogical starting point for such intellectuals is not the isolated student but individuals and groups in their various cultural, class, racial, historical and gender settings, along with the particularity of their diverse problems, hopes and dreams.

Transformative intellectuals need to develop a discourse that unites the language of critique with the language of possibility, so that social educators recognize that they can make changes. In doing so, they must speak out against economic, political and social injustices both within and outside of schools. At the same time, they must work to create the conditions that give students the opportunity to become citizens who have the knowledge and courage to struggle in order to make despair unconvincing and hope practical. As difficult as this task may seem to social educators, it is a struggle worth waging. To do otherwise is to deny social educators the opportunity to assume the role of transformative intellectuals.

Dilemma Language

Colin Lacey

Colin Lacey is a faculty member at University of Sussex, England.

Henry Giroux's book [*Ideology, Culture and the Process of Schooling*] has the benefit of an almost adulatory preface by Stanley Aronowitz who describes his approach as a "far cry from all previous theory" and as a "fecund work of *immanent critique.*" In addition, according to Aronowitz it contributes the "absolutely singular breakthrough in American literature" by offering us a critique of schooling within a framework which makes pedagogy an emancipatory activity.

In fact the introduction and six essays that make up the book are long on criticism and synthesis and short on new theoretical approaches. The critique, in each case, is developed within a now familiar framework. Giroux tells us that functionalism has been disposed of by the newer critical approaches of phenomenology and humanistic Marxism. . . . Giroux points out [that] the neo Marxist or economistic view, which provides [the] theory of class domination, presents an over determined view of correspondence between the effects of schooling and the economic structure.

Giroux wishes to produce a synthesis by demonstrating the contradictions within existing institutions and pointing to the degrees of autonomy that these contradictions confer within a class dominated society. He thus deals with an exceptionally important topic and certainly reminds us of the inadequacies of our understanding of many aspects of the school system. He reminds us of the degree to which many of our present practices and educational programmes support the class domination that many of us complain about. He reminds us of the importance of developing within our education, whether it be for our pupils or teachers in training, a critical

From "Dilemma Language," Reviews by Colin Lacey. © Times Educational Supplement, *1982.*

awareness of the commonsense assumptions that legitimize existing practices and forms of knowledge, that bolster this domination. He reminds us that the present crisis in education was not produced by education. It is a political and economic crisis with its roots outside the education system, which must not accept the blame for it.

Finally he proposes training programmes that will produce a new radical pedagogy welded to a new radical content, in which the learner and teacher collaborate in producing a new relationship and a new understanding of the multiple socio-economic and ideological connexions "that mediate between schools and the wider social structure." The revolution in education, he argues, must begin now but teachers will need to fight in each future generation for a better and more just society.

Despite my sympathy for the task he sets himself and the hard work he has put into reading, synthesizing and referencing the theoretical works of many writers my view is that he fails either to advance our theoretical understanding to any extent or to popularize the works of the writers on whom he depends for most of his concepts and ideas. It is in fact not at all clear whether he is writing for an academic audience or producing a popularizing account of the theoretical works of others meant to inform radical educators. The result is a text studded with terminology which often obscures and sometimes damages the analysis. For example, the term cultural capital is useful if it is used sparingly for those aspects of culture that resemble the use of capital by the capitalist class. If the term is used as synonymous with culture it loses any analytical quality and unnecessarily complicates the text.

A second major problem lies in the large gap left by the analysis between the theoretical debate and the problem and constraints of the classroom. In fact the author fails to identify these practical problems and frequently talks of the classroom as if it were a theoretical entity.

Although he acknowledges the important work done by sociologists studying the classroom he fails to make use of their findings. As a result many educationists will feel just as baffled by his suggestions as by the "pessimistic" "Orwellian" "economistic" sociologists whom he criticizes for trying to persuade educationists that change is not possible within education.

This last point leads to my third major criticism. Giroux's claim to a new synthesis of radical pedagogy and radical content depends on an intimate understanding of the classroom and the culture of the learner. Yet he makes absolutely no progress towards deepening our understanding of what this might mean. We are left with exhortation. As learners we have a right to be disappointed.

DISCUSSION QUESTIONS AND ACTIVITIES

1. Describe the technocratic approach in both teacher education and classroom pedagogy.
2. What are the shortcomings of the technocratic approach?
3. Collect information about your own teacher education program and observe the extent to which it follows a technocratic model. Which of the technocratic practices should be kept and which ones eliminated?
4. Why does Giroux believe it is better to conceptualize the teacher's role as a "transformative intellectual"?
5. Schools, it is said, are "contested spheres" that are "inextricably tied to the issues of power and control." What does that mean?
6. How can we make the "pedagogical more

political and the political more pedagogical"? Do you think that it is important to do so?

7. Lacey claims that Giroux's writing is replete with terminology that obscures analysis, and it is not clear for what audience he is writing. What is an author's responsibility to his or her audience?

8. Does Giroux fail to bridge the gap, as Lacey claims, between theory and practical classroom problems and constraints?

9. Does Giroux's attempt at a synthesis of radical pedagogy fail to provide "an intimate understanding of the classroom and culture of the learner"?

SUGGESTED READINGS

Books by Henry A. Giroux

Education under Siege: The Conservative, Liberal, and Radical Debate Over Schooling. South Hadley, Mass.: Bergin and Garvey, 1985. (with Stanley Aronowitz)

The Hidden Curriculum and Moral Education. Berkeley, Calif.: McCutchan, 1983. (with David Purpel)

Ideology, Culture and the Process of Schooling. Philadelphia: Temple University Press, 1981, paperback 1984.

Theory and Resistance in Education. South Hadley, Mass.: Bergin and Garvey, 1983.

Further Thoughts
on Reformers

Boyer addresses the problem of coherence in the curriculum by outlining six themes as connecting links. He also reemphasizes the role of general education at the secondary level. Some may question whether sufficient options would be built into his program to provide adequately for individual differences and diverse interests and aspirations.

In contrast to Boyer's subject curriculum, Sizer divides the curriculum into four broad areas as a more productive way to organize the high-school program. It is better, he believes, not to teach too many subjects but to teach them more thoroughly. Despite curricular flexibility, whether the cultural heritage can best be transmitted in such a curriculum is open to question.

Mortimer Adler is a perennialist. *Perennialism* derives its aims for education from human nature, holding that human nature is the same everywhere, both today and in the past; humans are, above all, rational animals. Since it stems from human nature, the function of persons is the same in every age and in every society. Rationality is the highest human attribute and therefore this attribute should be developed to its fullest extent. It can best be developed through educational institutions, whereas other attributes—morality and spirituality—can best be developed in different institutions (e.g., family and church). *Perennialism* holds that truth is absolute, and it is the task of education to impart these truths. These truths can largely be found in the great books of the past. Since the truth is the same everywhere and everyone is a rational being, all students study the same curriculum, as is the case with the Paideia Proposal. The reader is more likely to accept the proposal once the underlying philosophical grounds are accepted. Adler's reform rationale appeals to restoration by prescribing past ideals and standards and by reinstating a required curriculum.

If a science of behavior is possible, as Skinner contends, then more power-ful explanations and greater predictability of behavior will be possible, and learning failures and miseducative experiences will largely be a thing of the past. His investigations start with empirical data and proceed tentatively to limited-range generalizations. His positivistic approach is reminiscent of the tenor of August Comte's positivism, and his inductive method falls within the grand tradition of Francis Bacon and John Stuart Mill.

Yet one may still charge Skinner with a limited scientific methodology of description and observation. He is unable to deal with problems of motivation because of the unobservable and mentalistic concepts that may be needed in such a treatment.

Thus one is left with the question of whether Skinner's controlled environ-ment is more educationally valuable than a more open, nondirective envi-ronment with greater options. Skinner's reform rationale appeals to quality: educational institutions would utilize his model to bring about both an improved process based on positive reinforcement and better outcomes based on desired behaviors.

Looking at Kozol's approach to the problem of illiteracy, it is necessary, first of all, to determine what is meant by illiteracy and where the dividing line is drawn. Our definitional decision will determine the magnitude of the problem. Some people may be "undereducated" rather than illiterate. Even af-ter a decision is made about the definition, the significance of illiteracy for the nation as a whole as well as for illiterates needs to be considered. How impor-tant is literacy in the emerging postindustrial economy when a majority of the forthcoming job openings will likely be limited-skill service work? Are there more serious educational problems that should take precedence over illiteracy? The measures to ameliorate the problem should consider the respective respon-sibilities of illiterates, public schools, adult education, various community ser-vices, and special programs. It is also necessary to determine sources of fund-ing and how such funds can best be allocated.

Giroux wants schools to participate in developing a new society, and he sees teachers and students playing a key role in this process. One way that this is done is for teachers to avoid becoming technocrats and opt for a trans-formative intellectual role where they can understand and relate the pedagog-ical and political spheres. Giroux's reform rationale appeals to decision mak-ing. Here one needs to decide what the aims of education should be and, consequently, whether the aims proposed by Giroux are justifiable. How are aims determined? A number of approaches have been employed: (1) derive the aims from those values deemed to be of greatest worth (a hierarchy may be established, as Herbert Spencer did); (2) derive aims from human nature (as the perennialists do); (3) develop aims to meet societal needs; and (4) draw out aims from a preferred philosophy of education. Another approach, as suggested by R. S. Peters, is to claim that the search for aims is misguided because one is not asking for a statement of ends extrinsic to education; one is seeking instead to initiate the young into worthwhile activities that are intrinsic to the educational process. Dewey developed a similar line of thought: because the characteristic of life is growth, education is one with growing. Since growth is relative to nothing but further growth, education is not subordinate to anything except more education.

The reformers can be understood in various ways. How do they define education? In what respects do they differ in their conception of education? What educational aims are most important? What reasons are given for adopting a set of aims? Notice that some reformers seek to liberate the learner. What are they liberating the learner from, and what will the learner be able to do as a result of such liberation? What sort of institutions will nurture the type of person they believe education should develop?

Another common tendency for reformers is to offer an optimistic view of human nature by stating or, more often, implying that individuals are basically good and will become liberated in a nurturing environment. But how would reformers explain why institutions are oppressive when they are governed by individuals born with these same positive traits?

Certain methods of teaching are considered superior: Sizer advocates teaching less but studying each area in greater depth; Adler endorses three types of teaching (didactic, coaching, and Socratic questioning); Kozol proposes the use of "generative" or "dangerous words"; and Skinner seeks to individualize instruction through the use of teaching machines and programmed materials. Look at these different teaching approaches to see if they are consonant with the reformers' aims.

A PARTING SCENARIO

A number of guests, including yourself, are invited to a mountain lodge for a weekend retreat. To your surprise, the guests include all the reformers in Part I. They suddenly begin passionately debating the aims of education. What would they likely say? Who would you side with and why?

Part II

Innovations and Alternatives

Recent years have been marked by widespread dissatisfaction with public education and numerous attempts to find more successful approaches to educating the young. Not surprisingly, educators have sought to offer innovations and alternatives. Innovation is the introduction of any new idea, method, or device to improve some aspect of the educational process. The idea could lead to a new way of handling gifted or handicapped learners. The innovation may be the project method or the initiation of team teaching, and the device could range from educational television to microcomputers. In contrast, educational alternatives are systems and plans, both inside and outside public education that are different from the typical public school model.

Alternatives first appeared outside of public education as different types of schools (such as free schools), as new organizational plans for redistributing educational resources (vouchers), or plans for home instruction. Alternatives were developed in public education during the 1970s and ranged from schools for performing arts to the back-to-basics alternative.

Although there can be no innovation or alternative without change, most changes are not innovations or alternatives. Change is when something or someone becomes different and may be accidental. An innovation, since it is brought about by human agency to serve a particular purpose, rules out changes in nature and human changes that are unintentional. It is true that some innovations, just as scientific discoveries, are serendipitous. In such cases, however, it is still necessary to make the connection between the discovery and an educational goal and then visualize the innovation within an educational context.

Thus, by the time the discoverer finishes, the process has become highly deliberate.

But how novel does something have to be before it is counted as an innovation? Usually it will require some distinctive feature in at least one of the following aspects: rationale, organization, curriculum, or instruction. For instance, the rationale for accountability differs perceptibly from traditional rationales for school organization and evaluation; the organizational procedures of mainstreaming represent a sharp departure from earlier practices in handling handicapped children; and bilingual education differs significantly in curricula and instruction from traditional practices. Although innovations that are highly original are likely to leave a lasting impression, such innovations are also likely to meet with greater resistance from those that require less change. The following survey of key innovations and alternatives of the recent past will clarify these points.

THE CONTINUITY OF INNOVATIONS
AND ALTERNATIVES

Early Innovations in Instruction,
Curriculum, and Organization

The Dalton Plan.   This is a study plan based on instructional contracts for students. It was named after Dalton, Massachusetts, the district in which it was first introduced in 1920 by Helen Parkhurst. The plan actually attracted more followers overseas—in Europe, China, and Japan—than in the United States.

The plan called for a series of classrooms that were allocated to certain subjects. The classrooms were designated as laboratories and pupils as experimenters. In the English laboratory, pupils had access to significant literary works, and in the geography laboratory, the teacher helped pupils use models, maps, charts, and globes. Thus there was a laboratory for each subject taught in school.

The pupil was given a mimeographed guide sheet that listed all the work to be done for the month. The pupil then signed a contract to complete the assignments on the sheet by specified dates. There was no class teaching and pupils could move from one room to another as they chose in fulfilling their contract. It was initially thought that ideally each pupil would receive his or her own assignment sheet, but the burden proved too great for most teachers. One assignment sheet was usually compiled for everyone. Slower learners and indolent pupils required more supervision and direction. Some Dalton followers set aside afternoons for games, gymnastics, and social activities. Enrichment of English was through debates, public speaking, and histrionics; history was supplemented by discussion of current politics, the customs and manners of earlier eras, and other topics.

Despite greater freedom and individual attention than in traditional classrooms, the Dalton Plan came under criticism for insufficient socialization practices and lack of social education. This criticism, however, was more applicable to the original Dalton Plan and not to those that sprang up in various parts of the world where some attempt was made to balance individual learning with social education. Another criticism was that it did not actually individualize instruction because the assignments were not geared to the needs of each student. Nor did it break from the traditional subject curriculum, which some progressives deplored. The plan was suited for a subject curriculum and could be used with any standard subject, except perhaps with foreign languages.

The Winnetka Plan.   This plan was initiated in 1919 by Carleton Washburne (1889–1968) in Winnetka, Illinois, as a means of individualizing instruction at the elementary level. The curriculum was divided into two parts: the *common essentials*, the three Rs, sciences, and social studies; and *cultural and creative experiences*, which were taught in a group setting.

The common essentials were individualized at the beginning of the term by evaluating the child in each subject and then establishing assignments that were adjusted to the child's needs. Class recitation was discarded. Instead, pupils would read for the teacher one at a time while the others studied. Once a portion of their work was completed, they could ask the teacher for a test and then move on to the next assignment whenever the test was successfully passed. In the Winnetka Plan, children neither skipped grades nor failed. Thus studies were divided by the teachers into tasks and goals, and each child was given simple directions for proceeding independently.

Half the morning and half the afternoon sessions were dedicated to individual work with the common essentials, while the remaining half of the morning and afternoon was devoted to such cultural and creative experiences as plays, open forums, school journals, self-government meetings, workshops, excursions, shopwork, music, and art.

The Winnetka Plan was more genuinely individualized than the Dalton Plan; it enabled students to proceed at their own pace, whereas the Dalton Plan insisted that a pupil could not proceed in any subject until the entire monthly assignment was completed. Studies of the Winnetka Plan under Washburne's direction showed favorable results in terms of student performance or standardized tests, except in spelling where they lagged behind. Washburne used the Winnetka Plan for two decades. However, when adopted elsewhere, it was usually modified considerably to bring it more into line with traditional practices.

Some questions were also raised over what constituted "the common essentials" and whether these subjects were the ones that could best be individualized. Additionally, questions arose over how the two major areas of the program could be connected.

The Activity or Experience Curriculum.   This curriculum emerged in elementary schools during the progressive movement in the 1930s. It was based on the assumption that children learn best by experiencing things, rather than by the presentation of subject matter to them. Furthermore, units of study were constructed from a knowledge of their needs and interests. It was also based on the conviction that learning is an active affair, and involvement in activities will overcome the child's passivity and lack of motivation found in traditional schools. The program usually called for some pupil-teacher planning in which teachers ask children about their needs. Teachers and pupils worked together by using a problem-solving approach in planning, focusing on children's interests for organizational purposes.

This program was aimed at overcoming the interest and motivation problem in the subject curriculum, perhaps meeting some additional needs, and keeping students actively involved. One serious mistake, however, was the assumption that because learning is an active affair, then activity itself will lead to effective learning. One may learn by doing, but not all doing results in learning: Activity may be a necessary condition for some forms of learning but not a necessary and sufficient condition. Moreover, an activity curriculum tends to confuse overt activity with doing. Thinking, however, involves an active role by the learner but may not be observable. Another weakness is that since the child's range of experience is extremely limited, it is incumbent upon the school to broaden interests rather than stick to present ones. Finally, to use needs as a basis for curriculum planning may be untenable. To say that a need exists and that it should be fulfilled is to recognize that it exists to fulfill some objective. Whether or not an objective is desirable is determined by a set of values or the school's philosophy—not an appeal to needs.

The Project Method.   William Heard Kilpatrick (1871–1965) believed that the activities found in agriculture and extension work could be applied to other aspects of life through projects. His notion of a project, however, was much broader than the conventional one: "The presence of a dominating purpose." Thus building a boat, making a dress, or staging a play were considered projects, as well as any other activity with a dominating purpose. It was important, in Kilpatrick's view, that any given project would lead to other worthwhile projects, and it was better for each student to choose the project and plan it with teacher guidance, when needed. The Project Method, Kilpatrick believed, is valuable not just to sustain student interest but because life itself is composed of a series of projects, and therefore, this way of learning will be a suitable preparation for life.

Kilpatrick's definition of the Project Method, however, was too broad since it tended to equate any goal-directed behavior with a project, even though much of this behavior involved no project in the conventional sense of the term. Furthermore, the Project Method lacked structure, sequence, and organization; it was difficult to build a curriculum on the basis of projects. Moreover, classroom management was a problem because too many divergent activities were taking place simultaneously. Moving from one project into another was not always easy and children became bored and restless. Many projects may also tap only lower-level cognitive abilities. The bulk of organized knowledge, as well as skill development, was in danger of being lost with projects as the basis of curriculum. Today the curriculum is not built on projects alone; however, the "pure" Project Method can still be found in industrial arts, vocational agriculture, and the sciences.

The Platoon System.   Many American school districts adopted the platoon system early in this century. The first system was organized by William Wirt (1874–1938) in Bluffton, Indiana, in 1900, where Wirt served as school superintendent. The Platoon System divided the school population into two groups. While one group (Platoon A) received instruction in the three Rs for two hours daily, the second group (Platoon B) studied subjects in specially equipped facilities (shop, gym, art room) for the same length of time. Both groups exchanged places at a predetermined time. This was designed to achieve a balance between academic work and social-creative activities. Even the elementary grades followed this compartmentalized plan. This system increased pupil capacity by 40 percent without hiring additional teachers.

In 1907, Wirt became superintendent in Gary, Indiana, and established the Gary Plan. In addition to the Platoon System, Wirt adopted Dewey's idea of education as an embryonic community life in which the different community occupations were reflected in art, history, and science. Not only would the school provide greatly expanded educational opportunities in art and music rooms, swimming pools, gardens, and the like, but the school would become the community's center for intellectual and artistic life. The schools were open all day, twelve months each year, to persons of all ages, for the ultimate objective of bringing about community improvement.

A team of evaluators commended the Gary Plan for its boldness, organizational innovations, the application of democratic principles to school conduct and discipline, and the enrichment of community life through the schools. But it was also criticized for not always working well in practice: Some activities wasted time, others were enjoyable but not educative. School records were often inaccurate; instruction in the subjects was not well organized in many cases, sufficient in content, or presented other than conventionally. Despite these criticisms, over 200 cities had adopted the Gary Plan by 1929.

Early Alternative Schools

Francis W. Parker School.   An educational reformer who was credited by Dewey as the "father of progressive education," Francis W. Parker (1837–1902) became school superintendent in Quincy, Massachusetts, in 1873, and set about reforming the schools. Parker was a child-centered progressive: He sought to move the child to the center of the educative process and to make the curriculum convey greater meaning to the child. Parker's deification of the child suggests that this philosophy is closer to Rousseau's than Dewey's.

Parker abolished the formalities of the traditional classroom that insisted the child remain perfectly still and quiet and substituted instead observation, laboratory work, and the use of ideas in practice (as in the teaching of arithmetic). Inductive methods were employed in arithmetic; geography was taught by field trips as well as formal study. The emphasis was on observing, describing, and gaining a grasp of things before being introduced to more conventional studies. The program, which was dubbed the "Quincy System," achieved considerable recognition before Parker moved to the Cook County Normal School in Illinois. Here he continued his opposition, first expressed at Quincy, to traditional teaching and stressed instead activity, creative self-expression, the scientific study of education, and prepared special teachers for these subjects. In 1901, the Francis W. Parker School was founded in Chicago, staffed by many teachers prepared by Parker; it continued for more than thirty years.

Parker was a founding father of progressive education in the United States and set an example for others to follow. Criticisms of his approach are essentially those made earlier about progressivism of the child-centered variety.

The Dewey Laboratory School.   This experimental elementary school began in Chicago in 1896, reached its peak of 140 pupils in 1902, and closed in 1904 after a disagreement with the University of Chicago over the administration of the school. Whereas the Parker School began with practice and later moved to theory, Dewey sought to test theory in the Laboratory School. The school was an experiment in "cooperative living" whereby both individual interests and social life could be satisfied. Dewey sought to reconcile a host of dualisms in the larger culture: interest and effort, individualism and collectivism, work and play, labor and leisure, school and society, the child and the curriculum. The school was experimental and children were allowed to explore, create, and make mistakes in testing ideas.

The organizational focus for the Laboratory School was social occupations. Studying occupations, it was thought, would not only promote the social purposes of the school but would greatly enliven the school's activities and make the learning of routine skills more interesting. It would also promote a balance between intellectual and practical activities. Since, for Dewey, education was not a preparation for life but was life itself, children were to learn directly about life by the school producing in miniature the conditions of social life. And since many of the children would later become manual workers, they needed an understanding of industrial processes. School subjects in the conventional sense were dispensed with, and even the three Rs grew out of the child's activities. The social occupations represented human concerns about food, clothing, shelter, household furnishings, and the production, consumption, and exchange of goods. Four- and five-year-olds learned about preparing lunch before going home at mid-day; by the age of seven, the emphasis had changed from occupations in the home and neighborhood to an historical approach that traced the emergence of occupations beginning with earliest culture; finally, by the age of thirteen, the emphasis shifted to current events.

The Dewey Laboratory School was a bold experiment and represented the most salient ideas on the leading edge of the Progressive movement. It was criticized because it was difficult to achieve a balanced focus on both the individual (the child) and society. The individualistic or freedom side may have been given greater attention. Systematic follow-up studies were not conducted of the school's graduates and therefore no record is available of the school's impact on their lives. Yet from the records of the school and the extant examples of student work, it appears to have been a soundly managed school with quality teachers.

The Montessori School.   Maria Montessori (1870–1952), the first woman in Italy to receive an M.D. degree, worked with mentally defective children and then turned to normal children. Montessori believed that the child needs to escape from the domination of parents and teachers. Children in modern society are victims of adult suppression that compels them to adopt coping measures foreign to their real nature. Teachers must change their attitudes toward children and organize an environment in which children can lead lives of their own.

In Montessori schools children are placed in a stimulating environment where there are things for them to do and things to study. This environment should be free of rivalry, rewards, and punishments; instead, learning is to be through interesting activities. Teachers become directors who see that activities proceed according to a master plan; in fact, Montessori believed that one teacher could handle as many as forty-five children if necessary, but a class of thirty is more desirable. Special materials are used by children in a carefully organized environment. Through regular, graded use of didactic material, children gain skills of manipulation and judgment, and the special senses are separately trained by use of apparatus: Cubes of various sizes are used to build a tower so that children can learn about volume; several kinds of wooden insets exhibit breadth, depth, and volume; sticks of graduated length and cylinders of different sizes are to be placed in the correct blocks. Children learn to develop neuromuscular mechanisms for writing by pouring rice and picking up beans; they learn their letters through a combination of senses: visual, tactile, and auditory. And they learn to associate the sound of the word (sounded phonetically) with an object. In geography, children are given a sandpaper globe, tangible objects, and pictures of people from different cultures. Geography activities lead to the study of history, while learning one's language leads to the study of both subjects. Science, mathematics, and foreign languages are outgrowths of learning one's native language.

The Montessori system spread to many parts of the world prior to World War I, lapsed during the War but had a brief recovery in the 1920s, and was revived again in the United States in the 1950s. Despite their achievements, Montessori schools have been criticized for using equipment too complex and intricate for children, for failure to stimulate the imagination because no imaginary tales are used, for using overly planned and structured learning, and for not promoting social learning sufficiently.

Waldorf Education.   Rudolf Steiner (1861–1925), the founder of Waldorf education in 1913, believed in theosophy, a religious movement that originated in India that teaches about god and the world on the basis of mystical insight. Steiner later called his philosophy *anthroposophy.* It was his objective to provide a program of education from a spiritual point of view that recognized the child's physical, emotional, and intellectual development as manifested in three successive stages of growth in seven-year cycles. The first stage is characterized by imitation and expression in active movement. It is inappropriate, Steiner believed, to teach the three Rs at this stage. The second stage, from years seven to fourteen, features the development of feelings and imagination and is the period when basic skills are acquired. The third stage is where the pupil's thinking ability is emphasized through formal study.

During the first two stages, no specialization is permitted and pupils are grouped according to age and intelligence. The greatest need of the child, according to Steiner, is security; therefore, one teacher remains with a group of children throughout the first stage; similarly, another teacher remains throughout the second stage; and only in the final stage, when subject matter specialists are needed, is this pattern altered. No examinations are used because Steiner considered them of no educational value. In addition to traditional subjects, Waldorf education places emphasis on mythology, art, and eurhythmics (a music-based method of physical training). The Waldorf program strives to develop intellectual and manipulative skills, cultivate social conscience, promote self-expression, and encourage spiritual development. Waldorf schools have a non-denominational Christian outlook. By the 1980s, more than eighty of these schools were established in Europe and the United States.

Waldorf education offers a broad view of education, is holistic, and recognizes different stages (and suitable materials) of pupil development. It may not be appropriate for public education, not only because teachers are unprepared to handle this type of program but because it might raise questions about religious teaching in public schools. Steiner's stages of development do not reflect the latest research findings, and the practice of one teacher remaining with a group of pupils for many years is problematic on pedagogical grounds.

RECENT INNOVATIONS IN INSTRUCTION AND CURRICULUM

Instructional Innovations

Behavioral Objectives.   Behavioral objectives arose during the 1960s to move away from high-sounding educational goals on which performance could not be measured. Instead, behavioral objectives (or "instructional objectives," as they were later called) provide precise, observable, measurable statements of goals. Behavioral objectives state exactly what students can be expected to do after completing designated learning activities. (For example, after four weeks in an introductory typing course, students should be able to type at least twenty words per minute on a ten-minute typing test with no more than four errors.) Those planning a course are able to select materials designed to accomplish the objectives. Thus the teacher is able to plan more effectively as well as assess course effectiveness with greater precision. It also means teachers are more accountable for instructional activities, and the student is better informed about what is expected of him or her.

Behavioral objectives, however, have been criticized on a number of grounds. Since objectives for courses are set in advance, they make it difficult for teachers to change plans in the face of special learning needs. This leaves out much learning of an affective, aesthetic, and moral nature that cannot be stated as an objective. Although convergent thinking may in many cases be stated behaviorally, it is far less likely that divergent thinking can be stated or measured precisely (though it could be evaluated). Thus many of the more important objectives cannot be stated behaviorally. Emphasis on behavioral objectives may lead to neglect of principles, broad concepts, and understandings that give meaning to behavior. Even if behavioral objectives are sound, they are not feasible because of the enormous amount of time required for teachers to compose innumerable objectives.

Programmed Instruction and Computer-Assisted Instruction. The first teaching machine was developed in the 1920s by Sidney L. Pressey and was revived in the 1950s by B. F. Skinner in the form of programmed materials. These materials use a carefully planned sequence of learning tasks by breaking the material down into its smallest meaningful units. Students are expected to show mastery of each exercise before proceeding to the next one. Once the exercise is completed, the student knows if he or she has mastered the knowledge because the correct answer is given. If the student's answer is incorrect, he or she restudies the material (in a linear program) or is assigned a new exercise, as in alternate or branching programs developed by Norman Crowder.

Programmed instruction has some advantages over traditional teaching. Students have greater recall of material through programmed instruction, master knowledge and skills more rapidly than in traditional instruction, and enjoy the benefits of individualized learning through the use of branching. (Branching is when a learner temporarily ceases work with the main sequence of frames to study a subsidiary or remedial program.)

The disadvantages of programmed instruction are that these materials have not been used to teach higher-order skills and knowledge; students tend to become bored once the novelty has worn off; it is expensive (fifty or seventy-five hours of programming are needed for each student hour of instruction); it does not satisfy students whose learning objectives differ from the material; and it is atomistic and mechanistic.

Computer-assisted instruction (CAI) operates on similar principles of learning as programmed instruction. Students work individually with a programmed computer by typewriter, touch-manipulation board, or electronic pointer. The computer responds via typewriter, television, slides, recordings, or print. CAI can be used to individualize instruction, supplement classroom demonstrations, promote independent study, and diagnose student learning difficulties.

The advantages of CAI are that students learn faster than by using other methods; it may reduce student drop-out rates; it allows students to study at their own pace; students generally react favorably toward it; it is effective for students who do not perform well in traditional instruction; and it aids students to complete courses satisfactorily.

The disadvantages of CAI are that it is expensive; it is difficult to exchange programs because of many different computer languages; it is impersonal and lacking human interaction; student excitement over CAI is not easily sustained; teachers generally resist it; and it operates on an atomistic rather than a holistic model of learning.

Mastery Learning. This form of learning is based on the assumption that the mastery of a topic or a human behavior is theoretically possible for anyone given the optimum quality of instruction appropriate to each individual and given the time needed for mastery. Mastery learning began with the work of Henry C. Morrison in the 1920s and continued in the 1960s with further studies by J. B. Carroll and Benjamin S. Bloom.

Carroll's model uses five variables: aptitude, perseverance, ability to understand instruction, quality of instruction, and opportunity for learning. Taken together, these variables predict the degree of student learning for a particular learning task, and they also play an important role in Bloom's strategy for mastery learning. A mastery strategy involves deciding what will constitute mastery for a particular course, determining appropriate procedures, and deciding how mastery will be evaluated. Bloom supplements regular instruction with frequent evaluation to determine student progress and uses alternative methods and materials. Objectives are stated behaviorally; a preassessment of students is used before instruction to determine interest and ability; instruction is adapted to the learner; difficulties are frequently diagnosed; prescriptions for improvement are made; and postassessments are undertaken. A variety of instructional procedures are selected. Some are discarded and new ones added, based on feedback from ongoing instruction. Those students who fail to achieve mastery need to be assessed to determine the problems they are having and given more time to gain mastery.

Mastery learning has the advantages of being workable for virtually any level of schooling for any subject; potentially 90 percent of students can master a course; students can have a role in developing objectives; it can enhance a student's self-concept with a sense of accomplishment; and it promotes cooperation rather than competition for grades.

The disadvantages of mastery learning are that it is more appropriate for learning technical skills; it is unfair if most of the students receive the same grades because grades then become meaningless; teachers are unprepared for mastery learning because of the scarcity of reliable tests to assess the five variables; it is overly teacher-centered by ignoring credit for student effort not reflected on tests; and it overemphasizes outcomes to the detriment of learning processes.

Discovery Learning.　　This learning is inductive. The student is expected to formulate a rule, devise a formula, and recognize a generalization as a result of first-hand experience with cases or instances of some phenomena. Discovery learning was first advocated by Jerome S. Bruner who held that the most uniquely personal learning is that which the individual discovers for himself or herself. The student, for instance, can discover the generalization that lies behind a particular mathematical operation. Discovery is a process of going beyond the data to develop new insights. This process not only encourages mastery of fundamental ideas about a subject but promotes intellectual excitement about discovery and confidence in one's ability to perceive previously unrecognized relationships. Thus it helps the student acquire information in ways that make it more readily applicable; the student becomes less motivated by external rewards or fear of failure; the act of discovery provides a mode of inquiry in future learning, and the knowledge is more likely to be retained because it is organized in terms of learner interest.

Discovery learning has an outward similarity to Dewey's problem-solving or scientific method insofar as both promote independent, reflective thinking. Dewey's problem solving, however, is more structured, utilizing a step-by-step sequence; whereas discovery learning is not highly structured and more fully recognizes insight and intuition in the discovery of new knowledge.

One of the basic weaknesses in this area is that researchers have not specified what is to be discovered by the student. In some situations the student is left with almost no cues to discover a simple principle, but without cues it is unlikely that the student can arrive at the principle. However, if intensive cues are needed by the student, very little discovery will take place. In contrast to an expository approach (where the teacher provides background information and the correct answer), discovery learning is far more time consuming. It is probably true, though, that discovery methods are preferable to expository teaching if large amounts of time are not consumed by greater learning activity and involvement. Discovery, however, is only one way this involvement can be brought about. Expository teaching could be used to impart basic knowledge, and then students would become more actively involved by applying the knowledge to new situations.

Television Instruction.　　This form of instruction uses live or prerecorded television lectures or demonstrations in courses. It is used to enlarge slides, documents, pictures; to provide off-campus instruction; to share first-hand field experiences; to provide short demonstrations for videotapes; to observe one's own behavior, as in teaching, in order to improve performance; and to offer professionally prepared educational programs. Besides these uses, television instruction has certain advantages: It provides instruction to those unable to attend classes (in conjunction with a study guide or syllabus); the broadcasts can be aired repeatedly at convenient times; students generally prefer television instruction to regular lectures; and it enables viewers to see specimens, documents, and pictures more clearly.

Instructional television has some disadvantages: Except in the early grades, students prefer small-group discussion; it is essentially a one-way medium that provides no interaction or opportunity to raise questions (unless special provisions are made); it is inferior to other media for music broadcasts; it requires a large audience to be cost effective; and some teachers are averse to using it. When instructional television offers students an opportunity to raise questions and interact, it is at least as effective as other media and methods.

Curriculum Innovations

Structure of the Disciplines Approach.   This approach originated with scholars in the 1950s and 60s as a response to their findings of obsolete content and instructional practices in the subject curriculum. While retaining subjects as a framework for organization, the scholars revised and updated content, introduced discovery learning, and deemphasized rote learning in favor of teaching students how to grasp the structure of a discipline. This meant that fundamental axioms, concepts, and other building blocks of a discipline became the focus of learning so that students could comprehend the underlying structure, attempt to generate fruitful hypotheses, and perceive how scholars generate new knowledge. The concept of readiness was reassessed, and it was found that students could grasp concepts earlier if the concepts were formulated in terms of the student's cognitive development and how students learn best at different ages and levels of maturity. This led to earlier grade placement of subjects and concepts (in mathematics, for instance, set theory was introduced earlier).

The structure of the disciplines approach has certain advantages over the traditional subject curriculum: revision and updating and curriculum content are undertaken more frequently; the emphasis is on understanding a discipline's structure rather than learning facts for their own sake; stress is placed on critical thinking and intuitive judgment (in discovery learning); concepts are mastered earlier; and, as a consequence of these features, there is a greater likelihood of effective transfer of training.

Despite the promise of this approach and genuine progress in curriculum revision during the 1960s, some shortcomings should be noted. Students face problems in their daily lives that are not restricted to disciplines—problems of relations between the sexes, marriage and the family, racial matters, war and peace, ecology, shortages of economic resources, and numerous others that are better approached through interdisciplinary perspectives. Second, a subject or discipline approach to curriculum, as opposed to an interdisciplinary one, discourages examination of the curriculum as a whole in order to develop concepts progressively and provide proper continuity and articulation from one grade to the next. Third, this approach emphasizes cognitive learning and neglects social, emotional, and moral development. Stress on cognitive learning slants the approach to the more academically talented and is, in fact, used with highly motivated children in superior schools. A fourth difficulty is that children do not think like researchers in the disciplines, yet the program establishes models of this type of thinking and inquiry. Finally, this curriculum innovation gives little attention to goals and their justification, other than assuming that a mastery of disciplines is the most desirable end—an assumption that is not self-evident and needs to be demonstrated.

Compensatory Education.   These are programs that seek to overcome the educational disadvantages of children that arise from personal history, social background, or economic conditions. Research has indicated that retardation may be long-lasting or permanent unless intervention occurs at an early age; consequently, early childhood education programs such as Head Start have been developed. Compensatory education leaves responsibility for physical handicaps, brain damage, and genetic limitations to special education. Among the many approaches used in compensatory education are health programs, reading readiness and remediation programs, emphasis on developing a positive self-concept, expanded guidance services, and curriculum enrichment.

Compensatory education programs were funded under Title I of the Elementary and Secondary Education Act (ESEA) passed by Congress in 1965. This immediately provided $1 billion in Title I funds to supplement and improve the education of poor and minority-group children. By 1965, funds totaled $2 billion per year, or approximately $200 more for each disadvantaged child.

Despite ample funding and federal support, most of these programs were ineffective in raising the cognitive level of disadvantaged children. Numerous reasons account for these early failures: inadequately prepared teachers, a piecemeal approach, consultant fees paid for work improperly done, unethical methods of awarding grants, vague objectives, increased quantity of services without improved quality of program content, and poor evaluation procedures. Results since 1975 have been more favorable as some of these earlier deficiencies have been corrected, better monitoring procedures have been implemented, greater funding has been provided from state and local levels, and program evaluation has improved. Thus programs such as Head Start and Follow-Through have begun to succeed as student achievement in low-income schools in several metropolitan areas is shown to match or exceed the national average. Some studies of early childhood education programs have revealed that they have a lasting effect in raising achievement and IQ scores. The cost, however, of compensatory education is high—$3,000 annually per student—and it is questionable whether funds of this magnitude will be available during a recession or that the public will be willing to provide this level of support.

Organizational Innovations

Middle Schools.   During the 1960s the middle school was developed not only as a new form of organization but as a new approach for educating pupils in the sixth, seventh, and eighth grades (in some instances the fifth and ninth grades were also included). Proponents of the middle school believe that the junior high school has not been entirely effective and propose that a separate building and special programs be used to educate pupils in these grades. The middle school is designed to serve as a bridge between childhood and adolescence, a transitional period where existing programs are not suitable for this age group. Thus the middle school seeks to establish its own identity and mission. The program stresses such features as individualized study, team teaching, integration of extracurricular activities into the formal curriculum, use of a nongraded plan, and development of interdisciplinary programs.

One of the dangers is that the middle school will be little different than the conventional junior high school. In some cases middle schools have been used to accommodate excessive enrollments by transferring students to less overcrowded middle schools. Besides the problem of providing a distinctive program and recruiting teachers with the requisite abilities and interests, school buildings geared to these special programs are not always available. Considering it took junior high schools nearly fifty years to acquire buildings adequate for their programs, the likelihood of obtaining buildings does not appear promising. Additionally, the middle school movement has met considerable resistance from proponents of the junior high school; these proponents believe the criticisms of the junior high school are at best superficial. Middle school advocates, however, point to the junior high school as largely an administrative reorganization of secondary education that belatedly developed a curricular rationale, whereas the middle school is a curriculum response to the special needs of this age group. Moreover, the junior high school movement lacks a sufficiently broad research base to validate its effectiveness, whereas the middle school movement has recently accumulated greater data to support its claims.

Nongraded Schools.   These schools are a newer form of curricular and instructional organization and are found principally at the elementary level. Grade levels and all expectations associated with separate grades are eliminated. The goals are to individualize instruction and permit each student to learn at his or her own rate of speed. The problem of promotion and retention is overcome, instruction no longer has to be geared to the average student, and student progress is not delayed because of slower classmates. Different age groups work together and learn from one another. For example, a child may be advanced in arithmetic but slower to grasp social studies; consequently, this student will be placed with others of similar abilities in each subject and will work with them in large and small groups and spend some time working alone.

Nongraded plans, however, are no panacea for curricular and instructional problems. It is still necessary to have teachers adequately prepared for this form of organization and to have sufficient and appropriate curricular materials (which, generally, are in short supply). Without these two essential ingredients, it would be better to remain with graded plans. Moreover, in some schools the actual organizational pattern required has not been actually put into operation, though teachers and administrators usually assume the plan is nongraded. Other than different reading levels, many so-called nongraded plans are little different than graded ones. Thus many of these plans are conventional homogeneous groupings of pupils within the same grade; curriculum organization and instruction remain the same.

Despite these criticisms, research studies indicate that nongraded school children's achievement scores are significantly higher than those of graded children. Additionally, fewer children are retained, and nongraded schools are especially beneficial for blacks, underachievers, and boys. Most research on nongraded schools, however, was conducted in the early 1970s, and little research has been available since 1973.

Differentiated Staffing. This is a plan for structuring the teaching faculty so that instruction can be individualized by utilizing teachers in different types of assignments according to their competencies. Differentiated staffing is especially suited to merit plans. Public school teachers generally have little differentiation in assignments and responsibilities. People performing the same type of tasks are paid different rates in regular schools; whereas in differentiated staffing, teachers receive merit pay but for different types of responsibilities and tasks.

One model of differentiated staffing divides the staff into paraprofessionals and professionals. The paraprofessionals consist of clerical assistants and proctors, technical assistants and instructional assistants, instructional associates, and research assistants. These people serve as the supporting staff to provide clerical and proctoring services, assist in classroom management, supervise the school building and grounds, prepare transparencies and slide presentations, and carry out numerous other tasks that would allow the teacher to concentrate on instruction.

The professional staff consists of the intern teacher, probationary teacher, staff teacher, master teacher, and teacher specialist. The intern teacher is non-certified and teaches part-time or full-time, depending on the school system. The probationary teacher is equivalent to today's certified teachers who have yet to be awarded tenure. The staff teacher would be tenured and have a fifth year of preparation but not necessarily a master's degree. The master teacher has demonstrated ability to assume leadership in teaching. This teacher has a master's degree and assumes leadership on curriculum committees, serves as a team-teaching leader, assists in training of probationary and intern teachers, and undertakes related responsibilities. Finally, the teacher specialist has a doctorate or post-master's degree work and is responsible for research in the area of specialization, planning programs systemwide, demonstrations in experimental teaching situations, and related duties. The teaching specialist is employed on a twelve-month basis, whereas the master teacher is employed on a ten- or eleven-month basis.

Differentiated staffing, according to proponents, breaks the lockstep of traditional plans, affords far better staff utilization, and is more likely than traditional staffing to provide students with superior teaching and services. It also offers greater incentives and rewards for superior teaching, and it relieves teachers of more routine chores so that they can concentrate on professional activities.

Critics, however, say that there are problems in determining the different levels of responsibilities, assigning duties to these levels, and assessing competence. The plan also seems to be a surreptitious way of initiating merit pay. If this is the case a genuine plan of merit pay, based on performance, would be preferable to one based on roles assumed, degrees held, and the like. Second, differentiated staffing fosters specialization and moves the system away from a child-centered approach to one that is subject-centered. Third, the competent teacher is not necessarily the skillful supervisor or coordinator. Thus the Peter Principle may be operating here. Finally, some teachers resent a meritocratic system and a hierarchical arrangement. Although differentiated staffing enlists greater teacher participation in policy making, some administrators are reluctant to support such changes. If administrators are to make the plan work, they will need to involve teachers in organizing it, demonstrate that competencies can be accurately and impartially assessed, and clearly designate the specific types of responsibilities expected in each position.

Team Teaching.   This instructional arrangement breaks from the one-teacher-per-class system by involving two or more teachers who plan instruction and evaluation cooperatively for a group of students usually the size of two to five conventional classes. The class may range in size from 50 to over 180 students, two to six teachers may participate, and the class may be organized at times as one group, several small groups, or for individual instruction. Teams may be selected on the basis of the teacher's specialization or teachers who have special talents that complement one another. Usually a team leader with organizational and curriculum development abilities is selected. Differentiated staffing employs team teaching, but this hierarchical model is not a prerequisite for using team teaching, as some plans use teachers of equal or similar status. The ability of competent team members to work together cooperatively, agree upon objectives, and delegate responsibilities is essential for successful team teaching.

Among the advantages of team teaching are: it allows greater utilization of personnel, space, material, and equipment; it offers students an opportunity to find a teacher with whom they relate effectively; it permits students to work in large groups, small groups, and engage in individual study; and it is more likely to provide a more perceptive diagnosis of learning difficulties and a more objective evaluation of achievement because two or more teachers are involved. Teachers benefit as well. They receive stimulation from observing their colleagues, by being observed, and by sharing ideas. Teachers also prepare more carefully and exert greater effort when under observation, and it is an opportunity for more experienced teachers to help less experienced ones.

Yet despite these advantages, many difficulties have arisen in team teaching. One problem lies in organizing the team. Able team leaders and team members are hard to find; large amounts of time are required for preparation and planning and are not always available; and confusion arises at times over the team leader's role—whether to supervise teachers or instruct students. As for students, they may take advantage of different expectations of teachers and pit them against one another. Students may also find that members of the team have different grading practices.

Open Education.   This innovation emerged in Great Britian about twenty-five years ago and was popularized in the United States during the 1970s. It drew upon the findings of Susan Issacs and Jean Piaget. The term *open* may be somewhat misleading because it suggests large undivided spaces and removable partitions; however, open education can be conducted in classrooms that are traditional in a physical sense.

A number of characteristics are shared by open education classrooms. In the open classroom, the teacher may observe patterns of growth outlined by Piaget. The teacher instructs and guides learning in small groups or individually rather than instructing the class as a whole. Flexible scheduling is used, with many activities progressing simultaneously. And the abolition of a required curriculum permits children to make some decisions about their work. It is also characteristic that grading is deemphasized, that children learn at their own pace and in terms of their own learning style, and that the teacher's role is that of diagnostician, guide, and stimulator. Above all, "the whole child" is recognized—intellectually, emotionally, morally, socially, and physically.

Although open education shares similarities with the early progressive movement in the United States, it differs insofar as it is used more in public than private schools, is more structured, provides an active role for the teacher, and offers more of a planned environment than child-centered progressive schools. Open education also diverges from free schools (which will be discussed shortly) by usually placing more emphasis on cognitive development, providing greater curriculum structure, affording a more direct leadership role for teachers, and circumscribing more precisely the range and types of choices given to children.

The chief difference between open-space schools and open education is in the flexible architectural arrangements. Research evidence, however, does not support real differences in learning or teaching outcomes. Changes in architectural design in and of themselves do not make a difference. In open education, affective factors such as self-concept, creativity, independence, attitude toward school, and curiosity do show measurable improvement. Nevertheless, the divergent definitions of open education and the evaluative criteria are too varied to arrive at conclusive evidence that open classrooms are better than traditional ones.

Recent Alternatives

Education Vouchers.   Dissatisfaction with public education has led to alternative proposals for the use of resources. The voucher plan would finance elementary and secondary education through certificates given by government to parents of school-age children. The parents select the school of their choice—public, private, or parochial—and present the certificate as payment for instruction in the chosen school; the school then presents the voucher to the government and receives a check for a stipulated amount based on a formula.

Early voucher plans were essentially unregulated and posed threats of violating the separation of church and state and increasing segregated schooling. In contrast, Christopher Jencks and others have developed a highly regulated voucher plan that seeks to overcome the serious shortcomings of the earlier proposals.

Jencks's plan would create an Education Voucher Agency (EVA) at the community level for receiving government funds for financing schools. It would be locally controlled and would resemble a board of education except that it would not operate any schools of its own; responsibility for operating schools would be retained by public and private school boards. The EVA would determine the eligibility of public and nonpublic schools to participate in the plan.

The purposes of the voucher plan are to provide more education options, break the "monopoly" of the public schools, and enable poor parents to have the same choice as wealthy parents as to where they can send their children to school. The vouchers would offer each applicant roughly an equal chance of admission into any school by taking each student who applied to a particular school, except when the number of applicants exceeded the number of places, in which case a lottery would be used to fill half of its places. Each school would have to show that it had at least accepted as high a proportion of ethnic-group students as had applied. Vouchers from children of lower-income families would have higher redemption value because their education would likely be more costly. Additionally, EVA would pay the transportation costs of all children in order that low-income families would not be inordinately burdened. EVA would also disseminate information about all schools in the area, enabling parents to make intelligent choices.

The Office of Economic Opportunity made grants to several communities to study the feasibility of the voucher plan, but only the community of Alum Rock, California, with the aid of a federal grant, decided to try it. Alum Rock's plan, however, differed from Jencks's plan by using only public schools and providing alternative programs within them, and using the board of education in lieu of EVA. After four years of operation, it was found that teachers, students, and parents liked the plan but standardized test scores were either equivalent to national norms or, in some instances, were below them. In any case, the Alum Rock program does not actually test the original plan; it explores a new option instead.

Excluding Alum Rock, a number of serious deficiencies can be found in voucher plans. A basic tenet of voucher proponents is that public schools constitute a monopoly, and consequently, the use of vouchers would open many new options to parents. Voucher advocates frequently use the free-marketplace analogy that vouchers would do for education what free enterprise has done for the economy and its productivity. Schools, however, are relatively decentralized and do compete with private schools and with each other: in their sports programs, for teachers, appropriations, special projects, and the like. The market analogy is misleading insofar as profit-making firms sell their products to anyone who has cash or credit, whereas private schools are selective and not open to everyone. Moreover, for the voucher system to result in the benefits it purports to offer, nonpublic schools would have to be far more innovative and experimental in their programs and organizations; as of now only a small number exhibit these characteristics.

Furthermore, once nonpublic schools accept substantial state funds, they are likely to be more thoroughly regulated. It may mean that parochial schools would no longer be able to offer sectarian religious courses, and all nonpublic schools would be subject to desegregation rulings. Voucher plans make no provision for eliminating discrimination in the hiring of teachers. Nonpublic schools may also be required to observe judicial standards of academic freedom.

Public schools, under a voucher plan, would not likely receive additional tax funds but nonpublic schools would be free to increase their endowments, thereby leading to greater inequities. The voucher system could increase public costs by paying nonpublic-school tuitions, staffing and operating the EVA, creating new buildings and facilities for private schools, and underusing those of public schools (because of decreased enrollment, increased transportation costs, and inefficient use of tenured public-school teachers). Thus, in view of the substantial shortcomings of the voucher plan, it may be wiser to offer greater curricular alternatives in public schools.

Performance Contracting. This innovation, which rose and fell in the early 1970s, was one manifestation of the widespread concern that schools should be more accountable to the public at large. Performance contracting is a procedure by which a school system enters into an agreement with a private firm to take over from the school certain instructional tasks in order to achieve a set of designated objectives. The school system can contract with the firm to teach such subjects as reading and mathematics or to assume responsibility for the instructional program of an entire elementary or secondary school. For a stipulated sum of money the firm guarantees certain results within a designated time period. Should the company fall short of its goals, a lesser amount is paid; whereas, when goals are exceeded, some contracts award bonuses. An independent audit team is employed by the local education agency to monitor execution of the contract and certify results to the agency for purposes of payment.

In 1969, a Texarkana, Arkansas, school district entered into a contract with a private firm to take over part of their instructional program. Gary, Indiana, received a four-year grant in 1970 in excess of $2 million to experiment with performance contracting in an effort to overcome "gross underachievement." A number of the other school districts throughout the country have initiated performance contracting. The Office of Economic Opportunity (OEO) in 1970 sponsored eighteen experiments in performance contracting at a cost of $5 to $6 million. The test results at the end of the year for the experimental and control groups show that both groups did equally poorly in terms of overall averages, but these averages, with very few exceptions, are very nearly the same in each grade for the best and worst students in the sample. Thus the future of performance contracting as a means of insuring accountability—at least in its present form—is seriously in doubt.

Free Schools. As a response to the call for a new type of learning environment, free schools sprang up across the country in the late 1960s. Using city storefronts, old barns, barracks, abandoned churches, and even people's homes, these schools attempted to bring about greater freedom of learning through humanistic principles. Many of the directors of these schools believed that freedom was good, even though "freedom" was not always clearly defined or examined.

Although the majority of these schools are organized by middle-class white parents and attended by their children, occasionally integrated school settings can be found—in fact, there are a few free schools with little or no tuition located in economically depressed neighborhoods. The free schools utilize both early and neoprogressive methods, borrow ideas on child development from Piaget, and mix in here and there some practices from the English infant schools. Schools range from a Summerhill-type atmosphere to that of a more structured one, but generally children are not pushed to acquire basic skills before they show a readiness to learn.

The precarious financial basis upon which most free schools rest results in an average life span of about eighteen months—scarcely a beginning and surely no time to test out a program. Financial instability, joined with the more independent, idiosyncratic personalities who are drawn to establishing free schools, engenders a further basis for their transience. Additionally, free schools have been criticized for being accessible primarily to middle-class whites and for giving little emphasis to basic skills and vocational training that ethnic groups might find useful for their survival. With the emergence during the 1970s of alternatives within public schools, there has been less incentive to establish free schools and the movement has rapidly declined.

PLACING INNOVATIONS IN PERSPECTIVE

Educational Theories

Three educational theories that have been influential during the past several decades are behaviorism, essentialism, and progressivism. Proponents of each of these theories have contributed certain perspectives and sponsored or opposed certain innovations.

Behaviorism. Behaviorism has been the dominant American psychology since the militant behaviorism was first enunciated by John B. Watson in 1913. It spread into education through intelligence testing and then through a larger measurement movement that sought to make education scientific, as in the case of Edward Lee Thorndike who sought to propound laws of learning. Behaviorists study overt behavior and only those human and animal phenomena subject to measurement; thus they reject introspection and mentalistic concepts and rely instead on observing stimulus-response patterns. One of the chief applications of behaviorism in therapeutic situations is the rise of behavior modification.

In education, behaviorists have sponsored teaching machines, programmed learning materials, computer-assisted instruction, competency testing, some forms of accountability, and homogeneous groupings and tracking. One need not be a behaviorist to support one or more of these innovations; it is just more likely that a behaviorist would do so than someone who espouses a different theory or who is not entirely clear what theory to support. In seeking scientific precision, behaviorists are atomistic rather than holistic in approach; they seek to break things down into their smallest meaningful components for either study or educational use. Response patterns can be as simple as finger twitches or knee jerks. Similarly, programmed materials break learning bits to their smallest meaningful units. Since behaviorists also attempt to make accurate measurement of human abilities, they are usually interested in the classification of abilities and placing students in learning situations with peers of similar abilities. Thus they believe that homogeneous groupings will more likely ensure that no one will be held back by slower classmates or have to move more rapidly than they are able to do. Other behavioristic programs include competency education (which is based upon the assumption that human competencies can be identified), student acquisition of designated competencies, and tests designed to measure their attainment.

Essentialism.   Essentialism, one of the older theories in the history of education, was prominent in American education during the 1930s and 1950s and then again in the 1970s in the back-to-basics movement. Essentialism emphasizes transmitting the cultural heritage to all students, seeing that they are soundly trained in the fundamentals, and ensuring that they study the basic disciplines. In this way students will become educated persons and good citizens. Students, however, cannot always study what strikes their immediate interest, but must study what they need to enable them to assume responsible adult roles. This means that discipline and sound study habits should be stressed in order to master fundamental disciplines. Essentialists believe these disciplines are best grasped in a subject curriculum rather than vitiated in a broad fields curriculum or interdisciplinary programs.

The back-to-basics movement, since it focuses largely on the three Rs and firm disciplinary standards, is actually a truncated essentialist program because it fails to give equal weight to the other elements in the cultural heritage. In other words, it is generally consonant with essentialist principles but underdeveloped. Moreover, some back-to-basics programs advocate corporal punishment whereas some prominent essentialists would not do so. Essentialists would also want schools to be accountable, but the operational principles of accountability follow behavioristic lines more closely.

Progressivism.   Progressivism in American education began slowly around the turn of the century; as a formal movement it reached its zenith in the late 1930s only to decline precipitously by the mid-1950s. It rose again in the late 1960s in different forms and under new rubrics; it was largely submerged, however, by the overriding emphasis on accountability during the 1970s. Early progressives stressed the needs and interests of children and the importance of placing them in a learning environment where they could develop naturally, be free to express themselves, and nurture their creative development. This meant that the progressive teacher would shape learning experiences to students rather than the converse, that the subject curriculum would be modified to take into consideration individual differences, and that the teacher would be a guide, a facilitator of learning, rather than an authority figure.

Essentialists did not appreciate the progressives' departure from exact studies in the disciplines and their alleged abandonment of rigorous standards of scholastic achievement for projects based on immediate interests. Behaviorists found the atomistic approach in conflict with the holistic approach of humanistic education (a form that progressivism took during the 1970s). Rather than precise measurement of abilities and achievement in homogeneous groups, the neo-progressives stressed heterogeneous classrooms and evaluations of a qualitative type. Besides interdisciplinary programs and other departures from the subject curriculum, neo-progressives supported open classrooms, free schools, nongraded schools, alternatives within public schools, and various types of individualized instructional plans.

Ideologies in Education

Among the ideologies in education, meritocracy and egalitarianism have special bearing on innovations. Both of these ideologies have long been prominent in education, but egalitarianism has grown since the civil rights movement and the Elementary and Secondary Education Act of 1965.

The rewards in the meritocratic system go to those who achieve through demonstrated performance, rather than on the basis of race, religion, nationality, seniority, family background, politics, and other artificial distinctions commonly found in most societies. Instead, the abilities, skills, and types of performance are evaluated by merit. And those abilities most prized would be determined by the society's highest values and priorities. A meritocratic system is based on equal access to educational resources and opportunities so that those students with the potentials most valued by a given society would be in a position to best develop them and subsequently be rewarded for their use. Educational institutions are one of the chief mechanisms used by advanced industrial societies to screen and sort out those best qualified to assume careers and tasks that are highly esteemed and that demand greater abilities, responsibility, and leadership. Tomorrow's leaders will be sorted out through the process of schooling by its competitive system of grading, promotion, honors, and awards. Those who fail will be notified that they were given a fair chance and must now assume societal roles consonant with demonstrated abilities.

The meritocrat would want to maintain equal access to education to assure that all talented youth have an opportunity to be identified and developed; therefore, programs for the gifted and talented would be encouraged and competency education, if not construed too narrowly, would assure that certain measurable outcomes would be achieved. Meritocrats may at times join forces with essentialists in upholding standards, though the meritocrat would be more closely attuned than the essentialist to various sectors of society— government, business, industry, the military—to determine the standards needed.

Egalitarianism as an ideology renounces the policy of equal access because it fails to consider the handicaps and discrimination suffered by racial and ethnic minorities; thus equal access continues to give children of the white majority an unequal chance to advance. Egalitarians would either favor equal outcomes or substantive equality or both. Equal outcomes would assure that the overall average achievement scores of the different school populations are essentially the same, whereas substantive equality would require a redistribution of wealth in order to abolish poverty (just how this would be handled would depend on the particular plan). Those egalitarians who have not given up working with public education favor some compensatory education programs, community control of schools, bilingual education, multicultural education, and in some cases vouchers and free schools. These programs and plans, they believe, would best help the less advantaged and help to make society more just and egalitarian. The meritocrat would object to most of these proposals because they allegedly would result in the loss of a nation's talent and a subsequent rise of mediocrity. This would also bring about a leveling process whereby individual initiative and the achievement motive would be discouraged.

Whatever the respective merits of these theories and ideologies, one may want to look more closely at the basis for accepting or rejecting an innovation. It is no longer necessary to choose on an ad hoc basis if one wishes to adopt one of these theories or ideologies.

7

The Excellence Movement

The 1980s witnessed a flurry of policy reports detailing the state of American education, the problems besetting it, and the remedies needed to raise standards and vitalize the system. Among the commission reports were the National Commission on Excellence in Education, the Business-Higher Education Forum, the National Science Board Commission, the College Board, the Educational Commission of the States, and the Twentieth Century Fund. Prominent reform proposals also were issued by such educators as Mortimer Adler, Ernest Boyer, John Goodlad, and Theodore Sizer. Many states have placed education high on the agenda and passed legislation modifying teacher preparation, graduation requirements, student disciplinary policy, curriculum content, competency testing, and other areas.

One object of concern was the decline from 1963 to 1980 on the Scholastic Aptitude Test scores. Other problems were cited: the move away from a standard academic core curriculum for graduation, grade inflation, lower requirements for high-school graduation, functional illiteracy, and costly remedial instruction. These reported deficiencies occur at a time when the nation needs highly skilled workers and specialists.

Of the many commission reports of the 1980s, the one that probably captured the greatest attention and exerted the most influence was that of *A Nation at Risk: The Imperative for Educational Reform* (U.S. Government Printing Office, 1983), an assessment made by the National Commission on Excellence in Education under the auspices of the U.S. Department of Education. The report is written in a strident, urgent style employing military metaphors reminiscent of the Sputnik era. Drawing attention to some of the deficiencies cited above, the commission warned that the nation stands on the verge of losing its prominence as a world leader in industry and commerce because of its educational failures. The commission recommends a more rigorous high-school curriculum for all students, with additional work for college-bound students. Recommended also are more homework and a longer school day and school year. *A Nation at Risk* set the direction for state educational reform and some of the commission reports that followed.

A Nation at Risk: The Report of the National Commission on Excellence in Education

Milton Goldberg
James Harvey

Milton Goldberg, former Acting Director of the National Institute of Education, is Executive Director of the National Commission on Excellence in Education. James Harvey is a Senior Research Associate with the Commission.

Two hundred leaders of U.S. education, industry, and government gathered in the White House on April 26 to watch the ceremonial presentation to President Reagan of the report of the National Commission on Excellence in Education. Nearly five months later, the tumultuous reception of the report by the press and the public has yet to subside.

Such magazines as *Time*, *Newsweek*, and *U.S. News & World Report* have provided detailed coverage of the report, which has also been the focus of extensive discussions on several network television programs, among them "The McNeil-Lehrer Report," "Good Morning America," and "Nightline." Prompted by this publicity, the public demand for the Commission's report has been astonishing. The Government Printing Office, besieged by requests for the report, is now into the fourth printing; at least 200,000 copies of the text have been printed separately by various education publications, and an estimated three million readers have had access to shortened versions of the report in such newspapers as the *Portland Oregonian*, the *Washington Post*, and the *New York Times*.

The public's response suggests that Secretary of Education Terrel Bell, who created the Commission in 1981, is correct in hailing the report as a possible "turning point" in an era when U.S. schools face "the challenge of the postindustrial age." Bell also vowed not to allow the report "to be remembered as the warning our Nation failed to heed."

If the public response to the report has been remarkable, so are the activities already under way in response to it. The Pennsylva-

From Milton Goldberg and James Harvey, "A Nation at Risk: The Report of the National Commission on Excellence in Education," Phi Delta Kappan *(September 1983).* © *1983, Phi Delta Kappan, Inc.*

nia State Board of Education recently announced its intention to adopt new high school graduation requirements that will triple the amount of science and mathematics required for graduation and that will add computer science as a diploma requirement. Within weeks of the release of the report, the school board in Ypsilanti, Michigan, announced its intention to lengthen the school day for elementary students and to increase high school graduation requirements. The Tulsa, Oklahoma, superintendent published an extensive "Open Letter to the People of Tulsa," outlining the standing of schools in that city with respect to the National Commission's recommendations.

Not since the heady days following the launching of Sputnik I has U.S. education been accorded so much attention. Although the Commission released its report almost five months ago, major U.S. newspapers and network television programs continue to focus on the problems of education. President Reagan has already discussed the report at several regional forums, with other such forums scheduled for early fall. Individual members of the Commission and of the Commission staff continue to be deluged with requests to address meetings and convocations across the nation. Meanwhile, other prestigious individuals and panels have added their voices to the rising chorus of concern about the quality of U.S. schools; these include the Twentieth Century Fund, the College Board, and the Task Force on Education and Economic Growth (chaired by Gov. James Hunt of North Carolina).

The unprecedented attention now being paid to education is evidence of public concern. But this attention also provides—as the president of the American Federation of Teachers, Albert Shanker, pointed out to his constituents in early July—"unprecedented

opportunities" for education in the coming months.

THE IMPERATIVE FOR REFORM

What has generated all this fuss? The answer is: a deceptively short report to the nation, in which a panel of distinguished Americans warns that the "educational foundations of our society are presently being eroded by a rising tide of mediocrity that threatens our very future as a Nation and a people." Titled *A Nation at Risk: The Imperative for Educational Reform*, this report has sparked a national debate on education that could prove to be seminal to the development of an ethic of excellence in education and in American life.

COMMISSION AIMS AND PROCESS

That debate was quite consciously sought by members of the Commission, under the leadership of David Gardner, then president of the University of Utah, who has recently assumed the presidency of the University of California. It was Gardner's idea that the report be in the form of an open letter that would, in the words of Commission member Gerald Holton, serve as a "clarion call" to the American public. The call was intended to remind Americans of the importance of education as the foundation of U.S. leadership in change and technical invention and as the source of U.S. prosperity, security, and civility.

The National Commission conducted its work and collected its information in an extraordinary open manner, which also helped to encourage public response to *A Nation at Risk*. Practically everywhere one turned in the last two years, there was evidence of the Commission at work. Six public hearings and three symposia were held across the U.S., so that administrators, teachers, parents, and others could discuss their perceptions of the problems and accomplishments of American education. Forty papers were commissioned from a variety of experts and presented to the full Commission.

In virtually every city in which the Commission held a meeting or a hearing, the Commission members also visited local schools and corporate training facilities. It has been estimated that, during the 18 months between the first Commission meeting and the release of *A Nation at Risk*, Commission members were involved in a public event somewhere in the U.S. every three weeks. All of this highly visible activity created a national audience for the Commission's work; indeed, we knew several months before the report was issued that the response to it was likely to be unprecedented in education.

The Commission also examined the methods that other distinguished national panels had used to generate public and governmental reactions to their findings. The commissioners learned that the effective reports concentrated on essential messages, described them in clear and unmistakable prose, and drew the public's attention to the national consequences of continuing on with business as usual.

ESSENTIAL MESSAGES

The first essential message from the National Commission on Excellence in Education is found in the title of the report: the nation is at risk. It is at risk because competitors throughout the world are overtaking our once unchallenged lead in commerce, in-dustry, science, and technological innovation. As the Commission observed, the problem has many causes and dimensions; education is only one of them. But education is the primary factor undergirding our "prosperity, security, and civility."

The Commission is not the first national body to draw attention to the central importance of education to our national well-being. Indeed, in 1980 the President's Commission for a National Agenda for the Eighties reported that "the continued failure of the schools to perform their traditional role adequately . . . may have disastrous consequences for this Nation."

Just as assuredly, the Commission is not the last national body to draw attention to the central importance of education. One week after the release of *A Nation at Risk*, the Twentieth Century Fund Task Force called U.S. schools "the Nation's most important institution for the shaping of future citizens" and warned that "threatened disaster can be averted only if there is a national commitment to excellence in our public schools."

But the Commission may be the first national body to insist—as the essential first premise, not simply as an afterthought—that inattention to the schools puts the very well-being of the Nation at risk.

The second essential message from the Commission is that mediocrity, not excellence, is the norm in American education. *A Nation at Risk* paid tribute to "heroic" examples of educational excellence, but it made clear the fact that, on balance, "a rising tide of mediocrity" threatens to overwhelm the educational foundations of American society. And the consequences of that tide are staggering.

• On 19 international assessments of student achievement, U.S. students never ranked first or second; in fact, when compared only with students from other industrialized nations, U.S. students ranked in last place seven times.

- Some 23 million American adults are functionally illiterate.
- About 13% of U.S. teenagers (and up to 40% of minority adolescents) are functionally illiterate.
- From 1963 to 1980 a virtually unbroken decline took place in average scores on the Scholastic Aptitude Test (SAT).
- Similarly, a dramatic decline took place in the number of students who demonstrate superior achievement on the SAT.
- Between 1975 and 1980 the number of remedial mathematics courses offered in four-year public colleges increased by 72%.
- Only about one-fourth of the recent recruits to the Armed Services were able to read at the ninth-grade level, the minimum necessary to follow safety instructions.

The third essential message from the Commission is that we don't have to put up with this situation. We *can* do better, we *should* do better, and we *must* do better.

That message is found most clearly in a section of the report titled "America Can Do It." This section cites the remarkable successes of the American educational system in responding to past challenges as justification for the Commission's optimism that we can meet the current challenges. The past successes of U.S. education have included:

- the research and training provided by land-grant colleges and universities in the 19th century, which helped us develop our natural resources and the rich agricultural bounty of the American farm;

- the educated workforce that U.S. schools provided from the late 1800s through the mid-20th century, which sealed the success of the Industrial Revolution and provided the margin of victory in two world wars; and

- the school's role to this very day in transforming vast waves of immigrants into productive citizens.

The message that "America Can Do It" also appears in the letter from Gardner that accompanied the formal submission of the Commission report to Bell. Said Gardner: "The Commission deeply believes that the problems we have discerned in American education can be both understood and corrected if the people of our country, together with those who have public responsibility in the matter, care enough and are courageous enough to do what is required."

The message can be found as well in the first paragraph of the report, which notes that Americans can take "justifiable pride in what our schools and colleges have historically accomplished and contributed to the United States and the well-being of its people." But the Commission's optimism is perhaps most apparent in the recommendations it sets forth in *A Nation at Risk*. These recommendations provide more than a prescription for improving American schooling; they also provide a framework within which parents and educators across the U.S. can consider their own unique situations and then determine for themselves how best to proceed. The elements of this framework—the amount of time devoted to learning, the content to which students are exposed, the expectations we hold for ourselves and our children, the teaching, and the leadership—constitute, in the final analysis, the tools that local districts can use to improve the processes of education.

RECOMMENDATIONS

The Commission made five broad recommendations, each with several implementing recommendations.

Content

The recommendations regarding content was grounded in the Commission's conclusion that secondary school curricula have been homogenized, diluted, and diffused to such an extent that they no longer have a central purpose. According to *A Nation at Risk*, today's U.S. high schools offer "a cafeteria-style curriculum in which the appetizers and the desserts can easily be mistaken for the main courses."

The Commission recommended that all students seeking a high school diploma be required to lay a foundation in "five new basics" by taking four years of English, three years of mathematics, three years of science, three years of social studies, and one-half year of computer science. Several implementing recommendations suggested the kinds of skills that high school graduates should possess in each of these areas. The implementing recommendations also stressed the desirability of proficiency in a foreign language and stated that the teaching of foreign languages should begin in the elementary grades. In addition, the Commission recommended that the schools offer rigorous coursework in the fine and performing arts and in vocational education; that the elementary curriculum be improved and upgraded; and that such groups as the American Chemical Society and the Modern Language Association continue their efforts to revise, update, improve, and make available new and more diverse curricular materials.

Standards and Expectations

The Commission concluded that we expect far too little of our students and that we get, by and large, exactly what we expect. Evidence of our low expectations is widespread. For example:

- the schools are requiring less and less homework of students;
- two-thirds of the states require only one year of mathematics and one year of science for a high school diploma;
- one-fifth of the four-year public colleges and universities offer open admissions to all graduates of high schools in the state, regardless of the courses they have taken or the grades they have earned; and
- many U.S. colleges and universities reported lowering their admissions requirements during the 1970s.

The Commission recommended that high schools, colleges, and universities adopt more rigorous and measurable standards and higher expectations, both for academic performance and for student conduct, and that four-year colleges and universities raise their requirements for admission. The implementing recommendations focused on improving the reliability of high school grades as indicators of academic achievement, on raising college and university admissions requirements (including the scores required on standardized achievement tests in the five basics), on establishing a nationwide—but not federal—program of achievement testing for students who are passing from one level of schooling to another, on upgrading textbooks, and on the need for new instructional materials that reflect the most current applications of technology.

Time

The members of the National Commission were struck by the fact that many other industrialized nations have much longer school days and far longer school years than does the United States. Because the level of mastery of curriculum content is directly related to the amount of time that students devote to learning, the Commission made a number of recommendations designed to use available time more effectively and to prompt consideration of extending the amount of time available for learning.

The Commission recommended that significantly more time be devoted to learning the "five new basics." This will require more effective use of the existing school day, a longer school day, or a lengthened school year. The implementing recommendations included more homework, the provision of instruction in study and work skills, consideration of a seven-hour school day and of a 200- to 220-day school year, the reduction of disruption, the improvement of classroom management, and stronger policies on school attendance.

Teaching

The Commission concluded that too few academically able students are attracted to teaching; that teacher preparation programs need substantial improvement; that the professional working life of teachers is, on the whole, unacceptable; and that a serious shortage of teachers exists in key fields. The recommendation on teaching has seven parts, quoted here in full:

1. Persons preparing to teach should be required to meet high educational standards, to demonstrate an aptitude for teaching, and to demonstrate competence in an academic discipline. Colleges and universities offering teacher preparation programs should be judged by how well their graduates meet these criteria.

2. Salaries for the teaching profession should be increased and should be professionally competitive, market-sensitive, and performance-based. Salary, promotion, ten-

ure, and retention decisions should be tied to an effective evaluation system that includes peer review so that superior teachers can be rewarded, average ones encouraged, and poor ones either improved or terminated.

3. School boards should adopt an 11-month contract for teachers. This would ensure time for curriculum and professional development, programs for students with special needs, and a more adequate level of teacher compensation.

4. School boards, administrators, and teachers should cooperate to develop career ladders for teachers that distinguish among the beginning instructor, the experienced teacher, and the master teacher.

5. Substantial nonschool personnel resources should be employed to help solve the immediate problem of the shortage of mathematics and science teachers. Qualified individuals, including recent graduates with mathematics and science degrees, graduate students, and industrial and retired scientists, could, with appropriate preparation, immediately begin teaching in these fields. A number of our leading science centers have the capacity to begin educating and retraining teachers immediately. Other areas of critical teacher need, such as English, must also be addressed.

6. Incentives, such as grants and loans, should be made available to attract outstanding students to the teaching profession, particularly in those areas of critical shortage.

7. Master teachers should be involved in designing teacher preparation programs and in supervising teachers during their probationary years.

Leadership and Fiscal Support

Finally, the Commission recommended that citizens across the U.S. hold educators and elected officials responsible for providing the leadership necessary to achieve these reforms—and that citizens provide the fiscal support and stability required to bring about the reforms. The implementing recommendations in this area concentrated on the leadership roles of principals and superintendents; on the roles of local, state, and federal governments; and on the need for educators, parents, and public officials to assist in implementing the reforms proposed by the Commission. This section of *A Nation at Risk* concluded with these words: "Excellence costs. But in the long run mediocrity costs far more."

OTHER ISSUES

Although the overall response to the Commission's report is gratifying, several of us associated with the report have been disappointed at the scant attention paid to several major themes.

Learning Society

For example, the press has frequently misinterpreted *A Nation at Risk* as an attack on education and educators. Far from it. The report stands instead as an eloquent reaffirmation of education as a key element undergirding our society. Indeed, in light of new developments in computers, miniaturization, robotics, lasers, and other technologies, the report calls for the development of a learning society. The Commission states that:

> At the heart of such a society is the commitment to a set of values and to a system of education that affords all members the opportunity to stretch their minds to full capacity, from early childhood through adulthood, learning more as the world itself changes. . . . In our view, formal schooling in youth is the essential foundation for learning throughout one's life. But without life-long learning, one's skills will become rapidly dated.

Excellence

In similar fashion, little comment has been forthcoming about the Commission's careful definition of "excellence" in education, particularly the Commission's view of excellent individual performance. For the individual, the Commission defined excellence as performing on the boundary of individual ability in ways that test and stretch personal limits, both in school and in the workplace.

Implicit in this definition is the notion that each of us can attain individual excellence—although the boundaries that each of us tests and extends will clearly differ. This concept of excellence prompted the Commission to state that "our goal must be to develop the talents of all to their fullest." It also led the Commission to insist that the pursuit of excellence and the pursuit of equity are not incompatible educational goals and that we cannot permit one to yield to the other "either in principle or in practice."

Public Commitment

There has also been little attention given to the Commission's stand that, of all the tools at hand for improving education, "the public's support . . . is the most powerful." On the contrary, when informed of the report's findings and its recommendations, many educators and legislators have asked how these suggested reforms can possibly be funded. In the eyes of many of the commissioners, this response puts the cart before the horse. As one of them said, "If education demonstrates that it is willing to put its house in order, then the public will respond with increased support." As justification for this belief, the Commission cites results of national polls that indicate the public's steadfast regard for education as a major foundation of the nation's strength, the public's conviction that education is important to individual success, and the public's support for rigorous curricular offerings.

But it was toward another facet of the public's support for education that the Commission turned in seeking constructive reform:

> The best term to characterize [this facet] may simply be the honorable word "patriotism." Citizens know intuitively what some of the best economists have shown in their research: that education is one of the chief engines of a society's material well-being. They know, too, that education is the common bond of a pluralistic society and helps tie us to other cultures around the globe. Citizens also know in their bones that the safety of the United States depends principally on the wit, skill, and spirit of a self-confident people, today and tomorrow. . . .
>
> And perhaps more important, citizens know and believe that the meaning of America to the rest of the world must be something better than it seems to many today. Americans like to think of this Nation as the preeminent country for generating the great ideas and material benefits for all mankind. The citizen is dismayed at a steady 15-year decline in industrial productivity, as one great American industry after another falls to world competition. The citizen wants the country to act on the belief, expressed in our hearings and by a large majority in the Gallup Poll, that education should be at the top of the Nation's agenda.

Parents and Students

Finally, although our correspondence provides ample evidence that educators understand the importance of the Commission's message to parents and students, the message has received too little attention. Because the roles of parents and students in the improvement of educational quality are even more important than the responsibilities of teachers, administrators, or legislators, the Commission took the unusual step of addressing these groups directly in its report.

A Nation at Risk bluntly reminds parents of their responsibility to launch their children into the world with the soundest possible education, coupled with respect for first-rate work. It also reminds them of their right to demand the best that our schools and colleges can provide and of their obligation to serve as living examples of the kind of excellence the U.S. requires.

Students receive equally forthright advice: "You forfeit your chance for life at its fullest when you withhold your best effort in learning. When you give only the minimum to learning, you receive only the minimum in return. . . . [I]n the end it is *your* work that determines how much and how well you learn."

FROM RISK TO CONFIDENCE

Americans have not only lived with change in the past but also welcomed and encouraged it. Faced with the dangers of an uncharted continent, they spanned and mastered it; awed by the vastness of space, they investigated and explored it; perplexed by the mystery of the atom, they plumbed and solved it. Now a new challenge beckons: how to use our enormous educational system to turn to advantage the current risk to our values, our standard of living, and our international security.

The evidence that we can do so successfully is all around us. It can be found in the past successes of American education, from the development of the one-room schoolhouse to the development of our great research universities. It can be found in the attention paid to the Commission's report by the President and the secretary of education, as well as in the high visibility of education as a major issue on the national agenda. It can be found in the spirited debate we are witnessing on the issue of merit pay for teachers, for this issue touches on many of the elements we must address in seeking excellence — merit, reward for performance, evaluation, and the role and status of teaching.

The evidence can be found in the letters that the National Commission has received from students. Predictably, some students have complained about increased homework or a longer school day. One letter writer suggested that President Reagan contact his junior high school and cancel the book reports that teachers had assigned for the summer vacation. Other letters have been less amusing.

One seventh-grader wrote a six-page letter of despair. Teaching study skills during study hall would be fine, she wrote, "if there was anything to study, and if anybody did any studying. There isn't and they don't." She said she would opt instead for six demanding hours of history, math, composition, foreign languages, geography, literature, and science. "Then my school days would be worth getting up for. To lengthen our existing days would be merely to extend the monotony, boredom, frustration, and agony. . . ."

The evidence that we are up to the challenge is perhaps most apparent in the many schools, districts, and states that have already responded to the Commission's report or have appointed task forces and commissions of their own to chart their next steps. But it is also apparent in corporate and foundation boardrooms, in legislative cloakrooms, in meetings of the Cabinet, and in meetings of learned societies, where discussions of the report, of its implications for the nation, and of what the discussants should do about it are the order of the day.

All of this is as it should be, for it was precisely this kind of discussion, debate, and excitement about education that the Commission set out to provoke. If the level of interest remains high and leads to the kind of positive responses anticipated by the Commission, then we may eventually look back on the release of *A Nation at Risk* as a turning point in American education.

Clearly, the Commission's report has touched that chord in the American consciousness which governs the hopes, aspirations, and apprehensions of Americans about the future well-being of their children, their schools, and their society. The task for all of us now is to take this renewed commitment and dedicate it to the creation of a learning society. That responsibility does not belong solely to any one group. As *A Nation at Risk* concludes:

> It is . . . the America of all of us that is at risk; it is to each of us that this imperative is addressed. It is by our willingness to take up the challenge, and our resolve to see it through, that America's place in the world will be either secured or forfeited. Americans have succeeded before, and so we shall again.

The Worthless Debate Continues

Daniel W. Rossides

Daniel W. Rossides is a professor of sociology at Bowdoin College in Maine.

The current debate about education is worthless because the goals of education are stated in empty abstractions—so many years of English, and science, reasoning ability, excellence, etc. The current debate is worthless because the power of education is vastly exaggerated. The current debate is worthless because the debators are unaware of the real purposes of education. The current debate is worthless because all mistakenly assume that poor schools can be improved from within the educational system. Our poor schools cannot be improved until we increase the supply of good students and we cannot do that until we get control of our economy and eliminate the families that supply our schools with large numbers of children malnourished in body and spirit. And not much can be done unless we deal with our federal system in which federal money earmarked for the poor is put into general funds by our states, to be spent on all, thus leaving relative differences intact. And nothing can be done until we acknowledge the huge state and federal educational subsidies that we give to the middle and upper classes who attend colleges and universities while denying needed funds for school lunches and reading materials for the lower classes. Not only have our federal and state programs led to a growing gap between the well-educated and the less educated (for the first time in our history) but all indications are that the upper classes would have gone to school without the subsidies.

Over the past year or more many states have developed proposals to upgrade their academic offerings and requirements. Such proposals (if they are funded and implemented, which is doubtful) will probably increase academic test scores somewhat and provide a larger supply of students qualified in science, mathematics, and computer science. But imposing higher requirements on all is wasteful since academic skills have not been shown to be socially useful. If specific specialties and training are needed then these can be obtained more efficiently and at far less cost if the need is approached directly. But vested interests will not support specific reforms, especially if they suggest man-woman-power planning, and reformers must include everybody in their uplift proposals. The result? Raising academic standards will probably increase test scores somewhat but it will also serve to undermine vocational and artistic programs. Raising academic standards will serve to keep the lower classes in school longer, aggravating already serious problems of crowding and discipline and sending truancy and dropout rates even higher than they are now.

The philosophy of educational compe-

From Change *(April 1984). Reprinted with permission of the Helen Dwight Reid Educational Foundation. Published by Heldref Publications, 4000 Albemarle St., N.W., Washington, D.C. 20016. Copyright © 1984.*

tency (back to basics in reading, writing, and mathematics) is part of a vast world of things taken for granted in which means are turned into ends and victims into villains. The decline and failure in academic performance really stem from deep changes in American society. Remember that these declines have taken place along with the decay of American cities, especially in the Northeast, Midwest, and Middle Atlantic states. The declines are part of the buildup of a hardcore underclass bypassed by shifts in industry and services, and maintained by welfare, assorted charities, and other makeshift arrangements. The declines are part of a deteriorating school system marked by declines in enrollments, falling school budgets, and challenged by the rise of private secular and religious schools. Remember too that the declines are paralleled by a rise in one-parent homes (a condition that is associated with poorer educational achievement and biased treatment by schools), by a flood of illegal aliens and refugees, and by new burdens placed on the schools, especially the responsibility for educating the handicapped.

The back-to-basics movement is avoiding the real issues. A better-run economy and polity is the only way to achieve educational improvements. Crash educational programs, including those led by charismatic, concerned individuals like Jesse Jackson, cannot overcome the class, family, peer, and neighborhood experiences that form the lower classes. A back-to-basics movement is a good idea but only if it is oriented to competency in life, citizenship, and work.

But I have not even raised the real reason why the current educational debate is worthless. Discerning readers should already be saying to themselves, Aren't the worst schools in America the schools reeking with excellence, the elite high schools and colleges that complacently prepare their students, not to understand and direct their world, but to join it. Doesn't our mania for nonideological, inapplicable, pettifogging academic excellence shortchange everyone; isn't it bound to yield only skilled functionaries, compliant citizens, passive consumers, and a smoother application process for welfare and unemployment benefits?

Judged by its stated purposes, American education is an outright failure. Judged by *unintended* outcomes, American education is a resounding success—most students learn to accept failure and mediocrity as somehow stemming from their own inadequacies. Those who succeed feel they deserve their success as individuals and that somehow they are fit to lead. Above all, schools perpetuate the lie that innate talent is scarce, which really means that an artificial scarcity of good jobs is maintained under the cover of blaming scarcities in human nature. Despite the fact that the upper classes appear to be grossly overworked, little is done to increase the number of such jobs. In short, schools from kindergarten to liberal arts colleges and graduate-professional schools have succeeded in their main (latent) purpose: they provide a cloak of legitimacy for our concentrated, undemocratic, and ineffective economy, professions, and polity. Far from expressing and promoting democracy, the American educational system helps prevent it.

The surge of concern about education that emerged in 1983 has produced some ferment at the state level. A significant number of states are proposing costly reforms to strengthen academic performance. But the sociology of education prevents optimism. The large sums of money that are needed will not be forthcoming unless national priorities are reordered at the federal level. Unless changes are made in the American economy, and the economy and education are better coordinated, large segments of the working and lower classes will continue to flounder in middle-class schools. Above all, schools will continue to avoid political controversy and teach a bland consensus curriculum that favors the status quo. Bland, biased school texts will continue to be used. Sophisticated skills at political problem solving will be absent. And the apolitical, politically conservative emphasis on abstract reading and writing skills will continue. Even if reform succeeds, the only result will be better scores on life-removed subjects and skills.

Beyond the above secondary problems the real problem will continue unnoticed—our elite high schools and colleges which cannot show that they are producing better citizens or better professionals and leaders. And yet the heart of all proposed reforms is to stress doing more of what makes education irrelevant to our national life! The fewest changes, therefore, will take place where they are needed most—in our elite high schools and colleges. Abstract liberal arts will continue to dominate the curriculum and narrow and ineffective specialization will dominate the curriculum of graduate and professional schools. Since few realize that there is even a problem, there is little hope that American elites will give up the irrelevant education that favors them and their offspring. More science and mathematics will be taught but little will be said about the purposes of science or the threat to the environment posed by technology. Little will be said about the failure of economics to provide a better way to handle our economy. No realistic analysis of our stalemated political system will be forthcoming.

In recent years a number of policy programs have developed at both the undergraduate and graduate school levels in response to demands by government and legislators for useful knowledge and trained policy analysts. There seems to be a growing interest in social-policy research. In 1982, Harvard University announced reforms and proposals for reforms in its medical, law, and business schools, all of them pointed toward bringing the Harvard curriculum at least somewhat into line with the real world that graduates will face. Whether any of this will lead to any real change remains to be seen.

A democratic and effective education must ask: what kinds of competence does society need and what social institutions are needed to produce them? To prepare youngsters for concrete skills such as household budgeting, hygiene, home and appliance repairs, sexuality, fathering and mothering, first aid, preparing for death, drawing up a will or closing property deals, would require a vast transformation of education. To develop real competence as a consumer, a client, and a citizen would be well-nigh revolutionary, requiring deep alterations not only to education but to power relations in the economy, the professions, and the polity. Education for competence would be truly revolutionary if it brought honesty and science to the main questions of social science. What division of social labor is needed, what are the requirements for each position, and how are people to be selected and trained for social status? How should the public organize the economy? How should health-care resources be utilized? The true meaning of these questions cannot be grasped until it is realized that we have not even begun to ask them.

In education, as in employment, energy, transportation, health, housing, family life, and foreign policy, the United States lacks a coherent, realistic, and effective educational policy. As in these other areas, education's deficiencies will remain as long as the oligarchic institutions it is protecting remain. A first step in modernizing the United States is to discard the educational (social) myths that hide the real sources of our backwardness.

DISCUSSION QUESTIONS AND ACTIVITIES

1. Cite the data presented by the Commission to demonstrate "a rising tide of mediocrity."
2. Are there past successes in American education to indicate that the "mediocrity" can be overcome?
3. Standards are based on low expectations, according to the Commission. How are these low standards manifested in the curriculum, time on educational tasks, teaching, leadership, and fiscal support?
4. What does the Commission mean by "excellence"? Is it a meaningful definition or no more than a slogan?
5. What reasons does Rossides offer to demonstrate that the current debate about education is "worthless"? Do you agree or disagree with his line of argument? Explain why.
6. Why does Rossides contend that the imposition of higher requirements on all students is wasteful?
7. What areas of decline in American society have adversely affected the schools?
8. Why, according to Rossides, does the back-to-basics movement avoid the real issues?
9. Do our schools and colleges provide a cloak of legitimacy for "our concentrated, undemocratic, and ineffective economy, professions, and polity"?
10. What would a democratic and effective education that developed real competence actually be like?
11. Survey schools in your area to determine which ones have adopted some of the proposals from *A Nation at Risk*. Determine the relative success of these changes and report your findings to the class.
12. Organize a classroom debate on the merits of *A Nation at Risk* in terms of its underlying educational philosophy, the accuracy of its data, and the reasonableness and feasibility of its policy recommendations.

SUGGESTED READINGS

Academic Preparation for College: What Students Need to Know and Be Able to Do. New York: The College Board, 1983.

America's Competitive Challenge: The Need for a National Response. Washington, D.C.: Business-Higher Education Forum, 1983.

Goodlad, John I. *A Place Called School: Prospects for the Future.* New York: McGraw-Hill, 1983.

Gross, Beatrice, and Gross, Ronald, eds. *The Great School Debate: Which Way for American Education?* New York: Simon & Schuster, 1985.

Honig, Bill. "The Educational Excellence Movement: Now Comes the Hard Part." *Phi Delta Kappan* (June 1985): 675–681.

National Commission on Excellence in Education. *A Nation at Risk: The Imperative for Educational Reform.* Washington, D.C.: U.S. Government Printing Office, 1983.

National Science Board Commission. *Educating Americans for the 21st Century.* Washington, D.C.: National Science Foundation, 1983.

Ravitch, Diane. "The Continuing Crisis:

Fashions in Education." *The American Scholar* 53 (Spring 1984).

Spady, William G. "The Illusion of Reform." *Educational Leadership* (October 1983): 31–32.

Task Force on Education for Economic Growth. *Action for Excellence: A Comprehensive Plan to Improve Our Nation's Schools*. Denver: Education Commission of the States, 1983.

Twentieth Century Fund. *Making the Grade*. New York: The Fund, 1983.

8

Financial Reform

The excellence movement and its numerous reforms (see Chapter 7) have raised serious financial questions that have yet to be fully answered. Most school-related costs, except salaries, increased more rapidly than inflation in recent years. School board members have consistently ranked "lack of financial support" as the number one challenge with which they are faced. Yet the public, many of whom exhibit high expectations for public education, have in some communities staunchly opposed higher property taxes and defeated school board issues. Some critics contend that the form of tax sources allocated to public education are inequitable, create unintended economic distortions, and are unresponsive to changing economic conditions.

The center of financial reform in recent years has converged at the state level. In *San Antonio Independent School District* v. *Rodriguez,* the U.S. Supreme Court ruled that expenditure disparities between school districts in a state were not unconstitutional under the federal constitution but might be so under some state constitutions. Since the *Rodriguez* decision, a number of state courts have ruled that wide disparities in per-pupil expenditures between school districts are unconstitutional, and state legislatures have enacted laws to ameliorate these disparities. Some states employ a "foundation plan" that guarantees minimal annual expenditure per pupil; however, since such plans ignore taxable wealth, substitute plans have been introduced to provide expenditures in inverse ratio to the district's wealth. The major source of funding for new educational reforms in the 1980s stems from increased state taxes earmarked for public education. The bulk of financing for public education derives from local property taxes, state revenues from various sources, and about 7 percent from the federal government. But with considerable resistance by many residents to a rise in local property taxes, while at the same time a nationwide reform movement is in progress, new sources of revenue and imaginative financial plans are sorely needed.

Financing the Future

Joel D. Sherman

Joel D. Sherman is Associate Director, School Finance Project, U.S. Department of Education.

The Psychology of Decline has pervaded the educational establishment for nearly a decade. Declining enrollments, declining resources, and declining intergovernmental aid have been the buzzwords for the better part of the 1970s and early 1980s. The current recession only reinforces our predisposition to perpetuate a psychology of decline. The highest unemployment rates since the Great Depression, economic stagnation, and intense competition in international markets, a deteriorating infrastructure, and restrained resources at all levels of government all point to a future in which these bleak conditions seem likely to prevail.

Efforts to predict the future are obviously fraught with difficulty. Economists at this point seem no more able to accurately forecast economic growth levels in the 1990s than they are to predict next year's budget deficits. Nor can demographers predict with certainty that fertility rates will maintain their reversal of a long-term slide or that migration patterns will continue to shift the locus of population from one region or state to another as they have in the past. Yet some comprehension of the direction of future demographic and fiscal trends is essential if educators are to plan for the years ahead.

Starting with demography, the most important development forecast for the next decade and a half for elementary and secondary education is a reversal of the decline in the number of children of school age and an increase in school enrollments, starting in the mid-1980s.[1] The signs of that upturn are already in evidence. Between 1975 and 1980 the annual number of live births in the country rose by nearly 15 percent, and Census estimates suggest that this increase will continue through 1988. To be sure, this upturn can best be characterized as a "baby boomlet" when compared with the "baby boom" of the 1950s and early 1960s. Nonetheless, this development does mean that there are going to be more children of school age than there have been in recent years.

Moreover, a much larger proportion of

From Joel D. Sherman, "Financing the Future," Community Education Journal X, 4 *(July 1983): 5–6. Reprinted by permission.*

[1] The demographic projections that provide the basis of this discussion were drawn from George Masnick and John Pitkin, "Cohort Analysis of School-Age Population for States and Regions" (Cambridge, Massachusetts: MIT Harvard Joint Center for Urban Studies, 1982). This report was produced under contract for the School Finance Project at the U.S. Department of Education. Analyses of the implications of demographic and fiscal trends are drawn from "The Prospects for Financing Elementary Secondary Education in the States." This report was produced by the School Finance Project for the Secretary of Education as part of the congressionally-mandated study of school finance in Section 1203 of the Education Amendments of 1978.

children in the public schools is likely to come from minority backgrounds than in the past. The increased concentration of minority children is already evident in a number of our more populous states. In California and Texas, for example, the proportion of minority children rose from 35 to 43 percent and from 41 to 46 percent, respectively, between 1976 and 1980. Other states such as New York, New Jersey, Illinois, and Michigan saw a decline in the number of minority children, but an increase in their proportion of public school enrollments. With higher fertility rates among minority populations and increased immigration—both legal and illegal—from Latin America and Asia, this trend is likely to continue in the future.

These developments have important implications for the future finance of elementary and secondary education, the most important being additional resource requirements over the next several years. Most states will not benefit from the past period of enrollment decline to help them achieve real spending increases for schools. During the 1970s, real per pupil spending for elementary and secondary education increased by about 25 percent, but nearly half of this increase is explained by declining enrollments. Between 1985 and 2000, however, the school-age population is projected to increase nationally by about 18 percent. Without the benefit of declining enrollments, many states will have to increase total school spending more rapidly than in the past just to maintain real current resource levels for schools.

At the same time, there is evidence that the political constituency for schools may not be as strong as it has been in the past. In 1970, for example, children ages 5–17 represented nearly 26 percent of the total population of the country; by 1980, that proportion was down to about 21 percent; and for the balance of the century, it is projected to be in the range of 18 to 19 percent. Despite the increase in the number of school-age children, the relative size of the age cohort will remain small, as other sectors of the population will grow at least as rapidly as the school-age group.

One age group with large projected growth rates is the adult population over 65. Between 1985 and 2000, estimates of growth are in the range of 18 percent. Further, the proportion of adults in this age cohort is expected to increase from its current level of 11 percent to about 12.5 percent at the end of the century. While senior citizens may well support the expenditure of funds for education, they may also generate pressures for other types of social services or for continued tax and spending limitations. In sum, the change in the age structure of the population augurs lower political support for education and greater potential competition for resources from other interest groups.

What will the resource base be like? Will it be sufficient to meet the requirements of a large school-age cohort? This is, of course, a difficult question to answer, as the supply of revenues for public services is highly dependent on the state of the national economy. If the economy continues its sluggish performance, the consequences for school finance are apt to be adverse; should the economy take an upturn, the prospects will obviously be significantly brighter. Nonetheless, there have been a number of developments in state-local finance in the last few years which, if they continue in the future, suggest that the resource base for schools may not be as robust as it has been in the past.

First, the rapid growth in public spending that characterized the late 1960s and early 1970s was reversed by the end of the decade. Since 1975, state-local expenditures per capita have grown in real dollars by less than 1 percent per year; as a proportion of both personal income and gross national product, they have declined since that date. Moreover, there is little evidence that the increase of the earlier period is likely to recur. At best, the state-local sector is likely to remain relatively stable; at worst, it will continue to decline.

Second, elementary and secondary education's share of a relatively stable public sector has shown a continuous decline. In 1967, nearly 30 percent of state-local expenditures was devoted to elementary and secondary education; after a steady drop during the 1970s, the share was less than 25 percent in 1981. Part of this drop can be explained by declining enrollments, but the decline also reflected a shift in resources to other public functions, including health and welfare. The shift in resources from the elementary and secondary school sector seems to be part of a long-term trend that is likely to continue in the future as the average age of the population continues to rise and fewer adults have children of school age.

Finally, a discussion of recent fiscal trends would be incomplete without at least some reference to federal aid. Through most of the 1970s, federal aid to education increased both in real terms and as a proportion of school revenues. Beginning in 1978, however, federal aid has declined in real terms and as a proportion of school revenues. The Reagan budgets have produced a drop in current dollars as well. Certainly for the foreseeable future, this trend seems likely to continue, producing further fiscal constraints in states and school districts that are heavily dependent on federal aid for school revenues.

In sum, the future financial picture for education, when viewed from the national perspective, can best be characterized in the following way: increased demand for schools, higher concentrations of children with special education needs, constrained revenue bases, and increased competition for relatively stable public sector resources. Yet within this overall picture there is likely to be wide variability, both among states and among school districts within states. This is most evident in the area of demography.

For the next decade and a half, population projections generally show that states in the Northeast and Midwest will continue to have declining or stable enrollments, while states in the South Atlantic and Eastern Plains will experience moderate growth in their school-age populations, and Southern and Western States will grow quite rapidly. At the extremes, such states as New York are projected to show declines in the 5–17 age cohort of more than 15 percent, while states such as Utah, Idaho, Nevada, and Arizona will experience a growth rate well in excess of 50 percent. As a result, by the year 2000 nearly 60 percent of the school-age children in the country will be located in Southern and Western states.

On the fiscal side, there tends to be a mismatch between the potential demand for schools—as measured by the direction and magnitude of change in the projected size of the school-age population—and the state-local resource base. Interestingly, states with large projected increases in their school-age populations (greater than 25 percent increases between 1985 and 2000) tend to share a number of important fiscal characteristics that suggest potential funding problems in future years. For the most part, these states tend to be ones that currently have low expenditures per pupil for elementary and secondary education, below-average fiscal capacity,[2] and a relatively high level of dependence on federal aid. Moreover, many of these states have historically had higher concentrations of chil-

---

[2] The Advisory Commission on Intergovernmental Relations has developed a measure of tax capacity using a representative tax system. This discussion refers to that measure in assessing tax capacity.

dren with special educational needs, especially children from poverty and limited-English families. In contrast, states with school-age populations that are projected to increase moderately (under 25 percent between 1985 and 2000) or to continue to decline, tend to have more favorable fiscal conditions. Many currently spend at high levels per pupil, have relatively high levels of personal income and tax capacity, devote a relatively high proportion of their income to elementary and secondary education, and derive a relatively small proportion of their school revenues from federal aid. With relatively few new children to educate over the next few years, these states should be able to meet the demands of education with relatively little difficulty.

As a result of this mismatch between resource requirements and resource bases, the late 1980s and 1990s are likely to be a period when resource inequalities among states become more pronounced. We already have evidence of spending divergence among the states over the last few years, as states such as Alabama have fallen further behind national spending levels for education and high spending states such as New Jersey have pulled further ahead of the nation. Given the confluence of demographic and fiscal trends, we can expect this development to continue into the future.

Within states, there is some evidence that resource inequalities among school districts may parallel trends at the state level. Over the last few years there has been a shift back toward greater reliance on the property tax as a revenue source for education in a number of states, after a long period of upward shift in the responsibility for financing schools to the state level. While this may be a short-term development that is resulting from state revenue shortfalls associated with the current recession, the consequences for interdistrict equity are likely to be adverse. In addition, several state studies suggest a mismatch between enrollment changes and local property wealth in a number of high-spending states. For these states the overall funding situation may appear relatively good, but within them there are likely to be districts with severe funding problems.

The future financial outlook for elementary and secondary education is, at best, mixed. On the positive side, there will clearly be more children of school age, and the enrollment declines of the 1970s are, at least for a period, likely to be a memory of the past in many parts of the country. On the other hand, the fiscal outlook in many areas is less than promising. Even with an upturn in the economy, some states and school districts are likely to face tremendous revenue constraints. In sum, the rest of this century is likely to be a period of great challenge in the financing of schools.

Sources of Funding for Education Reform

Allan Odden

Allan Odden is Associate Professor in the School of Education and Director of the Southern California Policy Analysis for California Education (PACE) Center at the University of Southern California in Los Angeles.

Less than three years have elapsed since the release of *A Nation at Risk* and the accompanying calls to improve U.S. public schools. Yet a number of state legislatures have already acted on the basic recommendations of that and other, similar reports. Indeed, the education reform movement has moved faster than any public policy reform in modern history.[1] All the states have expanded their school improvement programs, nearly all have increased high school graduation requirements, most have stiffened college admission requirements, many are deepening the content of course offerings, and many are enacting a variety of policies to strengthen the teaching profession.

Moreover, signs in many states indicate that the reforms are being implemented as intended. A number of studies in California, for example, have shown that students are attending school longer, taking more and tougher academic courses, receiving better counseling about their secondary school programs and about college admission requirements, and scoring higher on achievement tests. Teachers are being paid more, and in some states they have new career-ladder options.[2] The swiftness of action, the breadth of the reform programs, and the multiple indicators of progress in the right direction give

reason for optimism about the ultimate success of the education reform movement.

A key issue in maintaining the momentum of the reform movement, however, is funding. Improving the quality of education is a costly endeavor. Early studies estimated that revenues would need to increase by at least 20% in order to pay for most of the proposed reforms.[3] At the same time, attention to the simultaneous pursuit of fiscal equity and educational excellence was being urged.

Encouraging action has taken place in the struggle for fiscal equity. Of the 11 reform states that I discuss in this article, four—Arkansas, Georgia, Kentucky, and Texas—enacted fundamental changes in their school finance formulas as part of their education reform packages. Six of the other seven states had enacted school finance reforms during the 1970s; most of these reforms promoted the equalization of resources among school districts. So far, equity in school finance seems to have fared well in states that are actively involved in the reform movement.

Furthermore, funding levels for programs for students with special needs have also fared well in most reform states—sometimes receiving the same percent increase as the general aid formula, sometimes receiving a higher increase.[4] Although more analysis is

From Allan Odden, "Sources of Funding for Educational Reform," Phi Delta Kappan 67 (January 1986): 335–340. Reprinted by permission.

needed on the ways in which funding changes have affected fiscal equity, the indicators above suggest that fiscal equity has not been forgotten in the pursuit of excellence – and indeed has shared center stage with excellence reforms in several states.

Less costly school improvement programs in the reform states have also expanded, both in number and in the amount of funding set aside for them. Missouri's recent reform program exemplifies the renewed attention being paid to initiatives designed to stimulate reform at the local level. Missouri enacted a set of education excellence initiatives to be financed at a level of $75 million from a separate fund. Programs supported by Missouri's Excellence in Education Fund include business/education partnerships, extended contracts for teachers and administrators, parent participation programs, instructional improvement projects, writing programs, high-technology projects, advanced placement programs, and opportunity classes for children at risk in grades 1 through 3. All are funded through some combination of state and local sources.

Finally, the gross indicators of funding for education reform look good. Arkansas, South Carolina, and Tennessee increased the sales tax by a penny in order to finance their reform programs. California and Texas each added more than a billion dollars to education in the first year of the reform, and Florida, Georgia, Missouri, and New York increased state aid to education by larger amounts than at any time in history. Kentucky's reform bill costs more than $300 million – just less than 30% of current state aid.

Now that the U.S. has several years of experience with the new wave of education reform, however, a more detailed look at the course of school funding suggests that optimism for fiscal growth needs to be restrained. Funds for education reform are actually in short supply. Two recent studies concluded that revenues for education – even in many reform states – will do well to stay even over the next five years, after adjustments for enrollment increases and inflation.[5] In the remainder of this article I will investigate the level of revenues that various sources of school financing have produced in recent years, and I will conclude with a prognosis for the fiscal needs of public education for the rest of the Eighties.

FUNDING PATTERNS

Nationwide, school funding has reversed the declines of the early 1980s and has begun to increase moderately.[6] Expenditures per pupil have increased 15.8% in the two years since the education reform movement started in 1983. When adjusted for inflation, the increase was only 7.2% – not the 20% that most of the reform plans will cost, but still better than the real losses of the preceding three years. Federal revenues have stayed about the same in nominal terms throughout the Eighties but have dropped in real terms from $6.7 billion in 1982 to $5.8 billion in 1985 (in 1979 inflation-adjusted dollars). During this period state and local revenues used for education increased in both real and nominal terms. Adjusted for inflation, state funds rose by 5.4%, and local funds rose by 6.4%. While there is comfort in the trends these figures reveal, the funding increases are modest. If education reform has helped to reverse the declining finances of the public schools, it has not opened a gushing faucet. The figures for per-pupil expenditures would be even lower had enrollments been rising during the early 1980s – as they are now beginning to do.

The individual states that have enacted comprehensive reform programs appear, at first blush, to have improved funding for education dramatically above the national averages. Tables 1 and 2 depict levels of funding and changes in funding for 11 education reform states between 1982–83 and 1985–86. Several of the changes are impressive. Arkansas increased state aid by 18.7% in the first year of its reforms, by 18.3% in the following year, and by 10.4% in the third year.

In the three years since its reform program began, California increased aid by $3.2 billion—a considerable amount by any standard. New York increased state aid by $613 million between 1983–84 and 1985–86, the largest aid increase in that state's history. When it enacted its reforms, South Carolina hiked state aid by 32.4%, bumping the total

Table 1
Level of State and Local Revenues for Public Schools, 1982–83 to 1985–86

	1982–83	1983–84	1984–85	1985–86 (est.)
		(millions of dollars)		
Arkansas				
State	509.8	605.3	716.3	790.7
Local	272.2	293.4	301.4	331.4
Total	782.0	898.7	1,017.7	1,122.1
California				
State	8,052.6	9,328.4	10,443.6	11,227.3
Local	2,675.0	2,886.0	3,289.1	3,459.9
Total	10,727.6	12,214.4	13,732.7	14,687.2
Florida				
State	1,898.9	2,122.9	2,353.0	2,575.4
Local	1,140.8	1,274.4	1,422.0	1,532.1
Total	3,039.7	3,397.3	3,775.0	4,107.5
Georgia				
State	1,367.0	1,460.0	1,630.0	1,755.0
Local	n.a.	n.a.	n.a.	n.a.
Total	n.a.	n.a.	n.a.	n.a.
Illinois				
State	2,103.2	2,236.1	2,352.9	2,697.9
Local	2,974.4	3,182.9	3,208.0	n.a.
Total	5,077.6	5,419.0	5,560.9	n.a.
Kentucky				
State	1,048.0	1,141.8	1,160.5	1,179.2
Local	279.5	314.8	359.0	409.3
Total	1,327.5	1,456.6	1,519.5	1,588.5
Missouri				
State	827.7	976.0	1,019.2	1,165.7
Local	1,058.9	1,228.2	n.a.	n.a.
Total	1,886.6	2,204.2	n.a.	n.a.

Table 1 (continued)
Level of State and Local Revenues for Public Schools, 1982–83 to 1985–86

	1982–83	1983–84	1984–85	1985–86 (est.)
		(millions of dollars)		
New York				
State	4,643.9	4,877.0	5,490.0	5,893.0
Local	6,459.7	7,085.0	7,130.0	7,531.9
Total	11,103.6	11,962.0	12,620.0	13,424.9
South Carolina				
State	745.9	803.8	1,064.1	1,117.3
Local	453.8	519.9	557.8	585.7
Total	1,199.7	1,323.7	1,621.9	1,703.0
Tennessee				
State	774.4	773.2	938.2	1,004.0
Local	706.8	741.7	778.8	817.7
Total	1,481.2	1,514.9	1,717.0	1,821.7
Texas				
State	3,620.0	3,734.6	4,701.8	4,851.2
Local	3,349.0	3,673.1	4,142.4	n.a.
Total	6,969.0	7,407.7	8,844.2	n.a.

Figures are not comparable across states. State revenues in Missouri include Proposition C funds. California figures exclude lottery revenues.

Table 2
Changes in State and Local Revenues for Public Schools, 1982–83 to 1985–86

	1982–83 to 1983–84 [millions of dollars (% change)]	1983–84 to 1984–85 [millions of dollars (% change)]	1984–85 to 1985–86 [millions of dollars (% change)]
Arkansas			
State	95.2 (18.7)	111.0 (18.3)	74.4 (10.4)
Local	21.2 (7.8)	8.0 (2.7)	30.3 (18.0)
Total	116.7 (14.9)	119.0 (13.2)	104.4 (10.3)
California			
State	1,275.8 (15.8)	1,152.0 (12.0)	783.7 (7.5)
Local	211.0 (7.9)	403.1 (14.0)	170.8 (5.2)
Total	1,486.8 (13.9)	1,518.3 (12.4)	954.5 (7.0)

Table 2 (continued)
Changes in State and Local Revenues for Public Schools, 1982–83 to 1985–86

	1982–83 to 1983–84 [millions of dollars (% change)]	1983–84 to 1984–85 [millions of dollars (% change)]	1984–85 to 1985–86 [millions of dollars (% change)]
Florida			
State	224.0 (11.8)	230.1 (10.8)	222.4 (9.5)
Local	133.6 (11.7)	147.6 (11.6)	110.1 (7.7)
Total	357.6 (11.8)	377.7 (11.1)	332.5 (8.8)
Georgia			
State	43.0 (6.8)	170.9 (11.6)	125.0 (7.7)
Local	n.a.	n.a.	n.a.
Total	n.a.	n.a.	n.a.
Illinois			
State	132.9 (6.3)	116.8 (5.2)	345.0 (14.7)
Local	208.5 (7.0)	25.1 (0.8)	n.a.
Total	341.4 (6.7)	141.9 (2.6)	n.a.
Kentucky			
State	93.8 (9.0)	18.7 (1.6)	18.7 (1.6)
Local	35.3 (12.6)	44.2 (14.0)	50.3 (14.0)
Total	129.1 (9.7)	62.9 (4.3)	69.0 (4.5)
Missouri			
State	148.3 (17.9)	43.2 (4.4)	146.5 (14.4)
Local	169.3 (16.0)	n.a.	n.a.
Total	317.6 (16.8)	n.a.	n.a.
New York			
State	233.1 (5.0)	613.0 (12.6)	403.0 (7.3)
Local	625.3 (9.7)	45.0 (0.6)	401.9 (5.6)
Total	858.4 (7.7)	658.0 (5.5)	804.9 (6.4)
South Carolina			
State	57.9 (7.8)	260.3 (32.4)	53.2 (5.0)
Local	66.1 (14.6)	37.9 (7.3)	27.9 (5.0)
Total	124.0 (10.3)	298.2 (22.6)	81.1 (5.0)
Tennessee			
State	−1.2 (−0.2)	165.0 (21.3)	65.8 (7.0)
Local	34.9 (4.9)	37.1 (5.0)	38.9 (5.0)
Total	33.7 (2.3)	202.1 (13.3)	104.7 (6.1)
Texas			
State	114.6 (3.2)	967.2 (25.9)	149.4 (3.2)
Local	324.1 (9.7)	469.3 (12.8)	n.a.
Total	438.7 (6.3)	1,436.5 (19.4)	n.a.

state and local revenues by 22.5%. Tennessee also increased state revenues by more than 20%, and Texas combined an increase in state aid of nearly $1 billion with a local revenue increase of nearly $500 million to bring total state and local increases to 19.4%. By any reckoning, these funding changes are large.

But if we analyze these funding changes over the long term, identify the trade-offs between state and local revenue changes, and adjust for enrollment growth and inflation, we find them modest overall. Consider the following examples. When California's funding increases are adjusted for enrollment increases (now averaging 100,000 students per year) and for inflation, revenues per pupil stayed even between 1984–85 and 1985–86, the third year of reform. Inflation and enrollment growth in California will require an additional $1.5 million dollars above what the reforms produced for each of the next few years in order to maintain a steady fiscal state. In South Carolina and Texas, large one-year increases were preceded and followed by lean years; in fact, with rising enrollments in Texas, state aid per pupil in nominal terms will drop in 1985–86 and in 1986–87. The state aid increase in New York between 1983–84 and 1984–85 – the largest in the state's history – seems to be almost completely offset by a lack of increase in local revenues for that year; in fact, combined state and local revenues increased by a larger amount in the year preceding that historic rise in state revenues. Put differently, New York's educational system fared better when state aid increases were more modest. Missouri's recent large increase in state aid came after three years of very small increases, though increased education revenues from the sales tax initiative (Proposition C) boosted education funding in the two years preceding the 1985 reforms.

The analysis above is not meant to criticize the Herculean efforts to increase education funding in the reform states. Rather, my point is that, even with extra effort, school funding has not increased all that much. Enrollment increase – a new phenomenon after a decade and a half of enrollment declines – will require a great many new dollars. Inflation, though modest, requires extra funding. State aid increases often can supplant local funds so that the net funding increase is modest. And large hikes in one year may not set a pattern for subsequent years. Over time, even in education reform states that have experienced the largest funding increases, these factors produce changes that are modest, that barely keep funding for the educational system from losing ground. More detailed analyses of the sources of these recent increases in funding for schools provide insight into the reasons why funding for education is unlikely to rise dramatically in the near future – even in reform states.

SOURCES OF FUNDS FOR REFORM

Federal Revenues

Revenues for public schools come from federal, state, and local governments, as well as from individuals and organizations in local communities. As I mentioned above, over the past few years federal education revenues have increased slowly in nominal terms and actually dropped when adjusted for inflation. Each year Congress introduces new education bills that would increase federal funding for education, but the bills usually do not make it to floor debate. Unless some dramatic change occurs in the issues pressing Congress, large federal deficits and growing noneducation expenditures make significant increases in federal aid to education an unlikely source of major new education revenues over the next five years.

State Revenues

As Tables 1 and 2 show, the states have been stalwart providers of recent increases in funding for education, and this pattern holds for the last decade and a half. States became the primary sources of education funding in part because of the school finance reforms of the 1970s. States also contributed three of every five new dollars for schools during the recession of the early 1980s.[7] Furthermore, states have been the fiscal engine that has powered the education reforms enacted since 1983.

Indeed, changes in state taxes proved to be the major source of funds for expensive education reforms—both directly, through such vehicles as sales tax increases dedicated to school reform (as in Tennessee, Arkansas, and South Carolina), and indirectly, through tax increases to balance state budgets.[8] Because of these actions, states claimed to be leaders in financing key domestic programs, including education. These politically courageous actions, coming at a time when the fervor to cut taxes and expenditures had not yet clearly waned, helped set the stage for a robust response to the funding needs of the proposed reforms.

The states that have enacted comprehensive education reforms usually raised state taxes to finance them. Five states increased the sales tax and devoted nearly all the extra revenues to education. In Arkansas, the December 1983 reform package increased the sales tax by a penny; the yield from that tax hike—$67 million for the last six months of the 1984 fiscal year—helped cover the $95.2 million increase in state aid in the first year of the reforms. In the next year, however, the extra penny brought in more than $155 million, while state aid for elementary and secondary education went up $110 million. South Carolina gave education the entire one-cent increase in its sales tax, estimated to

yield $202 million in 1985, $227 million in 1986, and $242 million in 1987. Tennessee's one-cent sales tax increase produced about $325 million in 1985, with elementary and secondary education receiving a hike of $165 million.

To garner public support for the one-cent tax increase in 1982, Missouri promised to use half of the proceeds to roll back local property tax levies. The rest, though, provided healthy revenue increases for education, boosting state aid by 18% in 1984. However, increases in education aid from general state revenues stagnated in the two years after Proposition C. Thus the hike in the sales tax supplanted a portion of natural increases in state aid.

Finally, Texas increased the sales tax modestly (from 4% to 4.125%) and expanded its base to provide the largest new, individual revenue source ($305 million) for its multi-billion-dollar education reform. During a special session of the legislature in 1984, Texas lawmakers increased several other taxes as well (including those on motor fuels, corporate franchises, insurance companies, and on the sale or rental of motor vehicles) to raise an extra $4.8 billion over three years to improve the state's schools and highways. From these sources, $2.7 billion was allocated for education, $1.4 billion for highways, and $700 million to balance the budget.

Illinois and Kentucky also increased state tax rates to fund education reform, but on a series of smaller items. Illinois raised a number of excise taxes (a 5% tax on long-distance telephone calls and an eight-cent cigarette tax) to fund its $92.5 million reform package. Kentucky restructured the depreciation schedules for its corporate income tax and increased the business inventory and corporation license taxes to help fund its $307 million reform program.

California and Florida enacted significant

modifications in various state taxes to raise the revenues needed to finance the reforms the states enacted in the summer of 1983. By making state tax codes conform to federal codes and by putting property on the tax roll when it is completed or using the new market value immediately when property changes hands, California raised an estimated $400 million that, when added to the $350 million that both houses of the state legislature had already agreed to add to education, nearly covered the $800 million first-year cost of the reforms. Florida made numerous adjustments to the way business income is taxed and to the general sales tax, in order to produce the extra $100 million it needed for education reform.

Georgia and Missouri—the two states that enacted no changes in the tax code and funded their reforms from natural revenue growth—actually delayed implementation of the reforms for at least one fiscal year. Time will tell whether available revenues a year hence will prove adequate.

Finally, three states seem to be banking heavily on lottery revenues to give education a fiscal boost. Missouri hopes that its new lottery, to begin in 1986, will produce funds to finance future costs of reform. California enacted a lottery by initiative in the fall of 1984; it began operating in October 1985. Net proceeds are expected to be approximately $400 million ($243 million for the current school year), which is about what is needed to "cover" one year of student enrollment increases—hardly a major revenue boost. Finally, the large increases in state aid in New York occurred during the year in which the lottery produced significant new revenues; but the next year, when actual lottery revenues exceeded estimates by $43 million, the general state appropriation for education was reduced by that exact amount. Furthermore, as noted above, when state aid in-

creased in 1985, local revenues fell, and the net gain was minimal. So in the first year, lottery revenues supplanted local funds, and in the next year, lottery funds supplanted state funds.

In short, education reform states have been quite aggressive in finding new sources of revenue for public schools. They have increased tax rates, expanded tax bases, adopted lotteries, and pledged natural revenue increases for the schools. They have taken these steps at a time when tax increases are even less popular than usual, though public support seems to be available if tax increases are specifically aimed at improving the quality of public education. In the main, though, the additional revenues have given education a one- to two-year fiscal shot in the arm, after which revenues per pupil will do well to stay even in real terms. In short, while the states have creatively tapped a variety of sources to fund education reform, they have not opened wide the fiscal floodgates. At a time when government growth is limited, it seems that state dollar increases to reform and improve the education system have so far been modest.

Local Revenues

As I mentioned above, local revenues have also played an important role in education finance in recent years. After the proliferation of property tax relief policies in the late 1970s, states turned once again—in the depths of the recession of the early 1980s—to the local property tax to help finance schools. Indeed, the large property tax increases between 1980 and 1982 were viewed with alarm by those who saw them as a reversal of gains made in the previous decade. Although the property tax continues to play a formidable role in school funding, it is unlikely to provide dramatic increases through higher tax rates, except perhaps in places where the tax is significantly underused. None of the education reforms discussed above, for example, was accompanied by mandatory increases in the property tax rates of the same order of magnitude as increases in state taxes, which changed as much as 25% in some states. In Arkansas, Florida, and Texas, however, modest property tax increases were required, and in Missouri requirements for increasing local property tax rates were loosened. Nevertheless, the property tax is still an unpopular tax,[9] and efforts to increase its use, except in times of severe fiscal stress, are likely to produce a backlash.[10] Thus higher property taxes are unlikely to be a source of new revenues for the schools.

There are several other potential sources of local revenue growth, however. The first includes local option sales and income taxes. Although these would create technical, administrative, and legal problems, they nevertheless are productive avenues to pursue for increasing local education revenues. In Tennessee, for example, the sales tax provides about 40% of local school revenues. Indeed, the popularity of the sales tax at the state level usually carries over to the local level as well; when put to a vote, taxpayers often support a local sales tax. Although local sales and income taxes are not widespread today, a growing number of communities are opting for their use, and they offer the potential for generating significant revenue in such states as California and Washington, where it is virtually impossible to increase local property taxes.

Other sources of local revenues include nontax income derived from various types of entrepreneurial activities. Lionel Meno identified three major sources of revenue of this kind:[11]

- donor funds, including direct cash donations to local districts, indirect cash donations through locally created educational foundations, and donations of goods and services;

- enterprise activities, such as leasing school services and facilities or charging user fees for various school materials and activities; and

- shared or cooperative activities with community colleges, other colleges and universities, and local government agencies, including sharing buses, parks, recreational centers, and pools.

Meno conducted an extensive study of the extent, nature, and amount of revenue produced by each of these categories of activities. He concluded that a district that used every one of them could possibly increase its budget by 9%. Meno found, however, that actual dollars raised varied from $1.57 per pupil to $75.57 per pupil. The largest actual revenue yield was about an additional 2% of the nationwide average expenditure per pupil.

In another study, Richard Yong and Alan Hickrod reached similar conclusions about the revenue-raising potential of entrepreneurial fund-raising activities.[12] Although the sums actually raised are not insignificant, the fact is that they do not offer much potential for enhancing local district revenues. Furthermore, many local enterprise activities entail new, shared school governance mechanisms—an understandable requirement, but perhaps too high a price to pay for the revenues that they yield.

On the other hand, the impact of well-organized local district educational foundations needs to be measured in terms beyond the revenues they yield directly. Foundation funds can expand community involvement in the schools, raise the interest of local businesses, and strengthen school/business partnerships. Noneducators involved in such foundations often develop a renewed appreciation for local schools and realize that schools do a pretty good job, given the complexity of the tasks they face and the level of resources they have available. Such activities can rekindle local support for schools that, over time, can become support for increased local funding and a catalyst for improving the schools. Viewed in this light, the seeming rise of local educational foundations across the U.S. could have significant positive effects on school funding.

No magic or secret sources of new funds for the schools exist. Local property taxes, state revenues from a number of tax sources, and federal aid will continue to provide the bulk of financing for our schools. These revenue sources have halted their decline of three years ago and are now increasing at modest rates. If the strength of education reform has reversed fiscal decline, though, it has not been sufficient—at least, given the fiscal evidence so far—to place funding for education on a sound course of improvement.

These current conditions, coupled with demographic trends for the future, make raising the level of education funding a challenge. Student enrollments are now on the rise; thus schools will need more money just to stay even with expenditures per pupil. More classrooms will be needed to house these students—another costly outlay. The rising public school enrollments will include larger numbers and percentages of minority, limited-English-proficient, poor, and learning-disabled students.[13] All these special categories of students will require extra services to meet their educational needs. And the quality of education for the rest of the population, though better than it was a few years ago, still needs to improve.

We must continue to increase school funding. Recent evidence shows that the educational system can change quickly when pub-lic demands for better quality are stated clearly and money for reform is provided. Continuing to improve the quality of public education will require sustained funding; providing education for a growing number of ever more diverse students will require sustained funding. If the nation responds in the next five years as it has in the past three, school funding can increase, and the quality of education can improve. We really have no other options.

ENDNOTES

1. Susan Fuhrman and Lorraine McDonnell, "The Political Context of School Reform," in Van Mueller and Mary McKeown, eds., *State Reform of Elementary and Secondary Education* (Cambridge, Mass.: Ballinger, forthcoming).
2. James Guthrie and Michael Kirst, eds., *Conditions of Education in California, 1985* (Berkeley: University of California, Policy Analysis for California Education, 1985).
3. Allan Odden, "Financing Education Excellence," *Phi Delta Kappan*, January 1984, pp. 311–18.
4. Allan Odden, *Education Finance in the States: 1984* (Denver: Education Commission of the States, 1984).
5. Allan Odden, "Education Finance 1985: Rising Tide or Steady Fiscal State?," *Educational Evaluation and Policy Analysis*, in press; and Jack Ossman, *Projections of Education Expenditures and Revenues in California to 1990* (Berkeley: University of California, Policy Analysis for California Education, 1985).
6. Odden, "Education Finance 1985. . . ."
7. Odden, *Education Finance in the States: 1984*, p. 2.
8. Steven Gold and Corina L. Eckl, *State Fiscal Conditions Entering 1984* (Denver: National Conference of State Legislatures, Legislative Finance Paper No. 42, 1984).
9. Advisory Commission on Intergovernmental Relations, *Public Attitudes on Governments and Taxes: 1984* (Washington, D.C.: ACIR, 1984).
10. Steven Gold, "State Tax Increases of 1983: Prelude to Another Tax Revolt," *National Tax Journal*, March 1984, pp. 9–22.
11. Lionel R. Meno, "Sources of Alternative Revenues," in L. Dean Webb and Van D. Mueller, eds., *Managing*

Limited Revenues (Cambridge, Mass.: Ballinger, 1984).

12. Richard Yong and G. Alan Hickrod, *Private Sector Support of K–12 Education: A Review of Selected Programs in Seventeen States and Recommendations for Illinois* (Normal: Illinois State University, Center for the Study of Educational Finance, April 1985).

13. Harold Hodgkinson, *All One System* (Washington, D.C.: Institute for Educational Leadership, 1985).

DISCUSSION QUESTIONS AND ACTIVITIES

1. According to Sherman, what is the most important development forecast for the next fifteen years in elementary and secondary education? What is the significance of this development?

2. Which demographic changes suggest that between 1985 and 2000 there may likely be lower political support for education and greater competition from other interest groups for services?

3. Why did public education's share of state and local expenditures decline since the late 1960s?

4. Wide variability is expected in school demographic trends both among states and among school districts within a state. What are the likely consequences of these trends?

5. Summarize the future financial picture for elementary and secondary education to the year 2000.

6. According to Odden, what are the signs that the reforms are being implemented as intended by many states?

7. What progress has been made in promoting fiscal equity?

8. Explain why funds for education reform are in short supply. What impact will this have on implementing reform proposals?

9. Cite the new sources of revenue for public schools and analyze the usefulness and problems associated with each one.

10. Survey the new sources of revenue for public schools in your state and report to the class on the relative effectiveness of these sources.

11. Make a class presentation on the problems and concerns over finance in your local school district.

SUGGESTED READINGS

Adams, E. Kathleen. "State Fiscal Conditions and Local School Financing." *NASSP Bulletin* 67 (November 1983):56–63.

Augenblick, John. "School Finance in the 1980s, Part II: State Issues for the 1980s." *Spectrum* 2 (Summer 1984):37–47.

Augenblick, John. "The States and School Finance: Looking Back and Looking Ahead." *Phi Delta Kappan* 66 (November 1984):196–201.

Burrup, Percey E., and Brimley, Vern. *Financing Education in a Climate of Change*, 3rd ed. Boston: Allyn and Bacon, 1982.

The Cost of Reform. Arlington, Va.: American Association of School Administrators, 1984.

Geske, Terry G., and Hoke, Gordon H. "The National Commission Reports: Do the States Have the Fiscal Capacity to Respond?" *Education and Urban Society* 17 (February 1985):171–185.

Guthrie, James W. "The Educational Policy Consequences of Economic Instability: The Emerging Political Economy of American Education." *Educational Evaluation and Policy Analysis* 7 (Winter 1985): 319–332.

Johns, Roe L.; Alexander, Kern; and Morphet, Edgar. *The Economics and Financing of Public Education*, 4th ed. Englewood Cliffs, N.J.: Prentice-Hall, 1983.

Jones, James R. "The Role of the Federal

Government in Educational Policy Matters: Focus on Finance." *Journal of Education Finance* 10 (Fall 1984):238–255.

Kirst, Michael W. "State Policy in an Era of Transition." *Education and Urban Society* 16 (February 1984):225–237.

Nelson, F. Howard. "Federal Economic Policy and the Finance of Elementary and Secondary Education in the Eighties." *Planning and Changing* 14 (Summer 1983): 91–100.

Odden, Allan. "Financing Educational Excellence." *Phi Delta Kappan* 65 (January 1984):311–318.

9

Private Schools

More and more parents are removing their children from public schools and placing them in private and parochial schools. Some do so on academic grounds; others do so for religious reasons; and still others wish to avoid integration. Those who favor aid to private schools generally believe private schools offer a better education than public schools.

Public high schools enroll over 90 percent of the total high school population and have an average of 750 students. Catholic schools enroll about 6 percent and average about 500 students, whereas other private schools enroll between 3 and 4 percent and average only 150 students. Pupil-teacher ratios in public and Catholic schools are similar, but the ratio is only about half as large as public schools in other types of private schools.

A study by James S. Coleman compares public schools with Catholic and other private schools in terms of discipline, problems of students, homework, achievement test scores, academic demands made on students, and aspirations for higher education. The study also evaluates the degree of religious segregation and economic segregation in American secondary schools. It concludes that Catholic schools have higher quality on the average and greater equality than public schools.

The public schools, Coleman has said elsewhere, are no longer a "common" institution because residential mobility has brought about a high degree of racial segregation in education, as well as segregation by income. He does not believe that the public interest in common institutions is an overriding public interest. Rather, it is relatively weak compared to interest in helping all children, especially the disadvantaged, receive a better education. Others disagree (see the selections by Butts and Rich in the *Suggested Readings*), citing the vital role that a public educational system can play in a democratic society.

In terms of policy, Coleman opposes the practice of assigning students on the basis of residence because it harms the nonaffluent and increases inequalities in opportunity. He prefers communities based on interests, values, and educational preferences. To support these plans, he would expand the different types of education supported by public funds.

Quality and Equality in American Education: Public and Catholic Schools

James S. Coleman

James S. Coleman (b. 1926) took his Ph.D. at Columbia University, taught at Johns Hopkins University, and is now Professor of Sociology at the University of Chicago. He is a member of the National Academy of Education, American Academy of Arts and Sciences, National Academy of Sciences, and the American Philosophical Association. His writing includes The Adolescent Society, High School Achievement *(coauthor), and the landmark USOE study,* Equality of Educational Opportunity *(coauthor).*

The report, "Public and Private Schools," of which I was an author, has raised some questions about certain fundamental assumptions and ideals underlying American education.[1] In this article, I shall first describe briefly the results that raise these questions. Then I shall examine in greater detail these fundamental assumptions and ideals, together with changes in our society that have violated the assumptions and made the ideals increasingly unattainable. I shall then indicate the negative consequences that these violations have created for both equality of educational opportunity in U.S. public schools and for the quality of education they offer. Finally, I shall suggest what seems to me the direction that a new set of ideals and assumptions must take if the schools are to serve American children effectively.

A number of the results of "Public and Private Schools" have been subjected to intense reexamination and reanalysis. The re-port has occasioned a good deal of debate and controversy, as well as a two-day conference at the National Institute of Education and a one-day conference at the National Academy of Sciences, both in late July. Part of the controversy appears to have arisen because of the serious methodological difficulties in eliminating bias due to self-selection into the private sector. Another part appears to have arisen because the report was seen as an attack on the public schools at a time when tuition tax credit legislation was being proposed in Congress.

I shall not discuss the controversy except to say that all the results summarized in the first portion of this article have been challenged by at least one critic; I would not report them here if these criticisms or our own further analyses had led me to have serious doubts about them. Despite this confidence, the results could be incorrect because of the extent of the methodological difficul-

From James S. Coleman, "Quality and Equality in American Education: Public and Catholic Schools," Phi Delta Kappan *63 (November 1981): 159–164. Reprinted by permission.*

ties involved in answering any cause-and-effect question when exposure to the different treatments (that is, to the different types of schools) is so far from random. Most of my comparisons will be between the Catholic and the public schools. The non-Catholic private schools constitute a much more heterogeneous array of schools; our sample in those schools is considerably smaller (631 sophomores and 551 seniors in 27 schools), and the sample may be biased by the fact that a substantial number of schools refused to participate. For these reasons, any generalizations about the non-Catholic private sector must be tenuous. Fortunately, the principal results of interest are to be found in the Catholic schools.

There are five principal results of our study, two having to do with quality of education provided in both the public and private sectors and three related to equality of education.

First, we found evidence of higher academic achievement in basic cognitive skills (reading comprehension, vocabulary, and mathematics) in Catholic schools than in public schools for students from comparable family backgrounds. The difference is roughly one grade level, which is not a great difference. But, since students in Catholic schools take, on the average, a slightly greater number of academic courses, the difference could well be greater for tests more closely attuned to the high school curriculum. And the higher achievement is attained in the Catholic schools with a lower expenditure per pupil and a slightly higher pupil/teacher ratio than in the public schools.

The second result concerning educational quality must be stated with a little less certainty. We found that aspirations for higher education are higher among students in Catholic schools than among comparable students in public schools, despite the fact that, according to the students' retrospective reports, about the same proportion had planned to attend college when they were in the sixth grade.

The first two results concerning equality in education are parallel to the previous two results; one concerns achievement in cognitive skills and the other, plans to attend college. For both of these outcomes of schooling, family background matters less in the Catholic schools than in the public schools. In both achievement and aspirations, blacks are closer to whites, Hispanics are closer to Anglos, and children from less well-educated parents are closer to those from better-educated parents in Catholic schools than in public schools. Moreover, in Catholic schools the gap narrows between the sophomore and senior years, while in the public schools the gap in both achievement and aspirations widens.

It is important to note that, unlike the results related to educational quality, these results related to equality do not hold generally for the public/private comparison. That is, the results concerning equality are limited to the comparison between public schools and Catholic schools. Within other segments of the private sector (e.g., Lutheran schools or Jewish schools) similar results for educational differences might well hold (though these other segments have too few blacks and Hispanics to allow racial and ethnic comparisons), but they are not sufficiently represented in the sample to allow separate examination.

The final result concerning educational equality is in the area of racial and ethnic integration. Catholic schools have, proportionally, only about half as many black students as do the public schools (about 6% compared to about 14%); but internally they are less segregated. In terms of their effect on the overall degree of racial integration in U.S. schools, these two factors work in opposing directions; to a large extent they cancel each other out. But of interest to our examination here, which concerns the internal functioning of the public and Catholic sectors of education, is the lesser internal segregation of blacks in the Catholic sector. Part of this is due to the smaller percentage of black students in Catholic schools, for a general conclusion in the school desegregation literature is that school systems with smaller proportions of a disadvantaged minority are less segregated than those with larger proportions. But part seems due to factors beyond the simple proportions. A similar result is that, even though the Catholic schools in our sample have slightly higher proportions of Hispanic students than the public schools, they have slightly less Hispanic/Anglo segregation.

These are the results from our research on public and private schools that raise questions about certain fundamental assumptions of American education. Catholic schools appear to be characterized by *both* higher quality, on the average, *and* greater equality than the public schools. How can this be when the public schools are, first, more expensive, which should lead to higher quality, and, second, explicitly designed to increase equality of opportunity? The answer lies, I believe, in the organization of public education in the United States, and that organization in turn is grounded in several fundamental assumptions. It is to these assumptions that I now turn.

FOUR BASIC IDEAS AND THEIR VIOLATION

Perhaps the ideal most central to American education is the ideal of the common school, a school attended by all children. The assumption that all social classes should attend the same school contrasted with the two-tiered educational systems in Europe, which reflected their feudal origins. Both in the beginning and at crucial moments of choice (such as the massive expansion of secondary education in the early part of this century), American education followed the pattern of common, or comprehensive schools, including all students from the community and all courses of study. Only in the largest eastern cities were there differentiated, selective high schools, and even that practice declined over time, with new high schools generally following the pattern of the comprehensive school.

One implication of the common-school ideal has been the deliberate and complete exclusion of religion from the schools. In contrast, many (perhaps most) other countries have some form of support for schools operated by religious groups. In many countries, even including very small ones such as the Netherlands and Israel, there is a state secular school system, as well as publicly supported schools under the control of religious groups. But the melting-pot ideology that shaped American education dictated that there would be a single set of publicly supported schools, and the reaction to European religious intolerance dictated that these be free of religious influence.[2]

The absence of social class, curriculum, or religious bases for selection of students into different schools meant that, in American schooling, attendance at a given school was dictated by location of residence. This method worked well in sparsely settled areas and in towns and smaller cities, and it was a principle compatible with a secular democracy. Two factors have, however, led this mode of school assignment to violate the assumptions of the common school. One is the movement of the U.S. population to cities with high population densities, resulting in economically homogeneous residential areas. The other is the more recent, largely post-World War II expansion of personal transportation, leading to the development of extensive, economically differentiated suburbs surrounding large cities.

The combined effect of these two changes has been that in metropolitan areas the assumptions of the common school are no longer met. The residential basis of school assignment, in an ironic twist, has proved to be segregative and exclusionary, separating economic levels just as surely as do the explicitly selective systems of European countries and separating racial groups even more completely. The larger the metropolitan area, the more true this is, so that in the largest metropolitan areas the schools form a set of layers of economically stratified and racially distinct schools, while in small cities and towns the schools continue to approximate the economically and racially heterogeneous mix that was Horace Mann's vision of the common school in America.

In retrospect, only the temporary constraints on residential movement imposed by economic and technological conditions allowed the common-school ideal to be realized even for a time. As those constraints continue to decrease, individual choice will play an increasing role in school attendance (principally through location of residence), and the common-school assumption will be increasingly violated. Assignment to school in a single publicly supported school system on the basis of residence is no longer a means of achieving the common-school ideal. And, in fact, the common-school ideal may no longer be attainable through *any* means short of highly coercive ones.

The courts have attempted to undo the racially segregative impact of residential choice, reconstituting the common-school ideal through compulsory busing of children into different residential areas.[3] These attempts, however, have been largely thwarted by families who, exercising that same opportunity

for choice of school through residence, move out of the court's jurisdiction. The unpopularity and impermanence of the court-ordered attempts to reinstitute the common school suggest that attempts to reimpose by law the constraints that economics and technology once placed upon school choice will fail and that, in the absence of those naturally imposed constraints, the common-school ideal will give way before an even stronger ideal—that of individual liberty.

It is necessary, then, to recognize the failure of school assignment by residence and to reexamine the partially conflicting ideals of American education in order to determine which of these ideals we want to preserve and which to discard. For example, in high schools distinguished by variations in curriculum—one form of which is a type of magnet school and another form of which is the technical high school—a more stable racial mix of students is possible than in comprehensive high schools. As another example, Catholic schools are less racially and economically segregated than are U.S. public schools; this suggests that, when a school is defined around and controlled by a religious community, families may tolerate more racial and economic heterogeneity than they would in a school defined around a residential area and controlled by government officials.

A second ideal of American education has been the concept of local control. This has meant both control by the local school board and superintendent and the responsiveness of the school staff to parents. But these conditions have changed as well. The local school board and superintendent now have far less control over education policy than only 20 years ago. A large part of the policy-making function has shifted to the national level; this shift was caused primarily by the issue of racial discrimination, but it has also affected the areas of sex discrimination, bilingual education, and education for the handicapped, among others. Part of the policy-making power has shifted to the school staff or their union representatives, as professionalization and collective bargaining have accompanied the growth in size of school districts and the breakdown of a sense of community at the local level.

The loss of control by school boards and superintendents has been accompanied by a reduced responsiveness of the school to parents. This too has resulted in part from the breakdown of community at the local level and the increasing professionalization of teachers, both of which have helped to free the teacher from community control. The changes have been accompanied and reinforced by the trend to larger urban agglomerates and larger school districts. And some of the changes introduced to overcome racial segregation—in particular, busing to a distant school—have led to even greater social distances between parent and teacher.

A result of this loss of local control has been that parents are more distant from their children's school, less able to exert influence, less comfortable about the school as an extension of their own child rearing. Public support for public schools, as evidenced in the passage of school tax referenda and school bond issues and in the responses to public opinion polls, has declined since the mid-1960s, probably in part as a result of this loss of local control. Even more recently, in a backlash against the increasingly alien control of the schools, some communities have attempted to counter what they see as moral relativism in the curriculum (e.g., the controversy over the content in *Man: A Course of Study*) and have attempted to ban the teaching of evolution.

Technological and ecological changes make it unlikely that local control of education policy can be reconstituted as it has existed in the past, that is, through a local school board controlling a single public school system and representing the consensus of the community. Individuals may regain such local control by moving ever farther from large cities (as the 1980 census shows they have been doing), but the educational system as a whole cannot be reconstituted along the old local-control lines. Again, as in the case of the common-school ideal, present conditions (and the likelihood that they will persist) make the ideal unrealizable. One alternative is to resign ourselves to ever-decreasing public support for the public schools as they move further from the ideal. Another, however, is to attempt to find new principles for the organization of American education that will bring back parental support.

A third fundamental assumption of American public schooling, closely connected to local control, has been local financing of education. Some of the same factors that have brought about a loss of local control have shifted an increasing portion of education financing to the state and federal levels. Local taxes currently support only about 40% of expenditures for public schooling; federal support amounts to about 8% or 9% and state support, slightly over half of the total. The shift from local to state (and, to a lesser extent, federal) levels of financing has resulted from the attempt to reduce inequalities of educational expenditures among school districts. Inequalities that were once of little concern come to be deeply felt when local communities are no longer isolated but interdependent and in close social proximity. The result has been the attempt by some states, responding to the *Serrano* decision in California, to effect complete equality in educational expenditures for all students within the state. This becomes difficult to achieve without full statewide financing, which negates the principle of local financing.

Yet the justification for student assignment to the schools within the family's taxation district has been that the parents were paying for the schools *in that district*. That justification vanishes under a system of statewide taxation. The rationale for assignment by residence, already weakened by the economic and racial differences among students from different locales, is further weakened by the decline in local financing.

A fourth ideal of American public education has been the principle of *in loco parentis*. In committing their child to a school, parents expect that the school will exercise comparable authority over and responsibility for the child. The principle of *in loco parentis* was, until the past two decades, assumed not only at the elementary and secondary levels but at the college level as well. However, this assumption vanished as colleges abdicated the responsibility and parents of college students shortened the scope of their authority over their children's behavior from the end of college to the end of high school.

Most parents, however, continue to expect the school to exercise authority over and responsibility for their children through the end of high school. Yet public schools have been less and less successful in acting *in loco parentis*. In part, this is due to the loss of authority in the society as a whole, manifested in high school by a decreasing willingness of high school-age youths to be subject to *anyone's* authority in matters of dress and conduct. In part, it is due to the increasing dissensus among parents themselves about the authority of the school to exercise discipline over their children, sometimes leading to legal suits to limit the school's authority. And, in part, it is due to the courts, which, in response to these suits, have expanded the scope of civil rights of children in school, thus effectively limiting the school's authority to something less than that implied by the principle of *in loco parentis*.

There has been a major shift among some middle-class parents—a shift that will probably become even more evident as the children of parents now in their thirties move into high school—toward an early truncation of responsibility for and authority over their adolescent children. This stems in part from two changes—an increase in longevity and a decrease in number of children—which, taken together, remove child rearing from the central place it once held for adults. Many modern adults who begin child rearing late and end early are eager to resume the leisure and consumption activities that preceded the child-rearing period; they encourage early autonomy for their young. But the high school often continues to act as if it has parental support for its authority. In some cases it does; in others it does not. The community consensus on which a school's authority depends has vanished.

An additional difficulty is created by the increasing size and bureaucratization of the school. The exercising of authority—regarded as humane and fair when the teacher knows the student and parents well—comes to be regarded as inhumane and unfair when it is impersonally administered by a school staff member (teacher or otherwise) who hardly knows the student and seldom sees the parents. Thus there arises in such large, impersonal settings an additional demand for sharply defined limits on authority.

This combination of factors gives the public school less power to exercise the responsibility for and authority over students that are necessary to the school's functioning. The result is a breakdown of discipline in the public schools and, in the extreme, a feeling by some parents that their children are not safe in school. Again, a large portion of the change stems from the lack of consensus that once characterized the parental community about the kind and amount of authority over their children they wished to delegate to the school—a lack of consensus exploited by some students eager to escape authority and responded to by the courts in limiting the school's authority. And, once again, this raises questions about what form of reorganization of American education would restore the functioning of the school and even whether it is possible to reinstate the implicit contract between parent and school that initially allowed the school to act *in loco parentis*.

The violation of these four basic assumptions of American education—the common school, local control, local financing, and *in loco parentis*—together with our failure to establish a new set of attainable ideals, has hurt both the quality and the equality of American education. For this change in society, without a corresponding change in the ideals that shape its educational policies, reduces the capability of its schools to achieve quality and equality, which even in the best of circumstances are uncomfortable bedfellows.

Next I shall give some indications of how the pursuit of each of these goals of quality and equality is impeded by policies guided by the four assumptions I have examined, beginning first with the goal of equality.

The organization of U.S. education is assignment to school by residence, guided by the common-school, local-control, and local-financing assumptions, despite those elements that violate these assumptions. In a few locations, school assignment is relieved by student choice of school or by school choice of student. But, in general, the principle observed in American education (thus making it different from the educational systems of many countries) has been that of a rigid assignment by residence, a practice that upholds the common-school myth and the local-control and local-financing myths.

It is commonly assumed that the restriction of choice through rigid assignment by residence is of relative benefit to those least well off, from whom those better off would escape if choice were available. But matters are not always as they seem. Assignment by residence leaves two avenues open to parents: to move their residence, choosing a school by choice of residence; or to choose to attend a private school. But those avenues are open only to those who are sufficiently affluent to choose a school by choosing residence or to choose a private school. The latter choice may be partially subsidized by a religious community operating the school, or, in rare cases, by scholarships. But these partial exceptions do not hide the central point: that the organization of education through rigid assignment by residence hurts most those without money (and those whose choice is constrained by race or ethnicity), and this increases the inequality of educational opportunity. The reason, of course, is that, because of principles of individual liberty, we are unwilling to close the two avenues of choice: moving residence and choosing a private school. And although economic and technological constraints once kept all but a few from exercising these options, that is no longer true. The constraints are of declining importance; the option of residential change to satisfy educational choice (the less expensive of the two options) is exercised by larger numbers of families. And in that exercise of choice, different economic levels are sorted into different schools by the economic level of the community they can afford.

We must conclude that the restrictions on educational choice in the public sector and the presence of tuition costs in the private sector are restrictions that operate to the relative disadvantage of the least well off. Only when these restrictions were reinforced by the economic and technological constraints that once existed could they be regarded as effective in helping to achieve a "common school." At present, and increasingly in the future, they are working to the disadvantage of the least well off, increasing even more the inequality of educational opportunities.

One of the results of our recent study of public and private schools suggests these processes at work. Among Catholic schools, achievement of students from less-advantaged backgrounds—blacks, Hispanics, and those whose parents are poorly educated—is closer to that of students from advantaged backgrounds than is true for the public sector. Family background makes much less difference for achievement in Catholic schools than in public schools. This greater homogeneity of achievement in the Catholic sector (as well as the lesser racial and ethnic segregation of the Catholic sector) suggests that the ideal of the common school is more nearly met in the Catholic schools than in the public schools. This may be because a religious community continues to constitute a functional community to a greater extent than does a residential area, and in such a functional community there will be less stratification by family background, both within a school and between schools.

At the same time, the organization of American education is harmful to quality of education. The absence of consensus, in a community defined by residence, about what kind and amount of authority should be exercised by the school removes the chief means by which the school has brought about achievement among its students. Once there was such consensus, because residential areas once *were* communities that maintained a set of norms, reflected in the schools' and the parents' beliefs about what was appropriate for children. The norms varied in different communities, but they were consistent within each community. That is no longer true at the high school level, for the reasons I have described. The result is what some have called a crisis of authority.

In our study of high school sophomores and seniors in both public and private schools,

we found not only higher achievement in the Catholic and other private schools for students from comparable backgrounds than in the public schools, but also major differences between the functioning of the public schools and the schools of the private sector. The principal differences were in the greater academic demands made and the greater disciplinary standards maintained in private schools, even when schools with students from comparable backgrounds were compared. This suggests that achievement increases as the demands, both academic and disciplinary, are greater. The suggestion is confirmed by two comparisons: Among the public schools, those that have academic demands and disciplinary standards at the same level as the average private school have achievement at the level of that in the private sector (all comparisons, of course, involving students from comparable backgrounds). And, among the private schools, those with academic demands and disciplinary standards at the level of the average public school showed achievement levels similar to those of the average public school.

The evidence from these data—and from other recent studies—is that *stronger academic demands and disciplinary standards produce better achievement.* Yet the public schools are in a poor position to establish and maintain these demands. The loss of authority of the local school board, superintendent, and principal to federal policy and court rulings, the rise of student rights (which has an impact both in shaping a "student-defined" curriculum and in impeding discipline), and, perhaps most fundamental, the breakdown in consensus among parents about the high schools' authority over and responsibility for their children—all of these factors put the average public school in an untenable position to bring about achievement.

Many public high schools have adjusted

to these changes by reducing their academic demands (through reduction of standards, elimination of competition, grade inflation, and a proliferation of undemanding-courses) and by slackening their disciplinary standards (making "truancy" a word of the past and ignoring cutting of classes and the use of drugs or alcohol).

These accommodations may be necessary, or at least they may facilitate keeping the peace, in some schools. But the peace they bring is bought at the price of lower achievement, that is, a reduced quality of education.

One may ask whether such accommodations are inevitable or whether a different organization of education might make them unnecessary. It is to this final question that I now turn.

ABANDONING OLD ASSUMPTIONS

The old assumptions that have governed American education all lead to a policy of assignment of students to school by place of residence and to a standard conception of a school. Yet a variety of recent developments, both within the public sector and outside it, suggest that attainment of the twin goals of quality and equality may be incompatible with this. One development is the establishment, first outside the public sector and then in a few places within it as well, of elementary schools governed by different philosophies of education and chosen by parents who subscribe to those philosophies. Montessori schools at the early levels, open education, and basic education are examples. In some communities, this principle of parental choice has been used to maintain more stable racial integration than occurs in schools with fixed pupil assignment and a standard educational philosophy. At the secondary level, magnet schools, with specialized curricula or intensive programs in a given area (e.g., music or

performing arts), have been introduced, similarly drawing a clientele who have some consensus on which a demanding and effective program can be built. Alternative schools have flourished, with both students and staff who accept the earlier autonomy to which I have referred. This is not to say, of course, that all magnet schools and all alternative schools are successful, for many are not. But if they were products of a well-conceived pluralistic conception of modes of secondary education, with some policy guidelines for viability, success would be easier to achieve.

Outside the public sector, the growth of church-operated schools is probably the most prominent development, reflecting a different desire by parents for a nonstandard education. But apart from the religious schools, there is an increasingly wide range of educational philosophies, from the traditional preparatory school to the free school and the parent-run cooperative school.

I believe that these developments suggest an abandonment of the principle of assignment by residence and an expansion of the modes of education supported by public funds. Whether this expansion goes so far as to include all or part of what is now the private sector or is instead a reorganization of the public sector alone is an open question. The old proscriptions against public support of religious education should not be allowed to stand in the way of a serious examination of this question. But the elements of successful reorganization remain, whether it stays within the public sector or encompasses the private: a pluralistic conception of education, based on "communities" defined by interests, values, and educational preferences rather than residence; a commitment of parent and student that can provide the school a lever for extracting from students their best efforts; and the educational choice for all that is now available only to those with money.

Others may not agree with this mode of

organizing education. But it is clear that the goals of education in a liberal democracy may not be furthered, and may in fact be impeded, by blind adherence to the ideals and assumptions that once served U.S. education—some of which may be unattainable in modern America—and by the mode of school organization that these ideals and assumptions brought into being. There may be extensive debate over what set of ideals is both desirable and attainable and over what mode of organization can best attain these ideals, but it is a debate that should begin immediately. Within the public sector, the once-standard curriculum is beginning to take a variety of forms, some of which the search for a new mode of organizing schooling. And an increasing (though still small) fraction of youngsters are in private schools, some of which exemplify alternative modes of organizing schooling. These developments can be starting points toward the creation of an educational philosophy to guide the reorganization of

American schooling in ways fruitful for the youth who experience it.

ENDNOTES

1. The other two authors are Thomas Hoffer and Sally Kilgore. A first draft of "Public and Private Schools" was completed on 2 September 1980. A revised draft was released by the National Center for Education Statistics (NCES) on 7 April 1981. A final draft is being submitted to NCES this fall. A revised version of the April 7 draft, together with an epilogue and prologue examining certain broader issues, is being published this fall by Basic Books as *Achievement in High School: Public and Private Schools Compared.*
2. It has nevertheless been true that in many religiously homogeneous communities, ordinarily Protestant, religious influence did infiltrate the schools. Only since the Supreme Court's ban on prayer in the schools has even nonsectarian religious influence been abolished.
3. The legal rationale for these decisions has been past discriminatory practices by school systems; but, in fact, the remedies have constituted attempts to overcome the effects of residential choice.

Oranges Plus Apples, Dr. Coleman, Give You Oranges Plus Apples

Joseph Rogers

Joseph Rogers, formerly a principal in Hudson, Ohio is superintendent of Windham Exempted Village Schools in Windham, Ohio.

James Coleman's 1981 research comparing private and public education, *Public and Private Schools*, leaves me frustrated and disheartened. Having worked in both systems, I could not help but feel that Coleman lacked insight into private and parochial education.

Whether the matter to be considered is quality, equality, or something else, it seems natural to compare private and public education as two sides of a similar reality. And therein lies the problem! Comparing them is not looking at two closely related variants. Rather, it is an attempt to span a chasm kindred to that of cultural difference.

Coleman's research indicates that Catholic and other private school students have higher academic achievement in the basic cognitive skills. And that should be the case! Because private schools have traditionally had more applicants than openings, applicants were screened and the academic cream accepted. During the '70s, tuition costs challenged the appeal of Catholic schools and they were faced with adopting more liberal admission policies. The result was the admittance of less able, but still significantly superior, students. On the other hand, public schools must educate all who have residential claim—regardless of academic achievement. Thus, Catholic and other private schools should be expected to surpass public schools in the area of purely academic achievement.

Coleman's study found that Catholic schools have a lower per pupil expenditure than public schools. And well they should! The lion's share of per pupil expenditure in public schools goes to salaries. Most Catholic schools have some religious members on the faculty and/or staff who do not have to support a family. Their salaries border on what the government cites as the poverty level. The salary of lay educators in Catholic schools is usually below that of public educators as well, even though public school educators are not highly paid. When Coleman commends Catholic education for its low per pupil expenditure, he overlooks this important difference.

Coleman notes that a large number of Catholic and other private school graduates go on to college. However, the number of these graduates who are college bound has nothing to do with the effectiveness of public education.

Seventy-five percent of Hudson (Ohio) High School's graduating class traditionally

From Joseph Rogers, "Oranges Plus Apples, Dr. Coleman, Give You Oranges Plus Apples," NASSP Bulletin 67 (October 1983): 107–109. Reprinted by permission.

attends college. In fact, many of them are admitted to the most demanding and exclusive colleges and universities. That does not make Hudson better than the surrounding schools. Rather, it says that we have an unusual student body for a public school district.

Catholic schools, for the most part, are oriented toward preparation for college. They should be expected to achieve their stated purpose.

"In both achievement and aspirations, blacks are closer to whites, Hispanics are closer to Anglos, and children from less well educated parents are closer to those from better educated parents in Catholic schools than in public schools," writes Coleman. Again, I have to wonder at Coleman's amazement. Two factors of private and Catholic education coalesce to ensure this result—greater homogeneity of student body and greater parental investment. Most Catholic high schools maintain entrance requirements that ensure much greater student body homogeneity than any public high school could ever have. This homogeneity is furthered by the fact that a student who is admitted but is unable to maintain the expected standards, can and will be removed—for all the right reasons. That student can receive more assistance in the public schools, which are better prepared—at least theoretically—to work with a wide range of abilities.

That Catholic and other private schools are doing a good job does not mean that public schools are not. All it indicates is that private and parochial schools are successful within their realm.

Even more ludicrous is Coleman's position that public schools, especially when compared with Catholic schools, have violated the four basic ideals of American education: common schools, local control, local funding, and "in loco parentis."

Coleman maintains that public schools today are no longer the common schools that they once were and are still meant to be. Residential restrictions, he contends, have made public schools segregated and exclusionary. Although there are public schools and school districts devoid of racial mix, there are few that lack a diversified student body. That a district has few minority students does not violate the concept of the common school.

Coleman alleges that local control of public education has been lost in the wake of state and federal funding. I would suggest that if the loss really has occurred, it has been more the result of the impact of teacher organizations, court interference, and escalating inflation than of state and federal funding. Residential or neighborhood schools help ensure some measure of real local control. The spread of student residence in many Catholic schools far exceeds what would be even loosely termed "the neighborhood." The typical Catholic high school would be hard pressed to specifically define its boundaries, let alone its neighborhood. Local control is, by necessity, surrendered to a board of trustees at best and the administration—diocesan or local—at worst.

The increasing need for and/or acceptance of outside funding does, however, affect the basic assumption that schools are supported by the neighborhood they serve. Coleman bemoans the loss of local financing for public schools. But is it really a loss of local financing when taxes paid by the residents of a district are returned to that district in the form of state or federal funding? If Coleman is correct in his contention that such funding damages the principle of local financing, what makes the violation any less when Catholic and private schools engage in the same pursuit?

Coleman contends that the ideal of "in loco parentis" has been lost to public schools for a variety of reasons. Chief among these is the current authority crisis and the size of public schools. It is hard to understand how public education can be faulted for a situation it did not create. Further, this crisis of authority is unquestionably on the wane. The appeal and ready acceptance of "assertive discipline" by both public schools and parent groups attests to this. There are, indeed, many overly large public high schools; however, many Catholic high schools have larger student enrollments than do the public schools. The challenge of "in loco parentis" and creative response enhances rather than diminishes this principle.

RENEWAL: THREE FORMS

The basic principles of American education have not been violated. Rather, they have developed as all vital and dynamic principles must. The major forces of American history—positive and negative—have influenced these principles. That they have taken on nuances absent from or only suggested in the original form is a tribute to a dynamic society and a sensitive system of public education. Public education does need assistance and renewal. That renewal, however, will not arise from a comparison with Catholic schools, but from serious introspection. Such renewal of public education must take three forms: reestablishment of the priority of education; development of alternatives to the present handling of due process and educational malpractice suits; and a resurgence of professionalism and public support of that professionalism.

Coleman, through his research, has explained why Catholic schools perform admirably and laudably. However, he has not told public education anything relevant. Oranges are not apples. Catholic schools are not public schools. Coleman has, however, provoked needed reflection. Now is the time for the American public and public school educators to look hard at the apple that is public education and to provide it the polish it needs and deserves. Making education a real priority, taking schools out of the courtroom, and intensifying the meaning of being an educational professional are, I believe, giant steps toward polishing the apple that is public education.

DISCUSSION QUESTIONS AND ACTIVITIES

1. In the Coleman study reported, do public-school or private-school students have higher expectations and aspirations?
2. Does being in a private school make any difference in educational achievement?
3. What are the characteristics of private schools that influence positive achievement?
4. Are private schools divisive along economic, religious, or racial lines?
5. Identify the different types of private schools in your community and visit one of each type. Describe each school's objectives, policies, and programs, then make comparisons with the public schools.
6. What are the methodological weaknesses of the Coleman study?
7. What effect will the tuition tax credit that Coleman advocates likely have on the redistribution of students and financial problems?
8. What are the dangers that race and class inequality in American society will be maintained or even increased?
9. Why are Coleman's proposals not useful for improving the public schools? What does Rogers advocate to bring about improvement?
10. Organize a class discussion involving

three groups of students: those who attended a parochial school, a secular private school, and a public school. Ask participants to compare school characteristics and evaluate the quality of their educational experiences.

SUGGESTED READINGS

Proponents

Coleman, James S. "Public Schools, Private Schools, and the Public Interest," *The Public Interest* 64 (Summer 1981):19–30.

———. "Response to Page and Keith." *Educational Researcher* 10 (August-September 1981):18–20.

———. "Response to Taeuber-James, Cain-Goldberger and Morgan." *Sociology of Education* 56 (October 1983):219–234.

Coleman, James S., et al. "Achievement and Segregation in Secondary Schools: A Further Look at Public and Private School Differences." *Sociology of Education* 55 (April–July 1982):162–182.

———. "Cognitive Outcomes in Public and Private Schools." *Sociology of Education* 55 (April–July 1982):65–76.

Coleman, James S., Hoffer, Thomas; and Kilgore, Sally. *High School Achievement: Public, Private, and Catholic Schools Compared.* New York: Basic Books, 1982.

"Reflections on the 1981 Coleman Study." *Momentum* 12 (October 1981):4–13. Three articles generally favorable to the Coleman study.

Critics

Breneman, David W. "Coleman II and the Credibility of Social Science Research." *Change* 13 (September 1981):13.

Culucei, Nicholas. "Should Public Schools Be Judged by Criteria which Symbolize the 'Private School'?" *Capstone Journal of Education* 2 (Winter 1981–82):18–28.

Crain, Robert L., and Hawley, Willis D. "Standards of Research." *Society* 19 (January–February 1982):14–21.

Goldberger, Arthur S., and Cain, Glen G. "The Casual Analysis of Cognitive Outcomes in the Coleman, Hoffer and Kilgore Report." *Sociology of Education* 55 (April–July 1982):103–122.

McPartland, James M., and McDill, Edward L. "Control and Differentiation in the Structure of American Education." *Sociology of Education* 55 (April–July 1982): 77–88.

Page, Ellis B., and Keith, Timothy Z. "Effects of U.S. Private Schools: A Technical Analysis of Two Recent Claims." *Educational Researcher* 10 (August–September 1981):7–17.

Page, Ellis B. "The Media, Technical Analysis, and the Data Feast: A Response to Coleman," *Educational Researcher* 10 (August–September 1981):21–23.

Ravitch, Diane. "The Meaning of the New Coleman Report." *Phi Delta Kappan* 62 (June 1981):718–720.

"Report Analysis: Public and Private Schools." *Harvard Educational Review* 51 (November 1981):481–545. This colloquium presents seven analyses of the report, *Public and Private Schools*, together with responses by the report's authors.

Policy Issues

Butts, R. Freeman. "The Public Schools: Assaults on a Great Idea." *The Nation* (April 30, 1973):553–560.

Coons, John E., and Sugarman, Stephen D. *Education by Choice: The Case for Family Control.* Berkeley: University of California Press, 1978.

Edmonds, E. L. "In Defense of the Private School." *Education Canada* 21 (Fall 1981):21–23, 48.

Everhart, Robert B., ed. *The Public School Monopoly*. Cambridge, Mass.: Ballinger Publishing Co., 1982.

NASSP *Bulletin* 66 (March 1982):1–95. A special issue devoted to nonpublic schools.

Phi Delta Kappan 63 (November 1981): 159–168. Five articles—one by Coleman, the other four mostly critical—about the Coleman study, and the policy issues it raises.

Rich, John Martin. "The Libertarian Challenge to Public Education." *The Educational Forum* 46 (Summer 1982):421–429. Condensed in *The Education Digest* 48 (December 1982):16–19.

10

Teacher Education

The first systematic arrangement for teacher preparation in the United States was the founding of the first normal school in Lexington, Massachusetts, in 1839. Normal schools spread slowly and grew at a rate of about twenty-five new schools each decade until after the end of the century. As the programs multiplied, a pedagogical literature developed in which study required two years beyond the high-school level. The teacher college was founded in the 1890s in New York state by converting the normal schools into four-year programs and offering greater work in general education. Yet it was not until the 1920s that there were more teachers' colleges than normal schools in the country. Teacher preparation was also introduced in the late nineteenth century as a part of state university programs, yet because of resistance, it was not until the 1920s that most universities undertook such programs.

This century has witnessed the establishment of accrediting bodies for teacher education, state certification of teachers, national teacher examinations, the development of tenure provisions for teachers, and the growth of sophistication in educational research. Despite these developments, a number of critics have charged that teacher education programs are inadequate. Arthur Bestor, Admiral Hyman Rickover, and other critics during the 1950s claimed that teachers are generally weakly grounded in their subject matter because their programs are overly crowded with education courses on *how* to teach rather than *what* to teach. One dominant solution would be to have all prospective teachers thoroughly educated in the liberal arts and greatly reduce or eliminate their requirements in education courses. The solution, as advocated by James Koerner in the 1960s, was to immerse the student in his or her specialty and in liberal arts studies.

In contrast, national studies by James B. Conant and Charles Silberman recognized responsibility by all parties: teacher educators, liberal arts faculty, and the public schools. Conant, along with most critics other than Silberman, failed to see the importance of education as a field of study in its own right; that is, building a system of scholarly knowledge and contributing to the development of professional consciousness.

Teacher educators have attempted to counter the critics' charges and, in turn, offer new programs and innovations. These include fifth-year programs, programs for culturally different learners, competency-based teacher education, microteaching, new forms of internship, and others. Still, the debate continues.

Alternative Futures
for Teacher Education

Bob Roth

Bob Roth is a former president of the Association of Teacher Educators. He has written and spoken extensively about teacher education reform. He is currently affiliated with Performance Learning Systems in Emerson, New Jersey.

INTRODUCTION

Numerous national reports have been issued which cite the inadequacies of teacher education programs and the poor quality of the students who enter and graduate from these programs. The National Commission on Excellence in their report, "A Nation at Risk," stated that "teacher preparation programs need substantial improvement."[1] The Southern Regional Education Board[2] made numerous recommendations regarding the means by which teacher certification and teacher education should be strengthened. The Council of Chief State School Officers (CCSSO) adopted a report on teacher preparation, certification and retention which cited several factors which needed significant improvement and recommended that "standards for teacher training should be strengthened through state program approval."[3] The Educational Testing Service also published a report which indicated that teacher education is mainly responsible for a "crisis of competence in teaching."[4]

Some of the specific concerns which have been identified in these reports can be summarized by the following:

a. There appears to be a lack of a specific body of knowledge in teacher education.
b. Teacher education courses and programs do not appear to have been particularly effective in producing competent teachers.
c. There appears to be little substance in teacher education programs and thus, their value is greatly questioned.

A net effect is that teacher education has attracted and graduated students with low academic ability as reflected by measures such as the Scholastic Aptitude Test (SAT) and Graduate Record Examination (GRE) scores. The response the teacher education profession makes will determine the future of teacher education. During this period of turmoil and criticism of teacher education, new directions for the entire profession are being formulated. It is thus a critical time since teacher education is being remolded and the actions of those in the profession at this time will in large measure dictate the future for the profession.

Three scenarios can describe the possible futures of teacher education. These will be identified and analyzed in the following paragraphs. The probability of each occurring and

From Bob Roth, "Alternative Futures for Teacher Education," Action in Teacher Education *6 (Winter 1984–85):1–5. Reprinted by permission.*

the reasons for that probability will also be reviewed.

STATUS QUO

One alternative for the future of teacher education is that it will basically stay the same as it exists. In effect, this scenario projects that the structure and content of teacher education will remain essentially unchanged at the end of this period of turmoil. Furthermore, although there is great ferment in the profession at this time, this wave of concern will pass and the public will turn its attention to other matters. When the public realizes the money needed to provide for the significant changes proposed, it may take a second look at the issue of reform and institute only nominal changes in view of the monetary constraints. The ultimate effects will be negligible.

Another factor supporting this scenario of no real change is that there is tremendous inertia in academia and in teacher education. Much change is not likely unless it would take place over a very long period of time and more through evolution than revolution. Also supporting this possible future is the tendency to look for "quick fixes" rather than comprehensive, meaningful change. State legislatures, for example, may require a teacher competency test in subject areas and assume that this single fact will cause improvement in the profession and ignore all of the other proposals or recommendations. The net effect of such single issue actions would be a rather negligible change in the total teacher education process. All of these factors suggest that teacher education will continue in essentially the same way it has.

There are factors, however, which suggest that there indeed will be a change of rather large proportions. There is significant pressure on the profession to initiate changes.

The national reports very strongly criticized the quality of teacher education graduates and the process of teacher education itself. Using this as a context, numerous recommendations have been made which urge the reform of teacher education. This has exerted considerable pressure and many teacher education institutions have responded with higher entrance and exit criteria and provisions for stronger assessment at the point of program exit. In addition, there are external forces which are actually creating changes rather than just exerting pressure to stimulate change. State legislatures, state boards of education, state school superintendents and the national and state accrediting bodies are some of the external forces which are imposing change by statutes, policy or regulation which actually put these changes into place.

The result of the external pressures on teacher education as well as the external forces that are actually creating change may operate to such an extent that teacher education may not be able to stay in its present form in the future. Some indications of this are the rapidly growing use of examinations in areas such as subject matter knowledge, basic skills, and pedagogy. Not only do these examinations alter the selection process, but also they have an effect on the teacher preparation curriculum itself. Other examples are required fifth year programs, internships, and alternative routes to teacher certification. It is more than likely that teacher education will change, but the probability of significant change is only moderate at this time.

DEMISE

A second major scenario for the future of teacher education is that it just may slowly disappear. This does not mean that it will merely change in form and substance but that it may practically cease to exist as a means for entry into the teaching profession. There are initiatives such as in Michigan, Connecticut and California which transfer some or all of the responsibility for the continuing education of teachers to local school districts or staff development agencies within the state. In certain instances the authority to issue certificates or grant credit toward certification is being shifted to these agencies as well.[5]

Several of the national reports on the reform of teacher education have made recommendations to eliminate formal teacher education as a means for entry into the profession. The SREB report suggested that arts and science graduates should be certified to teach without professional education. The report of the CCSSO recommended that states should support programs which provide opportunity for talented individuals who do not complete teacher preparation programs to enter teaching. These proposals suggest alternative routes which could entirely supplant existing structures. Furthermore, as a result of the proposals, there are initiatives in some states to implement alternative entry procedures. In New Jersey, for example, graduates with a baccalaureate degree and a liberal arts education enter teaching by passing a subject matter examination and by having no teacher education courses whatsoever. The State of Virginia also has a similar plan in operation. Several other states such as Vermont[6] and New Hampshire[7] are considering implementing alternative modes for entry into teaching without teacher education as a means to entice the academically capable individuals to enter teaching. This movement prompted an article in the *Wall Street Journal*, "Certification of Teachers Lacking Courses in Education Stirs Battles in Several States."[8]

It should be noted that in many of the national reports, recommendations provide for

standards which make it increasingly difficult for graduates of teacher education programs to enter the profession. In addition to more stringent requirements for certification, more requirements for the teacher preparation process and the use of examinations after completion of a preparation program have made it more difficult for these graduates of teacher education programs to enter the profession. What this implies is that teacher education courses have little or no value and that those who enter such programs should be carefully scrutinized and perhaps even more so than those who have not taken these courses. This is a tremendous indictment of the teacher education process.

All of these factors, such as the recommendations of the national reports and the steps actually being taken in some states, could result in the demise of teacher education programs at institutions of higher education. Teacher education would be "deprofessionalized" and those with a subject area concentration would be admitted to teaching and given little, if any, preparation in pedagogy.

If teacher education as it now exists cannot demonstrate that it has a body of knowledge, then the tendency to eliminate the teacher education requirements may continue to grow. Likewise, if teacher education programs cannot show that they produce a more effective teacher and that there is indeed substance in these courses and that highly academically capable students would be attracted to the programs, then the tendency to overlook these programs will continue to grow. Research in this area is just beginning.

It appears, then, that some of the responses to the negative perception of teacher education courses are not to improve teacher education, but to eliminate it entirely. If the current movement gains momentum because of the influence of the national reports and the need by state legislatures to respond, this second scenario could indeed become reality and there would be little future for teacher education.

NEW DIRECTIONS

The third scenario for the future of teacher education is that it will respond by striking out in new directions, and these directions will be significantly different so that evidence is provided that indeed teacher education is changing and is a viable process for the preparation of competent professionals. Teacher education has long struggled to gain its place and receive the recognition, status and prestige comparable to other academic fields in the university. In attempting to do this it has emulated the other academic areas so that it could also gain academic prestige. This could be one of the major reasons leading to the demise of teacher education. Instead of emulating academic areas it should recognize that teaching is not only a science with a body of knowledge but it is also a craft that is practiced, and as such is different in significant ways from the purely academic areas of study.

Teacher education should focus instead on what it should do, and that is to promote effective teaching. How often do other disciplines in the university turn to the college or school of education and ask that it provide preparation for faculty to improve their instructional effectiveness? If teacher education is to gain the respect it seeks, it must demonstrate that it indeed provides an exemplary model for instruction within the institution and that it can prepare others to be more effective teachers in their respective disciplines.

In order to move in this significant new direction, teacher education must seek to use existing research and knowledge. In doing so it should also demonstrate that there is a body of knowledge in teaching which must be learned in order to be an effective teacher. It must demonstrate that indeed the courses are effective and produce competent teachers, and that there is substance in the courses provided in the schools, colleges and departments of education. And this in turn will attract the better academically able students and enhance the profession.

In order to achieve this new direction teacher education programs must use new knowledge, but they need not create new knowledge to begin this new direction. New knowledge will be developed as more research is conducted, but there currently exists a body of knowledge which can provide this significant new direction for teacher education. This new knowledge is derived primarily from research on areas such as student learning styles, brain function, and communication techniques. There is a growing body of research which provides an important dimension to the improvement of instruction. Although there are some emerging publications[9] and there are exciting new courses that incorporate this research[10], little of this new knowledge has been integrated into preparation programs for teachers.

CONCLUSION

If teacher education is to survive then this last scenario is the one to pursue. Teacher educators, administrators, teacher education programs, and professional associations must move forward to incorporate this new knowledge base into teacher education programs. The future of teacher education is now being molded and the most likely way to provide that there indeed will be a future for teacher education is to move in this exciting and viable new direction.

REFERENCES

1. National Commission on Excellence in Education, "A Nation at Risk: The Imperative for Educational Reform," Washington, D.C., U.S. Government Printing Office, 1983.
2. Southern Regional Education Board, "The Need for Quality," Atlanta, 1981.
3. Council of Chief State School Officers, "Staffing the Nation's Schools: A National Emergency," Washington, D.C., 1984.
4. Educational Testing Service, "Teacher Competence," *Focus,* Princeton, N.J., 1982.
5. Michaels D. Rowls and Madlyn L. Hanes. "Teacher Recertification: The Shift Toward Local Control and Governance." *Journal of Teacher Education* (July/August, 1982).
6. Charlie Euchner "Vt. Board Seeks Training for Non-Education Majors," *Education Week* v. III, n. 23; Feb. 29, 1984, p. 7.
7. Susan G. Foster "N.H. Group Urges Expanded Access to Careers in Teaching." *Education Week* v. III, n. 23; Feb. 29, 1984, p. 7.
8. Virginia Inman "Certification of Teachers Lacking Courses in Education Stirs Battles in Several States," *The Wall Street Journal,* January 6, 1984.
9. Claudia E. Cornett "What You Should Know about Teaching and Learning Styles," Phi Delta Kappa Fastback #191, Bloomington, Indiana, 1983, and National Association of Secondary School Principals, *Student Learning Styles and Brain Behavior,* Reston, Virginia, 1982.
10. Performance Learning Systems, Inc., "Project T.E.A.C.H.," "P.R.I.D.E.," and "TEACHING through LEARNING CHANNELS," Emerson, New Jersey.

Making a Difference in Educational Quality Through Teacher Education

Carolyn M. Evertson
Willis D. Hawley
Marilyn Zlotnik

Carolyn M. Evertson is Professor, Department of Teaching and Learning; Willis D. Hawley is Dean, Peabody College of Vanderbilt University; and Marilyn Zlotnik is Research Associate, Vanderbilt University.

Teacher education probably has never received as much attention from public policy makers as it has over the past few years. Teacher educators have long felt neglected and unappreciated, but the recent scrutiny they have experienced may make many wish to return to their back seat status. Schools of education, and perhaps the state agencies and professional organizations that sustain them, are charged with lacking the necessary standards, competence, substance and academic rigor to do a quality job of educating America's teachers.

The response to the infamy now widely bestowed upon teacher education has been loud and not always coherent. State level policy makers generally perceive the solution to the problem in regulations that would restrict access to both teacher education and to teaching and that would prescribe specific courses of study and ways to teach. These regulatory actions are sometimes matched with incentives aimed at increasing the qual-ity and quantity of aspirants to teaching. A number of states created loan forgiveness programs to induce students to enter fields such as math and science where teacher shortages exist. A handful of states have increased significantly beginning teacher salaries. And, there is currently pressure to provide "alternative routes" to the teaching profession that presumably make teaching more attractive by allowing individuals with certain academic credentials to by-pass formal teacher preparation programs.

These actions, and more, have occurred largely without much involvement from teacher educators. Those who prepare teachers, however, are beginning to make their moves. The initiatives fall into two broad categories. The first initiative is to join the call for higher standards. In particular, teacher educators—at least those who speak out on the standards issue—are calling for higher grade point averages for admission to teacher education programs, minimum

From Carolyn M. Evertson, Willis D. Hawley, and Marilyn Zlotnik, *"Making a Difference in Educational Quality Through Teacher Education,"* Journal of Teacher Education *36 (May–June 1985):2–12.* Reprinted by permission.

course requirements and faculty qualifications, and preservice tests of teacher knowledge.

A second reform strategy is to require more extensive pre-entry coursework coupled with better supervised practica and internships. This strategy assumes that beginning teachers are less effective than they could be because they do not know as much as they need to know. An additional assumption underlying this position is that teaching is not as attractive to talented people as are other professions because requiring only a conventional undergraduate education for entry contributes to the low status attributed to a career in teaching. Advocates for this reform strategy are calling for five and, increasingly, six years of higher education prior to full entry to teaching. Perhaps because so-called "extended" or postbaccalaureate teacher preparation programs are likely to result in major shifts in student enrollment from private and small public institutions to large public universities, teacher educators are divided on this strategy. But there is little doubt that its advocates are growing in number and influence.

Most proposals for teacher reform are unburdened by evidence that the suggested changes will make a difference in the quality of students preparing to teach in elementary and secondary schools. They avoid questions such as: Can existing research provide guidance for how teacher education might be improved in a cost effective way? Before addressing this question, we acknowledge at the outset that although the number of studies related to teacher education is large, the research is often of dubious scientific merit and frequently fails to address the types of issues about which policy makers are most concerned. These types of limitations, however, apply to any number of policy questions, and our view is that it is better to be guided by what is known and to be concerned about

what is not known than it is to rest public policy decisions on intuition, commitment, and personal experience. We look first at the evidence related to whether formal teacher preparation can and does make a difference in the quality of teaching and learning in schools. Because the answer to that question appears to be affirmative, we will then turn to an exploration of strategies by which this difference can be enhanced. In particular we will examine three sets of reform proposals aimed at (a) improving the quality of students who get into and out of teacher programs, (b) extending and/or upgrading the curriculum of teacher preparation, and (c) almost independent of the content, teaching would-be teachers differently.

We do not deal with all of the types of research presently being conducted on teacher education and teaching that might be used to infer new directions. We have chosen to limit our review to studies that provide evidence that directly links teacher preparation programs to improvements in teaching or to student achievement. This constraint rules out dozens of studies based on teachers' own evaluations of their preparation as well as studies of how teacher education influences teacher attitudes or their academic achievement. It also excludes a growing body of interesting and useful research on how and why teachers make decisions that theoretically should influence their effectiveness. Our interest, in short, is more in how teacher education might enhance student learning than in how it might affect teachers.

DOES TEACHER EDUCATION MAKE A DIFFERENCE?

At the heart of the move to change the participants and the programs that prepare teachers is the assumption that teacher preparation is basically a waste of time. Though such an assessment is based to some extent on the frailties of teacher preparation programs, much of it seems to come from the view that teaching is an art rather than a science and can best be learned, as most college professors say they learned it, on the job.

There are two types of studies that address the question: Do preservice preparation programs teach teachers to teach effectively? The first of these involves comparisons on the effectiveness of teachers who participate in teacher education programs with the effectiveness of teachers who have little or no formal preservice preparation. The second body of research is composed of studies focused on efforts to teach preservice teachers particular ways of improving instructional practices.

Overall Effects of Teacher Preparation

To determine the overall effects of teacher preparation programs on teacher competence, most researchers compare the performance of regularly and provisionally certified teachers. Provisionally certified teachers, depending on the state, may have little or no formal preparation or they may be required to demonstrate progress toward satisfying the regular requirements for certification. Thus, the education courses and practical experiences of "provisional teachers" differ substantially within and among studies, and few studies explicitly take this into account. Nonetheless, comparing provisionally certified and regularly certified teachers provides the best way we have of assessing the overall effects of preservice teacher education on teacher performance.

Thirteen studies that compare regularly and provisionally certified teachers were reviewed. Four of these dealt directly with student achievement (Hall, 1962; Denton and Lacina, 1984; Taylor, 1957; Shim, 1965). The other studies used various formal rating systems administered by principals or trained observers to assess teacher performance (Gray, 1962; LuPone, 1961; Gerlock, 1964; Copley, 1974; Bledsoe, Cox and Burnham, 1967; Beery, 1960; Massey and Vineyard, 1958; two studies by Cornett, 1984).

In all but two of these studies (Shim, 1965; Cornett, 1984), regularly certified teachers rank higher in effectiveness than teachers with less formal training. Shim (1965) studied 89 elementary school teachers and found that the students taught by the uncertified teachers scored higher on tests of academic achievement. Shim also found that students of teachers with lower grade point averages tested better than students of teachers with higher grade point averages. Cornett (1984) compared principals' rankings of provisionally certified and regularly certified teachers in North Carolina and found no difference in the teachers' performance.

The investigations on teacher education effects do not represent a strong body of research. For example, most studies comparing teachers prepared through education courses and those not formally trained do not seek to control for possible differences in the intelligence or general academic competence of the teachers. This weakness in the research, however, is unlikely to result in overstating the positive effects of teacher education. Other background or context variables that might account for differences in teacher effectiveness are infrequently accounted for in selecting samples or analyzing data. For example, in a recent study (that was misreported in the national press), Cornett (1984) compared a principal's ranking of a small sample of regularly and provisionally certified teachers teaching in an urban Georgia school system. The regularly certified teachers were judged substantially more competent than the teachers with less professional training, but they also were more experienced in the classroom.

Evaluation of teacher expertise is an imprecise process. Some scholars suggest that evaluations are poor predictors of teachers' ability to foster student achievement (Soar, Medley, and Coker, 1983). On the other hand, little evidence exists to support the idea that teacher evaluations are invalid indicators of teachers' effectiveness; at least in two strong studies researchers found that principals rated higher those teachers whose students achieved greater growth in academic achievement (Armor et al., 1976; Murnane, 1975). Most of the procedures for evaluating teachers used in these studies rate teachers on their use of instructional strategies found to be correlated with student achievement.

Because the research reviewed examined a broad range of teacher behaviors, and because measures of effectiveness are not specifically tied, in most cases, to those behaviors, the available evidence does not allow identification of how differences in teachers' capabilities that might be related to their preservice preparation accounted for differences in their performance. Quite clearly, teachers learn to do some things through their education courses that might reasonably be expected to improve student achievement.[1]

Can Teacher Education Programs Teach Instructional Strategies?

The just-cited evidence that teacher preparation programs make a difference would be more persuasive if it could be shown that specific lessons and strategies that preservice teachers learn are reflected subsequently in their classroom performance.

Numerous studies show that particular efforts by education schools to structure preservice teacher learning have the desired effects on student teacher behavior in the short-run (Murphy, 1972; Francke, 1971; Collins, 1976; Gabrys, 1978; Joyce and Weil, 1972; Sweitzer, 1982; Howard, 1965; and Wal-

drop, 1978, Millett, 1969). The question of whether teachers take these capabilities into the classroom and sustain their use is another matter. Some preparation programs clearly have staying power (Adams, 1982; Hord and Hall, 1978), but others do not (Fullan, 1982). Overall, there is very good reason to believe that much of what prospective teachers learn in their formal college training is not transferred to their classroom behavior or even that many of the specific skills they acquire do not survive practice teaching (Locke, 1984). What schools of education can do to promote successfully the utilization and further development of the knowledge and skills they teach is not addressed adequately by the research; however, many teacher educators believe that continuing support during the first one or two years of teaching, the "induction period," is essential.

Summary

It seems clear that teachers who participate in preservice teacher preparation programs are more likely to be (or to be perceived by administrators as) more effective than teachers who have little or no formal training. Further, efforts to teach preservice teachers specific skills and knowledge invariably appear to be effective, at least in the short run.

PREPARING DIFFERENT PEOPLE TO BECOME TEACHERS

Many of the proposals for improving teacher education derive from the same logic that inspires the notion that we could have better prisons if we had better prisoners. Most of these proposals seem to be based on two assumptions:

1. restricting access to and exit from schools

of education would increase the number of academically able people who become teachers and this, in turn, would improve the quality of teaching in our schools; and,

2. more academically able students could handle more intellectually demanding courses.

The first of these assumptions seems reasonable, but we know of no study that demonstrates that the curricula of schools of education vary because of differences in academic selectivity.

The validity of the second assumption depends fundamentally on the development of screening mechanisms that discriminate between would-be teachers on the basis of their potential for instructional effectiveness and on the development of benefits and incentives that will attract able persons who do not now pursue teaching as a career.

SCREENING FOR POTENTIAL TEACHING EFFECTIVENESS

The measures traditionally used to screen students for admission and certification, and those most often advocated by state legislatures seeking reform, are overall scores on standardized admission tests, grade point averages, performance on the National Teacher Examination (NTE), or faculty evaluations of student teachers. The available research does not, however, provide much reason to believe that teachers' performance is correlated with scores on these measures. On the other hand, there is some reason to believe that teachers' or teacher candidates' verbal ability is correlated with student performance.

In general, principals' or supervisors' ratings of teacher performance are not related to scores on conventional measures of aca-demic aptitude such as the American College Testing *ACT* examinations, the Scholastic Aptitude Test *SAT* (Baker, 1970; Ducharme, 1970; Maguire, 1966), the Miller Analogies Test *MAT* (Young, 1977) or standardized achievement tests (Baker, 1970). Piper and O'Sullivan (1981) did find that National Teacher Examination *NTE* scores correlated positively with student teachers' ratings by university supervisors. (.43).

Evidence on the relationship between teacher performance on the job, as measured by principal's and trained observer's ratings, and college grade point averages is mixed. Some studies find a small positive association (Massey and Vineyard, 1958; Ducharme, 1970; Siegel, 1969; Druva and Anderson, 1983), and others find no relationship (Thacker, 1965; Baker, 1970), or a negative relationship (Shim, 1965; Cornett, 1984). Denton and Smith (1984) found no relationship between the grades of either education majors or nonmajors and the cognitive attainment of the students they taught.

Evidence on the ability of faculty who supervise student teachers to identify prospective teachers who will be evaluated highly by their on-the-job supervisors is also mixed (Thacker, 1965; Ducharme, 1970; Maguire, 1966).

Some researchers have found that supervisor's or principal's ratings of teacher or student performance are positively related to a student's score on the National Teacher Examination (Piper and Sullivan, 1981). Other studies, however, have found no such relationships (Thacker, 1965; Ducharme, 1970).

Evidence on the relationship between teacher scores on the NTE and student achievement is also limited and mixed. Lins (1946) and Sheehan and Marcus (1978) found a significant positive relationship between NTE scores an student achievement. Other studies, however, show no relationship between NTE scores and student achievement (Summers and Wolfe, 1977; Pugach and Raths, 1983). Ayers and Qualls (1979), Andrews, Blackmon and Mackey (1980), and Ducharme (1970) found an inverse relationship between teacher NTE scores and student achievement. The only study we could find regarding the validity to the revised NTE shows no significant relationship between teacher scores and either student gains in achievement or observers' assessments of teacher performance (Lovelace, 1984).

Many states have developed or are developing common tests of professional knowledge. Georgia is one of the first states to take this step. Little, however, is known about the ability of these tests to predict teacher effectiveness. Cornett (1984) recently examined the relative performance of Georgia teachers who were graduates of arts and science and teacher education programs on teacher certification tests. On a test of individuals' knowledge of their teaching fields, arts and science students with bachelor's degrees scored (.7) of a point higher than their teacher education peers (79.3 to 78.6). On the same test, teacher education students with master's degrees outperformed the master's degree arts and science educated teachers by 2.5 points.

In 1963, Getzels and Jackson reviewed the existing research on the association between teacher intelligence and effectiveness and found little evidence of such a relationship. More recent research, however, shows a modest relationship between the verbal ability of teachers and the verbal test scores of students, especially low income minority students (Summers and Wolfe, 1977; Winkler, 1972; McLaughlin and Marsh, 1978; Murnane and Phillips, 1978; Hanushek, 1977; Bruno and Doscher, 1981; Coleman et al., 1966). These findings are reinforced by an earlier study of Massey and Vineyard (1958) showing that principals ranked higher teachers who scored well on tests of English expression. (This research conflicts with the evidence that there is no relationship between the overall SAT scores and teacher performance, although the SAT scores include performance on mathematical tasks.)

In summary, raising admission standards to teacher education programs and testing teachers' knowledge prior to certification are among the proposed teaching preparation reforms on the nation's agenda, but there is little evidence that conventional ways of screening teachers—except, perhaps, tests of teachers' verbal ability—have predictable results. The research on this issue is limited, both in volume and quality, but is suggestive either of a need for caution or the need for more study before firm admission standards are set. Further, there is simply no way to know whether minimal standards for admission, either to college or to the teaching profession, would result in denying access to persons who would not subsequently be successful teachers.

It is difficult to know what the cut-off scores on various types of tests should be for admission to teacher education or for entry to the profession, but it is very clear that to the extent that such tests raise minimum standards of knowledge and competence, they will also restrict the supply of teachers (Ekstrom and Goertz, 1985; and Manski, 1985). At a time when an overall teacher shortage of significant proportions is anticipated (Darling-Hammond, 1984), efforts to improve teacher education by insisting upon greater selectivity will result in teacherless classrooms unless there are significant changes in both the intrinsic and extrinsic rewards teachers receive. The effects of such screens on the entry of minority persons to careers in education will be, and already have been, dramatic.

It seems likely that entry screens are a permanent feature of the teacher preparation landscape; nevertheless, it behooves teacher educators to be clear about what traits and competencies teachers should possess. When this is done, it is likely that more equitable and valid ways of assessing whether teacher candidates meet these standards can be developed.

Of course, there may be reasons for increasing college admission and career entry standards other than screening out persons who are likely to be ineffective teachers. These include gaining more status for teachers generally, setting basic levels of academic competence because teachers often serve as models for their students, or allowing the introduction of a more academically rigorous curriculum into teacher preparation.

TEACHING TEACHER CANDIDATES DIFFERENT THINGS

Critics of teacher education who are not involved in the preparation of teachers often focus on the curriculum that they variously characterize as being excessive in its emphasis on teaching methods, short on depth in the subjects teachers will teach, and insufficiently rigorous. Many teacher educators are critical of teacher education curricula on the grounds that so much more is known about teaching now than was the case a few short years ago, yet teacher candidates spend little time learning this new knowledge. The inadequate time given to professional studies is attributed both to the limited time available for coursework and to the fact that many faculty members are not familiar with recent research. Proposals for change in teacher education curricula are of three general types:

1. More emphasis should be placed on developing subject matter expertise.

2. More courses should be taken in the liberal arts.

3. More time should be given to the development of knowledge about teaching and the capacity to teach.

As we noted above, other more radical proposals are on the agenda that assume that not much is to be learned about teaching that cannot be learned on the job, perhaps in an apprenticeship to a "master teacher." The research cited earlier concerning the relative differences in the performance or in the effectiveness of teachers who have been certified in conventional ways as compared to teachers who did not complete a teacher education program suggests that improving rather than abandoning preservice teacher education would be more efficacious for student learning.[2]

Greater Subject Matter Expertise

It seems sensible to assert that one must know what one is teaching to be effective. But, how well must one know it? Most secondary teachers take a substantial number of courses in the field for which they are certified. Must a person major in the field he or she plans to teach? Must elementary teachers know calculus to teach arithmetic? Unfortunately, the available research is not very helpful in answering these important questions.

The most extensive assessment of the effects of subject matter knowledge on teaching effectiveness is a recent meta-analysis of 65 studies of science education (Druva and Anderson, 1983). Three conclusions from this study seem most relevant to our concerns with teacher education programs.

1. There is a relationship between teacher preparation programs and what their graduates do as teachers. Science courses, education courses, and overall academic perfor-

mance are positively associated with successful teaching.

2. The relationship between teacher training in science and cognitive student outcome is progressively higher in higher level science courses.

3. The most striking overall characteristic of the results . . . is the pattern of low correlations across a large number of variables involved. (p. 478)

With respect to the teaching of other subjects, the relationship between teacher expertise and teacher performance is not clear from the research. Massey and Vineyard (1958) found positive but small relationships as did Begle (1972) who characterized the association he found as "educationally insignificant." Maguire (1966), Siegel (1969), and Eisenberg (1977) found no or negative relationships between teacher knowledge (as measured by grade point averages and standardized tests) and student achievement. The General Accounting Office (1984) cites a 1983 synthesis of research by Colin Byrne that it characterizes as finding "no consistent relationship between the knowledge of teachers and the achievement of their students" (p. 33).

We emphasize, again, that this does not mean that good teaching can occur when teachers do not know their subject. The idea that the knowledge now typically required for certification in a given field contributes to teacher effectiveness finds support in the study by Hawk, Coble and Swanson that is reported in this issue of the *Journal*, which concludes that students of mathematics teachers who were certified "infield" showed higher achievement gain than the students of teachers who were certified to teach but did not hold mathematics certification.

In summary, the research suggests that knowing the subject matter does not necessarily make a person a good teacher of that subject. Furthermore, it seems reasonable to conclude that teachers with good instructional capabilities would be more effective if they had in-depth knowledge of the subjects they teach. This is, logically enough, more true of teachers of advanced courses. The research, however, provides little reason to believe that increasing teachers' knowledge of their subjects beyond that typically required for certification will significantly increase teacher effectiveness.

More Course Work in the Liberal Arts

Who can disagree with the idea that teachers should be well educated? For many people, being well educated means having a broad liberal arts education. Thus, it is not surprising to see the argument being made that professional teacher education plays too great a part in a prospective teacher's undergraduate education. We could not find any evidence in research on teacher education specifically or undergraduate education more generally that would provide support for the idea that a broad liberal arts education promotes the development of the values, analytical skills, love of learning, or other personal and intellectual characteristics one might reasonably attribute to teachers who care about their students and understand what it takes to facilitate learning.

The absence of evidence that greater emphasis on the liberal arts in the education of prospective teachers would result in greater teacher effectiveness does not, of course, prove that such changes are undesirable. Neither the empirical nor the theoretical case has been made. Moreover, recent research on the courses liberal arts students actually take raises doubts about the breadth and rigor of the typical undergraduate curriculum (Galumbos, Cornett, and Spitler, 1985). We hasten to add that we personally endorse, for reasons of our own, the idea that teachers should have to satisfy broad distribution requirements typically required of liberal arts students who major in an academic discipline. Furthermore, we see no reason why courses classified as "professional" could not be as intellectually rigorous and theoretically rich as courses described as "liberal arts."

Increasing the Pedagogical Components of Teacher Preparation

Much has been learned about teaching in recent years. Comprehensive reviews of the research include Brophy and Good (in press), Hawley and Rosenholtz (1984), MacKenzie (1983), and Rosenshine (1983). The research has emboldened many teacher educators (and others) to call for a more extensive pedagogical component to preservice teacher education.

Space limitations do not permit an adequate discussion of the knowledge base that might be covered in the preparation of teachers. There are several recent efforts to identify the types of instructional strategies and the theory necessary to implement them effectively that should be covered, and there appears to be substantial agreement on the topics that should be addressed (Smith, 1983; Egbert and Kluender, 1984; Berliner, 1985). Several researchers advocate that in addition to knowledge and competence in instructional strategies, teacher preparation programs should focus upon teacher decision making, attitude formation, and analytical skills (see, for example, Fenstermacher, in press; Feiman-Nemser and Buchmann, 1983; Tabachnick, et al., 1983; Joyce and Clift, 1984; Lanier, in press).

The many studies we noted above, demonstrating the efficacy of explicit efforts to train teacher candidates to believe in and to implement specific practices and habits of mind, provide good reason to believe that preservice teacher preparation programs, if structured

appropriately and if staffed by qualified faculty, can teach teachers the things being advocated as essential for beginning teachers to know and do. But no program of which we are aware has attempted to incorporate even a significant segment of the knowledge base many teacher educators argue that students should learn before they teach on their own.

Problems in Making Big Changes in What Preservice Teachers Learn

As we suggested earlier, little research exists to support the notion that making significant changes in what teachers learn before they begin their careers will significantly improve the quality of teaching experienced by most students in elementary and secondary schools. What if we did not let this deter us and we decided that significant changes should be required?

Few teacher educators or state agencies acknowledge that what is now taught teacher candidates should be eliminated (though this seems a worthy crusade). Furthermore, many proposals for improving the education of teachers urge at least two and often three of the types of curricular change previously discussed. The results, of course, are proposals to extend preservice teacher training to five and even six years.

Increasing the preservice period of required education naturally increases the cost of becoming a teacher. Because of earnings foregone, as well as tuition and other costs, requiring an additional year of college could double the cost of becoming a teacher. Unless salaries and other benefits are increased accordingly, requiring extended teacher preparation programs will likely result in a drop in both the quality and quantity of those entering the profession. Student stipends or other rewards could reduce those declines but could also result in a reallocation of funds from current priorities to teacher preparation.

Billions of dollars are involved, and a debate about the alternative uses of these funds vis-a-vis their potential impact on student learning seems to be in order.

The idea that significant additions to what teacher candidates should know and be able to do before embarking on a career in education not only has large economic costs, but there is reason to question whether students can learn and effectively transfer to practice all or even much of the pedagogical knowledge and skills that would be taught in extended programs. Considerable evidence exists that experienced teachers think differently about their work than do novices (see, for example, Koehler, 1985; Leinhardt, 1983; Erickson, 1984; Sprinthall and Thies-Sprinthall, 1983). Teachers may learn some things best, such as cooperative learning strategies, once they have an experiential base upon which to build.

TEACHING TEACHERS DIFFERENTLY

Whatever the content of teacher preparation programs, assuming it has some reasonable link to teacher performance, the fact remains that some ways of facilitating the learning of teacher candidates are more effective than others.

It seems safe to say that as teacher educators we frequently do not practice what we preach. That is, one seldom sees teacher educators modeling interactive teaching strategies, cooperative learning techniques, or problem-solving skills. Efforts to strengthen preparation programs must incorporate a strong modeling component and that modeling should reflect the body of research findings with respect to mastery learning, individualized instruction, cooperative grouping, competency based education, microteaching, and other approaches documented as effective

in strengthening prospective teachers' knowledge and skills. We draw attention from a research perspective to two of these approaches: competency based teacher education and microteaching. Other excellent reviews are available that support and provide greater documentation for the points we describe (see Gage, 1978). We then turn to the important problem of helping student teachers transfer what they learn during teacher education courses to their classroom behavior.

Competency Based Teacher Education

Generally, Competency Based Teacher Education (CBTE) refers to specific efforts to train prospective teachers to acquire competencies believed to be associated with effective teaching. The logic of this approach is similar to the pedagogy involved in teaching basic skills in elementary schools: be clear about what is to be learned, design lessons that fit that objective, teach the lesson, test for learning, provide feedback, redesign the lesson, and teach again. By the early 1970s, CBTE and its equivalents were seen by many teacher educators as the one best way to professionalize teacher preparation. But, CBTE came under attack for being too technical and for leading to the increasing specification and proliferation of skills that had no compelling link to student learning (cf. Sarason, 1978–79; Hamilton, 1973, as cited in Bush and Enemark, 1975). The idea that CBTE lacked a validated knowledge base has considerably less credibility now than it did six or seven years ago when attacks on CBTE were in full swing. This fact, plus the increasing propensity of states and school systems to develop performance-based teacher evaluation programs that spell out specific teaching behaviors, suggests that CBTE (no doubt in various disguises) is likely to be born again.

Research on the effects of CBTE on teacher attitudes and behavior seems to show positive results (Adams, 1982; Joyce, Wald and Weil, 1981; Piper and O'Sullivan, 1981; Borg, 1972).

Microteaching

Microteaching can take many forms but it essentially involves a prospective teacher's organizing and delivering a short lesson. Often, specific competencies are to be demonstrated in the lesson, such as planning, interactive questioning, etc., and the lesson is evaluated accordingly. Microteaching is, in short, a simulation technique that focuses on particular learning objectives for the teacher candidate through which evaluation and feedback are provided.

In general, it appears that microteaching—some versions of which are called minicourses—is an effective pedagogical device (Copeland, 1975; Boeck, 1972; Borg, 1972; Blankenship, 1970; Emmer and Millett, 1968; Kocylowski, 1970), although the acquisition of teaching competence does *not* always occur (Kallenbach and Gall, 1969).

One of the virtues of microteaching appears to be its facilitation of immediate feedback about an analysis of performance. As Gage and Winne (1975) conclude: "Evidence for the efficacy of feedback about teaching performance is fairly consistent. When the information is explicit, clear, and keyed to specific aspects of teaching behavior, feedback results in improvement in the trainees' ability to perform according to a model of teaching" (pp. 160–161). The usefulness of frequent and precise feedback as an instrument for promoting the improvement of teaching effectiveness is not limited, of course, to microteaching (cf. Flanders, 1970).

Student Teaching

Student teaching is usually identified by new teachers as the most rewarding and useful aspect of their preservice professional preparation (Griffin et al., 1983; Nemser, 1983). These claims by teachers, plus widespread skepticism about the rigor and scientific basis of many formal courses in teacher preparation, probably contributed to a rash of contemporary proposals that would place apprenticeship at the core of teacher preparation. The existing research, however, provides little reason to believe that supervised practical experience, in itself and as it is encountered in most student teaching situations, is a very effective way to educate teachers.

A decade ago, Peck and Tucker (1973) reviewed research on teacher education and concluded that "by the end of student teaching, there are some almost universally reported decrements in attitude and in teaching behavior, as compared with the starting position of students prior to their field experience" (p. 967). This conclusion still seems generally accurate. For example, in what may be the most intensive study of practice teaching yet conducted, Griffin and his colleagues (1983) found that little change occurred in the student teachers as a result of their field involvement.

Neither Griffin's research nor any other study we could find linked specific characteristics of the student teaching experience to teacher performance. The research suggests, further, that the role of practice teaching in the preparation of teachers may be over-rated.

Theoretically, student teaching, if structured properly, could engender teacher effectiveness. But it may also seem that the problems and costs of successfully implementing practice teaching programs are so great that other processes for achieving teacher education objectives should be explored more fully.

Induction

Some of the contributions that teacher preparation programs make to teacher effectiveness may be undermined by the experience first-year teachers have when they are inducted into the profession. As with practice teaching, the induction phase of a teacher's career more often narrows than expands the range of instructional strategies teachers perceive they can employ. The induction period of teaching is so chaotic and absent of support that teachers often focus on instructional strategies that stress controlling student behavior rather than facilitating student learning (Hawley and Rosenholtz, 1984, chap. 2). Induction is becoming a focus of attention as teacher educators come to think about teacher education along a professional continuum from preservice to inservice (Hall, 1982; Tisher, Fyfield, and Taylor, 1979). At the very least, knowledge about the problems that beginning teachers face as they start their teaching careers can provide important information for the design and evaluations of preservice teacher preparation programs.

Growing evidence indicates that unless teacher educators can mediate the experience teachers have in their first one or two years of teaching, much of what is taught in preservice courses will be seen by teachers as irrelevant (or will be undone). What implications does this conclusion have for teacher education? First, curriculum design can take into account the types of concerns teachers are likely to have by warning them about these realities and providing them with some analytical and problem-solving skills they can use to deal with the conditions that might undermine their effectiveness (cf. Stallings, 1984). Second, students should be introduced to the research on teaching in ways that provide them with an understanding of the variety of options they have, the contingencies that mediate the use of specific practices, and the theory that explains the efficacy of the practices. Efforts to increase the conceptual understanding of teaching by increasing

awareness of proven models and practices (Joyce and Showers, 1981; Joyce and Showers, 1982) and by training that includes theory, demonstration, practice, feedback and classroom application (Showers, 1983) seem likely to be productive. More fundamentally, however, we need to find ways to support the professional growth of teachers once they are surrounded by students of their own.

CONCLUSION

Despite the fact that teacher preparation programs have come under seemingly unprecedented criticism in recent months, the available research suggests that among students who become teachers, those enrolled in formal preservice preparation programs are more likely to be effective than those who do not have such training. Moreover, almost all well planned and executed efforts within teacher preparation programs to teach students specific knowledge or skills seem to succeed, at least in the short run.

The research we reviewed raises questions about the efficacy of a number of popular proposals for reforming teacher education, but it does *not* add up to a defense of teacher preparation as it exists in most institutions. Even the most aggressive apologists for teacher education acknowledge that improvements can and should be made in virtually all programs. Nonetheless, the research suggests, at least, that preservice teacher education programs can make contributions to effective teaching.

Based on our understanding of the research reviewed here and on other evidence relating the transfer of training to practice and adult learning, the model we find most intriguing is one that involves the following components:

1. A strong liberal arts undergraduate education.
2. The development of competence in the subjects to be taught, which would include the equivalent of a major in the primary field for high school teachers.
3. Professional education of 8–10 courses, many with a related practicum, to be taken either as an undergraduate or after the baccalaureate is received.
4. A year-long internship in a "teaching school" that would be similar in function and culture to a teaching hospital for physicians.
5. A one or two-year induction period with special support from the employing school system and a school of education.
6. Continuing professional development related to the learning needs of individuals that is distributed and organized in accord with their specific present and future instructional functions and with leadership roles of the individual.

Such a model, which obviously needs more specificity, would allow teacher educators to rethink what is needed to be taught to teachers at different stages of their development as professionals. We suspect, for example, that educational philosophy is a course best taught to teachers with two or three years of experience.

Hundreds of studies related to teacher education are available, but the lessons they teach do not add up to a particular model for improvement around which teacher educators should rally. Rather, this seems to be an opportune time for experimentation—and evaluation. If some models or elements prove to facilitate student learning more cost-effectively than others, we will be in a strong position to prescribe particular structures for implementing those strategies.

ENDNOTES

1. Popham (1971a) developed a set of *experiments* to examine whether pedagogical training adds to teaching effectiveness of persons with subject matter expertise. This research has been the subject of considerable debate (Glass, 1974; Turner, 1973; and Bausell and Moody, 1973). We are content to treat the work of Popham and his replicators as heuristic rather than determinative primarily because of its narrow focus and the artificial settings in which most of it was conducted.
2. For a research-based defense of teacher education, see Haberman, 1984.
3. The ground work for the developmental model has been laid—see for example, Fuller and Brown (1975), Gehrke (1981), Sprinthall and Thies-Sprinthall (1983).

REFERENCES

Adams, R. D. (1982). *Teacher development: A look at changes in teacher perception across time.* Paper presented at the annual meeting of the American Educational Research Association, New York.

Andrews, J. W., Blackmon, C. R., & Mackey, J. A. (1980). Preservice performance and the NTE. *Phi Delta Kappan, 61* (5), 358–359.

Armor, D., Conry-Oseguera, P., Cox, M., King, N., McDonnell, L., Pascal, A., Pauley, E., & Zellman, G. (1976). *Analysis of the school preferred reading program in selected Los Angeles minority schools.* Santa Monica, Calif.: Rand Corporation.

Ayers, J. B., & Qualls, G. S. (1979). Concurrent and predictive validity of the National Teacher Examinations. *Journal of Educational Research, 73* (2), 86–92.

Baker, L. W. (1970). *An analysis of some assumed predictors of success in teaching.* Doctoral thesis, United States International University.

Bausell, R., & Moody, W. (1973). Are teacher preparatory institutions necessary? *Phi Delta Kappan, 54* (5), 298.

Beery, J. R. (1960). *Professional preparation and*

effectiveness of beginning teachers. Coral Gables, FL: University of Miami.

Begle, E. G. (1972). *Teacher knowledge and student achievement in algebra* (School Mathematics Study Group Reports No. 9). Stanford University.

Berliner, D. (1985). *Reform in teacher education: The case for pedagogy.* Tucson: University of Arizona.

Blankenship, M. L. D. (1970). *The use of microteaching with interaction analysis as a feedback system for improving questioning skills.* Doctoral thesis, Pennsylvania State University.

Bledsoe, J. C., Cox, J. V., & Burnham, R. (1967). *Comparison between selected characteristics and performance of provisionally and professionally certified beginning teachers in Georgia.* Athens, GA.: University of Georgia. (ERIC Document Reproduction Service No. ED 015 553)

Boeck, M. A. (1972). *Stability of behavioral change: One year after precision micro-teaching.* Minneapolis: Minnesota University College of Education.

Borg, W. R. (1972). The minicourse as a vehicle for changing teacher behavior: A three-year follow-up. *Journal of Educational Psychology, 63,* 572–579.

Brophy, J., & Good, T. (in press). Teacher behavior and student achievement. In M. Wittrock (Ed.), *Handbook of research on teaching* (3rd ed.). New York: MacMillan.

Bruno, J. E., & Doscher, M. L. (1981). Contributing to the harms of racial isolation: Analysis of requests for teacher transfer in a large urban school district. *Education Administration Quarterly, 17* (2), 93–108.

Bush, R. N., & Enemark, P. (1975). Control and responsibility in teacher education. In K. Ryan (Ed.), *Teacher education: The Seventy-fourth yearbook of the National Society for the Study of Education.* Chicago: University of Chicago Press.

Byrne, C. (1983). *Teacher knowledge and teacher effectiveness: A literature review, theoretical analysis and discussion of research strategy.* Paper presented at the annual meeting of the Northeastern Educational Research Association, Ellenville, NY.

Coleman, J. S., Campbell, E. Q., Hobson, C. J., McPartland, J., Mood, A. M., Weinfeld, F. D., & York, R. L. (1966). *Equality of educational opportunity.* Washington, DC: U.S. Government Printing Office.

Collins, M. L. (1976). *The effects of training for enthusiasm displayed by preservice elementary teachers.* (ERIC Document Reproduction Service No. ED 129 773)

Copeland, W. D. (1975). The relationship between microteaching and student teacher classroom performance. *Journal of Educational Research, 68,* 289–293.

Copley, P. O. (1974). *A study of the effect of professional education courses in beginning teachers.* Springfield, MO: Southwest Missouri State University. (ERIC Document Reproduction Service No. ED 098 147)

Cornett, L. M. (1984). *A comparison of teacher certification test scores and performance evaluations for graduates in teacher education and in arts and sciences in three southern states.* Atlanta: Southern Regional Education Board.

Darling-Hammond, L. (1984). *Beyond the commissioned reports: The coming crisis in teaching.* Santa Monica, CA: Rand.

Denton, J. J., & Lacina, L. J. (1984). Quantity of professional education coursework linked with process measures of student teaching. *Teacher Education and Practice,* 39–64.

Denton, J. J., & Smith, N. L. (1984). *Alternative teacher preparation programs: A cost effective comparison.* Paper presented at the annual meeting of the American Educational Research Association, New Orleans.

Druva, C. A., & Anderson, R. D. (1983). Science teacher characteristics by teacher behavior and by student outcome: A meta-analysis of research. *Journal of Research in Science Teaching, 20* (5), 467–479.

Ducharme, R. J. (1970). *Selected preservice factors related to success of the beginning teacher.* Doctoral dissertation, Louisiana State and Agricultural and Mechanical College.

Egbert, R. L., & Kluender, M. M. (Eds.). (1984). *Using research to improve teacher education* (The

Nebraska Consortium). Washington, DC: Eric Clearinghouse on Teacher Education.

Eisenberg, T. A. (1977). Begle revisited: Teacher knowledge and student achievement in algebra. *Journal of Research in Mathematics Education,* 216–222.

Ekstrom, R. B., & Goertz, M. E. (1985). *The teacher supply pipeline: The view from four states.* Paper presented at the annual meeting of the American Educational Research Association, Chicago.

Emmer, E., & Millett, G. B. (1968). *An assessment of terminal performance in a teaching laboratory: A pilot study.* Austin: University of Texas, Research and Development Center.

Erickson, F. (1984). *Teachers' practical ways of seeing.* East Lansing: Michigan State University, College of Education.

Feiman-Nemser, S., & Buchmann, M. (1983). *Pitfalls of experience in teacher preparation* (Occasional Paper No. 65). East Lansing: Michigan State University, Institute for Research on Teaching.

Fenstermacher, G. (in press). Philosophy of research on teaching: Three aspects. In M. Wittrock (Ed.), *Handbook of research on teaching.* (3rd ed.). New York: MacMillan.

Flanders, N. A. (1970). *Analyzing teaching behavior.* Reading, Mass: Addison-Wesley Publishing Co.

Francke, E. L. (1971). *Pupil achievement and teacher behaviors: A formative evaluation of an undergraduate program in teacher preparation.* Doctoral thesis, University of Nebraska.

Fullan, M. (1982). *The meaning of educational change.* New York: Columbia University, Teachers College Press.

Fuller, F., & Brown, O. (1975). Becoming a teacher. In K. Ryan (Ed.), *Teacher education: The seventy-fourth yearbook of the National Society for the Study of Education.* Chicago: University of Chicago Press.

Gabrys, R. E. (1978). *The influence of a training intervention for business-like behavior on the business-like behavior and level of warmth of preservice elementary teachers.* Paper presented at the annual meeting of the Association of Teacher Educators, Las Vegas, January.

Gage, N. L. (1978). *The scientific basis for the art of teaching.* New York: Teachers College Press.

Gage, N. L., & Winne, P. H. (1975). Performance-based teacher education. In K. Ryan (Ed.), *Teacher education: The seventy-fourth yearbook of the National Society for the Study of Education.* Chicago: University of Chicago Press.

Galumbos, E., Cornett, L. M., & Spitler, H. D. (1985). *An analysis of transcripts of teachers and arts and sciences graduates.* Atlanta: Southern Regional Education Board.

Gehrke, N. (1981). A grounded theory of beginning teachers' role personalization through reference group relationships. *Journal of Teacher Education, 32,* 34–38.

General Accounting Office. (1984). *New directions for Federal programs to aid mathematics and science teaching.* (GAO/PEMD–84-5) Washington, DC: GAO.

Gerlock, D. E. (1964). *An analysis of administrators' evaluations of selected professionally and provisionally certified secondary school teachers.* Doctoral dissertation, Florida State University.

Getzels, J. W., & Jackson, P. W. (1963). The teacher's personality and characteristics. In N. Gage (Ed.). *Handbook of research on teaching,* (1st ed.). Chicago, IL: Rand-McNally.

Glass, G. (1974). Teacher effectiveness. In H. Walberg (Ed.), *Evaluating educational performance.* Berkeley, CA: McCutchan.

Gray, H. B. (1962). *A study of the outcomes of preservice education associated with three levels of teacher certification.* Doctoral dissertation, Florida State University.

Griffin, G. A., Barnes, S., Hughes, R., Jr., O'Neal, S., Defino, M., Edwards, S., & Hukill, H. (1985). *Clinical preservice teacher education: Final report of a descriptive study.* Austin: University of Texas, Research and Development Center for Teacher Education.

Haberman, M. (1984). *An evaluation of the rationale for required teacher education: Beginning teachers with and without teacher preparation.* Paper presented for the National Commission on Excellence in Teacher Education.

Hall, G. (1982). Induction: The missing link. *Journal of Teacher Education, 23* (3), 53–55.

Hall, H. O. (1962). *Effectiveness of fully certified and provisionally certified first-year teachers in teaching certain fundamental skills.* Doctoral dissertation, University of Florida.

Hamilton, P. D. (1973). *Competency-based teacher education.* Menlo Park, CA: Standard Research Institute.

Hanushek, E. (1977). The production of education, teacher quality and efficiency. In D. A. Erickson (Ed.), *Educational organization and administration.* Berkeley, CA: McCutchan.

Hawley, W. D., & Rosenholtz, S. J. (1984). Good schools: what research says about improving student achievement. *Peabody Journal of Education, 61* (4), 1–178.

Hord, S., & Hall, G. (Eds.). (1978). *Teacher education program evaluation and follow-up studies: A collection of current efforts.* Austin: University of Texas, Research and Development Center for Teacher Education.

Howard, J. L. (1965). *An analysis of change in teacher and pupil behavior: A study of the fifth-year program in teacher education at the University of North Carolina, 1963–64.* Doctoral dissertation, University of North Carolina at Chapel Hill.

Joyce, B. R., & Showers, B. (1981). *Teacher training research: Working hypotheses for program design and directions for further study.* Paper presented at the annual meeting of the American Educational Research Association, Los Angeles.

Joyce, B., & Showers, B. (1982). The coaching of teaching. *Educational Leadership, 40,* 4–10.

Joyce, B., & Cliff, R. (1984). The Phoenix agenda: Essential reform in teacher education. *Educational Researcher, 13* (4), 5–18.

Joyce, B., & Weil, M. (1972). *Models of teaching.* Englewood Cliffs, N.J.: Prentice Hall.

Joyce, B. R., Wald, R., & Weil, M. (1981). Can teachers learn repertoires of models of teaching? In B. R. Joyce, C. Brown, & L. Peck (Eds.), *Flexibility in teaching: An excursion into the nature of teaching and training.* New York: Longman.

Kallenbach, W. W., & Gall, M. D. (1969). Microteaching versus conventional methods in training elementary intern teachers. *Journal of Educational Research, 63,* 136–141.

Kocylowski, M. M. (1970). *A comparison of microteaching and conventional systems of preservice teacher education on teaching effectiveness.* Doctoral thesis, Wayne State University.

Koehler, V. (1985). Research on preservice teacher education. *Journal of Teacher Education, 36,* (1), 23–30.

Lanier, J. (in press). Research on Teacher Education. In M. Wittrock (Ed.), *Handbook of research on teaching.* (3rd ed.). New York: MacMillan.

Leinhardt, G. (1983). Novice and expert knowledge of individual student's achievement. *Educational Psychologist, 18,* 165–179.

Lins, L. J. (1946). The prediction of teaching efficiency. *Journal of Experimental Education, 15,* 2–60.

Locke, L. F. (1984). Research on teaching teachers: Where are we now. *Journal of Teaching in Physical Education, 2* (2), 1–86.

LuPone, L. J. (1961). A comparison of provisionally certified and permanently certified elementary school teachers in selected school districts in New York State. *Journal of Educational Research, 55,* 53–63.

MacKenzie, D. E. (1983). School effectiveness research: A synthesis and assessment. In R. Duttweiler (Ed.), *Educational productivity and school effectiveness.* Austin: The Southwest Educational Development Laboratory.

Maguire, J. W. (1966). *Factors in undergraduate teacher education related to success in teaching.* Doctoral dissertation, Florida State University.

Manski, C. (1985). *Academic ability, earnings and the decision to become a teacher: Evidence from the National Longitudinal Study of the High School Class of 1972* (Working Paper No. 1539). Cambridge, Mass.: National Bureau of Economic Research.

Massey, H. W., & Vineyard, E. E. (1958). Relationship between scholarship and first-year teaching success. *Journal of Teacher Education, 9,* 297–301.

McLaughlin, M. W., & Marsh, D. D. (1978). Staff development and school change. *Teachers College Record, 80* (1), 69–94.

Millett, G. B. (1969). *Comparison of teaching procedures for promoting teacher behavior and learner translation behavior.* Stanford, Calif.: Stanford University, School of Education.

Murnane, R. J. (1975). *The impact of school resources on the learning of inner-city children.* Cambridge, MA: Ballinger.

Murnane, R. J., & Phillips, B. R. (1978). *Effective teachers of inner city children: Who they are and what they do.* Princeton, NJ: Mathematica Policy Research.

Murphy, P. D. (1972). *Teaching strategies exhibited by first year teachers.* Fargo, ND: North Dakota State University.

Nemser, S. F. (1983). Learning to teach. In L. Shulman & G. Sykes (Eds.), *Handbook of teaching and policy.* New York: Longman.

Peck, R. F., & Tucker, J. A. (1973). Research on teacher education. In R. M. W. Travers (Ed.), *Handbook of research on teaching.* (2nd ed.). Chicago: Rand-McNally.

Piper, M. K., & O'Sullivan, P. D. (1981). The National Teacher Examination: Can it predict classroom performance? *Phi Delta Kappan, 62,* 401.

Popham, J. (1971). Performance tests of teaching proficiency: Rationale, development and validation. *American Educational Research Journal, 8* (1), 105–117.

Pugach, M. C., & Raths, J. E. (1983). Testing teachers: Analysis and recommendations. *Journal of Teacher Education, 34* (1), 37–43.

Rosenshine, B. (1983). Teaching functions in instructional programs. *Elementary School Journal, 83* (4), 335–351.

Sarason, S. B. (1978–79). Again, the preparation of teachers: Competency and job satisfaction. *Interchange, 10* (1), 1–11.

Sheehan, D. S., & Marcus, M. (1978). Teacher performance on the National Teacher Examinations and student mathematics and vocabulary achievement. *The Journal of Educational Research, 71,* 134–136.

Shim, C. P. (1965). A study of four teacher characteristics on the achievement of elementary school pupils. *Journal of Educational Research, 59,* 33–34.

Showers, B. (1983). *The transfer of training.* Paper presented at the annual meeting of the American Educational Research Association, Montreal.

Siegel, W. B. (1969). *A study of the relationship between selected undergraduate academic achievement variables and teaching success.* Doctoral dissertation, Washington State University.

Smith, D. C. (Ed.) (1983). *Essential knowledge for beginning educators.* Washington, DC: American Association of Colleges for Teacher Education.

Soar, R. S., Medley, D. M., & Coker, H. (1983). Teacher evaluation: A critique of currently used methods. *Phi Delta Kappan,* 239–246.

Sprinthall, N. A., & Thies-Sprinthall, L. (1983). The teacher as an adult learner: A cognitive-developmental view. In G. A. Griffin (Ed.), *Staff development: Eighty-second Yearbook of the National Society for the Study of Education.* Chicago: University of Chicago Press.

Stallings, J. (1984). Implications from the research on teaching for teacher preparation. In R. Egbert & M. Kluender (Eds.), *Using research to improve teacher education* (The Nebraska Consortium). Washington, DC: ERIC Clearinghouse on Teacher Education.

Summers, A. A., & Wolfe, B. L. (1977). Do schools make a difference? *American Economic Review, 67,* 639–542.

Sweitzer, G. L. (1982). *A meta-analysis of research on preservice and inservice science teacher education practices designed to produce outcomes associated with inquiry strategy.* Paper presented at the annual meeting of the National Association for Research in Science Teaching, Chicago.

Tabachnick, B., Zeichner, K., Densmore, K., & Hudak, G. (1983). *The development of teacher perspectives.* Paper presented at the annual meeting of the American Educational Research Association, Montreal.

Taylor, T. W. (1957). *A study to determine the relationships between growth in interest and achievement of high school science students and science teacher attitudes, preparation and experience.* Doctoral dissertation, North Texas State College.

Thacker, J. A. (1965). *A study of the relationship between principals' estimates of teaching efficiency and scores on National Teachers Examinations, academic averages, and supervisors' estimates of potential for selected teachers in North Carolina.* Doctoral dissertation, University of North Carolina, Chapel Hill.

Tisher, R., Ryfield, J., & Taylor, S. (1979). *Beginning to teach: The induction of beginning teachers in Australia* (Vols. 1 & 2). Canberra Australian Government Publishing Service.

Turner, R. (1973). Are educational researchers necessary? *Phi Delta Kappan, 54* (5), 299.

Winkler, D. (1972). *The production of human capital: A study of minority achievement.* Doctoral dissertation. University of California, Berkeley.

DISCUSSION QUESTIONS AND ACTIVITIES

1. According to Roth, what are the principal weaknesses of teacher education programs?
2. Three scenarios are presented by Roth. Which of the three is most likely to occur? Why?
3. What does teacher education need to demonstrate if it is to survive as a separate area of professional preparation?
4. Evertson, Hawley, and Zlotnik cite two reform strategies currently advocated. What educational consequences are likely to accrue should either of these be adopted?
5. What research evidence is available to show that teacher education programs make a difference in teacher effectiveness?
6. What likely effect will raising admission standards to teacher education programs and testing teachers' knowledge prior to certification have on the quality of teaching?
7. Will increasing teachers' knowledge of their subject beyond what is typically required for certification significantly increase teacher effectiveness? Why?
8. Why do Evertson, Hawley, and Zlotnik claim that the role of practice teaching in teacher preparation may be overrated?
9. Look at Evertson, Hawley, and Zlotnik's model (consisting of six components). What components would you accept? Reject? Explain why.
10. Gather data on changes in teacher education nationally, note salient trends, and report them to the class.
11. Analyze your own teacher education program as to whether research would actually support each aspect of the program.

SUGGESTED READINGS

Bestor, Arthur E. *Educational Wastelands.* Urbana: University of Illinois Press, 1953.

Carnegie Task Force on Teaching as a Profession. "A System of Pay, Autonomy, Career Opportunities." *Education Week* (May 21, 1986):11–18.

Conant, James B. *The Education of American Teachers.* New York: McGraw-Hill, 1963.

Houston, W. Robert, ed. *Exploring Competency-Based Education.* Berkeley, Calif.: McCutchan, 1974.

Koerner, James D. *The Miseducation of American Teachers.* Boston: Houghton Mifflin, 1963.

Lanier, Judith E. "Research on Teacher Education." In *Handbook of Research on Teaching,* 3rd ed., ed. M. C. Wittrock. New York: Macmillan, 1986, pp. 527–569.

Silberman, Charles E. *Crisis in the Class-*

room. New York: Vintage Books, 1970.

Teacher Education, ed. Kevin Ryan. 74th Yearbook, National Society for Study of Education, Pt. 2. Chicago: University of Chicago Press, 1975.

Tomorrow's Teachers: A Report of the Holmes Group. East Lansing, Mich.: Holmes Group, 1986.

11

Merit Pay

A number of national commission reports have expressed concern about teacher performance. *A Nation at Risk* (U.S. Government Printing Office, 1983) emphasized paying higher teacher salaries based on performance. Some school boards have taken the position that merit pay is a cost-effective approach of motivating teachers and providing higher quality instruction.

Merit pay rewards teachers with higher salaries for doing the same or a similar job better than their colleagues. *Career ladders* pay teachers more for performing duties different from those of their colleagues. Both plans require systematic, periodic assessment of faculty. In contrast, most school systems today base salary on formal education completed and the amount of teaching experience.

Proponents of merit pay argue that it stimulates individual improvement, rewards deserving teachers, promotes greater student achievement, and is consistent with practices in industry. Other reasons to support merit pay are that it is the main way to gain public support for higher salaries, and that such plans, when carefully developed, can be feasible.

Opponents suggest that merit pay will lead to politics and patronage rather than improved instruction, that there are not generally accepted criteria of teacher merit, that there are great difficulties in evaluating which of two good teachers is better, that evaluative judgment could be subjective and arbitrary, that the cost may be prohibitive if paid personnel are to do the rating, and that it may create serious morale problems.

In a 1986 Louis Harris poll, of the 72 percent of teachers who said that they were familiar with merit pay, 71 percent were opposed to such systems; 55 percent of principals agreed. Teachers were split in their views of career ladder programs, with 49 percent in favor and 46 percent opposed. Thus it can be seen that unless teacher attitudes change dramatically, teacher morale may decline under merit pay plans. Less threatening is the career ladder plan, which is being tried in a number of states and involves different levels of responsibility and pay for different jobs (such as probationary teacher as a classification for starting teachers, and master teacher for those who have demonstrated superior performance).

Merit Pay and Other Teacher Incentive Plans

Deborah Inman

Deborah Inman is Assistant Professor in the Department of Organizational and Administrative Studies at New York University.

The issue of merit pay is one of the most controversial in education today. The findings of the President's National Commission on Excellence in Education report, *A Nation at Risk: The Imperative for Educational Reform*, along with other national studies, have generated a momentum regarding quality education unlike any experienced in many years.

One of the underlying problems associated with the poor quality of public education is the low salary level of school teachers. As a result of these low salaries, many of the best teachers leave the classroom in an effort to upgrade their standard of living through other more lucrative employment. The departure of many competent teachers is one explanation for the lower standards of quality in our public schools. Merit pay was advanced by the Reagan administration as a solution to the issue of teacher competency, maintaining that such a plan would not only retrain the best teachers, but would also attract the "best and brightest" to the public schools. The education reform efforts of Governor Lamar Alexander of Tennessee and Governor Robert Graham of Florida added fuel to the flames and sparked various alternatives to teacher incentive plans nationwide. As a result, great interest in merit pay and other teacher incentive plans has been generated among school districts and across entire state systems.

Much of the blatant opposition to teacher incentive plans is caused by the confusion associated with traditional teacher merit pay schemes. This is largely due to the numerous discussions and the various commissions on merit pay. The fact that the concept of merit pay has continued to be rekindled time and again since its inception in 1908 suggests that while merit pay has not proven to be the answer to teacher competency, neither has it been completely discarded. The school districts that tried and then abandoned merit pay cited several reasons for doing so, including administrative problems, personnel problems, collective bargaining and financial problems. The area that created the most distress centered on personnel problems caused by unsatisfactory evaluation procedures, staff dissension and lack of proper funding.

In an effort to determine the feasibility of merit pay and other teacher incentive pay plans, a survey was conducted among nine local school districts with successful merit pay/teacher incentive programs. The survey was limited to school districts with successful

From Deborah Inman, *"Merit Pay and Other Teacher Incentive Plans,"* School Business Affairs 50 (October 1984):50–52. Reprinted by permission.

programs, in an effort to identify implementation problems and determine the feasibility of overcoming them. The selected district-wide administrators represented Bryan Independent School District, Texas; Charlotte-Mecklenburg School District, North Carolina; Evanston Public School, Illinois; Houston Independent School District, Texas; King William County Public Schools, Virginia; Ladue Public Schools, Missouri; Labanon Public Schools, Connecticut; Penn Manner School District, Pennsylvania; and Selling Public Schools, Oklahoma.

GENERAL FEASIBILITY OF MERIT PAY AND OTHER TEACHER INCENTIVE PLANS

There was unanimous agreement among the respondents that merit pay and other teacher incentive plans are indeed feasible. The most cited supporting statements were 1) It is the only way to gain public support for higher salaries for all teachers and 2) Administrators, teachers, parents and students already know who the best teachers are, so why can't we pay them more? After all, equal pay for unequals perpetuates inequality. Although everyone agreed that these programs are feasible, there were, of course, a few qualifying statements such as 1) Given reasonable criteria for distribution of funds and a reasonable means of implementing the criteria, merit pay and other teacher incentive plans are feasible; 2) They are feasible, but not without problems brought by opposition and 3) It will work if you define teachers as managers but will fail if you define teachers as workers. These responses suggest that even though merit pay and other teacher incentive plans are difficult, at best, to implement, local administrators are pleased with their plans and believe that, in general, merit

pay and other teacher incentive plans are feasible.

STATEWIDE VERSUS SCHOOL-WIDE OR DISTRICT-WIDE PLANS

The majority (67 percent) of the local administrators did not believe that statewide plans would be a better alternative to school-wide and district-wide plans. In fact, they were adamantly opposed to the concept of a statewide plan. Other responses were mixed, suggesting that the state should give support and direction, but the actual plan should be adapted to the district. It was believed that although statewide plans have merit, district-wide plans allow more diversity and can be designed to address needs at the district level. It was also emphasized that the teachers may feel more ownership of locally developed plans, a feeling which could contribute to the success of the plan. Only one respondent supported state-funded plans over individual locally funded plans.

The most commonly cited reasons by those who opposed statewide plans were 1) Most statewide plans create operational and paperwork burdens that tax the small district manpower; 2) Statewide plans are so unwieldy that they are not cost effective and 3) An effective plan should never be imposed on teachers or handed down from a central office or state agency. The job of the state should be to provide incentives for many small pilot projects, and then to carefully evaluate them. Pilot plans should be implemented in districts in order to discover those ideas that *will* work, and to eliminate those that will not. These responses are not surprising, considering the controversy that surrounds the shift of control and responsibility from the local to the state level in recent years.

POLITICAL FEASIBILITY OF MERIT PAY AND OTHER TEACHER INCENTIVE PLANS

Unanimous support from the local administrators was shown regarding the political feasibility of merit pay and other teacher incentive plans. In fact, most respondents indicated that teacher incentive plans are not only feasible but are a political necessity since parents, patrons and other taxpayers are demanding greater productivity. In response to the question, "What should be the roles, responsibilities, and impact of government and governmental agencies (state and national) in school improvement through teacher incentives?", the majority advocated various types of support by state and national governmental agencies. Only one percent strongly opposed any involvement from governmental agencies and that was based on the assumption that the plan would succeed or fail based on local support and involvement.

Suggestions from those supporting state and national involvement include 1) The state and federal governments should encourage districts to adopt merit and incentive plans, but not mandate them; 2) There should be sufficient incentives to attract, continually train, and provide proper resources for the teachers. Assistance in the form of developmental grants is one alternative at both the state and national levels and 3) The federal government should be involved in problem identification and clarification (research and evaluation).

ECONOMIC FEASIBILITY OF MERIT PAY AND OTHER TEACHER INCENTIVES PLANS

The respondents unanimously agreed that merit pay and other teacher incentive plans are economically feasible. However, the tone of their responses was not necessarily supportive of positive results. For example, merit pay in the form of small bonuses was said to be economically feasible, but a substantial incentive system was much more difficult to fund. Concern was expressed that merit pay might inadvertently be used to hold down salaries for the majority. Another perspective suggested that the cost of providing extra pay for exceptional teachers would actually be very low, since only a small percentage of the teachers would be eligible. This does not address the problems of the majority of teachers who would not be eligible, because they did not qualify or because there was a cap on the number of teachers who could be considered. It was therefore stressed that in order for a plan to be effective, each district must have an adequate (comparable to other school districts in geographical area) employee benefits package for all teachers before implementing merit pay for a few. Regarding cost effectiveness, there was concurrence that merit pay can result in a more efficient return for each school dollar, especially given the public's concern for teacher accountability. The public will support higher salaries for competence and experience but not higher salaries for everyone. The public demands that we reward differentially those teachers who exhibit meritorious service.

IMPACT OF MERIT PAY AND OTHER TEACHER INCENTIVE PLANS

Regarding the positive potential and limitations that such proposals may have for reshaping the teaching profession and improving the quality of our schools, the responses were varied. However, two major points did emerge. First, that without some radical restructuring, schools are certain to get worse. Doing something, therefore, is better than doing nothing. Secondly, the catchword of the past decade has been "accountability." Plans must be formulated to improve the profession. Evidence of such should be publicized and supported.

The positive potentials of merit pay and other teacher incentive plans include: 1) To keep master teachers in the classroom by recognizing them and paying them more; 2) To provide incentive for teachers to keep doing a good job, and to encourage other teachers to improve; 3) To influence weak teachers to leave the profession (those not weak enough to non-renew); 4) To attract and retain those high quality people who want to teach, but who also want a profession with resulting rewards for competence; 5) to emphasize quality and reward it and 6) To motivate staff.

The limitations of such plans are 1) It costs a little more if it is a true merit; 2) Everyone may not agree on who is meritorious; 3) Plans are limited by the ability of evaluators—training programs must be established: 4) It takes a great deal of time for administrators to make an adequate number of classroom observations and 5) Plans are limited by the amount of local funds available.

Overall, the findings suggest that while the implementation of merit pay and other teacher incentive plans may be difficult, it is not insurmountable. It is evident that we must attract and retain a quality staff; without this, educational excellence becomes an impossibility. Teacher incentive plans have the potential to attract bright individuals into education, and to help retain those individuals who would likely leave the profession to seek more lucrative salaries in the business world. Perhaps the development of a model school concept, with the purpose of utilizing merit pay and other teacher incentive plans to their fullest, would shed additional light on the effectiveness and feasibility of such plans.

Are Merit Raises Meritorious?

David Neil Silk

David Neil Silk is Associate Professor in the Indiana University School of Education at the Indiana University–Purdue University campus in Indianapolis. He has written about philosophy of education and cognate fields.

INTRODUCTION

Once recommended by the National Commission on Excellence in Education and endorsed by President Reagan, the status of merit raises for teachers as the new educational panacea was assured. However, like many previous educational panaceas, it will not even alleviate the problems it has been designed to cure. To merely say that it will not solve any educational problems obscures the fact that institutionalization of merit raises will be potentially more harmful than many of the innocuous educational trends of the past twenty-five years. A policy of merit pay for teachers will have a devastating effect on morale and collegiality among teachers. Even the chosen few who are identified as meritorious will be harmed in this sense, for they will have to rationalize their superior status among their peers, who are apt to take a cynical view of their ascribed merit.

To anyone who has not taught under a merit-pay system, it may appear quite sound. After all, "merit" is a good thing by definition. Disputing "merit" as a basis for paying teachers is the moral equivalent of impugning motherhood. However, practical experience with merit raises suggests the need for caution with respect to this latest cure-all for education.

TWO ERRONEOUS ASSUMPTIONS

How can something that appears so beneficial be so harmful? The answer lies in the fact that the merit-raise policy in education rests upon two erroneous assumptions. The first one is that the primary cause of underachievement in schools is poor teaching. Though poor teaching may be a factor, it is probably minor compared to other far more obvious problems. Research evidence can be cited to show that performance in schools would not be dramatically affected if weak teachers were eliminated. The work of Jencks and his colleagues at Harvard University are examples of such research.

> The data show that measures of school resources are a poor predictor of school performance, a conclusion reached not only by Jencks and his collaborators, but also by many other investigators. . . . If all schools were as "good" as the top 20% of all schools, national test scores would rise something like 3%. (1: pp. 115–116)

The second erroneous assumption is that "merit" in teaching is definable and identifiable. It may seem equivocal to claim that "merit" cannot be defined, but in effect this is true. There are so many divergent conceptions of "merit" in teaching that in a practical sense there are none. For example, some

From David Neil Silk, "Are Merit Raises Meritorious?" The Teacher Educator 20 (Winter 1984–85):23–26. Reprinted by permission.

teachers still prefer the lecture method of presentation, especially when difficult material is being introduced. Though this is not the current fashion among educators, it is by no means obvious that this kind of teaching is ineffective. Most of us have had a teacher who lectured exclusively, but whose classes were substantive and stimulating. I have always suspected that where the subject matter becomes very difficult, the lecture method prevails. Does such a teacher have a realistic chance of a fair evaluation when reviewed by colleagues who view lecturing as hopelessly outdated and authoritarian?

In addition to the problem of consensus with respect to what constitute merit in teaching, there is the notorious lack of objective, systematic evaluation procedures. Teacher evaluation is a sham in most schools, and it is the source of much cynicism among teachers. It is made tolerable to them only because they view it merely as an annual administrative ritual, having no real impact or significance. Merit-pay policies will convert this innocuous ritual into a potentially punitive practice. Without a fair and objective means of measuring effectiveness, merit-pay systems are worthless. Most evaluations are conducted on the basis of observations of classroom teaching. However, determining merit on the basis of classroom performance alone can be surprisingly misleading. A dramatic, innovative presentation before a class can be deceiving. Performances of this sort are rarely sustained on a day-to-day basis.

THREE IMPACTS OF MERITS RAISES

The impact of merit raises can be categorized into three broad areas. The first has already been mentioned: it will demoralize the majority of teachers and serve as a disincentive rather than an incentive. Merit raises

will introduce more competitiveness into teaching. Average and below-average performance is inherent in a competitive arrangement. No matter how highly selected and trained the participants, some are always more competent than others. Imagine what it would do to the morale and professionalism of physicians, for example, if some were publicly labelled "master physicians." This would carry the implication that the others were less than fully competent. Professionals are assumed to be competent because they are highly trained and selected. If some are not then the responsibility lies with the institutions that train and select them. A merit-raise system will not solve this problem, it will aggravate it.

The second negative effect is that it will create a political atmosphere in schools, based upon an inherently arbitrary system for the awarding of "merit raises." There is already an informal political structure within schools, but this will give it something more potent to feed on. It will create a monetary basis for applying leverage to teachers who are not fully complaint and for rewarding those who uncritically support administrative policies.

Third, its most serious effect will be to exacerbate the problem of low standards by making teachers hypersensitive to student classroom response. When teachers are evaluated on the basis of classroom performance rather than learning outcomes for their students, they begin to concentrate on being innovative and entertaining as ends in themselves. There is no inherent reason to believe that classroom practices that are innovative are necessarily effective. Some innovative techniques are excellent while some are silly. However, when teachers are evaluated on the basis of classroom performance, this becomes an inducement for more dramatic and unusual presentations. Students who are entertained appear to observers to be learning more. Often this is not the case. Some kinds of learning involve intense effort and are not easily made entertaining. Teachers being evaluated on the basis of observations of their teaching rather than on objective tests of student learning tend to avoid requiring students to do the difficult and sometimes quite tedious and unentertaining kinds of work.

Another aspect of this problem is that teachers tend to give higher grades when they know they are being evaluated on the basis of classroom observations of their teaching. Lower grades often result in more negative student perceptions of a class and its teacher. When teachers know they are being judged on the basis of student response, they tend to relax their standards to keep up student morale. This will aggravate the problem of "grade inflation" and low educational standards.

LEARNING: THE BEST MEASURE OF TEACHING

Ironically the most valid measure of good teaching is the one least used: learning. A good teacher is one whose students consistently meet or even exceed the learning expectations for that class. The best way to measure learning is by means of achievement tests. But few, if any, public school systems use standardized tests of learning to evaluate teachers. Evaluation is almost always based upon observation of classroom teaching. Yet most experienced teachers know that being well liked and having dramatic classroom presentations is no guarantee of effectiveness with respect to student learning.

Because we are unable to identify superior teachers by current methods, evaluation is inescapably arbitrary. It is notoriously difficult for a teacher to disprove a below-average evaluation. This invites exploitation of merit raises to support a patronage system in the school. Except for the few who are

among the "meritorious," teachers become demoralized, paranoid, and cynical in its atmosphere. This kind of competitiveness detracts from educational effectiveness.

There is a deep national concern over the alleged failures of our public schools. I suspect that the major attraction of the idea of merit raises for teachers is psychological rather than logical: it places the blame on the teachers, who supposedly have no incentive to do a good job unless their salaries are contingent upon it. Though this may be an attractive explanation to a public who appear to have a low regard for the professionalism of teachers, the belief that a teacher's primary motivation is money is simplistic and cynical. Teaching is the last profession that someone interested primarily in money would choose.

Educational problems are rooted in the circumstances of children's lives, in the economy, and in almost every aspect of the American way of life. Bad teaching and the lack of financial incentive to do a good job have little to do with underachievement and low standards. Solving these problems will require extensive changes that go far beyond school walls. These changes are likely to be expensive. It is not unduly cynical to speculate that political leaders are quick to endorse merit-raise policies because they involve relatively little additional cost. A more meaningful reform would be to raise salaries for all teachers, so that superior college students will find teaching a more attractive career to pursue. Paying a small percentage of teachers additional "merit pay" is tokenism and leaves unchanged the most obvious causes of ineffective education.

REFERENCE

Hurn, Christopher J. *The Limits and Possibilities of Schooling: An Introduction to the Sociology of Teaching,* Boston: Allyn & Bacon, 1978.

DISCUSSION QUESTIONS AND ACTIVITIES

1. Do you believe that merit pay is the "only way to gain public support for higher salaries for all teachers"?
2. Why would locally developed merit plans be better than statewide ones?
3. What are the positive potentials of merit pay?
4. Do you agree with Silk that the policy of merit pay will have a "devastating effect" on morale and collegiality of teachers?
5. Assess the evidence that performance in schools would not be dramatically affected if weak teachers were eliminated.
6. Can merit in teaching be satisfactorily defined?
7. Will merit pay likely create a political atmosphere in the school that rewards those who uncritically accept administrative policies?
8. Would it be better for teachers to be evaluated on objective tests of student performance rather than on observations of their teaching?
9. Trace the history of merit pay plans over the past twenty-five years and report your findings to the class.
10. Organize a classroom debate on merit pay.
11. Invite a speaker who has worked in a merit pay system to your class.

SUGGESTED READINGS

Brighton, Stayner, and Hannan, Cecil. *Merit Pay Programs for Teachers.* Belmont, Calif.: Fearon, 1962.

Calhoun, Frederick S., and Protheroe, Nancy J. *Merit Pay Plans for Teachers: Status and Descriptions* Arlington, Va.: Educational Research Service, 1983.

Coffman, Charlie Q., and Manarino-Leggett, Priscilla M. "What Do Teachers Think of Merit Pay? Study Lists Important Variables." NASSP *Bulletin* 68 (November 1984):54–59.

Cramer, Jerome. "Yes—Merit Pay Can Be a Horror, But a Few School Systems Have Done It Right." *American School Board Journal* 170 (September 1983):28, 33–34.

Johnson, Susan Moore. "Merit Pay for Teachers: A Poor Prescription for Reform." *Harvard Educational Review* 54 (May 1984):175–185.

"Merit Pay for Teachers: Worth Another Try." *American School Board Journal* (May 1983):8, 13.

Nickerson, Neal C. "Merit Pay—Does It Work in Education?" NASSP *Bulletin* 68 (March 1984):65–66.

"Only You Can Kill Merit Pay for Teachers." *American School Board Journal* 170 (September 1983):16, 18.

Shaten, N. Lewis. "Merit Does Not Have to Be a Four Letter Word." NASSP *Bulletin* 67 (December 1983):56–63.

Shreeve, Williams, et al. "Teachers Do Not Deal in Widgets." *Counseling and Values* 29 (October 1984):59–66.

Soar, Robert S., and Soar, Ruth M. "Teacher Merit Pay: Can Research Help?" *Journal of Human Behavior and Learning* 1 (1984):3–13.

12

Microcomputers in Education

Some hail it as a "revolution" while others claim, "It's just another fad." These disputes are over the introduction of the microcomputer in education. Some observers believe that within a few years the ability to program and use microcomputers may be as important as the ability to read, write, type, drive, or use a telephone.

Automated teaching devices began in the 1920s with the first teaching machine, which did not achieve popularity until the 1950s. As the work of these early machines could be handled in simpler, more economical ways, programmed materials supplanted them during the 1950s and 1960s. The emergence of computer-assisted instruction (CAI) in the late 60s was heralded as a breakthrough, only to find it constrained by prohibitive costs—to establish a CAI program in a school system costs in excess of $100,000.

In contrast, the spread of microcomputers stems largely from the cost reductions of microtechnology, with microcomputers available from $200–400 and up to $5,000–6,000. The National Science Foundation projects one million units available in elementary and secondary schools by 1985. Hardware development is outpacing software development and implementation, and the present microcomputers will probably be replaced in several years. In the next ten to twenty years networks will likely emerge that will permit microcomputers to access the resources of larger computers. Proponents claim, however, that present microcomputers can improve educational programs.

Computers have been widely adopted in business and various organizations. Most universities offer courses in computer science, graduate courses are available in computer-based education, and many computer literacy workshops are offered. Many school districts are identifying teachers who can be consultants for inservice sessions in the use of microcomputers. Still, there is no agreement on the precise knowledge needed for computer literacy.

The quality of programs is a problem in the field microcomputer, as in the case of CAI where the development of programs is an extremely time-consuming and expensive task. Thousands of programs written for CAI have limited instructional value. Suitable microcomputer programs for instruction are just beginning to emerge. Some serious problems, however, need to be addressed.

The new information technologies (including microcomputers) could lead to a further centralization of authority because they favor decentralization of activities while promoting centralized decision making. This technology contributes to the trend of large corporations making decisions for remote areas. The new technology also reduces personal contact and shrinks interpersonal communication.

Despite these shortcomings, the new information technology is likely to spread rapidly. Some observers envision future home instruction or neighborhood learning centers capable of providing basic instruction that consumes most of the school day, leading to a shift of accountability and competency education from the schools to the home. The role of teachers would be transformed from transmitters of knowledge to providers of higher-order learning experiences.

Shane explores the microcomputer breakthroughs in relation to larger developments in the information society, and then shows the likely changes that microcomputers may bring about in education. Slesnick debunks numerous computer myths and distorted popular thinking.

The Silicon Age and Education

Harold G. Shane

Harold G. Shane (b. 1914) has a Ph.D. from Ohio State University. He has been a teacher, principal, and superintendent in school systems in Ohio and Illinois. A former dean of the School of Education at Indiana University, he now is University Professor of Education. Professor Shane has been a consultant to USOE and other agencies, a recipient of awards, former president of the Association for Supervision and Curriculum Development, and the author of numerous books, including Education for a New Millenium.

"Change [must] be accepted . . . when it can no longer be resisted."
Victoria Regina (c. 1895).

The microchip is a tiny slice of silicon, an "electronic book" that stores information in a binary code consisting of zeros and ones.[1] Far too small to be seen by the naked eyes,[2] the chip requires a read-out terminal that converts the electronic transistor codes into the language of the viewer. Screens displays the textual material at viewer-controlled speeds.[3]

But this article is not concerned primarily with the technical aspects of silicon chips and other computer hardware. The implications of the computer revolution for reduction are my primary concern. Indeed, a large portion of the Western world already can be considered a computerized society. Our task is coping with and using constructively the new social environment that is emerging as computers approach an era of virtually exponential growth.

Human communication has gone through four distinct revolutions. The first was occasioned by our species-specific skills of complex speech—a development that created an important role for memory. It also permitted the nongenetic transfer of our human qualities, our mental achievements, from one generation to another.

The art of writing heralded the second revolution; its various forms—cuneiform, hieroglyphics, and the script of scribes—remained of prime importance for thousands of years. The art of writing became the victim of a third revolution, triggered by Johann

From Harold G. Shane, "The Silicon Age and Education," Phi Delta Kappan *(January 1982):303–308. Reprinted by permission.*

[1] The zeros and ones are symbolic representations of the presence or absence of electronic current.

[2] As of the early 1980s, the transistor or "chip" cell measured three microns. This is less than half the diameter of the seven-micron human red blood cell.

[3] Space constraints preclude more detailed information regarding computer hardware, but it is readily available in books by Christopher Evans and Robert Moody. See footnotes 5 and 6.

Gutenberg, who, in the 15th century, presumably became the first European to use movable type in his printing press. Soon thereafter the printed word was available to millions of people who could neither afford nor, in many instances, even read books lettered in medieval script.

The fourth and potentially most profound revolution—one still in the full vigor of its youth—has been wrought by the enormous advances in telecommunications in the span of a single lifetime. Although the telegraph, telephone, and radio played an important role, not until the last decade has our globe begun to become a "wired planet"—an infor mation society created by the microchip.

As John Platt points out in a superbly provocative essay:

> It is important to realize how far we have gone in the new direction. We are living already in what McLuhan has called the Electronic Surround. Half of the jobs in the American economy are now "tertiary" or information-handling jobs, and more and more of them have become computerized or electronic. Banks and businesses are linked together by credit cards and data processing. Government records, science, and the military are all dependent on big computers. Everywhere there are pocket calculators, transistor radios, citizens' band radios, and stereo sets with records and tapes. We have electronic monitors in stores and entryways, and videotapes for learning tennis. Telephone and television are linked by global satellites, while the home begins to have two-way cable electronic games, and video recordings on cassettes and disks.[4]

The revolution in telecommunications— the silicon chip revolution—and the resultant changes in the world of work demand that educators understand the new life patterns

and interactions that are coming into being. Not only our work in schools but our very ways of thinking, our global awareness, our concepts of power and political priorities— all must come under scrutiny.

BACKGROUND AND FUTURE PROSPECTS

The microprocessor is both the source *and* support system of the transitions already under way. In the computer, it is analogous to a combined heart and brain in humans. One may wonder why such an astute observer as Alvin Toffler failed to mention the microprocessor in *Future Shock.* The answer is simple. The microprocessor didn't exist in 1970!

According to Christopher Evans, the idea behind the computer is an old one. Charles Babbage, a British engineer born in 1791, first conceived the idea of a calculating machine but lacked the technology to build an efficient model. He and a gifted mathematician, Ada, the Countess of Lovelace (Lord Byron's daughter), probably deserve credit as the parents of what they called a "Difference Engine," the first primitive autocalculator.

But only within recent memory did the development of a general-purpose computing machine begin. ENIAC, the first digital computer, was built at the University of Pennsylvania in 1946.[5] It cost half a million relatively uninflated dollars to build, weighed 30 tons, and required the floor space of an average-sized house. Its 18,500 special vacuum tubes required 130,000 watts.

The development of a computer on a microchip—accomplished by Intel Corporation of Santa Clara, California, about 10 years ago—was the real breakthrough that

---

[4] John Platt, "Education in the Electronic Society," in John Y. Cole, ed., *Television, the Book, and the Classroom* (Washington, D.C.: Library of Congress, 1978).

[5] Robert Moody, *The First Book of Microcomputers* (Rochelle Park, N.J.: Hayden, 1978). pp. 3, 4.

presaged the silicon age. Evans describes what has happened as miniaturization techniques were used to etch complete, integrated circuits on a chip: "The units of which computers are made are getting smaller and smaller, shrinking beyond the range of ordinary microscopes into the infinites of the molecular world."[6]

By 1980 it was possible to etch the equivalent of 60,000 to 70,000 vacuum tubes on a microchip; by the spring of 1981, in a U.S. laboratory, 750,000 tube equivalents were squeezed onto a chip. Million-unit chips small enough to balance on a paperclip are just over the horizon. In fact, they may already have appeared by the time this issue of the *Kappan* is off the press. Already there are computers with a switching potential of nanoseconds—machines capable of billions of switchings in a one-second clock-tick. The incredible speed of the chip is, perhaps, more readily understood when one understands that a nanosecond is one thousand-millionth of a second.

Consider this: If a Rolls Royce had improved as much in cost-efficiency as the microcomputer has in the last decade, it would have a sticker price of just $3. A 1945 all-tube computer capable of doing the work of the present-day table-top computer would have had to be the size of New York City; it would have required more power than the whole of the city's subway system.

The microprocessor is the latest stage in the development of transistors (invented in 1947 by William Shockley) and a basic element in the computer. It is a small semiconductor with impurities that permit electrons to move under the impulse of an infinitesimal amount of energy. Its importance resides in the way it links three components: 1) *matter*

(the semiconductor's impurities); 2) *information,* expressed in a universal binary language; and 3) the actuating power of *energy.*

Before contemplating what the microprocessor may portend for education, let us examine some of the results of the marriage of computer technologies and telecommunications. The first commercially feasible microcomputer became available in 1975, just six years ago. Since then:

- As of the summer of 1981, about three million microcomputers had been sold in the U.S. alone, over a million of them as personal computers. The dollar value of the computer industry (including software) was $2.6 billion in 1980. If present trends in the sales of information processing equipment continue in the U.S., sales—including supplies and services—could exceed $62 billion in 1985.[7]

- In 1980 information workers (those who handled information and dispensed communications in their many forms) constituted approximately 50% of U.S. workers, far outstripping other service occupations (29%), industry (17%), and farm workers (4%).

- Within three to five years European televiewing will be saturated by three satellites that will beam a broad spectrum of commercial programs to 250 million Europeans. "Digital sound" equipment developed for use in Europe will permit many viewers (by pressing their choice from among four buttons) to hear programs dubbed in their own language.

---

[6] Christopher Evans, *The Micro Millennium* (New York: Pocket Books, 1979), p. 51.

[7] Estimate from G. T. T. Molitor, president, Public Policy Forecasting. Cf. the *Futurist* (April 1981) 23–30. *Time* magazine (5 October 1981, p. 69) reports that the cost of an Apple II personal computer (about $1,500) is only the beginning. One can also spend as much as $800 for eight softwear programs.

- By late 1981 physicians in New York and Tokyo exchanged information on the treatment of glaucoma by means of a "symposium" held via satellite.[8]
- "Smart machines" performing jobs formerly done by humans are proliferating; the field of robotics, made possible and profitable by the microprocessor, is becoming a major element in industry. About 4,000 robots are in use in the U.S., mostly in the auto industry, and more than 11,000 are at work in Japan, as of 1981. Some can be instructed to see, hear, feel, and even make simple decisions. Robots can now beat most humans at chess, they can perform, and they can "learn." General Motors is installing 10 "programmable universal machines for assembly" that can screw light bulbs into dashboard panels, spray paint, weld, load and unload parts, follow typed directions, and even respond to simple verbal directions. In handling hot casings, robots such as these have cut the number of rejects by 15% and increased production by 10% while reducing the need for human labor by 70%—all for $4.60 per hour.[9]

THE CHIP AND THE CURRICULUM

Following the example of Ned Lud, an angry worker who smashed two textile frames belonging to his Leicestershire employer, the Luddites in early 19th-century England literally attacked the new labor-saving machinery which they saw threatening them with wage cuts and unemployment. French work-

---

[8] *Indianapolis Star,* (4 October 1981); p. 1.

[9] The *Futurist* (vol. 15, nos. 1, 2, and 4, 1981) published a sequence of excellent and provocative articles on microelectronics and robotics.

ers also railed against the Industrial Revolution by jamming *sabots,* their wooden shoes, into the spinning equipment that was eliminating many of their jobs (thus the word *saboteur*).

Let me begin my discussion of the chip and its effects on the curriculum by suggesting that the teaching profession avoid an understandable urge to feel threatened by the microcomputer—lest we become educational Luddites. Rather, let us strive to anticipate the influence of the microchip and of telecommunications on 1) subject matter, 2) components of the educational community (preprimary through postsecondary), and 3) the ultimate goal of educating for a sustainable society. First, however, a quick review of terminology.

Schooling, Education, and Learning

As used hereafter, *schooling* refers to a program of planned and organized instruction designed to build a sense of identity with one's culture and to preserve or to transmit those values prized by the society. *Education* is used here in a broad sense to include the diverse experiences and continuing out-of-school learning of adults and youths. *Learning* refers to the sum of the internalized knowledge, values, and ways of thinking that determine behavior. The microchip is influencing each of the three.

Schooling and the Chip

The microprocessor is likely to encourage a number of desirable changes and innovations in the overall scope of the school. Increasing use of the hand calculator, greater use of videotapes and videodiscs, and increased use of suitable TV offerings should begin to permeate the classroom. The significant use of microcomputers will reside in the interactive relationship between learners and increasingly "smart machines"—not in the use of microcomputers as "electronic flash cards."

Computer literacy" will begin to receive more attention, too, and the idea and the basic purposes of "computer camps"[10] for pre-teen and teenage youngsters will probably be quickly co-opted within school walls. The National Education Association, for example, announced last summer that it was negotiating an agreement with Control Data Corporation to provide a computer literacy program for teachers.

As a part of this trend educators are forced to question the necessity of routine math drill when $10 calculators can instantly compute percentages and square roots. I suspect that tomorrow's schools will deemphasize the *mechanics* of ciphering but place more stress on pupils' acquiring a greater understanding of the *meaning* of numbers, including how to recognize reasonable solutions or answers to math problems fed to the calculator.

The microprocessor will also be used to facilitate work in traditional courses—mathematics, English, social studies—and a sprinkling of novel ideas will surface. By "novel ideas" I mean such strategies as using an IBM model 1620 to help teach singing: At Stanford University a computer has been used to print out notes to be sung by students. The machine compares the learner's pitch to true pitch an then selects proper remedial practice.

One puzzle yet to be solved is the future of computerized foreign language instruction.

It is quite possible that within two decades hand-held computers with voice input and output will provide translating devices virtually as fluent as and perhaps more grammatical than many native speakers. How will this affect practices and methods in the classroom? What might occur in the realm of bilingual education?

As the computer changes the work place, schools will find themselves pressured to modify vocational education and guidance programs to make them respond more rapidly to change. Lifelong education—including vocational reeducation or "retrofitting" for those replaced by robots—for mature (over 30) and senior (over 55 or 60) learners seems likely to open new, highly used social roles for the school. Retrofitting may become particularly important. Many of the persons who are likely to become unemployed as a result of developments in robotics will not necessarily have the skills needed to fill new jobs that are created by applications of the microcomputer.

I do not, however, see any radical or wrenching changes in schooling during the short-term future (five to 10 years) as a result of the silicon chip. Budget cuts and federal fiscal policies seem likely to impede major investments in computers and in material for at least another five years. (Even so, schools from the elementary level to the university are giving high priority to the equipment. For instance, the Indiana University School of Education, despite financial constraints, is installing 18 microcomputers for student an faculty education and use.) Moreover, computer-assisted instruction, at least in some fields of study, now has few advantages over a well-programmed text (although the availability of high-quality software seems likely to improve during the Eighties). Then too, some teachers will resist change either because they feel insecure in an electronic milieu or because they believe

---

[10] By mid-1981 the computer camp was enough of a growing phenomenon to command notice in such publications as *Time* and *Le Monde*. In the camps, children learn computer languages as BASIC and PASCAL, devise electronic games, learn programming skills, etc. (See *Time*, 3 August 1981, p. 70). A concomitant development in the opening of "computer stores" for children. In Indianapolis, for example, there is a store in which children pay tuition and receive instruction after school hours.

that any "computer takeover" would abort established routines or stifle creative planning and innovative teaching.

Perhaps one of the gravest impediments to the rapid development of suitable software is the lack of agreement among educators at all levels as to which methods of instruction are "best" and what the goals of education should be. Moreover, software producers (as well as educators) still have much to learn about the learning process and about individual differences in learning styles. Lacking such knowledge, we could end up merely cloning inadequacy more rapidly by means of the computer.

The Chip and Education

Education as a lifelong process will be more profoundly changed than schooling during the next 10 to 15 years. Learners of all ages are likely to find their homes becoming "electronic cottages," a term coined by Alvin Toffler in *The Third Wave*. In a knowledge-rich society many homes may become work places through the use of telecommunications, including 3-D holography—a development that could reduce the need for personal transportation as energy reserves wane.

Another important development—one with implications for both the electronic cottage and off-campus education—occurred in 1976–77 when the first commercial lightwave system were built. Bell, Corning Glass, and ITT, among others, succeeded in fabricating fiber glass cables—cables that carried lightwave communications made possible by laser beam technology. A 600-mile Boston-New York-Washington system planned by AT&T is expected to carry 80,000 telephone calls simultaneously through these new "glass pipelines." Within a few years fiber optics may link stores, homes, schools, and offices, and make "glass-wired" telecommunications inexpensive and commonplace.[11]

Telephone conferences, including doctoral orals for which the candidates remain overseas while their committees convene in the U.S. and special telephones that are linked to the resources of powerful computers already are feasible and available in a learning society. Fiber optics technology seems sure to facilitate such communications. However, as these changes occur, we must be careful not to confuse information with education. One is an *item,* the other a *process* to which the *item* may contribute.

As the robot revolution in industrialized nations creates the likelihood of a three- or four-day work week, education for the wise use of leisure takes on new importance. A shortened work week also should provide the hours needed to educate, or at least to retread, workers displaced by the robots that already perform some assembly-line tasks with greater skill, efficiency, and patience than humans. This and other opportunities for extending the schools' domain appear likely to characterize tomorrow's practices.

Furthermore, even widely acclaimed TV programs ("Sesame Street," for instance) tend to be stronger in production, in special effects, and in charisma than in sustained educational merit. Since this is likely to remain true for some time to come, there is sure to be a growing need for professionally prepared teachers, educational psychologists, and media specialists to work on the improvement of the population's general education via the media.

For both educators and the general public, novel technological innovations and new solutions also create new problems,[12] among them:

---

[11] See Daniel L. Askin. "The R & D Story," *Passages,* October 1981, pp. 54–66.

[12] For additional examples, see Jan Henrick Nyheim's list in "The Age of Doubt," *Intermedia,* March 1981, pp. 10, 11.

- the need to produce specialists and at the same time preserve the merits of a general education;

- the question of striking a balance between the amount of reference material that theoretically can be stored and the amount actually needed;

- learning to cope with the prospect that as many as half of the jobs in U.S. industry may be eliminated by 2000 or 2006;

- teaching learners to use information carefully rather than carelessly as it becomes more abundant and more available;

- educating the relatively few who master and direct the use of the new information technologies to use their advantage with prudence, integrity, and in the human interest;

- at least for the immediate future, dealing with "perhaps the most paralyzing aspect of the microelectronics industrial revolution": namely, "the inability of lawmakers and sociologists to cope with what is occurring, because no one knows where to begin";[13] and

- perhaps most important, striking a balance between what is made technically possible by microelectronics and what is educationally desirable in learning situations.

Telecommunications, the Chip, and Learning

In the long-range future (i.e., by 2000 or 2010), we may discover that the most significant socioeducational mutation wrought by the microprocessors in our Electronic Surround is what they do to enhance learning, the outcome of experiences that shape and improve our subsequent behavior. Advances in technology are already forcing us to think previously unthinkable thoughts. At a meeting in Paris last fall, a group of educators, predominantly scholars from the Third World, discussed at length the possible merits of totally by-passing the Gutenberg Revolution, moving immediately beyond the era of books, and introducing the world's illiterate masses to an unprecedented approach to learning: a new "electronic literacy" based on means of communication other than print.

A member of this UNESCO panel, a woman from the Ministry of Education in a Southeast Asian nation, said, "When I go to a village with a radio, I find all the people there gathering around me eager to listen. Can you imagine the drawing power that a large-screen TV set would have—and the way carefully developed programs may be designed to help those who are now blinkered and muzzled by their illiteracy to become more informed and effective humans."

As microcomputers and robots improve in their ability to *see* gestures, *feel* textures, *hear* commands, *accept* directions, and *speak*, extraordinary, almost preternatural, human-and-computer learning relationships may develop. Christopher Evans, an experimental psychologist and computer scientist, has discussed possibilities that are both exciting and vaguely disturbing. "The old teaching machines," he tells us:

> were electromagnetic gadgets, combining the subtle swiftness of electricity with the unhappy slowness of machinery. . . . Teaching computers, on the other hand, are basically all-electronic, with no moving parts—other than electrons—and are easy to mass produce . . . and they have the great advantage of being extremely reliable.
>
> Their value is not so much in *what* they teach as *how they will go about it.* The flexibility of a modern computer, small or large, is, to all intents and purposes, infinite, and the range of tasks it can perform is limited only by the range of programs which can be written for it.[14] [Emphasis in original]

[13] Adam Osborne, *Running Wild: The Next Industrial Revolution* (Berkeley, Calif.: Osborne/McGraw-Hill, 1979, p. ix.

[14] Evans, p. 193.

Evans contends that, by "learning" to recognize a student's voice patterns, computers will eventually be able to converse and to adjust their programmed responses to the learner "in a wide variety of ways, constantly giving the impression that they are 'interested' in teaching by the way in which they structure their communication to meet the needs of the moment."

Seymour Papert, an M.I.T. professor, contends that the "computer presence" actually can contribute to mental processes. To Papert, there is a world of difference between what computers can do to nurture learning and what society and its schools may choose to do with them as they face what may seem a threatening change. "It is hard to think about computers of the future," Papert says:

> without projecting on to them the properties and limitations of those we think we know today. And nowhere is this more true than in imagining how computers can enter the world of education. It is not true to say that [my] image of a child's relationship with a computer . . . goes far beyond what is common in today's schools. My image does not go beyond: It goes in the opposite direction.
>
> In many schools today, the phrase "computer-aided instruction" means making the computer teach the child. One might say the computer is being used to program the child. In my version, the child programs the computer and, in doing so, both acquires a sense of mastery over a piece of the modern and powerful technology and establishes an intimate contact with some of the deepest ideas from science, from mathematics, and from the art of intellectual model building.[15]

Contending that "it is possible to design computers so that learning to communicate with them can be a natural process . . . like learning French by living in France,"[16] Papert says that the computer presence will enable us to modify out-of-school learning environments to the point that "schools as we know them today will have no place in the future. But it is an open question whether they will adapt by transforming themselves into something new or wither away and be replaced."[17]

The "new curriculum" characteristic of our electronic age has certain features with which it is difficult for the school curriculum to compete. The TV and silicon age curricula are becoming ever more pervasive, often are more persuasive, combine images and narration, can provide immediate gratification, are relatively noncompetitive, and are irrefutable. This creates a fascinating potential development for educators: namely, that with the aid of computers some—perhaps many—of our young learners, a decade or two hence, may be taught the coping skills that life demands and that reading currently provides, with the help of an audiovisual-microchip support system.

Today it can take years for textbooks to begin to reflect current events. While textbooks will continue to be of value, schools of the eighties are likely to discover that they will need to install more computer terminals and other electronic equipment for using tapes, videodiscs, and the myriad of analogous resources that the Electronic Surround has begun to provide. While the microchip is not likely to cause a decline in the teaching profession, the status of teachers and what they *do* is likely to be different as they work at developing the planet's greatest resource: the valuable deposits of "gray matter" in the heads of young and old learners alike. With the help of the tools for improving teaching and learning that the chip provides, the skills of professionals should help to guarantee that the world retains the capacity to move toward a decent, civilized future.

[15] Seymour Papert, *Mindstorms* (New York: Basic Books, 1980), p. 5.

[16] Ibid., p. 6.

[17] Ibid., p. 9.

AN ULTIMATE GOAL

I have attempted to summarize some of the possible developments regarding schooling, education, and learning that are presaged by the silicon revolution. There is an ultimate goal, however, both short- and long-term, related to schooling, education, and learning. This is the goal of creating what Lester R. Brown has called a "sustainable society."

Today most of us are painfully aware of the great strains that humanity is placing on our planetary resources. Erosion, biological systems under stress, the changing prospects for maintaining food production for more than 4.6 billion people, the probable twilight of our petroleum-based culture, nuclear weaponry, and diverse socioeconomic stresses have been problems for 20 years or more.

To this end I believe that the curriculum should, at appropriate age levels, begin to educate for world society through:

- emphasizing the need to create a timetable for stabilizing world population;
- stressing the need to move from a throwaway society to a preserving, conserving society;
- directing attention toward more ways of powering the planet with unexploited energy sources;
- redirecting research and development in a context of global need rather than in the mere quest for ways to produce more material things;
- using school, community, and national *example* rather than *precept* to change values and shift priorities so that, in a resource-short world, we stop teaching our children and youths to want and expect what isn't there; and
- becoming more mindful of the social fis-

sures between the haves and the have-nots and beginning to patch them.

In effect, we have changed an old pattern of life in which many people often borrowed from their parents. Now, too many humans are borrowing from our children and grandchildren, many as yet unborn, as they seek to prolong their contemporary binge of conspicuous consumption. We need instead to move toward the voluntary simplicity that the future well-being of our posterity requires.[18]

How do these concluding points bear on education and on the marvels of the microchip? They bear on them because of the potential for improved communication, for more rapid problem identification, and for more effective problem solving that could characterize the silicon chip age. As Jean-Jacques Servan-Schreiber sees it:

Computerized infrastructures for the Third World could make it possible for whole stages of [socioeconomic] development to be by-passed. From abacus to the multiplication table to the logarithmic rule to adding machines to the first computers to transistors took centuries. And from this long series of innovations emerged the microprocessor—a wonderful device [in] which the . . . basic elements of all wealth converge. . . ."[19]

One hopes that the less-industrialized nations, thanks to the silicon revolution, can greatly improve the lives of their citizens through a blend of technological revolution and improved educational options. As a Dutch Nobel laureate, economist Jan T. Tinbergen, sees it, the information society can make pos-

---

[18] A number of points made above are developed in detail by Lester R. Brown, *Building a Sustainable Society* (New York: W. W. Norton, 1981).

[19] Jean-Jacques Servan-Schreiber. *The World Challenge* (New York: Simon and Schuster, 1980), p. 268.

sible a uniquely reconceived educational network with the potential for breaking down the festering poverty and continuing turmoil that is endemic in much of the Third World and thus avoid what otherwise could become an accelerating slide toward disaster.

Thus far, schooling and education have done relatively little to prepare us for the emerging information society. Nor has much been done to recognize or to remedy the need of less-developed nations for not merely a new *deal* but for a new economic *order*. Furthermore, teachers, the curriculum, and the media lag far behind in educating for a sustainable society. I am convinced that endeavoring to achieve this goal will prove to be education's greatest task and its more important responsibility as the 20th century winds down and a new millennium begins. And the microchip just might be the ally that puts the odds in our favor as the profession tackles the job.

Bunk! Computer Myths We Can Live Without

Twila Slesnick

Twila Slesnick is Senior Editor of the journal, Classroom Computer Learning.

Myths are not just innocuous fiction. People actually believe in them. It doesn't matter that they are by nature unverifiable; they are used to explain practices, beliefs and even natural phenomena when better explanations are not available.

In the brief 25 years since the computer first appeared in classrooms, we have adopted as truth many misconceptions about the machine. In fact, we have created an entire mythology that we use to justify how we use computers in education, to support our intuitions (or our fears) about the technology, and to explain phenomena (like obsessive hacking) that we don't understand. Although these misconceptions may entertain future generations and illuminate the zeitgeist of late twentieth-century America, they are not necessarily benign. The legends, predictions and promises about computers in education range from the insidious to the ridiculous, and it is time to debunk them.

From Twila Slesnick, "Bunk! Computer Myths We Can Live Without," Classroom Computer Learning *(February 1985):31–33. Reprinted by special permission of* Classroom Computer Learning, © *1985 by Peter Li, Inc., 19 Davis Drive, Belmont, CA 94002.*

PIE-IN-THE-SKY MYTHS

1 Computers Are Invaluable for School and Home Use

If all those computer commercials were effective, you probably ran out months ago to buy a computer for your kid, and your principal probably dashed out to purchase ten for the school. And now you both fret guiltily whenever the commercials come on—knowing there is an extra item in the hall closet or ten computers collecting dust in the computer lab.

People must realize that if they don't find computers useful at home or at school, it's not their fault. Finding applications for new gadgets as they appear on the market is not the responsibility of the consumer. Each new item should fill a need and if it doesn't, it won't sell—at least not for long.

Nonetheless, marketers of computer hardware and software insist that the machines are invaluable. And some people have been taken in by the hard sell. But in fact, using the computer for everyday household chores is still more trouble than it's worth. At school we spend much of our time trying to think of interesting ways to use trashy software. Or else we try to convince ourselves that programming is good for all kids.

If the struggle to make computers useful at home or at school continues to be difficult, their use in those places will disappear. Consumers will tire of inventing tasks for and spending money on items they don't use. If computer companies want to penetrate the market the way TV companies have, they must make computers easier to use and offer applications that consumers perceive as useful.

2 Programming Experience Means Job Security

Here's another message from the computer industry via the television: "If you don't buy your kid a computer, he might grow up to be an unemployed ignoramus." The implication is that if a kid knows how to program, he will always be able to get a job. There's probably not a programming teacher in the country who hasn't justified programming instruction—even for third graders—this way.

It's true that every now and then a big demand emerges for some particular skill, whether it's math teaching, engineering, nursing or boat building. Usually this demand is tied to recent developments in science or technology. The few people with these skills command high salaries and have little difficulty finding jobs. But inevitably the need is filled, and where once there was a shortage soon there is a surplus.

Computer programming skill is currently in demand. Market-research projections, however, suggest that in the future only 2 percent of the work force will be computer programmers. That percentage won't begin to represent the huge numbers of programming students who have descended upon computer science departments throughout the country. Furthermore, as the industry progresses toward the development of computers that can program themselves, diagnose their own malfunctions and, perhaps, even repair themselves, high-level jobs in technology will become scarce. Even now, for every high-level job opportunity in technology, there are nine unskilled job openings. Students should be encouraged to study programming if they like it and not because it promises financial security.

3 The Russians Are Coming, The Russians Are Coming

As more and more elements of society embrace the computer and its legendary powers, the pressures to incorporate computers into all aspects of the school curriculum increase. Among the most popular myths used to justify the current push for computers in our schools is the myth of Soviet superiority in education. The reasoning goes something like this: Soviet school children each take from one to ten more years of science and mathematics than do our children. Therefore, the number of technological experts in the USSR is increasing rapidly and the work of these experts will soon propel the Soviets into a position of economic and political supremacy.

This myth persists in spite of questionable statistics about Soviet education. Do we really know what it means to take nine years of physics in the Soviet Union? Is it an hour a day for nine years? An hour a week? And what about the quality of the courses?

Anyone who has recently been to the Soviet Union would be hard-pressed to imagine this nation leading the world in technology. Two years ago, few of the Soviet scientists with whom I spoke had even seen a microcomputer. Fortran was still the dominant language and calculators were expensive items. My money says the Russians aren't coming. They aren't even on the boat yet.

4 Teachers Will Develop Their Own Software

Optimists predict that since teachers know best what students need, the quality of educational software will improve once teachers begin developing their own programs. But curriculum development requires more skill and time than most people realize. Teachers can't whip out a quality piece of software during a 50-minute prep period. A good science simulation, for example, would require thorough research to ensure its validity. Such a program should allow students to alter values of variables, define new parameters and analyze outcomes. Its creation would challenge even a professional, experienced programmer. Expecting working teachers to produce software is not only un-

fair, it also encourages the development and use of inadequate software—the kind that's easy to write but contributes little to a child's intellectual growth.

5 Computers Increase Student Achievement

Widespread belief in this myth has stalled progress in computer education. The vast majority of computer-education research studies, which have investigated computer use as a *supplement* to the curriculum, report increased student achievement in classes that use computer software. But this news is hardly indicative of an educational revolution. In fact, *any* supplement to the curriculum is likely to produce gains. In cases where the software has been used as an *alternative* to other instructional methods, gains are nearly always negligible.

And yet, misleading reports of increased student achievement have perpetuated frivolous applications of computers while impeding curricular renovation. Years of research underscore the failure of computer-assisted instruction (CAI) as an alternative to teacher-directed instruction. It's time we heed the message.

6 Computers Make Good Teachers

For 30 years, money-conscious administrators have been looking for ways to replace teachers with computers. But even the most ambitious of these projects have wrought few changes in educational software. Tutorials are no more individualized than they ever were. (How could they be? Programmers rarely meet any of the students for whom their software is written.) Nor has the computer made much headway in discussion and dialogue capabilities. It can't yet learn to gather information on its own to make itself a better resource. And it can't provide tactile, living experiences for students.

The longer we cling to the myth that CAI and similar educational software will cure the ills of education, the more difficult it will be to let go of antiquated content and ineffective methods. Computers are not teachers. They are tools that extend efficiency and ease drudgery.

In fact, I have found no so-called educational program that I could not live without. Most are easily (and wisely) replaced with hands-on activities. If, for a while, classroom use of computers were focused on such applications as word processing, information retrieval and data manipulation, it would become clear that the computer can now do more efficiently much of what we are still teaching kids to do. Why not let the computer, for example, take over computations that are simply a means to an end? Why send a kid to the library to gather information from 20 different sources if the same information could be collected from a computer terminal? Why ask students to write and rewrite papers when a computer can cut the time for this chore in half? The absurdity of teaching children to do what computers can do is bound to strike home soon. And when it does, it will be the impetus to rid the curriculum of obsolete material. Only then will the revolution begin.

GLOOM-AND-DOOM MYTHS

The preceding myths serve to promote the use of computers in education. But there is another group of myths—proffered not by computer boosters but by the doomsayers among us—that also need debunking. Here are the three most popular.

7 Computers Will Divide the Haves and the Have Nots

Skeptics warn that because they are expensive, computers will widen the chasm between the rich and the poor. According to this myth, rich schools and rich homes give rich kids computer access, making those kids smarter and more employable.

Twelve years ago we listened to the same dire prognostications about calculators. And yet today, calculators, like TVs, can be found in virtually every American home. The computer phenomenon is analogous. Prices have fallen dramatically in the last decade and there is every indication that they will continue to do so. In the not-so-distant future, just about any individual or school that wants computers will be able to afford them.

Nonetheless, this myth is in danger of becoming a self-fulfilling prophecy. It suggests that whether or not you have an interest in or a use for computers, you are underprivileged if you don't have one. Thus, a person's social class is determined by whether or not she owns a computer, even though computers are not useful at home, have marginal value as they are currently used in schools and will not guarantee anyone a job.

We should not be so concerned about which students have or don't have access to computers—it's how the computers are used that makes the difference. When rich kids use computers for programming and practical applications while poor kids use them for punching out answers to rote questions, we exacerbate class disparity by depriving some children of exposure to new material, new ideas and new opportunities. And the problem is not so much that poor kids are not learning about new applications of computers, but that their time is being eaten up with rote work—on an off the computer.

8 Computer Experts Will Form an Elite Social Class

A related myth portends that unless we educate the masses, an elite class of computer experts will evolve. This myth pits the knows against the know-nots. The implication is that the knows will rise and oppress the know-nots since the know-nots will be dependent on the skills of the knows. In this myth, schools must counteract the danger by taking on a role as a great equalizer—teaching everybody everything.

But with the amount of information available today, being a generalist is not feasible. Although from time to time we are victimized by ignorance, specialization has become a necessity. Increasingly, we must rely on those who know more—expert auto mechanics, lawyers, teachers and now computer programmers and technicians. No one (not even computer experts) is immune from this dependence. To argue that we must teach everyone about computers is fatuous since the same argument could be applied to any subject area.

9 Computers Breed Social Misfits

Many people fear what might become of youngsters who spend a lot of time alone with a computer. The mythical computer freak is an idiot savant with rounded shoulders, glazed eyes and no friends.

The source of this fear is hard to trace. It can't really be the solitude that is objectionable. Reading, for example, is a highly respected solitary activity—one nurtured incessantly by schools. And besides, computing is no longer the isolated activity it was, as is evidenced by the rising popularity of electronic bulletin boards, through which computer users communicate with fellow students, subject-matter experts and potential friends and sweethearts.

We must also discount monomania as society's true objection to avid computing. After all, we greatly esteem scientists, musicians and artists who devote their entire lives to one discipline (and sometimes to one project). But computing for many people is just a hobby—an infatuation like coin collecting, Monopoly or chess—that is intense for

awhile and then abates or fades away.

I think the real source of the fear is simply ignorance of computers. Many adults remember spending hours (days? years?) playing chess or poring over coins and know that these passing infatuations left them unscathed. But since they have not experienced a childhood love affair with computers, today's adults *don't* know that kids will survive this particular obsession. As computers become more familiar, this fear will no doubt subside.

One day we may very well look back on these myths and chuckle. But attributing legendary feats to limited machines and making wild prognostications based on a modicum of evidence will only delay and subvert the widespread assimilation of computers into society.

DISCUSSION QUESTIONS AND ACTIVITIES

1. What are the four distinct revolutions, according to Shane, that human communication has experienced?
2. What technological breakthroughs made the microcomputer possible?
3. List four changes that the microcomputer is likely to bring about in school. Are all of these changes desirable?
4. What changes outside of schools are likely to result in the next ten to fifteen years from the dissemination of microprocessors?
5. What additional changes can be expected in the long-range future, by 2000 or 2010?
6. Shane believes that the curriculum should help educate for a world society. Evaluate the directions he outlines for the curriculum.
7. According to Slesnick, why is it not the fault of the consumer who does not find

computers useful at home or at school?

8. Does programming experience mean job security?
9. What effect do computers have on student achievement?
10. Rather than replace teachers with computers, what would be the most sensible use of computers?
11. Explore the courses available designed to promote computer literacy at your college.
12. Survey your local school district in terms of their use of microcomputers. Interview persons in charge of these programs, then assess the overall local effectiveness of this innovation.
13. Compare the more widely used microcomputers used in schools and colleges with those available for home instruction in terms of costs, programs, characteristic uses, and other features.
14. Invite an expert to speak in class and to provide an introductory demonstration of computer uses.

SUGGESTED READINGS

Becker, Henry Jay. "The Computer and the Elementary School." *Principal* 64 (May 1985):32–34.

Bell, Margaret E. "The Role of Instructional Theories in the Evaluation of Microcomputer Courseware." *Educational Technology* 25 (March 1985):36–40.

Bennett, Randy Elliot. "Evaluating Microcomputer Programs." *Special Services in the Schools* 1 (Fall 1984):83–90.

Bork, Alfred. "Computer Futures for Education." *Creative Computing* 10 (November 1984):178–180.

———. "Computers in Education Today—And Some Possible Futures." *Phi Delta Kappan* 66 (December 1984):239–243.

Culbertson, Jack A., and Cunningham, Luvern L. eds. *Microcomputers and Education,* Part I, 85th Yearbook of the National Society for the Study of Education. Chicago: University of Chicago, 1986.

Grube, Mark, "Evaluating the Educational Value of Microcomputers." *Computers in the Schools* 1 (Winter 1984):35–44.

Hoffman, Charles. "Access and Equity: Computers for Everyone." *Technological Horizons in Education* 12 (May 1985):72–74.

Moskowitz, Jay H., and Birman, Beatrice F. "Computers in the Schools: Implications of Change." *Educational Technology* 25 (January 1985): 7–14.

Pogrow, Stanley. "Helping Students to Become Thinkers." *Electronic Learning* 4 (April 1985):26–29, 79.

Schwartz, Arthur H. "Microcomputer Applications: Facts, Functions, Fads, and Fallacies." *Journal of Childhood Communication Disorders* 8 (Fall–Winter 1984): 89–111.

Shane, Harold G. "The Silicon Age II: Living and Learning in an Information Epoch." *Phi Delta Kappan* (October 1983): 126–129.

Sigg, S. F. "Computers in the Classroom." *Mathematics and Computer Education* 20 (Winter 1986):15–18.

Tucker, Mark S. "Computers in the Schools: What Revolution?" *Journal of Communication* 35 (Fall 1985):12–23.

Wagschal, Peter H. "A Last Chance for Computers in the Schools?" *Phi Delta Kappan* 66 (December 1984):251–254.

Webster, Staten W., and Webster, Linda S. "Computer Literacy or Competency?" *Teacher Education Quarterly* 12 (Spring 1985):1–7.

Wittich, Walter A. "Educational Technology: Sixty Years of Change." NASSP *Bulletin* 69 (April 1985):35–38.

13

Bilingual Education

Bilingual education has become an important part of American and Canadian education, marked by the testing of a number of approaches during the 1960s and the growth and spread of bilingual education during the 1970s. Historically, the United States has tended to assimilate foreign-speaking people from European backgrounds, but American Indians, Puerto Ricans, and Mexican-Americans have been less linguistically assimilated. In Canada, even before the Bilingualism and Biculturalism Commission's report (1968), educators urged the introduction of French (or English in French-speaking schools) in elementary grades at as early an age as possible.

Bilingual children traditionally tended to find that neither language served them well in coping with academic work. Educators, however, have generally underestimated the influence of the home language and culture. Those who survive academically are frequently asked to choose between their heritage and the dominant culture, a choice that may result in isolating themselves from their culture and their family.

Bilingual education seeks to overcome these problems. Bilingual education is designed to provide schooling fully or partly in a second language for the purpose of enabling students to acquire proficiency in the second language while simultaneously maintaining their proficiency in the first language and fully promoting their overall educational development. English is learned not as an end in itself but as one of many tools—the home language is another—for the development of skills, attitudes, and basic concepts.

At one time school officials, in those cases where there were few bilingual children, did nothing about the problem or perceived it as a problem of low IQ. Some early programs focused on vocabulary items without building a syntactic framework for using words. This was followed by an approach in the 1950s and early 1960s of teaching English as a second language by using drill exercises; however, this approach found little role for the mother tongue. As late as 1967 in the United States, the Bilingual Education Act developed curricula and Spanish language instruction but gave little attention to the development of bilingual teachers.

George Blanco distinguishes between equality and equity and seeks to determine whether bilingual education programs are effective and where the focus on bilingual education should be. However, *The Christian Science Monitor* contends that immersion in English is a better educational approach.

Equity, Quality, and Effectiveness in Bilingual Education

George M. Blanco

George M. Blanco (b. 1937) has taught at the elementary, high school, and the university levels. His main interests have been in the areas of second language teaching and learning and bilingual education. He held the position of Director of Foreign Languages at the Texas Education Agency and, later, that of Director of the Office of Bilingual Education at the University of Texas at Austin. He has served as a consultant to state and federal agencies, as well as to American schools in various Latin American countries. He currently teaches full time in the area of bilingual education at The University of Texas at Austin.

Federal and state attention to bilingual education in the United States during the past 18 years has been characterized by controversy and debate concerning its effectiveness, its cost to the taxpayer, its philosophy, and its lack of a conceptual framework with the necessary research underpinnings. Bilingual education during this period has also been characterized as compensatory in nature, i.e., designed primarily for lower socioeconomic students of limited English-language proficiency. It has also been implemented as a transitional program whereby the students' first language is eventually replaced altogether by English for instructional purposes.

Essentially, the goal of bilingual education in the United States has been to ensure that non-English speaking (NES) or limited English-speaking (LES) students acquire a good command of the English language and to succeed academically in the subjects that comprise the school curriculum.

This paper addresses the issue of equity of instruction for a segment of the student population referred to by Hawley (1982:207) as "children at risk." In his words:

> . . . children at risk are assumed to have special needs that set them apart, at least to some extent, from other children and, therefore, disadvantages . . . . What children at risk have in common is a set of circumstances which, while different, are likely to reduce the effectiveness or, in some cases make inappropriate, conventional educational practices. Business as usual for children at risk is risky business.

NES/LES children fall into the category of children at risk by virtue of the linguistic and cultural circumstances which make them different from the monolingual English speaker of the majority culture in the United States. The issue that NES/LES children are linguistically and culturally different has always worked to their disadvantage—the fact that they spoke a language other than Eng-

This essay was written especially for this book.

lish was *their* problem, not the school's, and it was *their* duty to conform to the school's all-English model from the outset. This was usually the case, despite the much touted maxim heard by several generations of future teachers: "Begin where the child is."

The U.S. Supreme Court case *Lau vs. Nichols*, decreed that English-only educational programs did not provide equal educational opportunity to Chinese-speaking students in San Francisco. In the educational arena, the terms "equal" and "equitable" have often been used synonymously. According to Salomone (1982:11) equality ". . . refers specifically to division, partition, and redistribution . . . it refers to numerical equality and to equal treatment or inputs. Equity, on the other hand, is a broader concept encompassing justice, equality, humanity, morality, and right."

Following this line of thinking, children at risk need not only educational opportunities that are equal, but also opportunities that are equitable. Educational equity for NES/LES students, as it is implemented in the schools, refers to special programs, strategies, and materials which go beyond those regularly in place for monolingual English-speaking students. The mounting of special programs for children at risk, then, is seen as a necessary step toward assuring that equity be present before true equality can exist. Given the fact, however, that programs for children at risk, such as bilingual education, are compensatory in nature, the question of quality, effectiveness, and excellence surfaces.

EDUCATIONAL QUALITY AND EFFECTIVENESS

While there is a considerable body of literature regarding bilingual education out-side the United States (Paulston, 1978), research in this country has been supported in a concerted manner by the federal government since 1979 through funding under Part C Research Agenda of ESEA Title VII. Prior to this effort, most of the research conducted fell into the area of program evaluation using a quantitative paradigm. Comparative studies using a quantitative paradigm required large student samples to provide reliable statistics. According to Goodrich (1980), the only language groups that have large enough numbers of students to warrant use of quantitative comparisons are the Spanish, French, and Navajo. Vázquez (1981) feels that this observation is important because cultural and linguistic differences affect such elements as educational practices, student achievement, motivation, etc., thus rendering interlanguage group comparisons less reliable. Research to show bilingual education effectiveness, or lack thereof, has been difficult to conduct. The evaluation of Title VII Spanish/English bilingual education programs conducted by the American Institutes for Research (AIR) (Danoff, 1978) has been criticized for its inadequacies (Gray, 1977 and 1978; O'Malley, 1978). Yet, Troike (1978) states that not all of the negative findings can be dismissed and that program weaknesses should be corrected. Both Saravia Shore (1979) and Vázquez (1981) feel that effectiveness is a relative term concerning several critical questions: What is to be measured? In relation to what? Using what criteria? Selected by whom?

Troike (1978 and 1981) in his reviews of bilingual education program evaluations in the United States concludes that quality programs can be effective in providing equal educational opportunities for NES/LES children. He feels strongly that if a program does not provide equal educational opportunities, there is something wrong with the program.

It is interesting to note that in the programs examined by Troike, the students in the bilingual education programs generally performed as well as, and in some cases better than, students in monolingual programs at the district or national levels in a variety of subjects. It is particularly noteworthy that the standardized tests used in these programs were in English. One of the main criticisms about bilingual education has been the notion that children are either not exposed sufficiently to the English language, or that time spent on instruction in the native language takes valuable time away from exposure to English.

There has been considerable research, both at the applied and the theoretical levels, to show that learning through two languages not only helps children learn the required subject matter, but that it also promotes their mastering the English language better than an all-English setting. Saravia Shore and Arvizu (in press) compiled a descriptive summary of a series of research projects which also support the general use of the students' native language for a portion of the instructional program.

We return to the issue of effectiveness, since its definition or definitions are of prime importance to the concept of bilingual education. The major part of the literature on effective instruction deals with monolingual settings. Even in such settings, it is highly improbable that there exist universal conditions of teaching, given the complex nature of the classroom teaching and learning (Tikunoff and Vázquez-Faría, 1982).

Barnes (1981:2) provides an operational definition of the "effective teacher":

> The "effective teacher" is the teacher whose classes regularly score higher on standardized achievement tests than do classes of other teachers of similar students after entering

differences among classes are statistically removed.

Barnes (1981:10) goes on to state that ". . . teachers who establish both a task or work-oriented atmosphere in the classroom and a warm, supportive environment for their students are providing those students with a successful learning environment." *The Significant Bilingual Instructional Features Study* (SBIF) (Tikunoff, et al., 1981) was based on the premise that effective instructional strategies are probably generic and are similar in monolingual and bilingual settings. The SBIF Study did not use traditional achievement test performance as a measure of effectiveness. Actual observation was used, based on an adaptation of the observation system used by Good and Grouws (1979). Two types of student outcomes were used for 232 students in 58 classrooms: Academic Learning Time (ALT), and establishing the students' competent participation in instructional work activity. ALT is the amount of time a student spends in a content area engaged in learning tasks with a high degree of accuracy. These students achieved a success rate of 80 percent, which averages to 84 minutes per student per day of ALT. The second student outcome, participation in instructional work activity, is particularly important for NES/LES students. Participation requires ". . . that a student understand what is going on, what the task requirements are, what the completed product must look like, what the steps are for completing the task, what the teacher's expectations are with regard to task completion, etc." (Tinkunoff and Váquez-Faría, 1982:249–50). It is obvious, then, that if students do not understand the language of instruction, they will not perform satisfactorily and will fall behind academically.

The SBIF Study speculates that the teacher sample used was effective, as judged by their use of active teaching behaviors and by their producing desired student performance in terms of ALT and student participation in instruction. Further, three skills or behaviors distinguish successful teachers in the sample from effective teachers in monolingual settings:

1. Teachers in the sample used *both* L1 and L2 [first language and second language] for instruction. . . . Particularly for NES/ LES who have no English or little English proficiency, this allows access to instruction.

2. Teachers focused some instructional time on English language development, using variations of the bilingual instructional strategies . . . designed to develop English language proficiency while concurrently ensuring that NES/LES will have access to regular instruction in the content areas so that they don't fall behind while learning English.

3. Preliminary analysis of the descriptions of instruction for teachers in the sample reveal frequent use of behavior which appears to be culturally relevant and specific for the ethnolinguistic group of NES/LES in a given classroom. . . .

For children to participate successfully in the instructional process, they must understand what is going on and what is expected of them. Equitable instructional programs, therefore, require that a school go above and beyond the regular school curriculum for children at risk who do not understand or speak the school language. Equally important, however, is the finding that effective teachers exhibit similar behaviors whether the setting being evaluated is monolingual or bilingual.

There are, of course, studies to support an anti-bilingual education stance. The AIR Study (Danoff, 1978) cited earlier, is perhaps, the best known example. Paulston (1978:188) states that "A study can be found to support virtually every possible opinion." The issue, then, is not so much whether bilingual education, ESL, or any other educational treatment "works" for the NES/LES children but whether students can participate actively in the instructional activities of the curriculum. Of the present options available, bilingual education seems to be the only approach that promotes understanding and thus encourages active participation by NES/LES students in the instructional activities, as far as the content areas are concerned.

Critics of dual-language instruction, however, are quick to point out that time learning subject matter in L1 is time taken away from the learning of English. As was shown by some of the studies reviewed by Troike (1978), participation in a sound bilingual education program does not retard student academic progress nor the learning of English. There is abundant anecdotal information regarding the academic success experienced by foreigners, such as Mexicans, who come to the United States and who often surpass their Spanish-speaking classmates born in this country (Lazos, 1981). The fact that foreign-born students often surpass their U.S.-born classmates in English (and consequently in the content areas) is, perhaps, best explained by the work of Cummins (1979) and the research conducted in Scandinavia by Skutnabb-Kangas and Toukomaa (1976) and Skutnabb-Kangas (1980).

Cummins has come forth with two hypotheses which may help to explain the anomalous situation of foreign-born students achieving a higher level of academic success than U.S.-born NES/LES students. The first is the Threshold Hypothesis which proposes that certain levels of L1 development must be attained by children to avoid cognitive deficits and to obtain cognitive benefits of bilingualism. If children's L1 is interrupted and discontinued before reaching the "threshold," around the age of 10 or 11, their cognitive development will be retarded. Cummins (1979) and Skutnabb-Kangas and Toukomaa (1976) have advanced the hypothesis that the cognitive aspects of L1 and L2 are interdependent and that proficiency in L2 is partially a function of the L1 proficiency level at the time the child was intensively exposed to L2. Since L1 and L2 Cognitive/Academic Language Proficiency are manifestations of the same underlying linguistic proficiency, literacy in L1 will have a direct bearing on literacy in L2. These hypotheses appear to be supported by the work of Skutnabb-Kangas and Toukomaa (1976) who indicate that, in general, the better students preserve their native language, the better are their prerequisites for learning a second language. These researchers report that the ability to do abstract thinking in the mother tongue is a prerequisite for learning mathematical concepts.

From the standpoint of cognitive development for NES/LES students, then, the research strongly supports the idea of ensuring L1 development until they have reached the "threshold" level and have attained the necessary literacy skills. From the point of view of English language development, the research also suggests a strong L1 base, since proficiency in L2 is directly related to proficiency in L1. This relationship has also been supported by some of the research reported by Saravia Shore and Arvizu (in press). An equitable solution to the dilemma would be to ensure a quantitative and qualitative *continuation* of the children's L1 for a longer period of time than is now commonly done. The issue does not revolve solely around the question of whether children can exit from a bilingual program to participate in an all English learning environment. Rather, it deals with the notion of ensuring the most efficient type of instruction for NES/LES students. By exiting students from the bilingual education program before L1 is firmly established, we may be truncating their cognitive/academic skills and their English language development.

LANGUAGE ATTITUDES

Sociolinguists maintain that the importance and prestige of a language are essentially based on the persons who use it, the audience, the purpose, and place where it is used (d'Angelan and Tucker, 1973; Fishman, 1972; Labov, 1966). If students perceive their native language to be unimportant by virtue of its minimal use or its use in a begrudging fashion, the result can only be negative. Tikunoff and Vázquez-Faría (1981:252–53) agree, stating that:

> A strong argument for bilingual instruction for NES/LES rests with the assumption that when instruction is provided only in English, a hierarchy of language use is constructed. At the top of that hierarchy is English, and those who can use it competently thereafter are perceived to be somehow "better" than those who cannot. If the NES/LES never hears his/her home language used in the classroom for instruction, or hears it only in a negative context for reprimands, attitudes might develop which place English in a positive frame and the child's home language in a negative frame.

Hansen and Johnson (1981), in their extensive review of the literature on language attitudes, found that language learning is related to self-esteem. "This literature clearly demonstrates that some language varieties are generally held to be inferior to others, and that children quickly adopt the dominant evaluations, perhaps to the detriment of their own self-esteem or cultural identity" (Hansen and Johnson, 1981:4). Positive self-esteem is seen as promoting positive attitudes toward learning and participating and succeeding in school work (Tikunoff and Vázquez-Faría, 1981).

The question of language attitudes in general and toward minority languages and minority groups in particular is an extremely complex one. Whatever the source of language attitudes or attitudes toward ethnolinguistic groups may be, it is quite evident that children adopt "dominant evaluations," to reiterate Hansen and Johnson's term. Children very often exhibit negative attitudes toward their native language, even in a bilingual education program. The pressure to abandon the native language in favor of English, exclusively, is significant, and it is pervasive throughout the educational system, the students' homes, and society at large.

The learning of English is one, if not the primary, goal of bilingual education programs in the United States, and it is vital that NES/LES students learn English and learn it well. The work of Cummins (1979) and the Scandinavian research cited earlier (Skutnabb-Kangas and Toukomaa, 1976), have a direct bearing on the ability of bilingual education students to learn English well. If children are tacitly or openly encouraged to abandon their native language in favor of English before reaching the threshold level, bilingual education will not go beyond a compensatory program with all of the negative opinions that accompany such programs. It is my contention that effective teaching in bilingual or monolingual programs is directly related to and, indeed, shaped by forces outside the school itself. The school, as one of the main purveyors of the mainstream culture, necessarily reflects the attitudes and values of that society. This perspective is not new, and it is supported in the literature on language attitudes and on social educational change.

FACTORS BEYOND THE CLASSROOM

Paulston (1978) contends that questions regarding bilingual education have shifted with more attention focused on factors outside the programs themselves as causal variables. Bilingual education has usually been looked on as the independent variable and the children's behavior as the dependent variable. Paulston (1978:191) goes on to state that:

We can begin to understand these questions only when we see bilingual education as the *result* of certain societal factors, rather than the *cause* of certain behaviors in children. Unless we attempt in some way to account for the sociohistorical, cultural, economic, and political factors which lead to certain forms of bilingual education, we will not be able to understand or to assess the consequences of that education.

The issue of research which focuses on the classroom, as opposed to research which looks at the larger context within which the classroom exists is examined by Akinasso (1981). This researcher states that the sociolinguistic studies of educational inequality have been criticized by such writers as Ogbu (1974) Karabel and Halsey (1977) for emphasizing micro rather than macrocosmic processes. These studies result in explanations that tell *how*, but not *why*. Gumperz (1980) feels that one cannot dismiss the classroom, altogether. Since students spend a significant part of their formative years in school, he says that what happens there can either change or reinforce values and attitudes brought from outside the classroom.

Hansen and Johnson (1981:2) synthesize this whole issue:

Classroom learning is seen as more than a simple acquisition of knowledge and skills such as reading, writing and arithmetic; it is seen as a process of active effort to understand and cope with the demands, opportunities and restrictions of the social environment of the classroom and school – demands, opportunities and restrictions that are themselves changing, and often are symbolically created not only by teachers, administrators and policy makers, but also by the child's community and family, and by new technologies of teaching, learning and living.

It is my opinion that the negative attitudes about minority ethnolinguistic groups and their languages have a direct effect on the nature of the instructional program and on the learning processes of the students themselves. We have evidence that bilingual education can be effective, that it can promote academic quality, that students can learn the required subject matter and that they can learn the English language . . . provided that the right educational and societal circumstances are present.

CONCLUDING REMARKS

The school and societal contexts in which programs for children at risk operate are as important, if not more so, than the actual instructional strategies used by the teacher. Programs, such as those using a dual-language approach, often operate as an appendage, as something to be tolerated, rather than as an integral part of the instructional and curricular program. The result is circular: the programs are appendages because of negative attitudes and the fact that the programs are appendages further reinforces these attitudes. The opinion held about such programs on the part of all teachers, administrators, parents, the community and society at large determines what the teacher can or cannot do. Negative attitudes about programs for children at risk and about their native language and cultural group breed equally nega-

tive attitudes, on the part of the students, about the special instructional efforts and about themselves.

Educational quality, achievement, effectiveness, and equity are not mutually exclusive concepts. Quite the contrary, these concepts should be mutually supportive to produce the desired educational results.

REFERENCES

Akinnaso, F. N. "Research on Minority Languages and Educational Achievement: A Synthesis and an Interpretation." 1981. ERIC Document ED 216 517.

Barnes, S. *Synthesis of Selected Research of Teaching Findings.* Austin, TX: The University of Texas at Austin, Research and Development Center for Teacher Education, 1981.

Cummins, J. "Cognitive/Academic Language Proficiency, Linguistic Interdependence, the Optimum Age Question and Some Other Matters." in *Working Papers on Bilingualism,* No. 19. Toronto: Ontario Institute for Studies in Education, 1979.

d'Anglejan, A. and Tucker, G. R. "Sociolinguistic Correlates of Speech Style in Quebec." In R. W. Shuy and R. W. Fasold, eds., *Language Attitudes: Current Trends and Prospects.* Washington, D.C.: Georgetown University Press, 1973.

Danoff, M. N. *Evaluation of the Impact of ESEA Title VII Spanish/English Bilingual Education Programs: Overview of Study and Findings.* Palo Alto, CA: American Institutes for Research, 1978.

Fishman, J. A. *Sociolinguistics: a Brief Introduction.* Rowley, MA: Newbury House Publishers, 1972.

Good, T. L. and Grouws, D. "The Missouri Mathematics Effectiveness Project: An Experimental Study in Fourth Grade Classrooms" *Journal of Educational Psychology,* 1979, 71, 335–362.

Goodrich, R. L. *Planning Factors for Studies of*

Bilingual Instructional Features. Bilingual Instructional Features Planning Study. Vol. 3. Washington, D.C.: National Institute of Education, 1980.

Gray, T. C. "Response to AIR Study." (Duplicated.) Arlington, VA: Center for Applied Linguistics, 1977.

———. "Challenge to USOE Final Evaluation of the Impact of ESEA Title VII Spanish/English Bilingual Education Program." (Duplicated.) Arlington, VA: Center for Applied Linguistics, 1978.

Gumperz, J. J. "Conversational Inference and Classroom Learning." In J. L. Green and C. Wallat, eds., *Ethnography and Language in Educational Settings.* Norwood, NJ: Ablex, 1980.

Hansen, D. A. and Johnson, V. A. *The Social Contexts of Learning in Bilingual Classrooms: An Interpretive Review of the Literature on Language Attitudes.* Rosslyn, VA: National Clearinghouse for Bilingual Education, 1981.

Hawley, W. D. Preface, "Effective Educational Strategies for Children at Risk." *Peabody Journal of Education,* 1982, 59 (4), 207–208.

Karabel, Jr. and Halsey, A. H. "Educational Research: A Review and an Interpretation." In J. Karabel and A. H. Halsey, eds., *Power and Ideology in Education.* New York: Oxford University Press, 1977.

Labov, W. *The Social Stratification of English in New York City.* Arlington, VA: Center for Applied Linguistics, 1966.

Lazos, Héctor. *A Study of the Relationship of Language Proficiency in the Motor Tongue and Acquisition of Second Language Reading Skills in Bilingual Children at Age Twelve.* Unpublished Doctoral Dissertation. The University of Texas at Austin, August 1981.

Ogbu, J. U. *The Next Generation: An Ethnography of Education in a Urban Neighborhood.* New York: Academic Press, 1974.

O'Malley, J. M. "Review of the Evaluation of the Impact of ESEA Title VII Spanish/English Bilingual Program." *Bilingual Resources,* 1978, 1 (2), 6–10.

Paulston, C. B. "Bilingual/Bicultural Education." In L. S. Shulman, ed., *Review of Research in Education,* 6. Itaska, IL: F. E. Peacock Publishers, Inc., 1978.

Salomone, R. M. "Public Policy and the Law: Legal Precedence and Prospects for Equity in Education." 1982, in press.

Saravia-Shore, M. "A Ethnographic Evaluation/Research Model for Bilingual Programs." In R. V. Padilla, ed., *Bilingual Education and Public Policy in the United States.* Ypsilanti, MI: Eastern Michigan University, 1979.

Saravia-Shore, M. and Arvizu, S., eds., *Cross-Cultural and Communication Competencies: Ethnographies for Educational Programs for Language Minority Students.* West Cornwall, CT: Horizon Communications (in press).

Skutnabb-Kangas, T. *Language in the Process of Cultural Assimilation and Structural Incorporation of Linguistic Minorities.* Rosslyn, VA: National Clearinghouse for Bilingual Education, 1980.

Skutnabb-Kangas, T. and Toukamaa, P. *Teaching Migrant Children's Mothertongue and Learning the Language of the Host Country in the Context of the Sociocultural Situation of the Migrant Family.* Helsinki: Finnish National Commission for UNESCO, 1976.

Tikunoff, W. J. and Vázquez-Faría, J. A. "Successful Instruction for Bilingual Schooling." *Peabody Journal of Education,* 1982, 59 (4), 234–271.

Tikunoff, W. J. et al. *Preliminary Analysis of the Data for Part I of the Significant Bilingual Instructional Features Study.* San Francisco: Far West Laboratory for Educational Research and Development, 1981.

Troike, R. C. "Research Evidence for the Effectiveness of Bilingual Education." *NABE Journal,* 1978, 3 (1), 13–24.

Troike, R. C. "Synthesis of Research on Bilingual Education." *Educational Leadership,* March 1981, 498–504.

Vázquez, J. A. "The Social, Political, and Instructional Contexts of the Bilingual Public Education Movement in the U.S.: A Brief Overview." In W. J. Tikunoff, et al., *Preliminary Analysis of the Data for Part I of the Significant Bilingual Instructional Features Study.* San Francisco: Far West Laboratory for Educational Research and Development, 1981.

Bilingualism Is Not the Way

The Christian Science Monitor

Of all the major educational issues confronting the American people, perhaps none is as contentious as that of bilingual education. Thousands of school-age children receive instruction in public schools primarily in their native language. Given the fact that public schools are now called upon to teach huge numbers of children from minority backgrounds, the bilingual approach is not surprising. In Texas alone, minorities make up close to half of the school-age population. About two-thirds of that group are hispanic. Many of those children speak only Spanish. In California, minorities comprise two-fifths of the school children. Again, many children can communicate only in their native language.

The motive for bilingualism, of course, is well-intentioned: namely, to ensure that the children have access to an appropriate and comprehensive education in the only language they understand, until such time as they acquire skills in English.

Unfortunately, good intention does not necessarily promote sound public policy.

There is strong evidence that bilingualism is short-changing for the long-range educational and social needs of the children and unduly burdening financially strapped school systems. Worst of all, a sentimental embracing of multiculturalism may be working against the assimilation so necessary to ensure that the United States remains a unified nation.

The better educational approach, it seems to us, is that recommended by the Twentieth Century Fund's task force on federal elementary and secondary education policy. The report stresses the importance of literacy in English as an overriding educational objective. It would achieve this through a preliminary program of total immersion in English language courses followed by a "catch up" period in courses such as mathematics, science, history, etc., which may have been neglected during the immersion process. This is the reverse of current practice.

Immersion in English—and moving away from bilingualism—makes sense. The issue is not one of denying children necessary instruction in their home language and culture. During a transition period teachers must be patient and not equate unfamiliarity with English with stupidity. And each school system should work out a program of immersion based on its particular circumstances—the children involved, which language they speak, their grade level, and so on. But the primary goal should be fluency in English.

To reject such an approach means continuing to subject school systems to impossible demands in finding foreign language instructors (as many as 56,000 would be needed for bilingual programs around the US, according to the Department of Education). Also, even if schools accommodate a use of languages other than English, this merely postpones the reality of the larger society, which does not.

From "Bilingualism Is Not the Way," The Christian Science Monitor (July 14, 1983). Reprinted by permission for the editorial page of The Christian Science Monitor. © *1983 The Christian Science Publishing Society. All rights reserved.*

The United States has always been a nation of many peoples, whose languages and cultures are respected. But English is the official and functional language of the United States. Its official records, its laws, its public discourse, its commerce have under almost all circumstances been conducted in English. It is that very commonality provided by the English language that has helped to give unity, shape, and direction to such a diverse society. At a time when young people need to know far more than the mere rudiments of good English just to obtain jobs in an increasingly sophisticated technological society, this would hardly seem to be the moment to create an educational system that downplays, minimizes, or even ignores English.

DISCUSSION QUESTIONS AND ACTIVITIES

1. Who are the "children at risk"?
2. What is the difference between *equality* and *equity*? Is it a valid distinction?
3. Why is research to demonstrate bilingual education effectiveness difficult to conduct?
4. Does time spent on native language take away valuable time from the study of English?
5. The issue, according to Blanco, is not whether bilingual education works but "whether students can participate actively in the instructional activities of the curriculum." What does he mean by this statement? Do you agree?
6. Should the focus in bilingual education be on the classroom? Forces beyond the classroom? Both?
7. Why does *The Christian Science Monitor*'s editorial claim that immersion in English is a better educational approach than bilingual education?

8. Will immersion in English place non-English-speaking students at a distinct disadvantage?
9. Do the needs of the larger society indicate that immersion in English, rather than bilingual education, is necessary?
10. What common values will immersion in English help support?
11. Observe bilingual programs in operation and report to the class on your observations.
12. Invite a bilingual educator to relate his or her teaching experience in the program.
13. Ask students who grew up in bilingual homes about their early school experiences.

SUGGESTED READINGS

Research Studies

Andersson, Theodore, and Boyer, Mildred. *Bilingual Schooling in the United States*, 2 vols. Detroit: Blain Ethridge, 1976.

Danhoff, M. N. *Evaluation of the Impact of ESEA Title VII Spanish/English Bilingual Education Program: Overview of Studies and Findings.* Palo Alto, Calif.: American Institutes for Research, 1978.

Dulay, H. C., and Burt, M. K. *Why Bilingual Education? A Summary of Research Findings*, 2nd ed. San Francisco: Bloombury West, 1978.

Fishman, Joshua. *Bilingual Education: An International Sociological Perspective.* Rowley, Mass.: Newbury House, 1976.

Hansen, D. A., and Johnson, V. A. *The Social Contexts of Learning in Bilingual Classrooms: An Interpretive Review of the Literature on Language Attitudes.* Rosslyn, Va.: National Clearinghouse for Bilingual Education, 1981.

Issues

Baker, Keith A., and deKanter, Andriana A. "An Answer from Research on Bilingual Education." *American Education* 19 (July 1983):40–48.

Barry, Joseph E. "Politics, Bilingual Education, and the Curriculum." *Educational Leadership* 40 (May 1983):56–60.

Carrison, P. "Bilingual–No!" *Principal* 62, no. 3 (1983):9, 41–44.

Cohen, Gaynor. "The Politics of Bilingual Education." *Oxford Review of Education* 10, no. 2 (1984):225–241.

Duhamel, R. J. "Bilingual Immersion." *Education Canada* 16 (Spring 1975):28.

Hechinger, Fred M. "How It's Done Elsewhere." *The New York Times Magazine* (November 10, 1985):50, 60, 75.

McFadden, Bernard J. "Bilingual Education and the Law," *Journal of Law and Education* 12 (January 1983):1–27.

Ovando, Carlos J. "Bilingual/Bicultural Education: Its Legacy and Its Future." *Phi Delta Kappan* 64 (April 1983):564–568.

Rohter, Larry. "The Politics of Bilingualism." *The New York Times Magazine* (November 10, 1985):1, 45.

Rotberg, Iris C. "Bilingual Education Policy in the United States." *Prospects: Quarterly Review of Education* 14, no. 1 (1984): 133–147.

Texas Monthly. "Double Talk." (July 1980): 78–83.

Waggoner, Dorothy. "The Need for Bilingual Education: Estimates from the 1980 Census." *NABE: The Journal for the National Association of Bilingual Education* 8 (Winter 1984):1–14.

14

Multicultural Education

When waves of immigrants were coming to American shores the melting pot ideology held sway over the thinking of educators. This ideology viewed the role of the school as that of assimilating the immigrant into the life of the culture by teaching the dominant values and beliefs. Many youth were assimilated and some rose in the socioeconomic scale but frequently at the cost of turning their backs on their own culture. Ethnic minorities today generally find public schools alien to their values and belief systems. Multicultural education has been proposed as a remedy. Multicultural education may emphasize ethnic literacy so that the different groups, including the white majority, will gain an understanding of cultural differences. Pluralists (proponents of multicultural education) believe that when assimilationists talk of promoting the common culture they often mean Anglo-American culture rather than a culture that reflects ethnic and cultural diversity. Through multicultural education, minority students not only acquire social and economic skills but skills to promote significant social change. Thus it will teach them how to bargain from a position of strength in order to gain full participation in society.

But critics note that such programs may exaggerate differences among groups and thereby be as harmful as the older practice of ignoring real differences. Additionally, should a situation arise where each group demands its own autonomy, it could cause fragmentation, cultural separation, and divisiveness. Usually it is assumed that racial bias is centered on the white middle class; however, ethnic minorities have prejudices that might be exacerbated by a narrow conceptualization of their grievances. Ethnic programs, critics add, assume monolithic groups and ignore variations in age, sex, occupations, social class, and the racially mixed background of many Americans. Though complaints may be sound about teaching a common culture founded on majoritarian values, and greater emphasis upon interdependence rather than competition may be more appropriate for a complex, interdependent society, some basic democratic values—liberty, justice, and equality—need to be taught.

In his essay, James A. Banks reviews different conceptions of multiethnic education and contrasts four leading hypotheses. M. Donald Thomas argues vigorously against certain pluralistic forms of multicultural education.

Multiethnic Education and the Quest for Equality

James A. Banks

James A. Banks (b. 1941) studied at Chicago City College, Chicago State University, and Michigan State University, has held an NDEA Fellowship for three years, and was a Spencer Fellow. He has taught in elementary schools and is presently Professor and Chairman, Department of Curriculum & Instruction at the University of Washington in Seattle. In addition to serving as a consultant on ethnic studies, he is the author of Multiethnic Education: Theory and Practice *(Allyn and Bacon),* Teaching Strategies for Ethnic Studies, *4th ed. (Allyn and Bacon), and other works.*

Multiethnic education requires that the total school environment be changed so that students from diverse ethnic and racial groups will experience educational equality. Many educators mistakenly assume that they can produce multiethnic education by simply infusing bits and pieces of ethnic content into the curriculum. Not so. Multiethnic education requires reform of the total school.

This reform must encompass staff attitudes and perceptions, the formal curriculum, teaching strategies, tests and testing procedures, and school-sanctioned languages and dialects.[1] Only when the total environment of a school promotes educational equality for all students can multiethnic education be said to exist.

Proponents of multiethnic education assume that schools have the power to substantially increase the academic achievement and life chances of minority students. This assumption contrasts sharply with the arguments set forth by theorists such as Christopher Jencks and by revisionists such as Samuel Bowles and Herbert Gintis, who contend that schools are severely limited in their ability to increase the educational equality that would seem to be a prerequisite of enhanced academic achievement and life chances.[2]

EQUALITY AND EQUITY

From the "separate but equal" Supreme Court ruling in *Plessy* v. *Ferguson* in 1896 until the mid-Fifties, black schools in the South had been unequal to white schools in terms of such input variables as teachers' salaries, facilities, instructional materials and supplies, and per-pupil expenditures. After the Supreme Court ruling in *Brown* v. *Board of Education* in 1954, however, southern and border states made major efforts to change all of that. During the Sixties and Seventies, many schools in economically depressed areas used funds authorized by the Elementary and Secondary Education Act of 1965 to make

From James A. Banks, "Multiethnic Education and the Quest for Equality," Phi Delta Kappan *(April 1983):582–585. Reprinted with the permission of James A. Banks and Phi Delta Kappa.*

their input variables more equal to those of schools in economically advantaged areas. By the end of 1979 the federal government had granted $23.2 billion under this act to local school districts.[3]

But the massive and controversial Coleman Report, released in 1966, indicated that such input variables as school facilities and curricula are not the most important correlates of academic achievement.[4] James Coleman concluded that such variables as the teachers' verbal ability, the children's sense of control of their environment, and the children's educational backgrounds play the most important role in academic achievement.

The gains made in equalizing such school input variables as teachers' salaries and school facilities during the 1960s and 1970s and the findings of the Coleman Report— coupled with the continuing failure of many minority students to attain educational parity with middle-class white youths—made the notion of measuring educational equality by inputs increasingly unpopular during the 1970s.[5] Instead, educators and social scientists began to define educational equality in terms of the results or effects of schooling. From this perspective, such groups as blacks, Chicanos, and Native Americans are thought to have equal educational opportunity only when their scores on standardized tests and other leading indicators of educational achievement are roughly equal to those of their white counterparts.

The output conception of educational equality, like other notions of equality, is both helpful and problematic. This conception does not explicitly recognize the clear relationship between school input variables and pupil achievement. But the school alone cannot bring about educational equality as measured by output; such other institutions as the family, the church, and the mass media also play powerful educational roles. Despite the prob-

lems inherent in the output conception of educational equality, this notion can help educators to set specific goals and to measure their progress toward closing the achievement gap between ethnic minorities and middle-class white students.

Clearly, educators must focus on educational equality, but this is not sufficient. They should also focus on the educational process, through which they can help children to experience educational *equity*. According to Patricia Graham, "Equity differentiates itself from equal educational opportunity by attention to the internal process of education, to the circumstances in which teaching and learning are embedded. The focus is not only on the 'input' (such as access) or 'output' (such as result) but on the educational process in between."[6] In other words, input variables, output variables, and the process of education are integrally interrelated; each must receive attention, if education is to help minority youths attain the literacy and other skills essential for survival in our technological society.

I agree with Graham that the process of education should receive the greatest emphasis, since educational outcomes rest to a considerable degree on the quality of this process. Moreover, I believe that multiethnic education offers the best hope of educational equity for minority students, because it focuses on reforming those variables of the school environment that now prevent minority students from having effective, enriching, and stimulating learning experiences.

During the 1960s and the 1970s educators increasingly realized that children whose family and community cultures differed markedly from the culture of the school were likely to find academic success more elusive than children whose home and community cultures were congruent with that of the school. For example, many Hispanic children

are socialized in the barrio. If they are to achieve on the same academic level as middle-class white youths, the school culture—whose norms, goals, and expectations are primarily white and middle class[7]—must be changed substantially. Merely treating such Hispanic children "equally" (i.e., the same as middle-class white children) will not help many of them to attain the knowledge, skills, and attitudes they need to function effectively in this highly technological society. Because of differing motivational styles, languages, and values, Hispanic and Anglo students may often have to be taught differently, if we expect them to learn the same skills and knowledge.[8] In other words, children from some ethnic groups may have different educational entitlements and needs. To reflect cultural democracy and to promote educational equality, the school may be required to provide specialized services, programs, and instruction for these students.

It is true that Jewish and Japanese-American students have been very successful academically; yet they have had no federally mandated bilingual programs in the public schools. (Both groups have established private, after-school language classes.) But the academic success of these groups does not necessarily imply that Hispanic children do not need bilingual education in order to attain educational parity with other students. *Some* Hispanic students may need bilingual programs; others may not.

EDUCATION AND SCHOOLING

The public school must play an important but limited role in bringing about educational equality. The family, the mass media, the community, the church, and the youth culture also play important roles in educating the young.[9] To the extent that these other insti-

tutions promote norms, behaviors, and values that contradict those that the school promotes, the school is hindered in achieving its goals. Thus policy makers must recognize both the possibilities and the limitations of the school in bringing about equal educational opportunity.

Within the last decade, the school has been handicapped in helping children to attain basic skills because it has received little help or support from the family, the community, and other important social institutions. The efforts of the school to teach children such values as justice and equality have often been undercut by practices in the larger society that contradict those teachings. Admittedly, the public school has not distinguished itself by its efforts to promote those values we think of as the American Creed. Nevertheless, it rarely gets much community support when it tries to do so. Although I will focus solely on the role of the school in bringing about educational equality, readers should keep in mind the severe limitations under which the school operates and the extent to which this institution is simply a reflection of the larger society. Our high expectations for the school should be tempered by these realities.

Minority youths are not likely to achieve full educational equality until other institutions within the society implement reforms that support those that I will propose here for the school. Educators should also realize that the notion of equal educational opportunity is an ideal toward which we should work. Working toward this ideal is a continuing process.

To help minority youths attain educational equality during the 1980s, educational programs should reflect the enormous diversity *within* ethnic groups. Too often, social scientists and educators describe ethnic minorities as monolithic groups, rather than as groups that display enormous socioeconomic, regional, cultural, and linguistic diversity. We have all heard or read such oversimplified and misleading statements as: "Blacks made continuous progress during the 1960s and 1970s," or "Indian children have low self-concepts." Such statements generally conceal more than they reveal and reinforce harmful educational practices.

Like educational programs, educational policy related to ethnic minorities should reflect the tremendous differences *within* ethnic groups. Most Puerto Ricans, blacks, Chicanos, and Native Americans are on the lower rungs of the socioeconomic ladder. But each of these groups also has a sizable middle class—with values, interests, behaviors, and educational needs that differ to some extent from those of the rest of the group.

Although these middle-class individuals usually identify to some extent with their ethnic groups, they also have strong social-class interests that bind them in many ways to other middle-class groups in the society. Middle-class members of ethnic groups often find that their class interests conflict with their ethnic allegiances, and their class interests are often more important to them than their ethnic attachments. Thus middle-class blacks and Chicanos often move to suburban communities and send their children to private schools—not to enhance their ethnic identities, but to live in a manner consistent with their social class. Many middle-class black and Chicano parents are more interested in having their children attain the requisite skills for admission to prestigious universities than they are in having their children enroll in schools sympathetic to black English or barrio Spanish. Many middle-class black and Chicano parents, like their white counterparts, are deserting the public schools.[10] Ethnicity remains a cogent factor in U.S. society, but it is often mediated by class interests.

Shaping and implementing educational policy for minorities in the Eighties will become increasingly complex as more members of lower-status ethnic groups join the middle class.[11] Most middle-class blacks, Chicanos, and Puerto Ricans wish to retain their ethnic identities without sacrificing the full benefits and opportunities afforded other members of their social class. They may encourage their children to apply to prestigious universities, but they also expect them to relate well to their cousins in the inner city and to take active roles in ethnic activities. During the 1960s and 1970s educators focused on helping lower-class minority children to achieve educational parity. Middle-class minority children were often overlooked—or the school assumed that they, too, were poor and "culturally deprived." Educators should be keenly sensitive to the class diversity within minority communities. This diversity is likely to increase throughout the 1980s.

Of course, ethnic minorities include other important subgroups besides the very poor and the middle class. Blue-collar laborers and their families make up one substantial and important segment of ethnic communities, and their educational needs must also be considered when educational policy is shaped for the 1980s. In many working-class ethnic families, both parents work. The children of such parents do not qualify for special programs that benefit children from poorer families. Yet these working-class parents often cannot afford the educational experiences, enrichment activities, and expensive colleges that are within the means of middle-class parents. Consequently, children from working-class ethnic families are often at a disadvantage; their parents simply do not make enough money to provide them with the educational opportunities they need and deserve.

The problems of educating minority and poor youths first attracted serious attention from educators and educational researchers in the 1960s. Yet our understanding of the reasons for the higher rate of academic failure among these youngsters than among other youths remains sparse and uncertain. We can make few conclusive statements about why minority youths often perform poorly in school and about what can be done to increase their academic achievement and emotional growth. Hypotheses abound, but most of the research is inconclusive and contradictory. As is true in other areas of social science, both the research and the hypotheses reflect the ideologies, assumptions, and values of the researchers and theorists.[12]

I do not intend to suggest that we should ignore the hypotheses and research that relate to the education of ethnic groups. Rather, as consumers of these hypotheses and of this research, we should be sensitive to the ideologies, assumptions, and values that underlie them. And we should be aware of our own goals and values as well. Only in this way can we use the hypotheses and the research appropriately, in ways that will enable us to help minority youths reach their full potential.

Hypotheses regarding the education of minority youths are diverse and conflicting. In the 1960s Arthur Jensen and William Shockley revived the genetic explanation for the low academic achievement of minority youths.[13] Richard Herrnstein, by contrast, hypothesized that intelligence is related to social class.[14] The geneticists argue that minority groups do not perform as well academically as nonminorities because of their genetic characteristics; consequently, the capability of the school to bring about educational equality is severely limited. When assessing the genetic hypothesis, educators should remember its history in the U.S. In earlier times, other theorists "explained" the intellectual inferiority of such groups as the

Irish and the Jews as a matter of genes. Moreover, in studies of intelligence in a nation such as the U.S., it is difficult to control for race. Racial purity is the exception, not the rule.

The cultural-deprivation hypothesis, which also emerged during the 1960s, maintains that poor youths do not achieve well in school because of the poverty-stricken environment in which they have been reared.[15] In these environments, the argument goes, they are unable to experience the kind of cognitive stimulation that develops intellectual skills. Unlike the geneticists, those who believe in cultural deprivation are confirmed environmentalists; they think that the school can and should play a significant role in establishing educational equality for poor youths. The school can do this, they believe, by intervening in the lives of poor youths at the earliest possible age and providing them with a rich and stimulating educational environment. Those who support the cultural-deprivation hypothesis believe that intensive, behaviorally oriented instruction will enable poor youths to greatly increase their academic achievement and emotional growth.

Another group of educators—the integrationists—emerged in the 1950s. The integrationists began to develop their arguments and research during a period of segregated schooling in the U.S. Integrationists contend that the best way to bring about educational equality for minority youths is to place them in racially desegregated, middle-class schools.[16] Like the cultural deprivationists, the integrationists are environmentalists who believe that the school can and should play a significant role in bringing about educational equality. The school, they say, can increase educational equality by creating environments in which students from diverse racial groups and social classes are free to interact and learn in an atmosphere that values and respects each group. School desegregation has become a major target of the neoconservative scholars who emerged during the 1970s.[17] Urban demographic trends have greatly diminished the likelihood of successful school desegregation in the 1980s. Yet the integrationists remain strongly committed to their dream of a racially integrated America.

A fourth group of scholars and researchers, who support the cultural-difference (or multicultural) hypothesis, emerged during the 1960s and the early 1970s. They reject the views of both the geneticists and the cultural deprivationists. They do not necessarily reject the ideas of the integrationists, but they have different priorities. Led by such researchers as William Labov, Geneva Smitherman, Joan Baratz, Manuel Ramirez, and Alfredo Castañeda,[18] those who support the cultural-difference hypothesis argue that ethnic minorities have rich and diverse, not deprived, cultures. Minority youths do not achieve well in school, these theorists suggest, because the school culture is alien to them and often in conflict with their home cultures. Moreover, the I.Q. tests used to assess the academic aptitude of these youths are invalid because they are grounded in the mainstream culture.[19] To help minority youths increase their academic achievement and emotional growth, they say, we must reform the culture of the school to make it more congruent with the cultures of ethnic minority youths.

Because of the thin, contradictory, and inconclusive nature of the hypotheses and research on the education of poor and ethnic minority youths, our policies and programs must be guided primarily by our own value commitments. In his classic work, *An American Dilemma*, Gunnar Myrdal argues that Americans believe deeply in the American Creed, which includes such core values as equality, justice, and human dignity.[20] But Americans face a dilemma, Myrdal wrote, because their treatment of blacks contradicts this creed. Myrdal believed, however, that the faith of Americans in the American Creed would help them to create a society that would become increasingly more humane and just.

I also believe that the American Creed is deeply embedded in the American conscience. It dictates that we choose hypotheses to guide the education of minority youths that are consistent with equality, justice, and human dignity.

Educational programs that spring from the idea of cultural deprivation show disrespect for students' home cultures. Educational programs that spring from the genetic hypothesis violate human dignity and other values set forth in the American Creed, because they deny the possibility of a dignified existence for many minority youths.[21] Views that foster cultural freedom for minority youths, such as the cultural-difference or multicultural hypothesis, provide the greatest possibility for an education that will engender justice and equity and thus improve the human condition.

ENDNOTES

1. For further discussion of these points, see James A. Banks, *Multiethnic Education: Theory and Practice* (Boston: Allyn & Bacon, 1981).

2. Christopher Jencks et al., *Inequality: A Reassessment of the Effect of Family and Schooling in America* (New York: Basic Books, 1972); and Samuel Bowles and Herbert Gintis, *Schooling in Capitalist America* (New York: Basic Books, 1976).

3. Patricia A. Graham, "Whither Equality of Educational Opportunity?" *Daedalus*, Summer 1980, pp. 115–32.

4. James S. Coleman et al., *Equality of Educational Opportunity* (Washington, D.C.: U.S. Government Printing Office, 1966).

5. James S. Coleman, "The Concept of Equality in

Educational Opportunity," in *Equal Educational Opportunity* (Cambridge, Mass.: Harvard University Press, 1969).

6. Graham. p. 123.

7. William Greenbaum, "America in Search of a New Ideal: An Essay on the Rise of Pluralism," *Harvard Educational Review*, August 1974, pp. 411–40.

8. Geneva Gay, "Interactions in Culturally Pluralistic Classrooms," in James A. Banks, ed. *Education in the '80s: Multiethnic Education* (Washington, D.C.: National Education Association, 1981).

9. Lawrence Cremin, *Public Education* (New York: Basic Books, 1976).

10. James S. Coleman, Thomas Hoffer, and Sally Kilgore, *Public and Private Schools* (Chicago: National Opinion Research Center, March 1981).

11. William J. Wilson, *the Declining Significance of Race: Blacks and Changing American Institutions* (Chicago: University of Chicago Press, 1978).

12. Philip Green, *The Pursuit of Inequality* (New York: Pantheon, 1981).

13. Arthur R. Jensen, "How Much Can We Boost I.Q. and Scholastic Achievement?," *Harvard Educational Review*, Winter 1969, pp. 1–123; and William Shockley, "Dysgenics, Geneticity, Raceology: A Challenge to the Intellectual Responsibility of Educators," *Phi Delta Kappan*, January 1972, pp. 297–307.

14. Richard J. Herrnstein, *I.Q. in the Meritocracy* (Boston: Little, Brown, 1971).

15. Carl Bereiter and Siegfried Engelmann, *Teaching Disadvantaged Children in the Preschool* (Englewood Cliffs, N.J.: Prentice-Hall, 1966).

16. Thomas Pettigrew and Robert L. Green, "School Desegregation in Large Cities: A Critique of the Coleman 'White Flight' Thesis," *Harvard Educational Review*, February 1976, pp. 1–53.

17. Peter Steinfels, *The Neoconservatives: The Men Who Are Changing America's Politics* (New York: Simon and Schuster, 1979).

18. William Labov, "The Logic of Nonstandard English," in Frederick Williams, ed., *Language and Poverty: Perspectives on a Theme* (Chicago: Markham Publishing Co., 1970); Geneva Smitherman, *Talkin' and Testifyin': The Language of Black America* (New York: Houghton-Mifflin, 1977); Joan C. Baratz, "Teaching Reading in an Urban Negro School System," in Williams, *Language and Poverty . . .* ; and Manuel Ramirez III and Alfredo Castañeda, *Cultural Democracy, Bicognitive Development, and Education* (New York: Academic Press, 1974).

19. Jane R. Mercer, "Testing and Assessment Practices in Multiethnic Education," in Banks, *Education in the '80s . . .* , pp. 93–104.

20. Gunnar Myrdal, *An American Dilemma: the Negro Problem and Modern Democracy, Vols. 1 and 2* (New York: Harper and Row, 1944).

21. Hannah Arendt, *The Human Condition* (Chicago: University of Chicago Press, 1958).

The Limits of Pluralism

M. Donald Thomas

M. Donald Thomas (b. 1926) studied at the University of Dubuque and the University of Illinois. He has been a high school teacher, counselor, principal, and is currently Superintendent of Salt Lake City School District. He is the author of monographs, workbooks, and teacher guides, and is the recipient of a number of awards.

My topic is not a popular one. And I must tread carefully, because my position may be so easily misconstrued. I am arguing against the accepted principle that pluralism is good for our schools. Here are my reasons for doing so:

- Pluralism in schools, at some point, destroys any sense of common traditions, values, purposes, and obligations. Without such commonly supported positions the schools lack unity and direction.

- Pluralism in schools, at some point, makes it impossible for them to teach a common body of knowledge. Pluralism diverts the schools' attention from their basic purpose—to educate for civic, economic, and personal effectiveness.

- Pluralism in schools, at some point, tends to create moral anarchy. It lends support to no-fault morality which claims that all values are of equal worth and that the ends justify the means. When no moral criteria exist, no obligations to adhere to those criteria are held.

I have arrived at these conclusions slowly over the past 10 years. They are the result of careful examination of what has happened to our schools under the influence of pluralism.

What began as a fresh breath of reform has grown stale and become another way by which schools have lost credibility and public support.

I am not arguing the need to preserve and to value the achievements of the diverse ethnic and racial groups of this country. There is certainly nothing wrong with racial and ethnic pride and the desire to give maximum freedom to each individual. What is unacceptable is the position that everything is of equal value, that the schools have a responsibility for teaching every possible belief and every perceived value, and that behavior is moral if it is believed to be so by any person or any group. There *are* limits to pluralism, and such limits must be articulated by schools and school leaders.

Nor am I a critic of U.S. public education. On the contrary, I believe that our public schools have served our nation well. I also believe that they are doing a good job at the present time. Public schools are and will continue to be the protectors of our freedoms and one of the bases for personal growth. I abhor critics who attack our schools without knowing and appreciating the contributions of schools to economic growth and social mobility. My point is simple: Pluralism, at some point, can diminish the effectiveness of pub-

From M. Donald Thomas, "The Limits of Pluralism," Phi Delta Kappan *(April 1981).* © 1981, Phi Delta Kappan, Inc. Reprinted by permission.

lic schools, and we should not permit that to happen.

A society cannot exist without a common ethos—a common set of beliefs, traditions, and values that glues it together. Without such unity there is no common bond that acts to motivate and to inspire. Without accepted obligations that are universally known there is no purpose or direction in most schools.

In particular, schools need a common set of assumptions to guide their work and measure their success. Schools were established to educate for the democratic ethos. That purpose is still a good one. If everyone is permitted to do anything he or she wishes, the work of the school may be left undone.

Schools should not be expected to deal with every social issue that arises, nor should they be torn apart by vested interests that wish to use the schools for private purposes. The historical purposes of our schools are clear: 1) to teach basic skills required for verbal and mathematical literacy, 2) to teach an understanding of political democracy and the ability to function within that system, 3) to prepare students for higher education or employment, 4) to develop personal discipline in students that will make it possible for them to live satisfying and productive lives.

Today, however, we have gone far beyond these purposes. In doing so we have gone far beyond our ability to establish purpose, meaning, and direction in our schools. We are trying to educate our students to satisfy the demands of a fragmented society, and we are failing. John C. Sawhill stated it well: "In thrusting the schools to the forefront of social change, we have diverted them from their basic purpose—education."

Pluralism in our expectations, in the services schools render, in the duties they perform, has deprived schools of a coherent set of principles—a common ethos. Schools can no longer teach basic historical beliefs about our country. They have no time to teach the basic tools of literacy, no curriculum to prepare students for higher education, and no funds for adequate vocational education. Cast adrift in a sea of pluralistic demands and conflicting interests, they have abandoned their traditional role of being the "glue" that keeps society's attention fixed on the national ethos, the *common destiny* of a varied people. Attention to dozens of ethnic and personal needs paralyzes the schools' ability to unite students for common purposes.

Pluralism in the curriculum has created weakness in teaching the basics. Demands to serve the needs of everyone have made it almost impossible to serve well the needs of anyone. With the present levels of funding, how can schools serve well the varying interests and values of all ethnic groups, all handicapped students, all gifted students, all undermotivated children, and all parents? It is an impossible task, and attempting it reduces our effectiveness in a primary responsibility—teaching a common body of basic knowledge to all children. Providing students with the skills to become effective citizens, able workers, and disciplined individuals is enough for schools to do.

However, we are asked to meet the various social, economic, and personal needs of minorities; we are asked to assist students with various language difficulties; and we are asked to participate in the "politics" of using the schools to solve all of our social and political problems. Pluralism has indeed gone mad. The efforts of schools have been atomized at the request of a thousand "me-first" groups. The schools simply do not have the personnel, the energy, and the skills to serve well all the needs of all the children, all the parents, and all the politicians who come into contact with them.

Among those things that schools can and have done well are:

- teaching most students basic linguistic and mathematical literacy skills,
- teaching most students the basic structure and purposes of a democratic nation,
- teaching most students skills necessary to succeed in higher education,
- teaching most students skills sufficient to obtain employment after high school graduation, and
- teaching most students skills required to continue learning on their own.

Among those things that schools have not done well are:

- teaching students how to be effective parents and family members,
- teaching students to be wise consumers and effective conservationists,
- teaching all handicapped students,
- teaching all students the culture of all the various ethnic groups that attend our schools, and
- teaching a second language to a large number of students.

The truth of the matter is that we are not now and perhaps never will be able to do these things successfully without massive new resources. My hope is that such tasks will be taken from the schools and given back to the home or to other agencies and institutions.

Requiring the schools to perform pluralistic jobs has spread out personnel so thinly that the basic responsibilities have been neglected. Pluralism has put an unbearable strain on the resources of the schools of this nation. It is time to put limits on pluralism and design the work of schools within those limits. If we continue the current trend toward greater pluralism, the end of public edu-

cation may indeed occur within our lifetime. Schools simply cannot teach everything that every person or group wishes them to teach. We have already gone too far, and it is time to call a halt.

Perhaps the most devastating effect of pluralism in our schools is the moral anarchy it breeds. Recent trysts with moral relativism have led to a "no-fault" morality and a do-it-yourself system of justice. Alastaire MacIntyre has written: "It is no wonder that the confusions of pluralism are articulated at the level of moral argument in the form of a mishmash of conceptual fragments."

The trend toward ethical pluralism has produced too many people all too willing to put success ahead of personal standards and cleverness ahead of character. Pluralism leads at its worst to no ethics and at its best to a school society with ambivalent ethics of conflict and confrontation. Without an emphasis on individual ethical responsibility, a common core of values that will unite our schools, we shall continue to sink deeper into the quagmire of the so-called "new morality" —which is not moral at all. It is a philosophy that favors ends over means, a philosophy that will, in the end, destroy all moral precepts.

Today there is too much credence given to slogans such as "morality is what I say it is." The belief is widespread that each individual defines moral action for himself or herself and that there exist no more universals to which the entire society is committed. However, the need remains for certain moral criteria: respect for individuals, respect for law, respect for property, common civility, honesty in our relationships, protection of personal liberties, freedom to learn without interference and conflict, and freedom from fear.

What is wrong with the values of pluralism is that they acknowledge no commonly accepted moral standards. Unrestrained pluralism results in a school society based on personal license and undisciplined personal behavior. Unfortunately, such behavior is common among students and adults in many schools. Each individual believes that moral behavior derives solely from personal judgment and that conscience alone arbitrates moral decisions. The problem is that conscience allows so many of us to cheat, disobey the law, interfere with the rights of others, harm others, use destructive means for personal ends, and do whatever conscience defines as right. The result is moral chaos and a fractured and fearful school society.

U.S. education has been and will continue to be the bedrock on which our political democracy is built. It will continue to provide the foundation for social stability and common purpose. It is still the best hope for free men and women all over the globe. We cannot, however, allow creeping pluralism to fragment our national unity, to divert us from our purpose, and to destroy that core of values that has made this country great. The future of this nation depends on our ability to confront pluralism and to bring it under control. The sooner we do so, the better our schools and our nation will be.

DISCUSSION QUESTIONS AND ACTIVITIES

1. What is the purpose of multiethnic education?
2. Explain the differences in the concepts of outputs, inputs, and equity.
3. What are the roles of institutions, other than educational ones, for bringing about greater equality?
4. What influence does social class have on ethnic groups?
5. Compare and contrast the following four hypotheses: geneticism, cultural-deprivation, integrationism, and cultural-difference. Which of the hyphotheses do you consider more valid? Why?
6. Should schools teach a common body of knowledge? According to Thomas, why does pluralism threaten such knowledge?
7. Does pluralism actually undermine educating for civic, economic, and personal effectiveness?
8. Can pluralism create moral anarchy? Does pluralism fail to acknowledge any commonly accepted moral standards?
9. Ask those class members of racial and ethnic minorities to comment on their own schooling in light of the essays.
10. Invite a teacher or administrator of a multiethnic program to speak to the class.
11. Survey what your local community is doing in multicultural education and make recommendations for needed programs.

SUGGESTED READINGS

Appleton, Nicholas. *Cultural Pluralism in Education.* New York: Longman, 1983.

Baker, Gwendolyn C. *Planning and Organizing for Multicultural Education.* Reading, Mass.: Addison-Wesley, 1983.

Bancroft, George W. "Do's and Don't's for Multicultural Living." *School Guidance Worker* 40 (January 1985):34–39.

Banks, James A. *Multiethnic Education: Theory and Practice.* Boston: Allyn and Bacon, 1981.

Capaldi, Nicholas. *Out of Order: Affirmative Action and the Crisis of Doctrinaire Liberalism.* Buffalo, N.Y.: Prometheus Books, 1985.

Freedman, Philip I. "Multiethnic/Multicultural Education: Establishing the Foundations." *Social Studies* 75 (September–October 1984):200–202.

Garcia, Jesus. "Multiethnic Education: Past, Present, and Future." *Texas Tech Journal of Education* 11 (Winter 1984):13–29.

Gibson, Margaret Alison. "Approaches to Multicultural Education in the United States: Some Concepts and Assumptions." *Anthropology and Education Quarterly* 15 (Spring 1984):94–119.

Glazer, Nathan. *Affirmative Discrimination*. New York: Basic Books, 1975.

Gollnick, Donna M., and Chinn, Philip C. *Multicultural Education in a Pluralistic Society*. 2nd ed. Columbus, Oh.: Merrill, 1986.

Grant, Carl A., and Sleeter, Christine E. "The Literature on Multicultural Education: Review and Analysis." *Educational Review* 37 (June 1985):97–118.

Harris, Larry B. "Multicultural Education and the Future of America." *Educational Considerations* 11 (Fall 1984):26–28.

Mock, Karren R. "The Successful Multicultural Teacher." *History and Social Science Teacher* 19 (December 1983):87–97.

Ogbu, John U. *Minority Education and Caste: The American System in Cross-Cultural Perspective*. New York: Academic Press, 1978.

Pratte, Richard. "Multicultural Education: Four Normative Arguments." *Educational Theory* 33 (Winter 1983):21–32.

Williams, Michael. "Multicultural/Pluralistic Education: Public Education in America 'The Way It's 'Spoze to Be.' " *The Clearing House* 56 (November 1982):131–135.

15

Mainstreaming

An increasingly widespread concern over the education of handicapped children and doubts about whether their special education is adequate to their needs have led to the development of mainstreaming. The movement was promoted by Public Law 94–142 and reinforced by the Education of the Handicapped Acts enacted by individual state legislatures. Mainstreaming involves moving handicapped children from their segregated status in special classrooms and integrating them into regular classrooms. Under mainstreaming, the handicapped child would be in a regular classroom for all or part of a day and receive the necessary support services of both special and general education. Mainstreaming for some students might only entail integrating with other students for nonacademic work such as physical education, but for others it might involve assignment to a regular classroom and provision therein for special education as appropriate. The theory of mainstreaming holds that children have a right, and would benefit from, participation in the least restrictive educational program they can manage.

The United States courts have so far decided that handicapped children have a right to participate in public education regardless of the classification or the severity of the handicap, and that an education should be furnished appropriate to individual learning needs, including treatment and therapy according to the disability.

One problem of labeling children with disabilities is that they may be misclassified, which might mean being almost indefinitely trapped in the wrong program and segregated from peers. Minority groups seem especially likely to be misclassified. At times children have been singled out for some behavior quirk or learning habit, labeled, and placed in a special classroom; this practice has led to emphasizing their differences rather than similarities with students in regular classes.

Even those in favor of mainstreaming recognize a number of difficult problems: regular classroom teachers need special preparation and assistance in working with handicapped children; these children may not be accepted by their classmates and may not receive special help needed from them in performing routine school activities; modification of the physical plant may be necessary; changes in curriculum and class size will be needed; and additional funding exclusively for such programs is essential. Moreover, research suggests that while the handicapped in regular classes learn more, those in special classes are better adjusted.

The Case for Keeping Mentally Retarded Children in Your Regular Classrooms

Martin Tonn

Martin H. Tonn (b. 1921) studied at the University of Iowa and held a USOE special education fellowship. He has been a speech therapist in the public schools, a consultant on speech and hearing to government agencies, and has held office in speech and hearing associations. In addition to articles in professional journals, he has written humorous articles and articles on child care for mass circulation magazines. Tonn is Director of Special Education at Moorhead State College, Moorhead, Minnesota.

Before the turn of the century, mentally handicapped children faced one of two rather bleak prospects: an isolated existence at home or institutionalization. In the early 1900s a third choice was opened for these children: special, segregated school (mentally handicapped children were placed in self-contained, special classrooms and taught by special education teachers). Only in the last decade or so has another option been offered: integration of handicapped children into the regular classroom program. It's something you should know more about.

The idea of placing mentally handicapped children in the mainstream of the school program gained impetus from a November 1968 magazine article published in *Exceptional Children*. The article's author, I. M. Dunn, spoke out against the exclusive use of self-contained classes for the educable mentally handicapped. Dunn did not call for abolishing all special classes, but he offered evidence to support the use of alternate programs. His article sparked further research and debate that, in turn have changed some of the traditional recommendations for teaching moderately retarded children.

Support for integrating educable mentally handicapped children into regular classes rests on these seven points:

1. Dunn and others say research shows that, with one exception, mentally handicapped children do better in regular classes than in special classes. The exception: peer acceptance.
2. Labeling and stigmatizing children by sending them to "retarded" classes may prove detrimental to them.
3. Special classes isolate children, preventing meaningful contact that could be helpful both to mentally handicapped and other students.

From Martin Tonn, "The Case for Keeping Mentally Retarded Children in Your Regular Classrooms," American School Board Journal *161 (August 1974):45. Reprinted with permission.*

4. Many special classes do not meet—in a real way—the educational and social needs of children.

5. Special classes have an unrealistically high proportion of minority children and children from low socioeconomic backgrounds. This lack of balance, researchers claim, is the result of a middle-class oriented test bias and of environmental deprivation, rather than of actual intellectual inferiority inherent in the child.

6. Isolating students in special classes is not in keeping with our democratic philosophy of education.

7. Results from standardized IQ tests are not sufficient evidence for placing children in special classes.

More about the final point: Psychologists and educators know that standardized IQ tests are subject to fluctuations caused by factors such as emotional problems, environmental deprivation, sensory defects, and special learning disabilities. At the educable level, children with IQs of 50 to 75 generally are placed in special classes. Studies have shown, however, that some students with moderate mental handicaps perform better (on a battery of various cognitive tests) than do children who have IQs above 75 and who attend regular classes.

Several alternative programs have been devised by school officials who are convinced that a number of mentally handicapped children can profit from experience in the regular classroom. In some districts, handicapped children are placed in ordinary classes when they reach a certain level of achievement in their special classes and when their special class teachers recommend the transfer. A mentally handicapped child who moves into the traditional classroom setting receives help each day from a special education resource teacher. This additional assistance is flexible—increased when the child is experiencing problems and decreased as he progresses with his school work. Resource teachers also can help classroom teachers plan curriculum programs for handicapped children.

A program called Individually Prescribed Instruction continually assesses and monitors the abilities and progress of a mentally handicapped child who attends a regular class. Special instructional materials are produced for the child as he reaches each new or different level of learning. This method allows a handicapped child to work at his own pace.

The Harrison Resource Learning Center in one of Minneapolis' inner-city schools provides prescriptive instruction to those moderately mentally handicapped youngsters who attend regular classes. The amount of time each child spends in the Resource Learning Center is flexible and based on individual needs. With the help of this program, a number of mentally handicapped children have been enrolled full time in regular classes.

No one is suggesting the elimination of all special classes for retarded children, some of whom may suffer from severe handicaps or a combination of emotional and physical problems. These children may be served best in special classes.

But this question *is* being asked: Do all special children necessarily need special classes? Donald MacMillan, writing in *Focus on Exceptional Children* poses the question this way: "To what extent, and under what circumstances, can a wider range of individual differences be accommodated in the regular class than is presently the case?"

School board members and superintendents should be aware of the district-wide implications of this trend to integrate certain handicapped children into the traditional classrooms:

1. More resource teachers and teacher aides will be needed.
2. Smaller classes will be beneficial, if not necessary.
3. Regular classroom teachers who work with mentally handicapped children will need more specialized inservice training.
4. Top school officials should ensure that administrators, teachers, parents, and the general community are aware of the goals and objectives of new programs for handicapped children within their districts.

Mainstreaming: A Formative Consideration

Harry N. Chandler

Harry N. Chandler is Associate Editor of the Journal of Learning Disabilities.

I do not think that it is as simple as a pendulum swing. In this case professional opinion seems to be changing before we see any theory to suggest a change. We rushed into deinstitutionalization with faith but little foresight, we stampeded into mainstreaming with panic and no preparation. Now things are getting sorted out, now are finding a center of gravity. Someday we might even witness a nearly unprecedented event: educators and social scientists attempting to plan instead of react.

There is little evidence that mainstreaming LD students results in better academic achievement. The mainstreaming argument was originally a civil rights move toward social equality and came most strongly from parents of retarded children. The limited research used to argue that special students did better in "regular" classrooms was dated and flawed.

Much of our present mainstreaming data has been on the social and emotional adjustment of retarded students. We have some studies of how teachers and peers view LD students and of how LD students feel about themselves. This conflicting evidence hints that mainstreaming has had some benefit to special students, their peers and their teachers. Many of these are not real studies but

From Harry N. Chandler, "Mainstreaming: A Formative Consideration," Journal of Learning Disabilities *19 (February 1986):125–26. Reprinted by permission of the publisher, Pro-Ed, Inc.*

articles of the "See how kind the third graders are to this Downs child" which, while heart-warming, is little more than a public relations performance.

Mainstreaming, especially at the secondary level, should be done to increase a child's academic, vocational or artistic skills. Mainstreaming for social reasons too often means that some authority has decided to stop trying to teach the child, that the only way to show growth is in a well advertised social placement. I am biased: I know that any good special education teacher can teach an LD, EMR or TMR child more basics than a regular class teacher. We can also better teach the basic concepts in content areas. Unless we have made a special study of a content area we might not have as complete a knowledge of the subject as the content teacher, but some content area teachers can only teach advanced concepts to equally advanced students.

At this point my liberalism bumps into my pedagogy, or, as my wife puts it, my dogma overcomes my karma. By teaching an LD child a content area subject am I not also deciding that the child cannot learn as much as an "average" child? Yes, I am deciding, but I'm deciding with the consent of the parent and the child. No, I am not giving up, any time the child wants to return to the regular classes he can with parental assent. Anytime I know the child is ready for more than I can teach, I will pass him on.

Given time and necessary resources it is possible to teach almost anyone almost anything. The catch: "time" and "resources." LD kids begin falling behind in kindergarten and keep on getting further and further behind. In some districts decisions about "tracking" begin as early as the fifth or sixth grade: will academics or a more vocational curriculum be given the child? In our democratic and, at times, egalitarian society we would like to leave options open as long as possible but another decision point comes in high school: What next? More schooling, work, the military, welfare . . . ?

One of our greatest problems is that our institutions are constantly forcing us into decisions: time moves on, children get older, resources dwindle or change. We find ourselves confronted with either mainstreaming or a self-contained classroom; either academics or vocational or pre-vocational training. No matter how we try to tailor a program for a child as implied in PL 94–142, opinions, prejudices, schedules, finances, theorists, anxious parents and impatient children force us into "cobbling up" poorly designed programs with few options.

Like euthanasia, medical triage or voting Republican, questioning mainstreaming is something a liberal educator does not like to do. Several recent happenings have forced me to look more closely than comfortable at mainstreaming: I re-read PL 94–142 so I could explain it to a student teacher, I reviewed the book *Perspectives in Special Education: Personal Orientations*, and I interviewed Pat Ellis, Associate Superintendent of Public Instruction for the State of Oregon and Director of the Division of Special Education and Student Services.

PL 94–142 reminded me that we should junk the term "mainstreaming" and use the more accurate but less picturesque "least restrictive environment." According to Pl 94–142 we are supposed to place children to the maximum extent possible with non-handicapped peers and they should be in a special class only when the nature or severity of their handicap prevents them from successfully being educated in regular classes with the use of supplementary aids and services. That phrase, "supplementary aids and services" was inserted when the framers of PL 94–142 thought the law would be fully funded. Few schools can afford those "aids and services" so, while the phrase is on the books, it is honored only by being ignored. Even state and federal audit teams do not look to see if a child could be successful in a regular class if given "aids and services." The "nature and severity" of the handicap is hard to determine since one has to take into account the handicaps of the school system and its teachers as well as the handicap of the child. The variables here are the teacher, the administration, the budget, the design of the school, and the nature of the student body. It is primarily the skill or incompetence of the regular class teacher which makes or breaks special students in the "mainstream."

The book *Perspectives in Special Education: Personal Orientations* by Burton Blatt and Richard J. Morris is the most thought provoking I have found in the area of special education (even better than Mann's *On the Trail of Process* or Ball's *Itard, Seguin, and Kephart*). It is the autobiographies of ten of special education's outstanding modern personalities (see the review in last month's *JLD*). I used the term personalities advisedly since all those represented are not only "experts" but have very personal ideas about the special education field—ideas which do not always square with conventional wisdom. Not all take up the topic of mainstreaming but all who do see that it has flaws. The greatest concern is that it was an attractive and humane theory which was rushed into law with no planning, no training of those responsible for making it work, and little funding to teach how to do it, to support it, or to monitor it. But, as I did in the book review, let the authors speak for themselves:

Seymour B. Sarason, professor of psychology at Yale and director of Yale's graduate program in Clinical Psychology and of the Yale Psycho-Educational Clinic:

"... I had very mixed feelings about 94–142. Of course, I was heartily in favor of it. At the same time, however, I was certain that neither the

proponents of that legislation nor school officials understood the resource problem. The problem and its amelioration were being defined in a way that was unrealistic and was setting the stage for backlash. Also, the fact that the word or concept of *mainstreaming* did not appear in the legislation said to me that the special class was in no way threatened—indeed it was implicitly receiving further legitimization. Finally and very important, in my travels around the country I learned that the bulk of school officials had no idea what PL 94–142 really said."

Samuel A. Kirk, professor of special education at the University of Arizona (and, of course, the man who coined the term "learning disabilities"):

I recommended to an advocate of mainstreaming many years ago that he teach a second- or third-grade of thirty children, accept into that class three or four mentally retarded, learning disabled, and emotionally disturbed children, and study exactly how mainstreaming could be accomplished adequately. He did not accept my suggestion. As everyone knows, it is easy to tell someone else what to do but it is more difficult to accomplish the task adequately and to describe exactly how it is done. We, as yet, have no detailed description of how mainstreaming is accomplished nor an exact distribution of responsibilities of both regular and resource teachers.

Herbert Goldstein, professor emeritus in educational psychology and special education, New York University:

In fact, recent data suggest that moving children about and occupying committees and teachers' time to cobble up IEP's are reducing students' and teachers' effectiveness ... The Individual Education Plans (IEPs) have generated a decade of professional deception—at least when it comes to disturbed youngsters [no, to all youngsters, my comment H.N.C.]. We seldom have the resources or are willing to make the investment necessary to make the significant difference. Our superficial appreciation of our business is its most depressing condition. I do not blame the teachers; their leadership has misled them.

James J. Gallagher, director of the Frank Porter Graham Child Development Center and Kenan Professor of Education at the University of North Carolina at Chapel Hill:

> The special education teacher and the regular education teacher are peers. If there is a disagreement, then how does it get settled? If the special educator wants to make a suggestion about how to change a student's program, how can it be done without offense? Who takes the lead in discussions or planning for the student? There is a range of role uncertainties cluttering the landscape on such issues and they make a difficult situation even more difficult.

Burton Blatt, the late dean of the School of Education at Syracuse University:

> Is mainstreaming a valid educational issue? I conclude that it is not! The program, the curriculum, the label, the organization—the most obvious components of education—are strangely irrelevant to the relationships we seek to understand. Those educational components which do matter—largely ignored in our research—are the teacher as a human being who teaches and learns, children as learners with potentials and rights, and the environment—rich, flexible and thoughtfully created.

Pat Ellis' remarks ranged over the field of special education but she kept coming back to special child programs. What follows are just a few of her remarks. Direct quotes are set off in quotation marks, the rest is a paraphrase which is, I hope, accurate and not colored by my biases:

How do we know what we are doing is correct for any special child? Are we being pressured into a position by parents who have been sold a bill of goods by theorists who have never tested their theory against the reality of everyday life? Mainstreaming special children makes them and their parents think that they will be mainstreamed in life after school, but life isn't like that. "Why strive for an appropriate education if they have nothing when they leave the education system?" Have we wasted our time and their money in special education when society will not treat them specially after they leave us?

We have not fulfilled the hope of PL 94–142 in testing or planning. We rely too much on tests and not enough on clinical data or on direct observation. We have to look at functional abilities and promote them in children. There are seldom enough people in the planning stages, too often just a teacher, quite often not even a parent. When we are planning for IEPs we should make it clear that a standard diploma is not realistic for most special children. We need a "meaningful completion document," and not just for students on IEPs. "Currently most diplomas are of very little value; they have no objective meaning as a certificate of high quality education."

There should be a close linkage between vocational education and special education. Vocational education is in trouble; if it is phased out, then special education is in equal trouble. We need to train students for jobs. We have to try to bring in social services, to look at housing and vocations of and for the students we serve. All of these things: education, homes, jobs, friends, and family make a whole person. Now each is treated separately by separate agencies with little communication among them. We need more alternative educational settings for all students. Schools cannot afford to keep students until they are twenty-one although they might have to as other social services close down.

As I wrote at the beginning of this article, this is not a pendulum swing yet. Some very respected people in the special education field are beginning to take a careful look at how we deliver educational services. Perhaps someday we might even get around to some long range planning. Stranger things have happened!

DISCUSSION QUESTIONS AND ACTIVITIES

1. What are the seven points that support the integration of educable mentally handicapped children into regular classes?
2. What alternative programs are provided for those mentally handicapped children who are mainstreamed?
3. Can those school systems that use mainstreaming dispense with all special education classes?
4. Gather evidence on school systems where mainstreaming has generally proven successful and those where the results have been unfavorable.
5. According to Chandler, why is mainstreaming for social reasons undesirable?
6. On what basis does Samuel Kirk (in the Chandler selection) claim that as yet we have "no detailed description of how mainstreaming is accomplished nor an exact distribution of responsibilities of both regular and resource teachers."
7. Will handicapped students be disillusioned because they will not be mainstreamed in life after school? Is this a reason for not mainstreaming them in school?

SUGGESTED READINGS

Proponents and Research Findings

Dunn, L. M. "Special Education for the Mentally Retarded—Is Much of It Justifiable?" *Exceptional Children* 34 (1968):5–22.

Gillet, Pamela. "Models for Mainstreaming." *Journal for Special Educators* 19 (Autumn 1982):1–12.

McCann, Scott, et al. "Reverse Mainstreaming: Nonhandicapped Students in Special Education Classrooms." *Remedial and Special Education* 6 (January–February 1985):13–19.

McCartney, Brian. "Education in the Mainstream." *Volta Review* 86 (September 1984):41–52.

Sabornie, Edward J. "Social Mainstreaming of Handicapped Students: Facing an Unpleasant Reality." *Remedial and Special Education* 6 (March–April 1985):12–16.

Salend, Spencer. "Factors Contributing to the Development of Successful Mainstreaming Programs." *Exceptional Children* 50 (February 1984):409–416.

Schneider, Barry H., and Byrne, Barbara M. "Predictors of Successful Transition from Self-Contained Special Education to Regular Class Settings." *Psychology Today in the Schools* 21 (July 1984):375–380.

Smith, Gayle, and Smith, Don. "Mainstreaming Program that Really Works." *Journal of Learning Disabilities* 18 (June–July 1985):369–372.

Strain, Philip S., and Kerr, Mary Margaret. *Mainstreaming of Children in Schools: Research and Programmatic Issues.* New York: Academic Press, 1981.

Widlake, Paul. "How Should We Respond to Change?" *British Journal of Special Education* 12 (June 1985):50–52.

Winzer, Margaret B. C. "Teacher Attitudes toward Mainstreaming: An Appraisal of the Research." *Journal of Special Education* 9, no. 2 (1985):149–161.

Critics

Bates, Louise. "Mainstreaming: We Have Come Full Circle." *Childhood Education* 58 (March–April 1982):238–240.

Gickling, E. E., and Theobold, J. T. "Mainstreaming: Affect and Effect." *Journal of*

Special Education 9 (Fall 1975):317–328.

Kunzweiler, Charles. "Mainstreaming Will Fail Unless There Is a Change in Professional Attitude and Institutional Structure." *Education* 102 (Spring 1982):284–288.

Longo, Paul. "Mainstreaming: The Promise and the Pitfalls." *Urban Education* 17 (July 1982):157–179.

Martin, Edwin W. "Some Thoughts on Mainstreaming." *Exceptional Children* 41 (November 1974):150–153.

Mosley W. G., and Spicker, H. H. "Mainstreaming for the Educationally Deprived." *Theory into Practice* 14 (April 1975):73–81.

Ringlaben, Ravic P., and Weller, Carol. "Mainstreaming the Special Educator." *Education Unlimited* 3 (Fall 1981):19–22.

Turney, David. "Mainstream or Quiet Eddy?" *Contemporary Education* 46 (Winter 1975):146.

16

Educating the Gifted

The gifted and talented are once more the object of attention after a period of relative neglect. When the Soviet Union launched Sputnik in 1957, alarm swept through the land that the United States had fallen behind in the space race and therefore more scientists, engineers, and mathematicians would be urgently needed. The National Defense Education Act of 1958 provided funds to promote the intellectually talented in those fields. But by 1965 with the Elementary and Secondary Education Act, interest in culturally different learners and compensatory education became a dominant concern; this trend was followed by provisions for handicapped children. Until recently many administrators assumed the gifted could make it alone. Now interest has again returned to the gifted and talented, and some important changes are evident since the earlier years.

An important development is that giftedness is no longer restricted to intellectual talent. In 1972, the USOE's Office of Gifted and Talented defined these two terms as referring to children capable of high performance in any one or more of these areas: general intellectual ability, specific academic aptitude, creative and productive thinking, leadership ability, visual and performing arts aptitudes, or psychomotor ability. By this definition, 3 to 5 percent of the school age population could be considered gifted. An elementary teacher with a class of thirty-five students would likely have one or two gifted children each year. Or, to use another example, out of a hypothetical roomful of one hundred children who represent all children in the fifth grade, sixty-eight of them are likely to be average learners, thirteen above average, thirteen below average, three retarded, and three gifted.

The two educational approaches to the gifted are acceleration and enrichment. Acceleration may involve early enrollment in kindergarten, skipping grades, advanced placement, and early high school and college entrance. Acceleration, however, removes the child from age mates and may cause social isolation. Enrichment programs, which are now part of many elementary schools, enable the child to spend most of the time in the regular classroom but meet several hours each week with other gifted children.

Federal education programs for the gifted were funded in 1976. Presently thirty states make some statutory provision for educating the gifted.

In the selections that follow, Donald Thomas surveys the present status of education for the gifted, including programs, legislation, type of teachers needed, and the role of parents. James J. Gallagher shows that Americans have generally had an uneasy and an ambivalent attitude toward the gifted, caught between the fear of a special elite as opposed to egalitarianism. Can these conflicting attitudes be reconciled? Will greater attention to the gifted neglect the handicapped and disadvantaged?

Gifted and Talented Children: The Neglected Minority

Donald Thomas

Donald Thomas (b. 1926) studied at the University of Dubuque and received a doctorate from the University of Illinois. He has been a high school teacher of English, speech, and remedial reading, and a counselor, principal, and superintendent in several school systems. He is presently Superintendent in Salt Lake City School District. Dr. Thomas has been a lecturer at a number of colleges and universities, a consultant to various organizations, and has contributed articles to many professional journals.

Youngsters with unusual talents number in the millions and many need special help in school. Some of our most gifted students have had difficulty in school, while others have passed through without using many of their talents.

Unfortunately, the education of gifted and talented students has not been given the attention it deserves. As a result, some of the brightest students have dropped out of school.

In the past decade our schools have made good progress in the education of handicapped students. Strides have been made in providing special services to the blind, the deaf, the retarded, the emotionally disturbed, the physically handicapped, and the disadvantaged. At the same time, however, little attention has been given to those who are gifted and talented.

GIFTED CHILDREN MISUNDERSTOOD

Some people may find it difficult to see why gifted children require special attention. The reason is that our schools are not equipped to deal with future Beethovens, Jeffersons, Newtons, and Einsteins. Such children often appear different, out-of-the-ordinary, and out-of-step with the rest of the class. They are often misunderstood, considered uncooperative, antisocial, or defiant.

Thomas Edison stopped going to school because his teacher claimed that he could not learn. Gregor Mendel failed an examination four times. Newton was considered a slow student. So were Darwin, Churchill, and Eisenhower. Shelley, Whistler, and Poe were expelled from school because they could not abide by the rules. Einstein found school to be so extremely boring that he learned mathematics from his uncle.

Those who study gifted children believe that a large number of these children simply do not survive the ordinary school programs. What is needed, they say, are learning activities especially suited to the needs of superior children. They need unique materials, highly skilled teachers, special attention, and sympathetic understanding.

From Donald Thomas, "Gifted and Talented Children: The Neglected Majority," NASSP Bulletin 60 (October 1976): 21–24. Reprinted by permission.

Now that schools have provided special services to the "disadvantaged" and the "handicapped," it is time that we better educate our most able children. The following questions and answers consider the current status of education for gifted and talented students.

Who Are the Gifted and Talented Children?

Gifted and talented children are those who have high potential or performance in one or more areas. Such students may be extremely bright. Some have leadership talent. Others are outstanding in the performing arts. Many show great decision-making ability. Their talents range from the ability to read far above their grade level to the ability to solve intricate social problems. Such children come from all walks of life, and are the children of parents from a wide spectrum of occupational fields.

How Many Gifted and Talented Children Are There?

Estimates vary widely. The U.S. Office of Education estimates that three to five percent of our children are gifted. This means that between 1.5 and 2.5 million gifted and talented children are in our schools. The School Management Study Group (SMSG) states that there are between three and five million gifted students in the public schools alone. Some educators who are authorities in the education of the gifted claim that the number of talented students is far higher than can be measured by our present tests. Others claim that all children are gifted in some way.

Why Should Gifted and Talented Children Receive Special Attention?

Being gifted is often as much a handicap in our schools as being retarded. These children need special programs to realize their potential. They need challenging learning activities, understanding teachers, and highly individualized learning opportunities. Without special assistance such children often conceal their talents, become bored, show hostile behavior, or withdraw from others. Human talent is the greatest resource possessed by any nation. It is the talents of our children that must be discovered and nurtured by our teachers.

What Kinds of Programs Exist for the Gifted and Talented?

Some 30 states have enacted legislation to implement programs for highly talented students. Twenty state departments of education have full-time directors to promote the education of gifted. Several states provide special funding as an incentive to develop educational programs for superior children. Five states that have strong programs for the gifted are Illinois, California, North Carolina, Idaho, and Ohio.

The Illinois Gifted Program was initiate in 1964, and provides supplementary funds to districts that voluntarily establish programs for gifted students. California has had the Mentally Gifted Minors (MGM) program for many years, and it has served thousands of bright children. The Marin County, Calif., "College for Kids" program has sufficiently shown that children can do more than is ever required of them.

Both Illinois and California define a gifted child as one who receives a high score on a test of academic ability. Some states have introduced the so-called "multiple-talent" programs promoted by Calvin Taylor, a psychologist at the University of Utah. Taylor believes that all children have "hidden" talents that must be nurtured and encouraged by teachers.

In explaining what happens to talented students, Taylor gives the example of a Utah mining process. In years past, miners extracted copper from the mountainside and deposited the waste products on the valley floor. Today we are discovering that what was believed to be waste contains metals of a larger value than the ones already extracted. Taylor believes that the talents of many gifted children are buried in underachievement.

What Is the Federal Government Doing in This Area?

The federal government has become very active in the education of gifted and talented. In March 1972, Congress received a major report, *Education of the Gifted and Talented*. Since then it has enacted the Education Amendments of 1974 to provide special funds in this area. In addition, the U.S. Office of Education operates a division of gifted and talented. It supports studies, provides information to Congress, awards grants to states and local school districts, and provides training in the education of the gifted and talented.

The U.S. Office of Education has taken a new interest in stimulating interest in the education of bright children. The office disseminates information, provides technical assistance, and encourages states to provide special help to extremely able children.

What Kind of Teachers Are Needed for Gifted and Talented Students?

Talented and gifted children need highly sensitive teachers. They should be trained in child development and learning theory. Without special training, some teachers are indifferent (or hostile) to the needs of bright children.

Generally, teachers who succeed with gifted children have special gifts themselves. Such teachers have a wide range of interests, a sense of humor, are student-centered, are enthusiastic about their work, and speak positively about children. They usually participate in renewal activities for themselves and can tolerate the divergent behavior of superior students. They are able to motivate, to encourage, and to nurture the "hidden" talents of their students.

What Can Parents Do to Stimulate Interest in Programs for Gifted and Talented?

Parents can work with local school districts to encourage special programs for talented children. They can work through the PTA, attend board of education meetings, and talk with state legislators. Parents can also become familiar with programs for the gifted. Information can be obtained from the local library, the superintendent of schools, or the state board of education. Free material can be obtained from the Office of the Gifted and Talented, U.S. Office of Education, Washington, D.C. 20202, or The Council for Exceptional Children, 1920 Association Dr., Reston, Va. 22091.

With the help of parents, local schools can provide special services to gifted children. Parents can develop talent banks, can assist teachers, and can supervise enrichment activities. Parents can also organize to assist the legislature to provide special funds for gifted programs. Schools welcome the help of parents in this area.

What Are the Benefits of Special Programs for the Gifted and Talented?

The gifted and talented youngster has the potential to make more than the average contribution to our troubled society. It is, therefore, in the national interest to provide special services for the gifted. Senator Jacob Javits said it well when he spoke to the Council for Exceptional Children: "Without the development of these neglected traits, the brightest individual is greatly handicapped and much of his potential is lost."

Special programs for the gifted and talented children may make it possible for hidden abilities to be discovered and for potential genius to be sympathetically encouraged. Such programs may reduce the loss of talent, the frustration of not being in tune with the rest of the class, and the boredom that occurs among so many bright children.

William James estimated that only 10 percent of human capacity is ever utilized. He believed it to be even less among the gifted.

The challenge of our schools, therefore, is great. It is our schools that must implement and establish programs for the education of gifted and talented children.

The vastness of man's potential can be seen in the "Grandma Moses effect." It illustrates that each boy and girl may have abilities that are never uncovered. Our hope, however, is that students will not have to wait until old age to find a new talent. It may be possible, with some special help, to uncover those gifts at an early age in our schools.

Issues in Education for the Gifted

James J. Gallagher

James J. Gallagher (b. 1926) is presently Kenan professor of education at the University of North Carolina at Chapel Hill. He studied at the University of Pittsburg and Pennsylvania State University, taught at several universities, and served in the Bureau of Education for the Handicapped, HEW. He is the recipient of several awards and has written Teaching the Gifted Child *and was editor of* Application of Child Development Research to Exceptional Children.

AMERICA'S LOVE-HATE RELATIONSHIP WITH THE GIFTED

The gifted scholars of tender years are often told by their elders that they are the future of the nation and that we are delighted with their academic performance and look eagerly to their forthcoming contributions to the society. These gifted students might well be confused by the conflicting messages they

From James J. Gallagher, "Issues in Education for the Gifted." In The Gifted and Talented: Their Education and Development *(ed. by A. Harry Passow). 78th Yearbook, Part I of National Society for the Study of Education. Chicago: The Society, 1979. Reprinted by permission.*

receive because even the most perceptive of them has a difficult time grasping the fundamental point that we adults do not say everything we mean, nor do we mean everything we say, about their talent.

A strong case can be made for the presence in the American society of a love-hate relationship with giftedness and talent. On one hand, we revere the gifted individual who has risen from humble background. We are proud to live in a society where talent can triumph over environment or family status. At the same time, since our origins came from battling an aristocratic elite, we are suspicious of attempts to subvert our commitment to egalitarianism. We do not wish a new elite class to develop, and as a result we seem to waver in our attitudes. We design our elementary and secondary programs for gifted students in ways that can be defended by careful administrators as giving no special favors, no tipping the scales in favor of the socially powerful or the specially endowed.[1]

Sometimes satire is the best way to illustrate the ambiguous positions in which we find ourselves. Kurt Vonnegut, Jr. has carried one of the common feelings about the gifted in our society to a logical conclusion in a short story entitled *Harrison Bergeron*, set in some future society:

> The year was 2081, and everybody was finally equal. They weren't only equal before God and the law, they were equal in every which way. Nobody was smarter than anybody. No one was better looking than anybody else.[2]

The reason for this enforced equality was that people who were outstanding in various ways were given handicaps. Those that could

dance well had to wear sandbags on their feet, those who were strikingly good looking would have to wear a mask so as not to embarrass those who did not have those characteristics. And those with high intellectual ability?

> George, while his intelligence was way above normal, had a little mental handicap radio in his ear. He was required by law to wear it at all times. He was tuned into a government transmitter. Every twenty seconds or so, the transmitter would send out some noise to keep people like George from taking unfair advantage of their brains.[3]

The essentially destructive approach to "equality" does not really pass until we reach higher education when a miraculous transformation takes place. The United States has created the most complex and extensive higher education and professional school establishment in the world. We do not call the Stanford Medical School or the Harvard Law School a program for gifted students, but we know that they are and no apologies are made that only the "best" students should be allowed to attend. After all, some of us may need a good lawyer from time to time, others may need an excellent surgeon, and others would like to get some good advice from a competent psychiatrist.

As we view the needs of the society, the agenda of unsolved problems such as pollution, population, energy, and a lacking sense of national purpose, we feel the need for the best and the brightest to be well prepared and well motivated, not only to achieve their individual destiny, but also to aid the society as a whole.

At the local, state, and federal levels we vacillate in our public school program between the need to be "fair" and the need to be "effective." At times when the society

---

[1] John Gardner, *Excellence: Can We Be Equal and Excellent Too?* (New York: Harper and Row, 1961).

[2] Kurt Vonnegut, Jr., *Welcome to the Monkey House* (New York: Dell, 1950), p. 7.

---

[3] Ibid.

seems to be threatened, such as in the Sputnik era and recently with the variety of problems surrounding energy shortages, we lean toward the productive use of all talent. In more placid eras such as the early 1950s, the post-World War II decade, when there seemed to be little to worry and threaten us, we sought "equality" as a more appropriate goal. At the very least, we need to make these conflicting values visible so that a more mature societal decision can be made.

DISCUSSION QUESTIONS AND ACTIVITIES

1. How do we determine who are the gifted and talented? Are they likely to be found primarily in certain segments of the population?
2. What are the arguments used to support special programs for the gifted? Are the arguments valid?
3. What special characteristics do teachers of the gifted need?
4. Why do some democratic societies evince an ambivalent attitude toward the gifted?
5. How would you explain the fact that in the United States during certain periods the gifted are given special attention and in other periods are neglected? Cite examples. Can you think of any societies in which the gifted are consistently given preferential treatment?
6. Investigate what provisions have been made in your home community for educating the gifted, and determine the adequacy and success of these programs.
7. Invite a teacher or administrator experienced in working with the gifted to your class to speak.
8. In his *Excellence: Can We Be Equal and Excellent Too?* John Gardner sought to find a place in a democratic society for both

equality and talent. Read his book to determine whether he was able to do so convincingly.
9. In John Rawls's *A Theory of Justice* (Cambridge, Mass.: Harvard University Press, 1971) he articulates two fundamental principles: (1) each person is to have an equal right to the most extensive total system of equal basic liberties compatible with a similar system of liberty for all; and (2) social and economic inequalities are to be arranged so that they are both (a) to the greatest benefit of the least advantaged, and (b) attached to offices and positions open to all under conditions of fair equality of opportunity. Although the first principle has priority over the second one, would we still assume that the gifted would receive less resources if these two principles were adopted? In other words, would the second principle allocate extra resources to the handicapped, mentally retarded, and culturally disadvantaged? Thus what would be just and fair in the use of scarce societal resources for educating the gifted?

SUGGESTED READINGS

Alexander, Patricia A., and Mula, Joseph A. *Gifted Education: A Comprehensive Roadmap.* Rockville, Md.: Aspens Systems Corp., 1982.

Anthony, John B., and Anthony, Margaret M. *The Gifted and Talented: A Bibliography and Resource Guide.* Pittsfield, Mass.: Berkshire Community Press, 1981.

Baskin, Barbara H., and Harris, Karen H. *Books for the Gifted Child.* New York: R. R. Bowker, 1980.

Bruch, Catherine B. "Schooling for the Gifted: Where Do We Go From Here? *Gifted Child Quarterly* 28 (Winter 1984):12–16.

Colangelo, Nicholas. "A Perspective on the Future of Gifted Education." *Roeper Review* 7 (September 1984):30–32.

Feldhusen, John F., and Hoover, Steven M. "A Conception of Giftedness: Intelligence, Self-Concept and Motivation." *Roeper Review* 8 (February 1986):140–143.

Feldhusen, John F., et al. "Problems in the Identification of Giftedness, Talent, or Ability." *Gifted Child Quarterly* 28 (Fall 1984):149–151.

Gagne, Francoys. "Giftedness and Talent: Reexamining a Reexamination of Definitions." *Gifted Child Quarterly* 29 (Summer 1985):103–112.

Gardner, John. *Excellence: Can We Be Equal and Excellent Too?* New York:Harper & Row, 1961.

Getzels, Jacob W., and Jackson, Philip W. *Creativity and Intelligence.* New York: Wiley, 1962.

Karnes, Frances A., and Collins, Emily C. *Assessment in Gifted Education.* Springfield, Ill.: C. C. Thomas, 1981.

Karnes, Frances A., and Koch, Susan F. "State Definitions of the Gifted and Talented: An Update and Analysis." *Journal for the Education of the Gifted* 8 (Summer 1985):285–306.

Khatena, Joe. *Educational Psychology of the Gifted.* New York: Wiley, 1982.

Maker, C. June. *Curriculum Development for the Gifted.* Rockville, Md.: Aspen Systems Corp., 1982.

Marland, Sidney P., Jr. *Education for the Gifted and Talented, Vols. I and II: Report to the Congress of the United States.* Washington, D.C.: U.S. Government Printing Office, 1972.

Ormrod, Jeanne E. "Issues in the Identification of Gifted and Talented Students," *Texas Tech Journal of Education* 12 (1985):63–77.

Passow, A. Harry. *The Gifted and Talented: Their Education and Development.* 78th Yearbook, Part I. Chicago: National Society for the Study of Education, 1979.

Richert, E. Susanne. "The State of the Art of Identification of Gifted Students in the United States," *Gifted Education International* 3 (1985):47–51.

Roach, Patricia, and Bell, David. "Finding the Gifted: Problems and Promises," *Contemporary Education* 57 (Winter 1986):95–97.

Stanley, Julian C.; George, William C.; and Solano, Cecilia H. *The Gifted and the Creative: Fifty Year Perspective.* Baltimore: Johns Hopkins University Press, 1977.

Taylor, Calvin W. "Cultivating Multiple Creative Talents in Students." *Journal for the Education of the Gifted* 8 (Spring 1985):187–198.

Terman, L. M., et al. *Genetic Studies of Genius.* Stanford, Calif.: Stanford University Press, 1925.

Terman, Lewis M. *The Gifted Group at Mid-Life.* Stanford, Calif.: Stanford University Press, 1967.

Torrance, E. Paul. *Guiding Creative Talent.* Huntington, N.Y.: R. E. Krieger, 1976.

17

Cognitive Moral Development

The concern over moral education is not new. Educational systems in various cultures since antiquity have usually espoused more than cognitive outcomes. These systems sought, in most cases, to develop a certain type of individual, a person, among other things, of sound character. And character, of course, was formulated according to the dominant norms of society or the values of those who controlled the educational system. Leading educators, both past and present, usually expressed their educational philosophy in terms not only of intellectual changes but moral outcomes as well.

Yet ostensibly educational systems may go through different cycles. One reaction in the United States to the Soviet Union's launching of Sputnik during the late 1950s, for instance, was to place greater emphasis on science, mathematics, and cognitive learning in general. Following a period of attention to culturally different learners in the late 1960s, there has been a recrudescence of interest in moral education—not only in the United States but in Canada and England as well. Thus it is much more than a post-Watergate phenomenon; among the many factors, an emerging world of eroding traditions and temporary, fragmented social relations contribute to a heightened interest in the examination of values.

Values are no stranger to schools. Value decisions are involved in choosing aims and selecting the means for their achievement, in allocating funds in terms of a set of priorities, in determining curriculum content, in attempting to establish desired outcomes for the instructional process, and in developing a professional code of ethics. Whether consciously or not, the teacher influences the student's behavior and his or her attitudes toward learning the teacher's choices and the example he or she sets. Not only the content of the message but the teacher's voice, facial expression, and muscular tension are also important. Today more educators believe that value acquisition should not be left to informal cues and chance but must be deliberately developed in the most effective way.

In the development of moral judgment, theories of moral development describe how children learn a moral code and how thought and action change. These developmental changes have usually been stated in terms of stages of moral growth and judgment. Such theories serve to clarify moral judgments and to apprise educators of what to expect so that a suitable program can be established.

Lawrence Kohlberg's cognitive-developmental approach is indebted to Jean Piaget's pioneering work and was influenced by Dewey's psychological writings. Kohlberg's studies have yielded six developmental stages allotted to three moral levels. These stages are based on ways of thinking about moral matters. Kohlberg believes that a necessary, but not sufficient, condition for morality is the ability to reason logically. His theory, he claims, is both psychological and philosophical, and his findings generate a philosophy of moral education designed to stimulate moral development rather than teach fixed moral rules. Kohlberg believes that a philosophic concept of morality and moral development is required, that moral development passes through invariant qualitative stages, and that moral development is stimulated by promoting thinking and problem solving. Justice, Kohlberg holds, is the key principle in the development of moral judgment.

R. S. Peters's reply acknowledges the importance of Kohlberg's research but he chides him for generally ignoring his critics and thereby failing to make a number of needed changes in his approach.

Moral Development:
A Review of the Theory

Lawrence Kohlberg
Richard H. Hersh

An expert in developmental and social psychology, Lawrence Kohlberg (b. 1927) had clinical psychological experience during and after his studies at the University of Chicago. He has been a fellow at the Institute for Advanced Study in Behavioral Science and held faculty positions at Yale University and the University of Chicago, where he was Director of the child psychology training program before assuming his present position with the Laboratory of Human Development at Harvard University. Professor Kohlberg is internationally recognized for his significant research in moral development and moral education.

Richard H. Hersh (b. 1942) is Professor of Education and Associate Dean of Teacher Education at the University of Oregon.

. . . Whether we like it or not schooling is a moral enterprise. Values issues abound in the content and process of teaching. The interaction of adults and students within a social organization called a school results in human conflict no less so than does such interaction in social organizations labeled "families." Yet moral education has been viewed as the exclusive province of the family and/or church. Disregarded or misunderstood has been the nature of the school as an important moral education institution. Because schools have not been viewed as legitimate institutions of moral education, society has avoided concepts of morality and ethics in evaluating the effects of these institutions on the social development of children and adolescents. Terms like "socialization" or "acculturation" or "citizenship" have been used to refer to the moral impact on students. Such terms ignore the problem of the standard or principle of value implied by such terms. We must face the issue of choice as to whether the outcome of the growth and education process is the creation of a storm trooper, a Buddhist monk or a civil rights activist. All are equally "socialized" in terms of their social group. To consider "socialization" or the "acquisition of values" as moral education, is to consider the moral principles children are developing (or are not developing). It is also to consider the adequacy of these principles in the light of an examined concept of the good and right (the province of moral philosophy) and in the light of knowledge of the moral processes of human development (which is the province of psychology).

We are concerned with the traditional prohibition of schools from teaching values or "morality" normally felt to be the province of the home and church. In keeping family, church, and school separate, however, educators have assumed naively that schools have

From Lawrence Kohlberg and Richard H. Hersh, "Moral Development: A Review of the Theory," Theory Into Practice *16 (April 1977): 53–59, College of Education, The Ohio State University. Reprinted by permission.*

been harbors of value neutrality. The result has been a moral education curriculum which has lurked beneath the surface in schools, hidden as it were from both educators and the public. This "hidden curriculum"[1] with its emphasis on obedience to authority ("stay in your seat, make no noise, get a hallway pass"; and the feeling of "prison" espoused by so many students), implies many underlying moral assumptions and values, which may be quite different from what educators would admit as their conscious system of morality. Schools have been preaching a "bag of virtues" approach—the teaching of a particular set of values which are peculiar to this culture or to a particular subculture, and which are by nature relativistic and not necessarily more adequate than any other set of values. But the teaching of particular virtues has been proven to be ineffective. We wish to go beyond this approach to moral education and instead to conceptualize and facilitate moral development in a cognitive-developmental sense— toward an increased sense of moral autonomy and a more adequate conception of justice.

Moral development, as initially defined by Piaget[2] and then refined and researched by Kohlberg,[3] does not simply represent an increasing knowledge of cultural values usually leading to ethical relativity. Rather, it represents the transformations that occur in a person's *form* or structure of thought. The content of values varies from culture to culture; hence the study of cultural values cannot tell us how a person interacts with his social environment, or how a person goes about solving problems related to his/her social world. This requires the analysis of developing structures of moral judgment, which are found to be universal in a developmental sequence across cultures.[4]

In analyzing the responses of longitudinal and cross-cultural subjects to hypothetical moral dilemmas it has been demonstrated that moral reasoning develops over time through a series of six stages. The concept of stages of cognitive development refers to the structure of one's reasoning and implies the following characteristics:

1. Stages are "structured wholes," or organized systems of thought. This means individuals are consistent in their level of moral judgment.

2. Stages form an invariant sequence. Under all conditions except extreme trauma, movement is always forward, never backward. Individuals never skip stages, and movement is always to the next stage up. This is true of all cultures.

3. Stages are "hierarchical integrations." Thinking at a higher stage includes or comprehends within it lower stage thinking. There is a tendency to function at or prefer the highest stage available.

The stages of moral development are defined by the following characteristics:

DEFINITION OF MORAL STAGES

I. Preconventional Level

At this level, the child is responsive to cultural rules and labels of good and bad,

[1] P. Jackson, *Life in the Classrooms*, (New York: Holt, Rinehart & Winston, 1968).

[2] J. Piaget, *The Moral Judgment of the Child* (1932), (New York: Free Press, 1965).

[3] L. Kohlberg. *Stages of Moral Development as a Basis for Moral Education*, in C. Beck and E. Sullivan (eds.), *Moral Education*, (Toronto: University of Toronto Press, 1970).

[4] L. Kohlberg, "Moral Stages and Moralization: The Cognitive Developmental Approach," In T. Lickona (ed.), *Moral development and behavior: Theory, Research, and Social Issues*, (New York: Holt, Rinehart & Winston, 1976).

right or wrong, but interprets these labels either in terms of the physical or the hedonistic consequences of action (punishment, reward, exchange of favors) or in terms of the physical power of those who enunciate the rules and labels. The level is divided into the following two stages:

Stage 1: The punishment-and-obedience orientation. The physical consequences of action determine its goodness or badness, regardless of the human meaning or value of these consequences. Avoidance of punishment and unquestioning deference to power are valued in their own right, not in terms of respect for an underlying moral order supported by punishment and authority (the latter being Stage 4).

Stage 2: The instrumental-relativist orientation. Right action consists of that which instrumentally satisfies one's own needs and occasionally the needs of others. Human relations are viewed in terms like those of the marketplace. Elements of fairness, of reciprocity, and of equal sharing are present, but they are always interpreted in a physical, pragmatic way. Reciprocity is a matter of "you scratch my back and I'll scratch yours," not of loyalty, gratitude, or justice.

II. Conventional Level

At this level, maintaining the expectations of the individual's family, group, or nation is perceived as valuable in its own right, regardless of immediate and obvious consequences. The attitude is not only one of *conformity* to personal expectations and social order, but of loyalty to it, of actively *maintaining,* supporting, and justifying the order, and of indentifying with the persons or group involved in it. At this level there are the following two stages:

Stage 3: The interpersonal concordance or "good boy–nice girl" orientation. Good be-

havior is that which pleases or helps others and is approved by them. There is much conformity to stereotypical images of what is majority or "natural" behavior. Behavior is frequently judged by intention–"he means well" becomes important for the first time. One earns approval by being "nice."

Stage 4: The "law and order" orientation. There is orientation toward authority, fixed rules, and the maintenance of the social order. Right behavior consists of doing one's duty, showing respect for authority, and maintaining the given social order for its own sake.

III. Postconventional, Autonomous, or Principled Level

At this level, there is a clear effort to define moral values and principles that have validity and application apart from the authority of the groups of persons holding these principles and apart from the individual's own identification with these groups. This level also has two stages:

Stage 5: The social-contract, legalistic orientation, generally with utilitarian overtones. Right action tends to be defined in terms of general individual rights and standards which have been critically examined and agreed upon by the whole society. There is a clear awareness of the relativism of personal values and opinions and a corresponding emphasis upon procedural rules for reaching consensus. Aside from what is constitutionally and democratically agreed upon, the right is a matter of personal "values" and "opinion." The result is an emphasis upon the "legal point of view," but with an emphasis upon the possibility of changing law in terms of rational considerations of social utility (rather than freezing it in terms of Stage 4 "law and order"). Outside the legal realm, free agreement and contract is the binding element of obligation. This is the "official" morality of the American government and constitution.

Stage 6: The universal-ethical-principle orientation. Right is defined by the decision of conscience in accord with self-chosen *ethical principles* appealing to logical comprehensiveness, universality, and consistency. These principles are abstract and ethical (The Golden Rule, the categorical imperative); they are not concrete moral rules like the Ten Commandments. At heart, these are universal principles of *justice*, of the *reciprocity* and *equality* of human *rights*, and of respect for the dignity of human beings as *individual persons.*[5]

Given that people have the psychological capacity to progress to higher (and therefore more adequate) stages of moral reasoning, the aim of education ought to be the personal development of students toward more complex ways of reasoning. This philosophical argument is based on the earlier contributions of John Dewey:

> The aim of education is growth or development, both intellectual and moral. Ethical and psychological principles can aid the school in the greatest of all constructions—the building of a free and powerful character. Only knowledge of the order and connection of stages in psychological development can insure this. Education is the work of supplying the conditions which will enable the psychological functions to mature in the freest and fullest manner.[6]

Like Piaget, Dewey's idea of development does not reflect an increase in the *content* of thinking (e.g., cultural values) but instead, a qualitative transformation in the *form* of the child's thought or action. This distinction has been elaborated elsewhere:

> What we examine in our work has to do with form rather than content. We are not describing or classifying what people think is right or wrong in situations of moral conflict, for example, whether draft-evading exiles should be given amnesty or thrown in prison if and when they return to this country, or even changes in what individuals think as they grow older. Nor are we assuming that we can specify a certain behavioral response as necessarily "moral" (in the descriptive or category sense, as distinguished from non-moral), for example "cheating," and then discuss moral-development in terms of the frequency with which individuals engage in this behavior as they grow older, perhaps in different kinds of situations ranging from spelling tests to income tax. As distinguished from either of these two avenues of research that might be said to be dealing with moral content, our work focuses on the cognitive structure which underlie such content and give it its claim to the category "moral," where "structure" refers to "the general characteristics of shape, pattern or organization of response rather than to the rate of intensity of response or its pairing with particular stimuli," and "cognitive structure" refers to "rules for processing information or for connecting experienced events." From our point of view it is not any artificially specified set of responses, or degree of intensity of such responses, which characterizes morality as an area of study. Rather, it is the cognitive moral structurings, or the organized systems of assumptions and rules about the nature of moral-conflict situations which give such situations their meaning, that constitute the objects of our developmental study.[7]

Based on this crucial difference between form and content, the aim of moral education should be to stimulate people's thinking abil-

---

[5] L. Kohlberg, "From Is to Ought," in T. Mischel (ed.), *Cognitive Development and Epistemology* (New York: Academic Press, 1971), pp. 164–164.

[6] J. Dewey, "What Psychology Can Do for the Teacher," In R. Archambault (ed.), *John Dewey on Education: Selected Writings* (New York: Random House, 1964), p. 207.

[7] D. Boyd and L. Kohlberg, "The Is-Ought Problem: A Developmental Perspective," *Zygon*, 1973, *8*, 360–361.

ity over time in ways which will enable them to use more adequate and complex reasoning patterns to solve moral problems. The principle central to the development of stages of moral judgment, and hence to proposals for moral education, is that of *justice.* Justice, the primary regard for the value and equality of all human beings and for reciprocity in human relations, is a basic and universal standard. Using justice as the organizing principle for moral education meets the following criteria: It guarantees freedom of belief; it employs a philosophically justifiable concept of morality, and it is based on the psychological facts of human development. The stages may be seen as representing increasingly adequate conceptions of justice and as reflecting an expanding capacity for empathy, for taking the role of the other. And in the end the two are the same thing because the most just solution is the one which takes into account the positions or rights of all the individuals involved. The expansion of empathy thus, in turn, leads to an expansion of points of view and this expansion defines the three levels of moral judgment into which the six stages subdivide.

At the first or preconventional level the individual sees moral dilemmas in terms of the individual needs of the people involved. Situations of moral conflict are seen as situations in which needs collide and are resolved either in terms of who has the most power in the situation (Stage 1) or in terms of simple individual responsibility for one's own welfare (Stage 2) except where bound by simple market-place notions of reciprocity.

These formulations are perfectly consonant with the child's experience. For a young child power is perhaps the most salient characteristic of his social world (Stage 1) and as he learns to see conflicts between conformity to power and individual interests, he shifts to a notion of right as serving in-

dividual interests. However, as the child becomes increasingly involved in mutual relationships and sees himself as a sharing and participating member of groups, he sees the individual point of view toward morality as inadequate to deal with the kinds of moral conflicts which confront him. He has then two choices: he can hold on to his preconventional philosophy and simplify experience, or he can expand his philosophy so that it can take into account the expanding complexity of his experience.

The second two stages of moral development are termed "conventional" in that moral conflicts are now seen and resolved in group or social terms rather than in individual terms. Right or justice is seen to reside in interpersonal social relationships (Stage 3) or in the community (Stage 4). At the conventional levels there is an appeal to authority but the authority derives its right to define the good not from greater power as at Stage 1, but from its social sharedness and legitimacy.

However, if society defines the right and the good, what is one to think when one recognizes that different societies choose differently in what they label as good and bad, right and wrong? Eskimos think it is right to leave old people out in the snow to die. When abortions were illegal in this country, they were legal in Sweden. With the increasing exposure of everyone to how others live, there is a greater recognition of the fact that our way is only one among many.

If one cannot simply equate the right with the societal and the legal, then what is one to do? We have found that adolescents may go through a period of ethical relativism during which they question the premises of any moral system. If there are many ways to live, who can presume to say which is best? Perhaps everyone should do as he or she chooses.

The way out of this moral relativism or

moral nihilism lies through the perception that underneath the rules of any given society lie moral principles and universal moral rights, and the validity of any moral choice rests on the principles that choice embodies. Such moral principles are universal in their application and constitute a viable standard against which the particular laws or conventions of any society can and should be judged. When obedience to laws violates moral principles or rights, it is right to violate such laws.

At the last two stages, then, choice is based on the principles that supersede convention, just as previously the claims of society or convention were seen as the grounds for adjudicating differences between individuals. This, then, is the sequence of moral development.

What spurs progress from one stage to another and why do some individuals reach the principled stages while others do not? Moral judgment, while primarily a rational operation, is influenced by affective factors such as the ability to empathize and the capacity for guilt. But moral situations are defined cognitively by the judging individual in social interactions. It is this interaction with one's environment which determines development of moral reasoning.

Social interaction requires the assumption of a variety of roles and the entering into a variety of reciprocal relationships. Such relationships demand that one take others' perspectives (role-taking). It is this reworking of one's role-taking experiences into successively more complex and adequate forms of justice which is called moral development. Thus moral development results from the dialogue between the person's cognitive structure and the complexity presented by environment. This interactionist definition of moral development demands an environment which will facilitate dialogue between the self and others. The more one encounters situations

of moral conflict that are not adequately resolved by one's present reasoning structure, the more likely one is to develop more complex ways of thinking about and resolving such conflicts.

What can teachers and schools do to stimulate moral development? The teacher must help the student to consider genuine moral conflicts, think about the reasoning he uses in solving such conflicts, see inconsistencies and inadequacies in his way of thinking and find ways of resolving them. Classroom moral discussion are one example of how the cognitive-development approach can be applied in the school. Much of the moral development research in schools has focused on moral discussions as the vehicle for stimulating cognitive conflict. But such discussions, if too often used, will become pedantic. The classroom discussion approach should be part of a broader, more enduring involvement of students in the social and moral functioning of the school. Rather than attempting to inculcate a predetermined and unquestioned set of values, teachers should challenge students with the moral issues faced by the school community as problems to be solved, not merely situations in which rules are mechanically applied. One must create a "just community."

At present, the schools themselves are not especially moral institutions. Institutional relationships tend to be based more on authority than on ideas of justice. Adults are often less interested in discovering *how* children are thinking than in telling them *what* to think. The school atmosphere is generally a blend of Stage 1, punishment morality, and Stage 4, "law and order," which fails to impress or stimulate children involved in their own Stage 2 or Stage 3 moral philosophies. Children and adults stop communicating with one another, horizons are narrowed and development is stunted. If schools wish to foster morality, they will have to provide an atmosphere in which interpersonal issues are settled on the basis of principle rather than power. They will have to take moral questions seriously and provide food for thought instead of conventional "right answers."

We do not claim that the theory of cognitive moral development is sufficient to the task of moral education. . . . There are three major areas in which the cognitive development approach to moral education is incomplete: 1) the stress placed on form rather than content 2) the focus on concepts of rights and duties rather than issues of the good 3) the emphasis on moral judgment rather than behavior.

We have previously mentioned the distinction between form and content. That we have chosen to delineate the form or structure of moral judgments does not deny the importance of the moral content of school curriculum. That textbooks and other curricula materials have reflected and perhaps reinforced racism, sexism and ethnocentrisms is to be decried. It is imperative that the content of curriculum for moral education be construed so as to avoid unfair characterizations of others as well as promote opportunities for structural development. The integration of curriculum content is exemplified by articles in this issue by Lickona, Bramble and Garrod, and the Ladenburgs. Additional work in this content dimension is required if educators wish to incorporate the cognitive developmental approach to moral education in the curriculum.

We have stressed in this "theory" the concern for what is right, what is just or fair. To ask "what is right?" or "what ought I do in this situation?" presumes that notions of what is "good" are in conflict. But,

We are not describing how men formulate different conceptions of the good, the good life, intrinsic value, or purpose. Nor are we discussing how men develop certain kinds of character traits and learn to recognize these traits in judgments of approbation and disapprobation. Instead, we are concentrating on that aspect of morality that is brought to the fore by problematic situations of conflicting claims, whether the conflict is between individuals, groups, societies, or institutions, and whether the source of the conflict lies in incompatible claims based on conceptions of the good, beliefs about human purpose, or character assessments. In short, we intend the term "moral" to be understood in the restricted sense of referring to situations which call for judgments involving denotological concepts such as right and wrong, duty and obligation, having a right, fairness, etc., although such judgments may (or may not) involve either or both of the other two basic concepts or their derivatives.[8]

This is not to say that questions of "good" are less important or need not to be asked. Rather it is an acknowledgement that the cognitive developmental approach is limited in scope and requires that attention be paid to such issues in the development of any moral education program.

The relationship between moral judgment and moral behavior is not fully defined. That is, moral judgment is a necessary but not sufficient condition for moral action. Other variables come into play such as emotion, and a general sense of will, purpose or ego strength. Moral judgment is the only distinctive *moral* factor in moral behavior but not the only factor in such behavior. Educators who are looking for answers as to how to "get children to behave" often meaning to rid themselves of discipline problems will not find *the* answer in one theory. We hypothesize that behavior when informed by mature moral judgment is influenced by level of

_____

[8] *Ibid.*, p. 360.

moral development.[9] Further research in this crucial area is needed.

[9] The relationship between moral judgment and moral behavior is more fully discussed in: Kohlberg, 1976 "Moral Stages," L. Kohlberg, "Stage and Sequence: The Cognitive Developmental Approach to Socialization," in D. A. Goslin (ed.) *Handbook of Socialization Theory and Research*, vol. I (New York: Russell Sage Foundation, 1964), pp. 383–432.

Cognitive developmental moral education is rooted in a substantial empirical and philosophical base. The theory is complex and as suggested above insufficient to the task claimed by "moral education." Within limits, however, the theory has informing power for the practitioner. Resourceful practice is required both to validate and inform the theory.

A Reply to Kohlberg
"Why Doesn't Lawrence Kohlberg Do His Homework?"

Richard S. Peters

Someone said to Bernard Shaw that he was like the Venus de Milo. What there was of him was excellent. The same, I think, needs to be said of Kohlberg. The trouble is, however, that Kohlberg remains quite impervious to criticisms of the limitations of his view of moral education. He has never answered, for instance, a series of very constructive criticisms leveled against him by myself and Bill Alston in the Binghampton conference of 1969.[1] It is not that the stuff he continues to ladle out is not very good. It is, and I have

made much use of it myself.[2] It is simply that he remains oblivious of the many other important aspects of moral education, and there is a danger that the unwary will think he has told the whole story. In a commentary of this length, I can only list the main omissions.

1. He suffers from the rather touching belief that a Kantian type of morality, represented in modern times most notably by Hare and Rawls, is the only one.[3] He fails to grasp that utilitarianism, in which the principle of

[1] See Theodore Mischel, *Cognitive Development and Epistemology* (New York: Academic Press, 1971).

[2] See articles collected in Part 2 of Richard S. Peters, *Psychology and Ethical Development* (London: Allen and Unwin, 1974).

From Richard S. Peters, "A Reply to Kohlberg," Phi Delta Kappan, LVI (June 1975): 678.

justice is problematic, is an alternative type of morality and that people such as Winch have put forward a morality of integrity in which the principle of universalizability is problematic.[4] I think this can be carried forward, actually. A morality of courage as exemplified by train robbers, the old "virtue" of Machiavelli's *Prince*, is a defensible morality. So also is a more romantic type of morality such as that of D. H. Lawrence, in which trust must be placed in "the dark God within." It is either sheer legislation to say that Kohlberg's morality is the true one, or it is the worst form of the naturalistic fallacy which argues from how "morality" is ordinarily used to what morality is.

2. He does not take "good-boy" morality seriously enough either from a practical or from a theoretical point of view. Practically speaking, since few are likely to emerge beyond Kohlberg's States 3 and 4, it is important that our fellow citizens should be well bedded down at one or the other of the stages. The policeman cannot always be present, and if I am lying in the gutter after being robbed it is somewhat otiose to speculate at what stage the mugger is. My regret must surely be that he had not at least got a conventional morality well instilled in him. Theoretically, too, the good-boy stage is crucial; for at this stage the child learns from the inside, as it were, what it is to follow a rule. Unless he has learned this well (whatever it means!), the notion of following his *own* rules at the autonomous stage is unintelligible. Kohlberg does

not appreciate, either, that moral rules have to be learned in the face of counter-inclinations. Otherwise there would, in general, be no point to them. Hence the necessity at these stages for the type of reinforcement advocated by Skinner and others and for the modeling processes so stressed by Bronfenbrenner in his *Two Worlds of Childhood*.[5] In particular, he ignores the masterly chapter on "The Unmaking of the American Child." He seems sublimely unaware, too, of the mass of evidence about other aspects of moral education collected by Hoffman in Musen's *Carmichael's Manual of Child Psychology*.[6]

3. As Bill Alston stresses in his article[7] and I stress elsewhere, Kohlberg, like Piaget, is particularly weak on the development of the affective side of morality, of moral emotions such as "guilt," "concern for others," "remorse," and so on.

4. Finally, Kohlberg, in his references to ego strength, sees the importance of will in morality, but offers no account of the type of habit training which encourages or discourages its growth.[8]

I and others have written a great deal about these other aspects of morality and moral learning and development; it is a pity that Lawrence Kohlberg does not start doing some homework!

[3] See Richard S. Peters, *Reason and Compassion* (London: Routledge and Kegan Paul, 1973) and Iris Murdock, *The Sovereignty of Good* (London: Routledge and Kegan Paul, 1970).

[4] See Peter Winch, *Ethics and Action* (London: Routledge and Kegan Paul, 1972) and Sören Kierkegaard, *Purity of Heart* (London: Fontana Books, 1961).

[5] Urie Bronfenbrenner, *Two Worlds of Childhood* (London: Allen and Unwin, 1971).

[6] Paul H. Mussen, *Carmichael's Manual of Child Psychology* (New York: Wiley, 1970).

[7] See Alston's remarks in Mischel, op. cit., and Richard S. Peters, "Moral Development: A Plea for Pluralism," in the same volume.

[8] See Richard S. Peters, "Moral Development: A Plea for Pluralism," in Mischel, op. cit., and "Moral Education and the Psychology of Character," in Richard S. Peters, *Psychology and Ethical Development*, op. cit.

DISCUSSION QUESTIONS AND ACTIVITIES

1. How has moral education been handled by schools lately? In what respects are such activities inadequate?
2. Why has Kohlberg established stages of moral development? On what principles do they rest?
3. What is Kohlberg's aim of education? Is this aim an adequate one?
4. Explain the role that the principle of justice plays in Kohlberg's system.
5. What promotes progress from one stage to another, and why do some individuals reach the principled stages while others do not?
6. How can student's moral development best be stimulated according to Kohlberg's theory?
7. What is the relation between moral judgment and moral behavior?
8. Examine some samples of dilemmas used by Kohlberg to promote moral development, and assess their likelihood for doing so.
9. Administer these sample dilemmas to students at various age levels and try to ascertain their particular stage of moral development.
10. Has Kohlberg overlooked alternative forms of morality and, if so, is this oversight as serious as Peters would have us believe?
11. Does Kohlberg underestimate the importance of Stage 3 (the good boy–nice girl orientation)?
12. Is Kohlberg's theory weak on the development of the affective side of morality?
13. What role should habit training play in moral development?
14. Check what programs of moral education are used in your local community. Visit classrooms and, even if Kohlberg's approach is not employed, see what types of moral judgments are made and classify them according to the six stages.

SUGGESTED READINGS

Principal Works by Lawrence Kohlberg

"Continuities and Discontinuities in Childhood and Adult Moral Development" *Human Development* 12 (1969):92–120. (with R. B. Kramer)

"The Development of Children's Orientations toward a Moral Order: 1. Sequence in the Development of Moral Thought." *Vita Humana* 6 (1963):11–3.

"The Development of Moral Character and Moral Ideology." In *Review of Child Development Research*, Vol. 1, ed. M. L. Hoffman and L. W. Hoffman. New York: Russell Sage Foundation, 1964, pp. 383–431.

"Early Education: A Cognitive Development View." *Child Development* 39 (1968): 1031–1062.

"Education for Justice: A Modern Statement of the Platonic View." In *Moral Education: Five Lectures*, ed. Nancy F. and Theodore R. Sizer. Cambridge, Mass.: Harvard University Press, 1970, pp. 57–83.

"From Is to Ought: How to Commit the Naturalistic Fallacy and Get Away with It in the Study of Moral Development." In *Cognitive Development and Epistemology*, ed. T. Mischel. New York: Academic Press, 1971.

The Just Community Approach to Corrections: A Manual, Part I (with others). Cambridge, Mass.: Education Research Foundation, 1973.

The Meaning and Measurement of Moral Development. Worcester, Mass.: Clark University Press, 1981.

Moral Stages: A Current Formulation and a

Response to Critics. New York: S. Karger, 1983. (with A. Hewer)

"Moral Stages and Moralization: The Cognitive Development Approach." In *Moral Development and Behavior: Theory, Research, and Social Issues*, ed. T. Likona. New York: Holt, Rinehart & Winston, 1976.

"Moral Development and Moral Education." In *Psychology and Educational Practice*, ed. G. Lesser. Chicago: Scott, Foresman, 1971, pp. 410–465. (with E. Turiel)

The Philosophy of Moral Development: Moral Stages and the Idea of Justice. San Francisco: Harper & Row, 1981.

The Psychology of Moral Development. New York: Harper & Row, 1983.

"Stage and Sequence: The Cognitive Development Approach to Socialization." In *Handbook of Socialization Theory and Research*, ed. D. S. Goslin. Chicago: Rand McNally, 1969, pp. 347–480.

"Stages of Moral Development as a Basis for Moral Education." In *Moral Education*, ed. C. Beck and E. Sullivan. Toronto: University of Toronto Press, 1970.

Proponents

George, Paul S. "Discipline, Moral Development, and Levels of Schooling." *The Educational Forum* 45 (November 1980): 57–67.

Gross, Francis L., Jr. "Teaching Cognitive-Moral Development in College (A Generalist Approach)." *Journal of General Education* 32 (Winter 1981):287–308.

Herring, Mark. "Social-Moral Development and Individualized Instruction." *The Educational Forum* 46 (Fall 1981): 23–30.

Hersh, Richard H.; Paolitto, Diana Pritchard; and Reimer, Joseph. *Promoting Moral Growth: From Piaget to Kohlberg*. New York: Longman, 1979.

Lapsley, Daniel K., and Serlin, Ronald C. "On the Alleged Degeneration of the Kohlbergian Research Program." *Educational Theory* 34 (Spring 1984): 157–174.

Larsen, John A. "Applying Kohlberg's Theory of Moral Development in Group Care Settings." *Child Welfare* 60 (December 1981): 659–668.

Leming, James S. "Curricular Effectiveness in Moral/Values Education: A Review of Research." *Journal of Moral Education* 10 (May 1981):147–164.

Levine, Charles, et al. "The Current Formulation of Kohlberg's Theory and a Response to Critics." *Human Development* 28 (March/April 1985):94–100.

Modgil, Sohan, and Modgil, Celia. *Lawrence Kohlberg: Consensus and Conflict*. Philadelphia: Falmer Press, 1986.

Mosher, Ralph L. "Parenting for Moral Growth." *Journal of Education* 163 (Summer 1981):244–261.

Novak, Barbara. "Morality Reasoning among High School Students." *The Clearing House* 55 (October 1981):73–79.

Olson, John R. "Curbing Vandalism and Theft." *Educational Horizons* 59 (Summer 1981):195–197.

Rorvik, Harald. "A Comparison of Piaget's and Kohlberg's Theories and Tests for Moral Development." *Scandinavian Journal of Educational Research* 25, no. 3 (1981): 99–124.

Rosen, Hugh. *The Development of Sociomoral Knowledge: A Cognitive-Structural Approach*. New York: Columbia University Press, 1980.

Critics

Anawalt, Howard C. "Moral Development and the Quest for Justice." *Liberal Education* 70 (Summer 1984):43–52.

Codd, John S. "Some Conceptual Problems in the Cognitive Developmental Approach to Morality." *Journal of Moral Education* 6 (May 1977):147–157.

Conroy, Anne R. and Burton, John K. "The Trouble with Kohlberg: A Critique." *The Educational Forum* 45 (November 1980): 43–55.

Evans, Charles S. "Reliability of Moral Judgment Interview: Written Version." *Journal of Moral Education* 11 (May 1982): 200–202.

Falikowski, Anthony. "Kohlberg's Moral Development Program: Its Limitations and Ethical Exclusiveness." *Alberta Journal of Educational Research* 28 (March 1982): 77–89.

Frankel, Jack R. "The Kohlberg Bandwagon: Some Reservations." *Social Education* 40 (April 1976):216–222.

Gibbs, John C. "Kohlberg's Stages of Moral Judgment: A Constructive Critique." *Harvard Educational Review* 47 (February 1977):43–58.

Peters, R. S. "Moral Development: A Plea for Pluralism." In *Psychology and Ethical Development*. London: George Allen & Unwin, 1974, pp. 303–335.

Reid, B. V. "An Anthropological Reinterpretation of Kohlberg's Stages of Moral Development." *Human Development* 27 (March–April 1984):57–64.

Rich, John Martin. "Moral Education and the Emotions." *Journal of Moral Education* 9 (January 1980):81–87.

Schmitt, Rudolf. "The Steps of Moral Development—A Basis for an Educational Concept?" *International Review of Education* 26, no. 2 (1980):207–216.

Sichel, Betty A. "The Relation Between Moral Judgment and Moral Behavior in Kohlberg's Theory of the Development of Moral Judgments." *Educational Philosophy and Theory* 8 (April 1976):35–67.

Sullivan, Edmund V. *Kohlberg's Structuralism: A Critical Appraisal.* Toronto, Ont.: Ontario Institute for Studies in Education, 1977.

Wallwork, Ernest. "Sentiment and Structure: A Durkheimian Critique of Kohlberg's Moral Theory." *Journal of Moral Education* 14 (May 1985):87–101.

West, John D., and Bursor, Davele E. "Gilligan and Kohlberg: Gender Issues in Moral Development." *Journal of Humanistic Education and Development* 22 (June 1984):134–142.

18

Values Clarification

Values clarification is one way to help students choose their values freely while maintaining an open mind. It was initiated by Louis Raths and further developed by Sidney Simon, Howard Kirschenbaum, and Merrill Harmin. It is widely used in the United States today in many areas of the curriculum, including drug education, social studies, environmental education, reading, language arts, vocational education, marriage and family life, and other areas.

The program avoids indoctrination and inculcation of a fixed set of values; instead, it is based on a valuing process for examining, clarifying, and accepting or rejecting values. It posits values based on three processes: choosing, prizing, and acting. Choosing should be (1) freely done, (2) from alternatives, (3) after thoughtful consideration of each alternative. Prizing involves (4) cherishing and being happy with the choice and (5) willingness to affirm the choice publicly. Acting consists of (6) doing something with the choice and (7) doing it repeatedly, in some life pattern.

The teacher's role is to help students become aware and appreciative of their value position. The teacher does this by eliciting value statements from students, accepting their ideas nonjudgmentally, and raising questions that will help them think about their values. Many different strategies are used: "values voting" permits students to indicate publicly what they believe and discover what others believe; "rank ordering" enables students to choose among alternatives and explain their choices; "name tag" asks students to look more closely at themselves and tell others about one's values. Other strategies employed are values sheets, discussions, role playing, and interviews. Many classroom materials are available.

Roberta P. Martin's interview conveys the evolution and present status of values clarification, in what areas and settings it is used, its relation with other movements, and why certain criticisms of it are unwarranted. Alan L. Lockwood identifies and explains what he considers to be five shortcomings of values clarification.

Values Clarification: The State of the Art for the 1980s

An Interview with Sidney Simon and Howard Kirschenbaum

Roberta P. Martin

Roberta P. Martin is an assistant professor in the Department of Counselor Education, Mississippi State University. Sidney Simon is a professor at the Center for Humanistic Studies, University of Massachusetts, Boston. Howard Kirschenbaum is Co-Director of Sagamore Institute and Executive Director of the National Coalition for Democracy in Education, Saratoga Springs, New York.

Values clarification is a process that has been used widely in the past two decades by counselors and teachers in almost every facet of the educational world. The following is an interview conducted in August 1980 with Drs. Sidney Simon and Howard Kirschenbaum, two major leaders in the field. The interview attempts to assess the impact of values clarification during the preceding 20 years and to project the future directions of values clarification in the 1980s. The interviews were conducted separately, but since the same basic questions were asked to both Dr. Simon and Dr. Kirschenbaum, they have been combined for clarity and continuity.

Roberta Martin: Sid, you have been a major leader in values clarification since the beginning. What is your assessment of what has happened in the values clarification movement? Did it change, and if so, how?

Sid Simon: Well, the 70s were the great verdant, vibrant opening expansion of values clarification. The word was first used in 1957, to my recollection, and that was by my teacher, Louis Raths, when I was a graduate student at New York University. He first came up with that phrase, and how exciting those times were, Roberta. The next few years were spent in trying to refine strategies and in beginning to understand the theory better. That finally culminated in our book in 1966, *Values and Teachings* (Raths, Harmin, & Simon, 1966), a book which had phenomenal success. I am not sure many people realize it, but that book sold well over a half million copies and was adopted by hundreds of colleges and teacher education institutions. Well, that took us into the 1970s, and in 1972 we published *Values Clarification: A Handbook of Practical Strategies for Teachers and Students* (Simon, Howe, & Kirschenbaum, 1972), which was clearly the thing that gave the movement its momentum. That book also sold over a half million copies and from what I understand it is one of the books most widely ripped off at libraries and from teachers' desks. I'm not sure exactly if I should be proud of that, but it does happen!

The Values Clarification Handbook led to dozens of workshops all around the country. People came out in droves to learn values clarification. So, the 70s for us was the great sweeping introduction and attracted thousands of people to the values clarification work. Kirschenbaum recently made an estimate, and he said that to his best guess, a million people probably have had a values clarification workshop or seen a presentation on values clarification—that's a lot of people—so values clarification is known.

The years of the 1970s saw the extension of the values clarification strategies approach, and this was best expressed in two other major books. One was *Clarifying Values Through Subject Matter* (Harmin, Kirschenbaum, & Simon, 1973), which raises the notion that we can teach subject matter content with the values clarifying approach. It is a very useful book, and I hope that people who are reading this article are familiar with it. The other was a book of *Readings in Values Clarification* (Simon & Kirschenbaum, 1973), which is expansive articles on theory and application of values clarification. From that point on, the remainder of the 1970s began to see an abundance of books—books on values clarification in teaching foreign languages, books on values clarification teaching English, books on values clarification teaching human sexuality, et cetera. Values clarification began to be the underpinning of a whole range of discipline. It was during this time that more and more counselors became aware of values clarification, and I doubt that there are many counselors in these days who do not use values clarification as one of the tools in their repertoire. So we have seen the word spread, we have seen it go off in new directions, and we see it now coming . . . at clearly a crossroads in its existence.

Martin: Where do you see values clarification work going in the 80s? What will the changes be?

Simon: Well, I anticipated the spreading to audiences that have not yet been reached. For example, I think we'll see the health professions use values clarification in its practices, in its training, and in its applications. It is clear that nurses' daily tasks are dominated by values issues. Physicians, too, have come to realize that the simple problem of getting a patient to take his or her medications is a values issue. The physician can prescribe it and have hopes that it will cure the diagnosed disease or ailment, but until a patient makes a commitment to take the medication nothing much can transpire. The physicians are finding that it is very difficult to prescribe an exercise program or a diet change. These are also values issues that must be dealt with by that profession. I think we will also see more and more applications of values clarification in industrial centers. Business is coming to realize that, clearly, choices are based on values, and value choices dominate the market and also dominate employee relationships and personnel policy. We will see a use of values clarification in industrial business efforts. We will also see, I hope, an increasing use of values clarification in child rearing and the family setting.

All of these are places where values clarification needs consideration. Just this afternoon we had an exercise in asking people to decide where they spent the last four Saturday nights. We are coming to realize that these kinds of choices are things that many of us need to consider more carefully. It is not only teenagers who need to make those choices. We need to take a closer look at our lives. I continue to believe the phrase that Emerson said, "The unexamined life is not worth living." Values clarification strategies and the theory which supports those strategies create enormous possibilities of getting people to live life at a deeper intensity and help them to reach the fullest of their potential.

Martin: Howie, you too have been deeply involved in the development and growth of values clarification. What are your thoughts on the future of values clarification in the next decade?

Howard Kirschenbaum: It occurs to me that to some extent I give a response to that question in the book *Advanced Values Clarification* (Kirschenbaum, 1977), in the chapter under the "Futures of Values Clarification." I talk about what I think are some of the paradoxical trends. In many cases values clarification will become integrated and absorbed into peoples' professional styles, and it will fade from the scene as a separate approach; yet, at the same time more people who have not had prior exposure will be discovering values clarification. I think that graduate students will continue to do a considerable amount of doctoral research on it. I think the techniques will be taught in colleges of education and inservice programs, but not necessarily called values clarification. The techniques of values clarification are part of the education profession and other helping professions now, and they will be passed on. Some people will use values clarification to teach decision-making skills, other to teach value-clarifying skills, others as moral development strategies, others as just strategies to help students work more effectively in

groups—but the activities are here to stay.

I think the basic thing that values clarification does—which is to identify an important issue that has value dimensions and to provide an effective way for young people to identify their own beliefs and feelings on this issue and to share these and to interact with others—is something that is a part of quality education and something that is going to continue to take place.

Martin: You have mentioned that values clarification is becoming integrated with other approaches. This brings another question to mind. How will the interfacing or blending of values clarification with other aspects of humanistic education affect values clarification?

Simon: Well, what are the threads of humanistic education? One is an awareness of the whole person which includes the transpersonal, the spiritual, and–or intuitive. Values clarification is in perfect harmony with that. We happen to be more grounded in cognitive exercises, but we have a deep respect for the part that the transpersonal and the spiritual play in our lives. In addition, the benefits of touch and the tactile senses, the kinesthetic, have deep commitment in my own work. It is a natural extension of values clarification. I see values clarification being in perfect harmony with some of the therapies that are clustered under humanistic psychology or related to humanistic education. Glasser's Reality Therapy is so compatible with values clarification and so is Ellis's Rational Emotive Therapy. I think the threads of Gestalt and transactional analysis and reevaluation counseling all can be enhanced by the use of values clarification because the insights that have come from therapy need to be translated into change, and values clarification has always had its focus on change. So it is absolutely compatible with so many branches of humanistic education.

Martin: Are there any other changes that either of you see?

Simon: Well, I'm sure values clarification will have to face and deal with the "return to basics" movement. It's hard to deal or to talk to parents who are anxious about the economy who feel that unless their own children get all of their training in basics that are needed, they will not be suitable for the job market. It is hard to talk with them and show them what in Joel Goodman's phrase is "a return to the basics and a forward move to fundamentals." One of the basic fundamentals has got to be values clarification—how to make choices, how to know what you really love, how to take action, how to look at alternatives, examining the consequences. All of these processes are essential to what we would call a basic education. But we are going to have to do our homework and we are going to have to talk to parents and administrators in non-threatening ways to convey this message. Maybe we ought to do an article on how to talk to parents or to administrators about values clarification and why we have it.

Kirschenbaum: One of the main things we can say to parents and administrators is that values clarification can be combined with teaching subject matter so that students learn even more of the basics that they would otherwise. I describe research in *Advanced Value Clarification* showing how this assertion was supported in elementary reading, in high school biology, in driver education, and in other areas. The reason is not difficult to understand. Values clarification activities help the students relate the subject matter to their own lives—their feelings, choices, and

behavior. This dramatically increases the students' motivation with respect to the subject. It also makes class a lot more interesting, enjoyable, and memorable.

Martin: The 80s obviously set forth some strong challenges for values clarification, challenges which will require homework as you say. There are those who say that values clarification is a fad that is passing. It is my observation in watching school districts really become involved in values clarification over a period of time that changes are taking place slowly, gradually, gently. Is it not possible that the seeds planted during the prolific fast-moving 70s are just now beginning to show growth? There is a time for forging ahead and there is a time for waiting. Does that make sense?

Simon: Yes, it does. I think you have outlined the problems very, very carefully. The numbers of people coming to workshops have fallen off. There still are millions of people that need to know about values clarification, but there will not be the period of time of enthusiasm of the 1970s. And what we are in is what you have clearly outlined—a period of carefully filling in the holes—of people doing methodical, thoughtful work, to see that curricula contain values clarification, to see that work with the parents is done ever more effectively, to build support groups for teachers who do values clarification. We're out of the period of the flashy work and we're into what you call the solid building of the waiting work, and I think that it is very important that it be done and be done well.

Martin: There are those who oppose humanistic education in general and values clarification in particular. How are such groups affecting or going to affect values clarification?

Kirschenbaum: There are attempts to ban values clarification. Every now and then a piece of legislation or a school board decision says that values clarification cannot be used in schools. But that is untenable. That's like saying school teachers cannot identify an important issue for students to talk about and that teachers and students cannot talk to one another about their ideas on a topic. You can't ban that. Among other things, it is protected by the Constitution. Students and teachers have a right to think for themselves and say what they think.

But I think it's yet to be seen what effect certain elements will have in their attacks on humanistic education and education in general. It's becoming increasingly clear that there are well-organized and well-financed oppositions to humanistic education, values clarification, sex education, students' choosing some of the directions of their education, and so on. I think that it starts with the attack on humanistic education and, if that is successful, it goes on to banning sex education of any type in the schools, and then it goes on to eliminating a large number of books in the school library and reading programs, and it goes on to disallowing certain people who are different—whether they are homosexual or have liberal beliefs—from the teaching profession. And who knows where it will go from there.

So, I think as this becomes increasingly clear, as I hope it will, that those who have belief not only in the importance of humanistic education but in the importance of free thought and quality education in the schools will recognize that some very important issues are at stake and will get together to see what needs to be done to enable our schools to remain a very important part of our democratic system. I don't know which way it is going to go. I would like to be optimistic and say that people are going to realize pretty soon what's happening, and that the major organizations in the education profession, like the NEA and the UFT, will be among the leaders in standing up for the rights of professionals to do a good job of educating students for democratic living.

Martin: Two of the specific contentions of those who oppose humanistic education are that values clarification and humanistic education are amoral and atheistic. How do you address these concerns?

Kirschenbaum: I think that most humanistic education approaches are highly moral approaches. Basic to so many of them is the respect for persons, an advocacy to tolerance within the classroom, and emphasis of the importance of people understanding one another and working out their conflicts in a way that respects the rights and beliefs of all individuals. I think many of the humanistic education approaches and the curriculum that have come out of the field have encouraged young people to take a look at the real issues and problems in the real world outside and get involved in working on them. I think many of the approaches of humanistic education have asked students and taught students to take responsibility for their own behavior and to recognize the consequences of their behavior on other people. So it seems that some of the basic moral values of respect for persons, positive conflict resolution, communication among family, friends, and colleagues, and social responsibility—some of the great moral concerns that both conservatives and liberals share—are very much reflected in humanistic education.

In terms of religion, humanistic education doesn't take a stand on religious issues. It is not meant to. Reading programs in schools are *nontheistic,* which is different than *a* theistic. Most science curriculums are nontheistic. Math is nontheistic. Some of the skills that humanistic education teaches are nontheistic. What that simply means is that humanistic education, like most other aspects of public schools, doesn't attempt to tamper with people's religious beliefs and values. The fact is that many humanistic educators are priests, ministers, rabbis, and lay people who have firm religious beliefs! I would imagine that some humanistic educators are atheists and agnostics as well. I think many of the moral values of humanistic education are consistent with the moral values of most world religions, but it's not a theistic system and was never meant to be.

Simon: Well, values clarification and humanistic education have been attacked by certain fundamentalist groups in this country. And I feel sad about that because I can't think of anything that is being done in the schools that has a deeper base in paralleling what wise, sensitive parents are doing with their children at home. I clearly don't understand what the furor is about. But what we are doing seems utterly consistent with Christian beliefs expressed by almost any person who calls himself of herself a Christian. And still we are working in a secular setting. We try very, very hard to give equal voice, to allow people to express their opinions. But not just anything is called a "value." A value in our framework has a most demanding set of criteria—it must be prized and cherished, chosen after considering consequences, acted upon, et cetera. We insist on a rigorous search for values. What parents don't want their kids to look at the consequences of their choices or act on their beliefs? What I would dream of would be that the fundamentalists would become allies, realizing that millions of children don't get a fundamental background at home at all. And they come to school without any guid-

ance training whatsoever. The genuine concern that is expressed by some fundamentalists are concerns that we have, too. What we need, however, is that they actually read our materials and present their arguments in context with things they have difficulty with. We don't need uninformed reactions that come from propaganda because then no dialogue can ensue.

Kirschenbaum: With regard to values clarification being amoral, I just think the critics are wrong. I think it is as powerful a tool for building good people who live respectable and responsible lives as any set of tools I know. Just the rigors of the seven criteria which demand critical thinking, which demand the testing of consequences, and which demand closing the gap between your creeds and your deeds make it an extremely moral discipline. What some people are concerned about is that we raise moral issues at all, and that's true. We do sometimes raise questions, as the students raise questions about sexuality, religion, politics, families, money, and the like. Some people would ban these topics from the classroom. Well, that can't be done. If it relates to the subject area being considered—and there are certainly a fair share of moral issues connected to social studies, literature, science, and health, among other subjects—then I think the First Amendment and the traditions of academic freedom say the teacher and student have every right to read about, to write about, and to share their views on these topics.

Martin: Is there anything either of you would like to add?

Simon: Yes. Louis Raths died in 1978. This was 30 years after his conception and his brilliant innovation, and how proud I am to be carrying on work which that noble man started.

REFERENCES

Harmin, M.; Kirschenbaum, H.; & Simon, S. *Clarifying values through subject matter.* Minneapolis: Winston, 1973.
Kirschenbaum, H. *Advanced values clarification.* La Jolla, Calif.: University Associates, 1977.
Raths, L.; Harmin, M.; & Simon, S. *Values and teaching.* Columbus, Ohio: Charles E. Merrill, 1966.
Simon, S.B., Howe, L.; & Kirschenbaum, H. *Values clarification: A handbook of practical strategies for teachers and students.* New York: Hart, 1972.
Simon, S.B., & Kirschenbaum, H. (Eds.). *Readings in values clarification.* Minneapolis: Winston, 1973.

What's Wrong with Values Clarification

Alan L. Lockwood

Alan L. Lockwood is Professor of Education at the University of Wisconsin and has written widely on moral education.

I deliberately chose this negative title because I assume that Howard Kirschenbaum will try to explain what is right with Values Clarification. He has a much tougher job than I do. There are a number of serious conceptual, ethical, and practical flaws with the Values Clarification approach to values education.[1] Among them are:

1. The failure to distinguish moral from non-moral value issues.

2. The embodiment of an unacceptable moral

From Alan L. Lockwood, "What's Wrong with Values Clarification," Social Education 41 (May 1977): 399-401. Reprinted with permission of the National Council for the Social Studies.

[1] The position taken in this commentary is a distillation of more detailed argumentation developed in other papers. A. Lockwood, "A Critical View of Values Clarification," *Teachers College Record*, September, 1975. A. Lockwood, "Values Education and the Right to Privacy," unpublished mimeo, University of Wisconsin-Madison. G. Wehlage, and A. Lockwood, "Moral Relativism and Values Education," in *Moral Education . . . It Comes With the Territory,* Purpel and Ryan (eds.) McCutchan, Berkeley, 1976.

point of view best characterized as ethical relativism.

3. The reliance on assumptions and methods of approaches to therapy.

4. The use of methods which jeopardize the privacy rights of students and their families.

5. The absence of a persuasive body of research to support claims of effectiveness.

In the remainder of this commentary, I will briefly summarize these five shortcomings of Values Clarification.

THE FAILURE TO DISTINGUISH MORAL FROM NON-MORAL VALUE ISSUES

Values Clarification asks students to clarify their values on a wide variety of topics ranging from favorite foods to whether mercy-killing should be legalized. For example, suggested questions for the "Public Interview" strategy cover such topics as one's views on welfare policy, community injustices, career preferences, favorite sports, and current toothpaste preferences.

It appears that, for the advocates of Values Clarification, a value issue is a value issue; that there are no fundamental distinctions between decisions affecting the rights and welfare of other persons and decisions regarding one's personal tastes. Clearly, however, not all value issues are of the same type. A decision to support policies involving the termination of human life is different from a decision involving one's preferences in entertainment. Decisions of the former type are moral value decisions, while the latter are non-moral value decisions.

The moral/non-moral distinction is not always easy to make, but to pretend that it does

not exist is a serious shortcoming, especially in curricula used by social studies teachers. Social studies teachers have a general responsibility to engage in citizenship education. As part of this responsibility we should help students recognize the importance of social-ethical issues and the need to make considered, defensible decisions when confronted with such issues; we have no compelling interest in how citizens decide on matters of personal taste. Curricula, such as Values Clarification, which blur the distinction between moral and non-moral value issues are a disservice to one of the major goals of citizenship education.

THE EMBODIMENT OF ETHICAL RELATIVISM

Simply put, ethical relativism is the view that no value beliefs can be proven better than others; so, therefore, all value beliefs are equally valid. Two features of Values Clarification suggest that it, perhaps unwittingly, holds the relativistic point of view: (a) the advocacy of a non-judgmental classroom environment, and (b) the absence of justificatory requirements in the seven-step valuing process.

Participants in Values Clarification are urged to be non-judgmental in their treatment of others' point of view. The desired atmosphere is one of acceptance, nurturance, and unconditional positive regard. Disagreement over the rightness or wrongness of persons' views is discouraged; empathy, supportiveness, and trust are encouraged. The stress is on helping students make decisions with which they feel personally comfortable, rather than on helping them make decisions which they believe are morally justified.

In addition to the general absence of ethical argumentation, the recommended seven-step valuing process does not include any suggestions or criteria for such debate. Indeed, the seven criteria fit an almost limitless array of value positions. For example, the views of Adolph Hitler, Charles Manson, Mahatma Gandhi, and Jesus Christ clearly fulfill the Values Clarification criteria for possession of a value. Surely Values Clarification does not intend to nurture morally indefensible points of view, but, as currently formulated, it does nothing to inhibit them.

Any values education curriculum which rules out debate on the propriety or defensibility of moral value decisions is susceptible to charges of promoting ethical relativism. Relativism may be quite acceptable in the realm of non-moral value decisions, but is inadequate for making moral value decisions. Moral judgments require sound justifications, not simple expressions of personal taste. If not, how could we fairly and rationally oppose the views and practices of Hitlers, Mansons, Watergaters, and the like?

THE RELIANCE ON ASSUMPTIONS AND METHODS OF THERAPY

A variety of Values Clarification strategies and assumptions are drawn from therapeutic theory and practice. For example, note the strategies "Rogerian Listening," "Self-Contracts," "Chairs or Dialogue With Self," "Partner Risk or Sharing Trios," "R D As," and others in *Values Clarification* by Simon, Howe, and Kirschenbaum.[2] Similarly, the general orientation presented in *More Values Clarification*, by Simon and

Clark,[3] is in the tradition of self-disclosure group therapies.

Currently, most teachers are neither trained in nor authorized to engage in therapy with their classes. (Whether they should be is a separate question.) Inexperienced, amateur therapists in public school classrooms are likely to do more harm than good. I believe most teachers recognize this and would not intentionally choose to play a role without training and public acceptance/authorization for the performance of therapy.

The advocates of Values Clarification occasionally assert that Values Clarification is not therapy. This blanket claim is most misleading given many of their recent recommendations to teachers. Values Clarification should admit the therapeutic derivation and orientation of many of their suggestions and strategies and present them separately from the more conventional strategies. This would allow teachers and other curriculum decision-makers to better decide what aspects, if any, of Values Clarification they feel competent and justified in employing.

PRACTICES WHICH JEOPARDIZE PRIVACY RIGHTS

Many Values Clarification strategies are designed to encourage students to disclose information about themselves and their families. This is done through both explicit questioning and the use of projective techniques. Some examples of explicit questions are: Do you have any brothers or sisters? How do you get along? What does your mother do? Does she like it? Reveal who in your family brings you the greatest sadness, and why. How did you first learn to kiss? Did you ever cheat on

---

[2] Sidney B. Simon, Leland W. Howe, and Howard Kirschenbaum, *Values Clarification* (New York: Hart Publishing Co. 1972). Strategies are on pages 295, 319, 221, 177, 358 in the order mentioned above.

[3] Sidney B. Simon and Jay Clark, *More Values Clarification* (San Diego, California: Pennant Press, 1975).

tests? How many of you are in love right now?

In addition to explicit questions designed to obtain personal information, projective techniques are used. One example is the sentence completion type of strategy in which students fill in the blanks for such statements as Secretly I wish . . . My parents are usually . . . I'd like to tell my best friend . . . I'm trying to overcome my fear . . . Another projective strategy, "My House," asks students to draw a picture of their house and its family occupants. Then, students are instructed to write in what the people are saying to each other. Another strategy, "If I Were a Dog," is recommended to teachers as ". . . one way to discover how younger students feel without asking them openly."

Privacy rights should be respected unless there is grave social need for their abridgment. In public schools especially, we need to be conscious of persons' rights to privacy because schooling is compulsory, classroom discourse occurs in the presence of many others, and teachers have the authority to set and evaluate student performance. The potential for privacy violations in institutions characterized by coercion, publicity, and power is high. The usual privacy protections of prior informed consent rarely explicitly operate in public schools, so the application of strategies designed to elicit personal information is a genuine threat to the privacy rights of students and their families.

THE ABSENCE OF PERSUASIVE RESEARCH SUPPORT

The advocates of Values Clarification make a variety of claims regarding the positive effects of their approach on such variables as school achievement and attitudes, drug usage, reading ability, general self-concept, and classroom behavior. I recently completed an in-depth review of thirteen studies on the effects of Values Clarification and have concluded there is little evidence to support such claims of effectiveness.

For example, one study suggested that reduced drug usage was an outcome of Values Clarification.[4] The suggestion was based on a statistically significant difference between pre-test scores and post-test scores on a questionnaire in which students indicated the frequency with which they used various drugs. A closer look at the data and instrumentation is revealing. The largest obtained change was from a pre-test mean of 2.47 (according to the questionnaire this falls between drug usage "almost never" and "every few months") to a post-test mean of 1.96 ("almost never"). Given the questionable validity of self-reporting instruments on drug usage and the dubious distinction between "every few months" and "almost never," one should have little confidence, based on the study, that Values Clarification contributes to reduced drug usage.

Seven studies employed some measure of general self-concept, adjustment or esteem. With the exception of one study, the research on these variables was flawed by unwarranted statistical manipulations or interpretations. Space does not permit an analysis of these studies, but it is fair to conclude that even when well-designed and interpreted studies have found a statistically significant change, that change is very small numerically and, as a result, of questionable education significance.[5] Given these small changes

---

[4] Reported in Jay Clark, *Operation Future: Third Annual Report* (San Diego, California: Pennant Educational Materials, 1974), pp. 1-24.

[5] A. Lockwood, "The Effects of Values Clarification and Moral Development Curricula on School-Age Subjects: A Critical Review of Recent Research," *Review of Educational Research* 48 (Summer 1978): 325-364.

and the difficulty of measuring elusive, affective variables, one should be extraordinarily cautious in claiming that research supports the effectiveness of Values Clarification.

FINAL COMMENTS

Values Clarification is admirable for the simplicity and specificity of its recommended classroom strategies, as well as for the clarity of its general rationale. To this extent, hard-working, busy teachers may find it easy to incorporate into their instructional plans. There can be no question that Values Clarification has caught on. The rate of acceptance of Values Clarification appears to have outdistanced that of most recent educational fads. It is now time for a careful critical assessment of the approach. My criticisms are offered in that spirit with the hope that the advocates of Values Clarification will take them seriously and that teachers will be more selective in their usage of this approach to values education.

DISCUSSION QUESTIONS AND ACTIVITIES

1. Does the widespread use of values clarification in many different subjects and educational settings definitively demonstrate its worth and soundness?
2. Will values clarification likely get people "to live life at a deeper intensity and help them to reach the fullest of their potential"?
3. How is values clarification related to humanistic psychology and to certain therapies?
4. Does values clarification conflict with back to basics, or can it help students learn the basics?

5. Is values clarification amoral and atheistic?
6. Is it necessary for values clarification to adopt an ethical relativist stance in order to avoid indoctrination?
7. Why is it unsuitable for teachers to use therapeutic approaches? Are Lockwood's criticisms on the matter well founded?
8. Examine the literature to determine what research studies support the values clarification approach.
9. Investigate the type of classroom materials available for use with values clarification.
10. Invite a teacher who has successfully used a values clarification approach to class for a presentation.

SUGGESTED READINGS

Proponents
Aspy, David. "Fulfilling the Great Tradition through Interpersonal Honesty: A Response to Wynne." *Educational Leadership* 43 (Dec.–Jan. 1985–86):13–14.

Burton, Grace M. "Values Education for PreService Teachers: A Basic." *Contemporary Education* 53 (Fall 1981): 39–42.

Havens, Robert, and Morrison, Kenneth. "Values Counseling: A Clarifying Approach." *Counseling and Values* 27 (October 1982):36–39.

Howe, Leland W., and Hart, Gordon. "Counseling with a Focus on Values." *Education* 97 (Spring 1977):237–241.

Kautz, Carol. "Encouraging the Development of Value Clarification and Life-Coping Skills in Any Classroom Setting." *Illinois Teacher of Home-Economics* 21 (March–April 1978):177–178.

Kinsler, Karen Taber, and Sinatra, Richard. "Promoting Language Arts through Values Clarification." *Reading Teacher* 31 (November 1977):173–178.

Kirschenbaum, Howard. *Advanced Values Clarification.* Minneapolis: Winston Press, 1973.

Knapp, Clifford E. "The Values of Values Clarification: A Reaction to Critics." *Journal of Environmental Education* 13 (Winter 1981–82):1–4.

Logan, Donald, et al. "The Impact of Classroom Values Clarification Program." *Counseling and Values* 21 (February 1977):129–135.

McAninch, Amy Raths. "A Response to Boyd and Bogdan on 'Values and Teaching,'" *Educational Theory* 35 (Summer 1985): 321–330.

McEniry, Robert. "Values Clarification: An Aid to Adolescent Religious Education." *Counseling and Values* 27 (October 1982): 40–51.

McGinnis, Mary D. "Values Clarification." *Volta Review* 83 (December 1981): 466–474.

Martin, Roberta P. (ed.). "Values Clarification: State of the Art." *Counseling and Values* 26 (July 1982):220–274. Eight articles about values clarification: its history, issues, application, and future.

Piercey, Fred, and Schultz, Kay. "Values Clarification Strategies for Couples' Enrichment." *Family Coordinator* 27 (April 1978):175–178.

Raths, Louis, et al. *Values and Teaching*, 2nd ed. Columbus, Ohio: Merrill, 1978.

Schwarberg, Helene. "Let's Develop Survival Skills." *School Shop* 37 (September 1977): 33–34, 66.

Simon, Sidney B., and Clark, Jay. *Beginning Values Clarification: A Guide for the Use of Values Clarification in the Classroom.* La Mesa, Calif.: Pennant Press, 1975.

Simon, Sidney, et al. *Values Clarification: A Handbook of Practical Strategies for Teachers and Students.* New York: Hart, 1972.

Stanely, Toll. "An Implementation Strategy for 'Values Clarification'." *Clearing House* 50 (May 1977):385–389.

Thompson, David G., and Hudson, George R. "Values Clarification and Behavioral Group Counseling with Ninth Grade Boys in a Residential School." *Journal of Counseling Psychology* 29 (July 1982): 394–399.

Turner, Thomas N. "Critical Readings as a Values Clarification Process." *Language Arts* 54 (November/December 1977): 909–912.

Warnick, Barbara. "Arguing Value Propositions." *Journal of the American Forensic Association* 18 (Fall 1981):109–119.

Critics

Baer, Richard A., Jr. "Clarifying My Objections to Values Clarification: A Response to Clifford E. Knapp." *Journal of Environmental Education* (Winter 1981–82): 5–11.

Bennett, William J., and Delattre, Edwin J. "Moral Education in the Schools." *The Public Interest* 50 (Winter 1978):81–98.

Boyd, Dwight, and Bogdan, Deanne. " 'Something' Clarified, Nothing of 'Value': A Rhetorical Critique of Values Clarification." *Educational Theory* 34 (Summer 1984):287–300.

Eddy, James M., et al. "A Re-Examination of Values Clarification for the Health Educator." *Health Education* 16 (February–March 1985):36–39.

Feldmesser, Robert A. and Cline, Hugh F. "To Be or Not to Be: Moral Education in the Schools." *New York University Education Quarterly* 13 (Spring 1982):11–20.

Gluck, Phyllis Gold. " 'Values Clarification': The Engineering of Consensus." *Teachers College Record* 79 (December 1977): 267–274.

Kazepides, A. "The Logic of Values Clarification." *Journal of Educational Thought* 11 (August 1977):99–111.

Lockwood, Alan L. "The Effects of Values Clarification and Moral Development Curricula on School Age Subjects: A Critical Review of the Literature." *Review of Educational Research* 48 (Summer 1978): 325–364.

Loggins, Dennis. "Clarifying What and How Well?" *Health Education* 7 (March/April 1976) 2–5.

McGough, Kris. "Values Clarification: Your Job or Mine?" *Social Education* 41 (March 1977):404, 406.

Partington, Geoffrey. "(Im)moral Education in South Australia." *Journal of Moral Education* 13 (May 1984):90–100.

Smith, John K. "Values Clarification and Moral Nonexistence." *Journal of Thought* 12 (January 1977):4–9.

Suttle, Bruce B. "Moral Education versus Values Clarification." *The Journal of Educational Thought* 16 (April 1982): 35–41.

Wagner, Paul A. "Simon, Indoctrination and Ethical Relativism." *The Journal of Educational Thought* 15 (December 1981):187–194.

Wynne, Edward A. "The Great Tradition in Education: Transmitting Moral Values." *Educational Leadership* 43 (December–January 1985–86):4–9.

19

Sex Education

Various countries had different motives in the introduction of sex education in schools. Sweden, the nation with probably the longest tradition of sex education, introduced it in the 1920s to cope with problems of sex hygiene. In Norway in the 1920s, teachers involved in social welfare initiated school courses in reproductive processes. Universal and compulsory sex education is found today in European school systems in only five countries: Sweden, Norway, Denmark, the German Democratic Republic, and the Federal Republic of Germany.

Sex education began in the United States as a response to a societal concern about unwed mothers. After World War I the public became aware that youth had little knowledge about conception and reproduction; therefore, early courses were biologically oriented. Sociopolitical motives in the 1960s led to programs on family planning. Sex education has now broadened to include understanding one's sexuality and developing sensitivity to others'; programs draw from interdisciplinary sources. Sex education programs may refer to programs to help parents teach their children, to a single course for students, or to a spiral curriculum where the topic is repeatedly taught in school with increasing levels of comprehensiveness and depth.

Few sex education programs are found in elementary schools and, when discussed, the topic is usually incorporated into such other subjects as health, science, or social studies. At least 50 percent of secondary students receive some kind of instruction, but less than 10 percent enroll for a separate course. It has generally been found that knowledge increases as a result of sex education, but there is no clear pattern as to its effect on behavior. Methodological problems in sex education are of three types: the belief that knowledge alone will change behavior, the use of human subjects, and inadequate measuring devices.

Sex Education: An Overview of Current Programs, Policies, and Research

Asta M. Kenney
Margaret Terry Orr

Asta M. Kenney is an Associate for policy development at Allan Guttmacher Institute in New York City, where Margaret Terry Orr is a Senior Research Associate.

In June 1981, the Alexandria, Virginia, school board ventured into new territory. It approved an eighth-grade sex education course that included discussion of masturbation, homosexuality, incest, venereal disease, and contraception—all placed in the context of personal values. One board member voiced his surprise at the ease with which the course was adopted, as compared with an earlier experience in neighboring Fairfax County. "I thought we'd have a tremendous fight about the Fairfax Five [birth control, venereal disease, abortion, homosexuality, and rape and incest]," he said, "but we didn't." Is the Alexandria experience indicative of a new climate for sex education?

The sharp increases in sexual activity, pregnancy, abortion, and out-of-wedlock births over the past decade (see Tables 1 and 2) are of profound concern to many Americans. Almost 40% of today's 20-year-old women have had at least one pregnancy while in their teens. Twenty-one percent have had at least one birth, and more than one in seven have had at least one abortion.[1]

The reasons for statistics such as these are complex and not fully understood. Many experts believe that they are related to such factors as changing societal values that make sexual activity and out-of-wedlock childbearings more acceptable, changing family structures, the portrayal of sex in the media, the earlier maturation of teenagers today, and the ready availability of methods of birth control. To some extent, however, a situation that has always existed is simply more visible because more comprehensive data have become available.

In the face of a host of societal pressures favoring early sexual experiences, it is remarkable that births to teenagers declined significantly over the past decade, that pregnancies increased more slowly than might have been expected in light of the sharp increase in sexual activity, and that the out-of-wedlock birthrate climbed less sharply than

From Asta M. Kenney and Margaret Terry Orr, "Sex Education: An Overview of Current Programs, Policies, and Research," Phi Delta Kappan 65 (March 1984):491–496. Reprinted with permission from the authors.

in the 1960s.² These trends are certainly due, at least in part, to the increased availability of information and contraceptive services and to the legalization of abortion nationwide in 1973.

The need for sex education is confirmed by the fact that 36% of first premarital pregnancies occur in the first three months of sexual activity, before most of the young women have sought effective methods of contraception.³ Society has few ways of preventing unintended teenage pregnancies. Sex education is one method that offers two great advantages: it can reach all young people before they become sexually active, and information

can be provided to them at a relatively low cost through the schools and other delivery systems.

For several decades, sex education sought to help young people understand the physical changes associated with puberty, the biology of reproduction, and the responsibilities of family life. Today, however, most Americans believe that sex education should also address the complex problems of human sexuality that young people face. But a few people still believe that sex education—particularly when it covers methods of contraception—actually increases teenagers' sexual activity, causes an upswing in unintended

Table 1
Teenage Pregnancies and Their Outcomes: 1980, 1973, and 1970

	Pregnancies*	All Births	Out-of-Wedlock Births	Abortions*	Miscarriages*
1980					
Ages 13–19	1,181,000	562,000	272,000	460,000	159,000
Under 18	469,000	208,000	131,000	199,000	62,000
1973					
Ages 13–19	1,008,000	617,000	205,000	243,000	148,000
Under 18	442,000	251,000	111,000	128,000	63,000
1970					
Ages 13–19	997,000	656,000	201,000	190,000	151,000
Under 18	370,000	235,000	107,000	80,000	55,000

*Figures for pregnancies, abortions, and miscarriages for 1970 are estimates.
Sources: Pregnancies: *Factbook on Teenage Pregnancy, Tables and References for Teenage Pregnancy: The Problem That Hasn't Gone Away* (New York: Alan Guttmacher Institute, 1981); and Alan Guttmacher Institute, unpublished data. Births: National Center for Health Statistics, *Advance Report of Final Natality Statistics, 1980* (Washington, D.C.: Department of Health and Human Services, 1982); and idem, *Teenage Childbearing: United States, 1966–75* (Washington, D.C.: Department of Health, Education, and Welfare, 1977). Out-of-wedlock births: National Center for Health Statistics, *Advance Report . . .*; idem, *Teenage Childbearing . . .*; and Alan Guttmacher Institute, unpublished data. Abortions: Stanley K. Henshaw and Kevin O'Reilly, "Characteristics of Abortion Patients in the U.S., 1979 and 1980," *Family Planning Perspectives*, January/February 1982, p. 5; *Factbook . . .*; and Alan Guttmacher Institute, unpublished data. Miscarriages: *Factbook . . .*; and Alan Guttmacher Institute, unpublished data.

Table 2
Proportion of Unmarried Teenage Females and Males in Metropolitan Areas Who Were Sexually Active at Selected Ages, 1979 and 1971

	Age 15 %	Age 17 %	Age 19 %
Females			
1979	22	48	69
1971	14	26	46
Males			
1979	–	56	78

Source: *Factbook on Teenage Pregnancy, Tables and References for Teenage Pregnancy: The Problem That Hasn't Gone Away* (New York: Alan Guttmacher Institute, 1981).

pregnancies among that age group, and undermines the family unit. Thus sex education remains controversial.

Not suprisingly, sex education programs today are enormously diverse. They range from a short unit on menstruation to comprehensive family-life education programs that begin in kindergarten and continue through grade 12. Program goals are equally diverse. They include helping young people feel more comfortable about their sexuality, contributing to a better understanding between the sexes, and, in some cases (albeit relatively few), preventing teenage pregnancies. In addition to public and private schools, the sponsors of sex education programs include YWCAs, YMCAs, Boys and Girls Clubs, church groups (including Catholic ones), Scout troops, family-planning clinics, local health departments, and many other organizations and institutions.

Given the wide variety of programs, it is difficult to present a full and coherent picture of them all. We will focus primarily on those programs operated by public high schools—particularly those programs that seem likely to contribute to a reduction in unintended teenage pregnancies. But we must first point out the fact that relatively little research on sex education has been conducted, and much of the existing research consists of small-scale studies of local programs or suffers from the lack of a uniform definition of "sex education." Although we have made every effort to present the findings of the largest and most reliable studies, these data are by no means all-inclusive or conclusive.

PUBLIC SUPPORT

Numerous polls demonstrate broad support for sex education in the schools. In a National Broadcasting Company/Associated Press (NBC/AP) poll in 1981, for example, 75% of respondents said that they approved of sex education in the public schools.[4] More recently, a 1982 survey by the National Opinion Research Center found that 82% of adult respondents supported such programs.[5] Moreover, as Table 3 shows, such approval has been growing since the mid-Sixties.

Polls also show strong support for including information on methods of birth control in sex education courses. In a 1981 survey of voters by Yankelovich, Skelly, and White, 70% of the respondents said that they approved in disseminating information on birth control in sex education classes.[6] And, as Table 3 shows, a 1977 Gallup poll found that 69% of the respondents approved of this practice.

Parents strongly support sex education in the schools. Indeed, they are more likely to be supportive than other adults—by a margin of 80% to 70%—according to the 1981 NBC/AP poll. Moreover, the 1977 Gallup poll

Table 3

National Opinion Research Center (NORC) and Gallup Poll Findings on Sex Education In the Schools

	NORC*			Gallup**			Gallup†		
	Approve %	Disapprove %	No Opinion %	Approve %	Disapprove %	No Opinion %	Approve %	Disapprove %	No Opinion %
1982	82	15	3						
1977	77	21	2	77	16	7	69	6	2
1975	76	20	4						
1974	79	17	4						
1970				65	28	7	36	23	6
1969				71	22	7	55	12	4
1965				69	22	9	46	18	5

*Question: "Would you be for or against sex education in the public schools?"

**Question: "Do you approve or disapprove of schools giving courses in sex education?"

†Question: "Would you approve or disapprove if [sex education] courses discussed birth control?

Sources: *General Social Surveys, 1972–1982: Cumulative Codebook* (Chicago: National Opinion Research Center, 1982); and "Growing Number of American Favor Discussion of Sex in Classroom," news release from the Gallup Organization, Princeton, N.J., 23 January 1978.

showed no major differences between men and women, whites and nonwhites, Catholics and Protestants, or Democrats and Republicans in their support of sex education.[7]

Teenagers also believe that sex education is important. A University of Michigan survey of high school seniors in 1978 showed that 84% of those who had received sex education in school—and 88% of those who had studied birth control—considered these studies worthwhile. Seventy-eight percent of seniors who did not have any instruction and 77% of those who did not have instruction that included information on birth control wished that they had received such instruction.[8] A 1978 Gallup youth survey found that, among 13- to 18-year-olds, 82% of those who had taken part in a sex education course thought it helpful; instruction that included birth control information was almost twice as likely to be rated "very helpful" as instruction that did not.[9]

Opinions among educators are consistent with opinions among other segments of the population. A 1982 survey of school board members and school superintendents in Indiana showed that 82% approved of sex education in their schools, 49% considered contraception an essential topic, and an additional 31% believed that this topic should "probably" be included.[10]

Although Americans support sex education in the schools, they still believe that parents have the *primary* responsibility for talking to their children about sex-related topics. In a 1979 survey by Yankelovich, Skelly, and White, 84% of the parents of teenagers said that it was up to them to teach their youngsters about birth control.[11] However, parents say that they want assistance.

A 1981 survey in Fresno, California, showed that 81% of a large sample of parents with children between the ages of 10 and 17 thought that they "should not be the only ones to provide sex education"; 70% believed that the schools should also provide such instruction.[12]

Clearly, parents prefer to have some say about whether their youngsters will be exposed to sex education and what form that instruction will take. Public support for sex education drops significantly if it is offered without parental consent: a 1980 Gallup poll found that 79% of adults supported sex education with parental consent—but only 34% approved of such instruction without parental consent.[13]

Consistent with their support for sex education, most Americans also think that such instruction is likely to be beneficial. According to the 1981 NBC/AP poll, 67% of adults believe that sex education classes give students a healthy view of sex; moreover, parents of school-aged or younger children are more likely than other adults to hold this view. Fewer than 20% of the parents who were surveyed said that such instruction gives children an unhealthy view of sex. Meanwhile, only 12% of adults (9% of parents and 14% of nonparents) said that they believed that sex education will "encourage" students to become sexually active.

Several studies show that virtually all parents translate their support of sex education into practice by permitting their youngsters to enroll in sex education courses when they are offered. For example, a recent evaluation of family-life education programs in 12 California school districts, in which 18,000 junior and senior high school students participated, showed that 81% of the parents supported the program; over a two-year period, fewer than 2% of the parents chose to keep their children from participating.[14]

Finally, controversy about a program does not always indicate community opposition to sex education. Rather, it may reflect concern about the topics to be included, the lack of parental involvement, or the teacher's credentials. In most cases, an airing of these concerns does not jeopardize the program. A 1971 study of a national sample of large school districts found that three-fourths of the districts that considered instituting sex education actually adopted a program; of those that initially turned down sex education, many later reconsidered and adopted it. Furthermore, once a program was in place, fewer than 10% encountered opposition strong enough to lead to its elimination or curtailment. Indeed, almost half of the districts later expanded their programs as a result of the opposition.[15]

PREVALENCE OF SEX EDUCATION

Sex education is more prevalent than it used to be. The 1971 study of large school districts showed that approximately 55% of them offered sex education programs.[16] In 1977, 36% of public high schools (*not* school districts) offered *separate courses* in family-life or sex education, according to a 1977 survey by the National Institute of Education.[17] Meanwhile, an Urban Institute survey of almost 200 school districts in large U.S. cities in 1982 showed that three out of four school districts with junior and/or senior high schools offered some sex education—though not necessarily separate courses on that subject—in some or all of their schools.[18] An analysis of school and community characteristics using data from the NIE survey, revealed that no one type of school or community is significantly more likely than others to offer a sex education course.[19]

Surveys of students to determine whether they have received sex education reinforce these findings. For example, a Johns Hopkins University study in 1979 found that, in a national sample, 76% of females between the ages of 15 and 17 and of males between the ages of 17 and 18 had received some classroom instruction on human sexuality.[20] A 1978 University of Michigan survey of U.S. high school seniors showed that 60% had taken a unit on sex education while in high school.[21] A Gallup poll of 13- to 18-year-olds that same year found that 43% had taken a separate sex education course.[22]

CONTENT AND PRACTICE

Two major national studies provide insight into the content and organization of sex education in public secondary schools. One is an analysis by the Alan Guttmacher Institute (AGI) of a 1978 National Institute of Education survey of sex education teachers in more than 200 public high schools that offered sex education courses.[23] The other is the 1982 Urban Institute survey of almost 200 school districts in large cities.[24] Despite the five-year interval between these studies and their different approaches, their findings are remarkably similar.

Sex education courses have many titles (family-life education, human growth and development, and health education, to mention only a few), and these titles often reflect the differing content and emphases of the courses. Regardless of what they are called, these courses are considered a part of basic education, according to the school officials who responded to these surveys. The primary goals of the courses, these officials say, are to increase students' knowledge about human sexuality and to help them make responsible decisions about their lives. In only 37% of the programs described by the AGI study is the reduction of teenage pregnancy considered a primary goal. This holds true whether sex education is taught separately or as part of another course. Moreover, instruction is re-

markably comprehensive; about 18 topics—ranging from "drugs, alcohol, and sex" to "love and marriage"—are generally covered.

Given the goals of most sex education programs, it is not surprising that both surveys show the most frequently covered topics to be anatomy and physiology, pregnancy and child-bearing, and venereal disease (Table 4). Approximately 75% of the programs also provide information about contraception, abortion, and the likelihood of teenage pregnancies. This information, according to the Urban Institute survey, is usually introduced in grade 9 or 10. But these topics are apparently not covered in depth; only 60% of the districts that provide sex education devote one or more class periods to contraception, according to the Urban Institute survey—although 82% of the districts devote at least that much time to the study of bodily changes during puberty.

The 1978 University of Michigan survey of high school seniors reported that 49% had studied birth control in school, and the 1978 Gallup poll of somewhat younger teenagers found that 31% had been taught about contraception. A national survey in 1979 of unmarried females between the ages of 15 and 19 and of unmarried males between the ages of 17 and 21 found that about 65% had studied contraception—a higher figure that is probably explained by the facts that this study involved older teens in metropolitan areas and that the question covered both school and nonschool instruction.[25]

Topics such as alternatives to abortion, avoiding unwanted sex, and other moral issues are often included in the curriculum. But such controversial issues as masturbation, homosexuality, and (particularly) sexual techniques are covered more rarely, according to both surveys.

If not taught as a separate course, sex education is almost always integrated into such other subjects as family living, home economics, biology, or physical education and, according to the Urban Institute survey, generally occupies six to 20 hours of class time per year. The AGI study found that most instructors reported that their high school *courses* in sex education last five to 20 hours per semester, and 92% said that these courses are coeducational. The Urban Institute found that, at the junior high level, instruction is more frequently segregated by sex, with only 70% of the classes enrolling both boys and girls.

The AGI study found that teachers of high school sex education courses generally are certified in physical education, home economics, science, or social studies. Most teach these subjects in addition to sex education, and more than half had taught sex education for five years or more at the time of the survey. The average age of the teachers was 38, and slightly more than half were male. The most commonly used instructional methods were lectures and group discussions; 86% of the teachers used commercially developed instructional materials, but many also said that they prepared their own supplementary materials.

State laws and policies strongly encourage (and, in some cases, mandate) paren-

Table 4
Content of School Sex Education Programs

Alan Guttmacher Institute/ National Institute of Education (1978)		Urban Institute (1982)	
Topic	Frequency of Inclusion %	Topic	Frequency of Inclusion %
Anatomy and physiology	90	Physical differences	98
Pregnancy and childbirth	96	Pregnancy and childbirth	90
Venereal disease	97	Sexually transmitted diseases	96
Teenage pregnancy	90	Consequences of teen pregnancy	85
Contraceptive methods	78	Contraceptives	72
		Sources of family planning services	77
		Most likely time in cycle for pregnancy	79
Abortion	78	Abortion	47
Abortion alternatives	73		
Avoiding unwanted sex	65	Resistance to peer pressure for sex	76
Moral values	70	Personal values	82
Sexual techniques	6		
Masturbation	53	Masturbation	57
Homosexuality	52	Homosexuality	40

Sources: Margaret T. Orr, "Sex Education and Contraceptive Education in U.S. Public High Schools," *Family Planning Perspectives*, November/December 1982, p. 304; and Freya L. Sonenstein and Karen Pittman, "Sex Education in Public Schools: A Look at the Big U.S. Cities," paper presented at the annual meeting of the National Council on Family Relations, Washington, D.C., October 1982.

tal and community participation in planning for sex education. Surprisingly, the AGI study found that only 28% of the high schools that offered sex education had involved parents in the development of the curriculum. A similar proportion of these high schools (29%) require parental permission for students to participate; many others undoubtedly allow parents to request that their children be excused from instruction. Only 12% of these high schools actually involve parents in classroom discussions. However, the AGI study showed that, when parents are involved in curriculum development, more topics (and more controversial topics, such as masturbation and homosexuality) are included in the sex education program.

EFFECTS OF SEX EDUCATION

One of the most complex and least explored issues related to sex education is the critical question of its effectiveness. Sex education programs face an awesome task: attempting to modify, in a few hours of classroom instruction, the messages that young people receive every day from their friends, the mass media, and other sources. Furthermore, the link between knowledge and behavior is tenuous and difficult to prove, particularly since parents and educators may be reluctant to ask students sensitive questions about their knowledge of sex-related topics, their behavior; and their values.

Very few sex education programs have been systematically evaluated, and most of the evaluations that have been conducted have focused on college, rather than high school, classes. There have been virtually no attempts to conduct follow-up studies to ascertain the long-term effects of sex education on students' knowledge attitudes, and behavior.

However, a new nationwide study, conducted by researchers at Johns Hopkins University, does address the central question of the relationship between sex education and adolescent sexual activity, the use of contraceptives, and pregnancy.[26] The authors concluded that "the data seem to provide overwhelming support for the claim that the decision to engage in sexual activity is not influenced by whether or not teenagers have had sex education in school." They also found no association between sexual activity and courses that cover contraception. Perhaps the most important finding is that, if teenage females are sexually active, those who have had sex education seem less likely than others to become pregnant. Approximately 60% more white females and 70% more black females became pregnant if they had *not* received sex education than if they had. The researchers also found that young women who had received sex education that included discussions of contraceptive methods appeared somewhat more likely to use contraception the first time they engaged in intercourse and thereafter than those who had not received such instruction.

A federally funded review of the literature three years earlier reached one of the same conclusions arrived at by the Johns Hopkins researchers: no evidence supports the beliefs that sex education will increase *or* decrease the sexual activity of participants.[27] Meanwhile, other earlier studies have shown that sex education increases knowledge, as measured by tests before and after instruction. Studies of the long-term retention of such knowledge are lacking; however, a national survey in 1976 found that, among a large sample of 15- to 19-year-old females, those who had taken a sex education course at some point in their lives were 40% more likely than others to know the time of the month when pregnancy is most likely to occur.[28]

Studies of attitude changes among high school students as a result of sex education are rare, but available evidence indicates that students who are exposed to such instruction do not develop more permissive attitudes toward sexual activity. A recent study of 100 eighth-graders found that sex education increased students' knowledge but did not reduce their guilt feelings.[29] Another study of 100 high school students showed that these teenagers did not become more permissive in their attitudes toward sexual behavior as a result of sex education. However, they did become more confident in their ability to make "correct" decisions about their own behavior and more "liberal" in their thinking on family planning and abortion.[30] The evaluation of family-life education in 12 California school districts—and some earlier studies, as well—found that sex education could have a positive effect on students' self-esteem and decision-making skills, two qualities that appear to be strongly related to responsible behavior.[31]

One of the most important findings concerning the effects of sex education on behavior is that such instruction can lead to better communication between parents and children. In the evaluation of family-life education in California, about 70% of the parents reported that the program had improved their communication with their youngsters.

PUBLIC POLICY

Although sex education generally is—and traditionally has been—an issue handled at the local level, 31 states and the District of Columbia have adopted laws or policies to guide school districts' efforts.[32] In the remaining states, the decision to provide sex education and the methods of doing so are determined entirely by the local school districts.[33]

Maryland, New Jersey, and the District of Columbia are the only jurisdictions that have mandated the inclusion of sex education in the curriculum. Eight other states—Delaware, Illinois, Iowa, Kansas, Minnesota, Montana, Pennsylvania, and Utah—encourage such instruction. No state prohibits it, although Louisiana bars sex education prior to grade 7.

Where they exist, the state laws and policies generally encourage local school districts to involve parents and community members in planning of sex education programs. Eight states—Arizona (for elementary programs only), Idaho, Maryland, Michigan, Nevada, New Jersey, Washington, and Wisconsin—mandate such involvement. Moreover, most such laws and policies either require or recommend that local districts make provisions for pupils to be excused from instruction at the request of their parents. In addition, many states provide some guidance on program content. For example, seven states (Connecticut, Illinois, Maryland, Michigan, Minnesota, New Jersey, and North Dakota) and the District of Columbia support covering family planning in sex education programs; three states (Kansas, Ohio, and Utah) restrict it; and three states (Connecticut, Louisiana, and Michigan) restrict instruction that has to do with abortion. The District of Columbia alone requires that instruction on contraception and abortion be provided.

Small groups of parents have gone to court from time to time to challenge the constitutionality of sex education. Their most frequent argument is that such instruction constitutes the establishment of a religion, thus interfering with their rights under the First Amendment. Beginning with *Cornwell* v. *State Board of Education* in Maryland in 1969,[34] the courts have held that sex education is a public health measure that neither establishes any particular religious dogma nor denies religious freedom—as long as parents have the right to request that their children be excused. In *Smith* v. *Ricci* in 1982,[35] the U.S. Supreme Court dismissed an appeal by a group of parents who had challenged the mandate by the New Jersey State Board of Education that family-life education be provided in the public schools. This decision allowed the mandatory program to stand in New Jersey (where parents can exclude their children from such instruction). The courts have also made it clear that educational programs that cover birth control information are "neutral" in terms of religion, as long as they give equal time to all methods of contraception.[36] Finally, when parents have argued that their right to teach their children about sexual matters precludes school instruction, the courts have ruled that these parents cannot prevent other students from participating in sex education.[37]

Apart from the emerging constitutional framework we have just noted, there is no federal law on sex education. A policy statement issued in 1966 by the U.S. Office of Education (USOE) stresses the authority of *local* communities and educational institutions over sex education and proffers the support of the USOE (now the Department of Education) in initiating or improving programs. In practice, the department's role has been limited to providing technical assistance, on request, through a special projects section in the Office of the Assistant Secretary for Elementary and Secondary Education. However, legal authority exists for states and localities to fund sex education activities under Chapters 1 and 2 of the Education Consolidation and Improvement Act of 1981.[38]

In the Department of Health and Human Services (DHHS), the Office of Family Planning has spent approximately $3 million since 1970 to support a variety of projects, most of them related to curriculum development,[39] and the Bureau of Health Education in the Centers for Disease Control spent close to $2 million between 1978 and 1980 for several sex education research projects.[40] A relatively new federal program, the Adolescent Family Life Act of 1981, authorizes expenditures for family-life education programs that focus on "the problems associated, with adolescent premarital sexual relations"; approximately $3 million was spent on such programs in 1982.[41] All the DHHS programs have involved extensive community input and have been designed to meet community needs and standards.

Despite the perception of continuing controversy over sex education programs in the schools, it is clear that a broad base of support for such instruction exists. Sex education programs are also more widely available and broader in scope than has previously been assumed. Moreover, these programs are generally designed to reflect the needs and standards of the local communities, and the teachers who serve as instructors usually have considerable experience in teaching sex education and have relevant training in related fields.

It is also clear that young people can benefit from sex education. At best, programs that are carefully designed to provide information on the responsibilities of parenthood and on methods of birth control may help to reduce unwanted pregnancies. At the very least, sex education programs seem likely to increase youngsters' knowledge about the otherwise mysterious and confusing topic of human sexuality.

In locales where the schools do not yet offer sex education programs, individuals who are willing to propose that the schools consider doing so will find support among parents, students, and educators. Although a fear of controversy has probably deterred many supporters of sex education from proposing such programs, this fear appears to be exaggerated. With parental and community involvement, comprehensive sex education programs can be implemented successfully.

Where such programs *do* exist, however, it is probably unrealistic at this time to expect sharp declines in teenage pregnancy and sexual activity. Current sex education programs do not appear to have been designed to contend specifically with these problems. If the reduction of teenage pregnancy were made a major goal, better results might perhaps be achieved. Clearly, strong public support exists for including information on contraception in the sex education curriculum—presumably because the public perceives a relationship between such knowledge and a reduction in the number of unintended teenage pregnancies. Thus the topic of contraception should no longer be considered unduly controversial. Those communities that wish to see a reduction in teenage pregnancies may wish to reexamine their sex education programs in light of this information.

However, sex education in the schools will never be a panacea. Medical services have to go hand-in-hand with education. And, ultimately, the family will continue to play a far more pivotal role than any school or outside agency in setting an example and establishing values for young people and in providing them with the information they need in order to behave wisely.

ENDNOTES

1. Christopher Tietze, "Teenage Pregnancies: Looking Ahead to 1984," *Family Planning Perspectives*, July/August 1978, p. 205.
2. The Alan Guttmacher Institute, "Family Planning and Teenagers: The Facts," *Issues in Brief*, January 1982.
3. Michael A. Koenig and Melvin Zelnik, "The Risk of Premarital First Pregnancy Among Metropolitan Area Teenagers: 1976 and 1979," *Family Planning Perspectives*, September/October 1982, p. 239.
4. "Poll Results, NBC News September National Poll No. 70," news release, National Broadcasting Company, New York, 8 October 1981.
5. *General Social Surveys, 1972–1982*: Cumulative Codebook (Chicago: National Opinion Research Center, 1982), p. 161.
6. "It's Rightward On," *Time*, 1 June 1981, p. 12.
7. *Gallup Opinion Index, Report No. 156* (Princeton, N.J.: American Institute of Public Opinion, 1978), p. 28.
8. Jerald G. Bachman, Lloyd D. Johnston, and Patrick M. O'Malley, *Monitoring the Future: Questionnaire Responses from the Nation's High School Seniors, 1978* (Ann Arbor: Survey Research Center, Institute for Social Research, University of Michigan, 1980).
9. "Gallup Youth Survey: Teens Claim Sex Education Classes Helpful," news release, Gallup Organization, Princeton, N.J., 4 October 1978.
10. David Marini and Herb Jones, *Beliefs of Indiana Public School Policy Makers on the Role of the School in Education About Sexuality: Its Responsibility, Its Quality, Its Direction* (Muncie: Planned Parenthood of East Central Indiana, 1982).
11. *The General Mills American Family Report, 1978–79: Family Health in an Era of Stress* (Minneapolis: General Mills, 1979).
12. Memorandum to Solem and Associates on baseline survey, Public Response Associates, San Francisco, 28 October 1981.
13. *American Families-1980*, report submitted to White House Conference on Families (Princeton, N.J.: Gallup Organization, 1980).
14. Lynne Cooper, *Final Report on the Secondary Component of the Family-Life Education Program Development Project* (Santa Cruz, Calif.: E.T.R. Associates, 1982).
15. James Hottois and Neal A. Milner, *The Sex Education Controversy* (Lexington, Mass.: Lexington Books, 1975).
16. Ibid.
17. A parallel survey by the National Institute of Education found that 35% of all nonpublic high schools offered family-life or sex education; 38% of Catholic high schools and 24% of other nonpublic high schools offered such courses. Both of these surveys are referenced in Margaret Terry Orr, "Sex Education and Contraception Education in U.S. Public High Schools," *Family Planning Perspectives*, November/December 1982, p. 304.
18. Freya L. Sonenstein and Karen Pittman, "Sex Edu-

cation in Public Schools: A Look at the Big U.S. Cities," paper presented at the annual meeting of the National Council on Family Relations, Washington, D.C., October 1982.

19. Orr, "Sex Education and Contraceptive Education. . . ."

20. Melvin Zelnik and Young J. Kim, "Sex Education and Its Association with Teenage Sexual Activity, Pregnancy, and Contraceptive Use," *Family Planning Perspectives*, May/June 1982, p.116.

21. Bachman, Johnston, and O'Malley, *Monitoring the Future. . . .*

22. "Gallup Youth Survey. . . ."

23. Orr, "Sex Education and Contraceptive Education. . . ."

24. Sonenstein and Pittman, "Sex Education in Public Schools. . . ."

25. Zelnik and Kim, "Sex Education and Its Association. . . ."

26. Ibid.

27. Douglas Kirby, Judith Alter, and Peter Scales, *An Analysis of U.S. Sex Education Programs and Evaluation Methods* (Atlanta: Bureau of Health Education, Centers for Disease Control, Department of Health, Education, and Welfare, 1979).

28. Melvin Zelnik and John F. Kantner, "Sexual and Contraceptive Experience of Young Unmarried Women in the U.S., 1976 and 1971," *Family Planning Perspectives*, March/April 1977, p.55.

29. Guy S. Parcel and Dave Luttmann, "Evaluation of a Sex Education Course for Young Adolescents." *Family Relations*, January 1981, p. 55.

30. Loren L. Hoch, "Attitude Change as a Result of Sex Education." *Journal of Research in Science Teaching*, vol. 8, 1971, p. 363.

31. Cooper, *Final Report on the Secondary Component . . .* ; Hoch, "Attitude Change as a Result of Sex Education"; and Douglas Kirby, "The Effects of School Sex Education Programs: A Review of the Literature," *Journal of School Health*, December 1980, p. 559.

32. The 31 states are Arizona, California, Connecticut, Delaware, Florida, Georgia, Idaho, Illinois, Iowa, Kansas, Louisiana, Maryland, Massachusetts, Michigan, Minnesota, Montana, Nebraska, Nevada, New Jersey, New Mexico, New York, North Carolina, North Dakota, Ohio, Oklahoma, Pennsylvania, Tennessee, Utah, Virginia, Washington, and Wisconsin.

33. Asta M. Kenney and Sharon J. Alexander, "Sex/Family Life Education in the Schools: An Analysis of State Policies," *Family Planning/Population Reporter*, June 1980, p. 440; and the Alan Guttmacher Institute, unpublished, updated material, Washington, D.C. 1983.

34. 314 F. Supp. 340 (1969), affd., 428 F.2d 471 (4th Cir. 1970), cert. denied, 400 U.S. 942 (1970).

35. 89 N.J. 514 (N.J. Sup. Ct. 1982), appeal dismissed sub nom. *Smith* v. *Brandt*, 51 USLW 3331 (U.S., 1 November 1982) (No. 82-309).

36. *Citizens for Parental Rights* v. *San Mateo County Board of Education*, 1 Civil No. 33547 (Calif. Ct. App. 1st Dist. Div. 2, 28 August 1975).

37. *Supra*, at 32 and 34.

38. P.L. 97-35.

39. Personal communication with Elsie Sullivan, Division of Family Planning, Health Resources and Services Administration, Department of Health and Human Services, Rockville, Md.

40. Personal communication with Dr. Walter Gunn, Bureau of Health Education, Centers for Disease Control, Department of Health and Human Services, Atlanta.

41. Personal communication with Lucy Eddinger, Office of Adolescent Pregnancy Programs, Office of the Assistant Secretary for Health, Department of Health and Human Services, Washington, D.C.

Turning Children into Sex Experts

Jacqueline Kasun

Jacqueline Kasun is Professor of Economics at Humboldt State University.

The notion having long prevailed that anyone questioning the value of sex education must be some sort of unenlightened crank, it is small wonder that the topic receives so little scrutiny. There are, nevertheless, elements in the emerging sex-education movement that must raise questions in even the most accepting hearts.

It may come as a surprise to other parents, as it did to me, that the contemporary sex-education movement does not focus primarily on the biological aspects of sex. The movement's leaders and disciples are not biologists but mainly psychologists, sociologists, and "health educators." Their principal concerns are less with the physiology of procreation and inheritance than with "sexuality," a very broad field of interest running the gamut from personal hygiene to the population question, but largely concerned with attitudes and "values clarification" rather than with biological facts.

Thus, though the new sex programs are rather thin on biological facts, they do not skimp on information about the various types of sexual activity. From instruction in "French" kissing to the details of female masturbation, the information is explicit and complete. The curriculum guide for the seventh and eighth grades in my city of Arcata, in Humboldt County, California, specifies that "the student will develop an understand-

ing of masturbation," will view films on masturbation, will "learn the four philosophies of masturbation—traditional, religious, neutral, radical—by participating in a class debate," and will demonstrate his understanding by a "pre-test" and a "post-test" on the subject. A Planned Parenthood pamphlet, *The Perils of Puberty*, recommended by my county health department for local high school use, says: "Sex is too important to glop up with sentiment. If you feel sexy, for heaven's sake admit it to yourself. If the feeling and the tension bother you, you can masturbate. Masturbation cannot hurt you and it will make you feel more relaxed."

Homosexuality receives similarly thorough and sympathetic treatment in the new sex curriculum. In an article on "Sex in Adolescence: Its Meaning and Its Future," reprinted from *Adolescence* and distributed to high school teachers by Planned Parenthood, author James W. Maddock stresses that "we must finish the contemporary sex 'revolution' . . . our society must strive to sanction and support various forms of intimacy between members of the same sex." The sex-curriculum guide for elementary schools in my city specifies that children will "develop an understanding of homosexuality," "learn the vocabulary and social fads" relating to it, "study the theories concerning it," view films and engage in role playing about homosexu-

From Jacqueline Kasun, "Turning Children into Sex Experts." Reprinted with permission of the author from: The Public Interest, *No. 55 (Spring, 1979), pp. 3–5, 8–14. © 1979 by National Affairs, Inc.*

ality, and take tests on it. The teaching stresses the sociological, rather than biological, nature of sex "roles." A suggested class outline distributed to teachers by Planned Parenthood emphasizes the "cultural basis of sex: 'masculine' vs. 'feminine' behavior; how we *learn* society's defined sex roles."

Another noteworthy feature of the contemporary sex-education movement is its emphasis on separate individual sexual gratification, rather than on sex as an interpersonal act. Thus, authors John Burt and Linda Meeks, in their *Education for Sexuality* (W. B. Saunders, 1975), a text for teachers of sex, describe coitus briefly but dwell for pages on the "four phases of sexual response" of the separate individuals concerned. They liken sexual response to an individual's "jumping off a diving board" and suggest that junior high school teachers discuss in depth with the class "the person's [singular] feelings about sexual excitement and orgasm."

The instruction makes it clear that the source from which the person obtains these individual pleasures of sex—whether from married intercourse or from masturbation or from homosexual relations—is entirely a matter of personal preference. In a "sexuality" course for teachers, given recently by my county health department, I heard the instructor deplore the fact that so many otherwise well-informed girls and women "have never been told anything about masturbation" and "don't even know they have a clitoris."

AN EARLY START

To most persons first encountering the new "sexuality" instruction, probably its most striking feature is its precocious intensity. The Burt and Meeks kindergarten-through-twelfth-grade model curriculum begins with a mixed-group "bathroom tour" in the first grade, accompanied by the naming and explanation of the male and female genital parts. Children receive detailed instruction in male and female genital anatomy and human sexual intercourse in the fourth grade. Moreover, proponents of the new sex programs want them to be compulsory for all students from kindergarten through at least two years of high school.

Here in California state law still permits parents to keep their children out of sex classes by written request. Parents report, however, that they receive so little information about the times and nature of the instruction that they are unable to send in their requests at the right times. And whereas for most school activities requiring parental permission a signed permission slip is necessary, the law allows a child to receive sex instruction unless his parent specifically requests that he *not* receive it.

Planned Parenthood instructions urge sex teachers to maintain an "open atmosphere" in which students can "share" their feelings and "open up and talk freely about their concerns." One Humboldt County curriculum guide urges students to "thoroughly discuss their problems" in their sex classes and to engage in "total sharing" in such discussions. Teachers can accomplish these objectives and can "change teenagers' intentions" by "becoming the best friends in the adult world that many of these students have ever had," according to the Humboldt County *Family Planning News,* edited by Planned Parenthood officials and distributed by the county health department to sex teachers.

The "intention-changing" techniques are worthy of note. Rather than having the class register opinions by merely raising hands or casting ballots, the teachers of a sexuality class I attended would ask students holding various views to move to designated places in the room. Holders of minority opinions would thus find themselves conspicuously isolated in space.

With subject matter varying between the coyly sentimental and the grossly explicit, most class activities consist of seemingly innocuous, but clearly directional, mental-conditioning "exercises." Thus the Burt and Meeks teaching unit on homosexuality begins by having students discuss the changes which have occurred in male and female roles. Students then decide whether these changes have been beneficial for society. After this, they "role play" the parts of effeminate men and masculine women, and then they "collect magazine . . . articles . . . and pictures of famous persons who possess attributes of the opposite sex." The unit culminates with a vocabulary list of such words as *fellatio* and *cunnilingus*. Needless to say, the thrust of the conditioning process in this instance is obvious. A similar progression can be observed in all elements of the "sexuality" teaching.

By the time children are in the seventh grade, they will have been taught—and will begin to review—ovulation, intercourse, fertilization, anatomy (including ovaries, Fallopian tubes, uterus, vagina, hymen, labia, clitoris, scrotum, penis, testes, prostate, Cowper's glands), erection, ejaculation, orgasm, genetics, embryonic development, the several stages of birth, breast-feeding and bottle-feeding, and birth control. The curriculum in my city provides for seventh- and eighth-grade children to spend one-fifth of the school day for four weeks each year in "sexuality" instruction. During this time they are to review the above subjects and also take up new material on contraception, venereal disease, the "effects of overpopulation," the "need for mature and responsible decisions regarding population stabilization," homosexuality, masturbation, the "intelligent choice of a sexual life style," genetics, and abortion. They receive information about the legality and safety of abortion and the "services available" to them (i.e., the availability of abortion through the county health department or Planned Parenthood to any girl without her parents' consent or knowledge).

The teaching methods are as intense as the subject matter. Burt and Meeks recommend that teachers have students in every grade "take notes on the discussion and carefully organize them into separate units to compile a notebook on human sexuality." The authors say teachers should "encourage outside reading and the inclusion of additional materials in the notebook," and should have students "do some research and report to the class on the differences between human sexuality and the sexuality of lower animals." The National Sex Forum distributes for dissemination to school children pages of details regarding the male and female genital response during sex. The curriculum guide drawn up for schools in Ferndale, California, suggests that high school students work as boy-girl pairs on "physiology definition sheets" in which they define "foreplay," "erection," "ejaculation," and similar terms. Whether or not students are satisfied with their "size of sex organs" is suggested as a topic of class discussion in this curriculum.

The teacher of a "sexuality" class I attended distributed instructions for "Group Drawing of Female and Male Reproductive Anatomy," in which high school students are to "break up into groups of four to six persons, with men and women in each group." Each group then makes a drawing of the female and male reproductive organs and genitals, including the penis, scrotum, testes, vagina, clitoris, cervix, labia, and other parts. When the groups have finished, the teacher instructs them to check their drawings against accurate ones which she projects on the wall to "correct them" and to "talk about inaccuracies." The instructions for this exercise state that its purpose is "to provide a relaxed 'non-academic' means of reviewing the basic sexual physiology," to "provide a setting in which ignorance about physiology may be revealed without shame," and to " provide an opportunity to work as a group on a task." This activity has been included in the curriculum proposed for one city in my county. The guide suggests that though students may be permitted to work on this "exercise" as individuals, "the group experience . . . can help in . . . building . . . trust and sharing." In conclusion, the guide instructs the teacher to have students "discuss how they felt about 'drawing sex organs.' "

This enthusiastic pursuit of "self-awareness" in an "open atmosphere" extends to all aspects of sex education, including the programs for the mentally retarded. In their *Sex Education for the Developmentally Disabled* (Baltimore: University Park Press, 1973), Henry L. Fischer, Marilyn J. Krajicek, and William A. Borthick present explicit drawings of men and women masturbating and tell the teacher to elicit discussion by using four-letter words. The authors admit that parents may have "an underlying fear . . . that such talk about sex will create uncontrollable overstimulation." They nevertheless insist that parents and teachers should seize opportunities to discuss sex with retarded children, since the children know about it already or will find it out elsewhere. The fact that in either event the instruction is unnecessary raises a logical difficulty for all types of sex instruction, which its promoters counter by hinting darkly that all other purveyors of sex information are peddling mere "obscenities," in the words of Fischer and his colleagues.

SOME COSTS

In evaluating modern "education for sexuality," one natural question is: Is it worth it? In the spring of 1978 Carter Administration representatives testified before the House Select Committee on Population and suggested an additional $142 million be spent on the Federal government's teenage sex-education and birth-control program. Nor is this all. Numerous agencies within the Department of Health, Education, and Welfare channel millions of dollars into sex-education programs. Every hour, every day spent on sex education is time not spent on other school subjects. What returns can we expect from this huge investment? Though the increasing wealth of our society permits us to lavish on students more movies, books, pamphlets, wall-size anatomical drawings in full color, and other "instrumental aids" than ever before, the basic educational resource—students' time—has not increased. Children who are absorbed in "sexuality" instruction are not learning arithmetic, spelling, grammar, history, or music. Though some school administrators insist that reading and spelling can be "integrated" into subjects such as "sexuality," the evidence on this score is not encouraging: There were seven misspelled words on one page of the sex-curriculum guide drawn up for teachers in my city.

Still, large benefits can justify a costly program. Perhaps intensive sex education will reduce venereal disease or births to unwed mothers. There is, however, no evidence of any such results. In a recent pamphlet, "What Parents Should Know About Sex Education in the Schools," the National Education Association admits that "While many feel that sex-education programs are necessary to halt the spread of venereal disease and the rise in the birth rate of illegitimate children, there is as yet only meager evidence that such programs reduce the incidence of these phenomena." In her study, *Illegitimacy* (University of California Press, 1975), Shirley Foster Hartley noted that in Sweden—where sex education became compulsory in 1956—the illegitimacy rate (the number of illegitimate births per thousand females of child bearing age), which had been declining, subsequently rose for every age group except the older group, which did not receive the special sex education. Swedish births out of wedlock now amount to 31 percent of all births, the highest proportion in Europe, and two-and-a-half times as high as in the United States.

Proponents of sex education are aware of these facts. They accordingly deny that sex education should be expected to reduce illegitimacy or venereal disease (though they often cite such phenomena as "proof" of the need for sex education). They claim instead that its purposes are loftily intangible; ". . . to indicate the immense possibilities for human fulfillment that human sexuality offers," according to Dr. Mary Calderone, quoted in the Humboldt County *Family Planning News* of Fall 1977. Thus armed with inspirational purpose and millions of Health, Education, and Welfare Department dollars, the supporters of sex education promote it with missionary zeal. The superintendent of schools in my city rapturously described how the sex program would "dispel ignorance." In a long, suggested "Speech to Introduce Sex Education to the Community," authors Burt and Meeks promise that sex education is "education for love" which "will enable the individual to evaluate and effectively handle the consequences of his sexual behavior." Perhaps the summit of foggy aspirations is reached in two Humboldt County curriculum guides which promise that sex education will "develop a spiral of learning experiences to establish sexuality as an entity within healthy interpersonal rela-

tionships"—suggesting that, whatever else it may do, sex education will not advance the cause of literacy.

However, just in case the public is not as enthusiastic as the sex-education promoters, there are instructions for ramming the programs through. "Pack the board room with your supporters," advises Planned Parenthood of Alameda-San Francisco in its pamphlet *Creating a Climate of Support for Sex Education,* and ". . . avoid a public encounter . . . with the opposition."

RUGGED INDIVIDUALISM

The ethics behind "sexuality" education seem simple: "Stress what is right for the individual," advises the curriculum guide for seventh and eighth grades in my city. In making an "Intelligent Choice of a Sexual Life Style," the seventh-grader in my city is advised to set for himself a purely "personal standard of sexual behavior." No religious views, no community moral standards are to deflect him from his overriding purposes of self-discovery, self-assertion, and self-gratification. Carrying out these themes are a host of books targeted at junior high and high school students. In *Values, Rights, and the New Morality* (Prentice Hall, 1977), Jack L. Nelson advises high school students that much of previous history has consisted of sexual inhibitions imposed by the Catholic Church and similarly repressive institutions. He urges them to make up their own minds—under the guidance of their sex teachers, of course—about sexual morality, pornography, sex education itself, abortion, and euthanasia.

Despite the billing as "education for love," love itself is thoroughly debunked in the new programs. Sex is simply something with which one feels "comfortable," in the new view. A "sexuality" teacher whose class I attended guided her students through a lengthy list of "reasons why young people have sex" ("they want to prove their masculinity or femininity," "everybody else is doing it," etc.) without once mentioning love or marriage. "Romantic love," as portrayed in *Romeo and Juliet,* is an especially dangerous illusion, according to the new sex cult. It offers instead "rational love," which, according to University of Washington psychologist Nathaniel Wagner in his film *Human Sexuality,* can surmount the romantic impulse by envisioning the beloved sitting on the toilet passing wind while nosepicking and scratching.

Though rejecting traditional moral values, the new teaching is far from value-free. The new ethic, embraced and taught with all the fervor of the New England preaching tradition, is "responsible sex"—i.e., sex without parenthood, except under rigidly circumscribed conditions and in extremely limited numbers. Indeed, according to the Humboldt County *Family Planning News,* which is distributed to teachers, it is good to realize that one may not be "parent material" and to forego parenthood entirely. If people insist on having children, the *News* advises that there are "practical advantages to the one-child family," including "marital fulfillment," "lessened pressures from population growth," and "freedom to organize family activities without conflicts among children."

One school curriculum guide in my county carries out these themes by asking children to decide whether they are "parent material" by discussing "the problems that would be eliminated if I were the only child" and by lengthy discussions of family "conflicts" and "sibling rivalry." The guide offers a list of "reasons for having children," including the "desire to prove your femininity or masculinity (I *can* do it!)," "to make up for your own unhappy childhood," the "desire to be punished for having sexual relations," "to get back at your parents," and other motives

suggesting that persons who want children must, at the least, be socially inadequate, and, more probably, psychologically deranged.

The literature stresses how difficult it is to raise children and how unattractive they are: "Babies are *not* sweet little things. They wet and dirty themselves, they get sick, they're very expensive to take care of," warns one Planned Parenthood pamphlet distributed for student use. One local curriculum guide warns that "it is estimated that it takes $70,000 to $100,000 (not including mother's loss of income) to raise a child these days," that "babies need attention and care 24 hours a day," and that they often spoil marriages by making their fathers "jealous" and rendering their mothers "depleted."

But above all, babies add numbers to the population. Though modern sex education claims to relieve students from all anxiety regarding any means of sexual expression, it imposes its own burden of guilt: Those who add to the population "explosion" are guilty of unforgivable sin. The promotional literature makes it clear that the population-control purposes of sex education override any interest in "education for love" or "healthy positive attitudes." Fully one-quarter of the Burt and Meeks "Speech" is concerned with the "major problem of our times"—the population "explosion." The Speech states that the so-called "explosion" is responsible for unemployment, pollution, poverty, and starvation. The Speech tells listeners they have already "encountered the problem" on a personal basis while "attempting to get a bowling alley," "waiting your turn to play golf," and "looking for a place to hunt, fish or camp."

Not content with thus playing upon middle-class impatience at waiting in any line for any reason, the authors erroneously claim that "world population is increasing at a rate of 2 percent per year whereas the food supply is increasing at a rate of 1 percent per year." (In fact, the world food supply in the period since World War II has increased substantially faster than population, and per-capita food supplies are now at their all-time highs, despite attempts by several countries to curtail production.) The Speech threatens that unless the so-called "population explosion" is brought under control, average world food intake will decline to mass-starvation levels by the year 2000.

Nor is the Speech exceptional. The leading proponents of sex education have all frankly espoused it as the most effective and politically acceptable form of population control. In its *Implementing DHEW Policy on Family Planning* (1966), the Department of Health, Education, and Welfare touted its sex-education projects as a means of "effective fertility control," especially among minorities. Planned Parenthood and the Sex Information and Education Council of the U.S. (SIECUS) have long taught that sex educators have the duty to change people's values so as to reduce their fertility. As Dr. Mary Calderone, a leader in both of these organizations, put the problem of inducing people to want and to beget fewer children, "If man as he is, is obsolescent, then what kind do we want in his place and how do we design the production line? ... In essence, that is the real question facing ... sex education."

The sex curriculum adopted in my city places major emphasis on "population stabilization" and the "effects of overpopulation ... crowded housing, lack of farmland ... famine and eventual death." Seventh-grade students in my city are told to "consider future generations" and are shown films on the "overpopulation" threat. The teaching unit on "Contraception and Population Stabilization" instructs these seventh-graders in the contraceptive methods which they can use to avert the horrors of overpopulation. They are also instructed in "the permanent methods of

birth control—vasectomy and tubal ligation," which they can use to defend themselves against this threat, and are told where they can obtain this protection. To maintain the pressure, local health departments throughout the country distribute impassioned warnings about the population "explosion" in periodic newsletters; here in Humboldt County the *Family Planning News* regularly sounds the population alarm by reprinting and distributing to teachers sundry threats of the calamities to ensue from "excessive fertility." The so-called "teenage pregnancy epidemic" stimulates additional alarms.

The "values clarification exercises" so much emphasized in modern sex classes carry out these themes. The following "exercise" appears in Sidney B. Simon's widely-used *Meeting Yourself Halfway: 31 Value Clarification Strategies for Daily Living* (Argus, 1974):

> The population problem is very serious and involves every country on this planet. What steps would you encourage to help resolve the problem?
> [1] volunteer to organize birth-control information centers throughout the country
> [2] join a pro-abortion lobbying group
> [3] encourage the limitation of two children per family and have the parents sterilized to prevent future births

But, above all, the teaching emphasizes that the student should take responsibility for limiting his own procreation by means of contraception, sterilization, or abortion. Also, "if you're not supposed to go after a girl ... masturbation is a perfectly acceptable, useful, comforting thing," counsels Planned Parenthood in *The Problem with Puberty*, distributed for use in schools. Finally, homosexuality also achieves the movement's goal of separating sex from reproduction.

Though a full discussion of the population question would be beyond the scope of this article, it should be noted that the doomsday view of the subject is not universally, or even very widely, shared by knowledgeable specialists in economics and demography. The significant point, however, is that under the guise of providing publicly-funded sex education, a particular interest group has found the opportunity to promote its unique view of the population "crisis." In undertaking to finance and promote a multi-million-dollar program of public sex education, the government has entered very heavily into the promotion of a particular world view and the establishment of a chosen ideology, a kind of secular religion. That is a posture the public and Congress would do well to examine anew.

BIOLOGY OR IDEOLOGY

Future policy should avoid excess—even though the extreme actions of the sex lobby invite extreme responses. Sex, taught as a part of biological science, is a valid study—from eggs and chickens in kindergarten to the miracle of human reproduction studied in higher grades. Indeed, this is the way good schools, both public and private, have traditionally taught sex. Numerous excellent biology textbooks and other teaching materials are in existence to support this traditional scientific instruction. Nor is there any reason why those students whose parents want them instructed in various methods of birth control should not receive this information from their physical-education teachers.

The question of the degree to which schools should be concerned with "values clarification," however, is a thorny one. Schools have traditionally been entrusted with the task of "molding character," but this responsibility offers as well an opportunity for ideologues to propagandize. Clearly, the emerging sex lobby is making every effort to use the schools to mold minds in the direc-

tion of a new morality which claims that though sex should be freely and widely enjoyed, the principal human responsibility is to limit human numbers.

Those who oppose this reduction of all philosophical and ethical thought into a grotesquely simplistic capsule cannot ask that the schools teach *no* values, since this would be both logically and practically impossible. But what values? Certainly, at the very least, parents have the right to demand that the schools *not* be used to induce guilt in children and young people for aspiring to become parents. As an immediate, practical recommendation for sex education, the advice of a citizens' group in this county may have been as good as any: It recommended that sex be taught as a biological science, with the permission of parents, and it recommended that the teaching of values be regarded as family responsibility primarily, with the schools teaching "respect for the traditional moral values shared by most groups in our society."

The objectionable feature of the programs now being promoted by Planned Parenthood, the public-health establishment, and other members of the sex lobby is not that they teach sex but that they do it so badly, replacing good biological instruction with 10 to 12 years of compulsory "consciousness raising" and psychosexual therapy, and using the public schools to advance their own peculiar world view. One can only hope that not only biological science, but education itself, can withstand the assault.

DISCUSSION QUESTIONS AND ACTIVITIES

1. What plausible explanations can be offered for sharp increases in pregnancy, abortion, and out-of-wedlock births among teenagers over the past decade?

2. To what extent does public opinion support sex education, and what does the public usually want taught in such courses?

3. What topics are most frequently covered in sex education programs? What topics, if any, do you believe are neglected?

4. What effect does sex education have on students' knowledge, attitudes, and behavior?

5. What legal rights do parents have who object to sex education in public schools?

6. Do the types of materials found by Kasun in sex education courses differ from those reported by Kenney and Orr?

7. Kasun contends that sex education, as taught in terms of a new morality, is not worth the large costs because of its results; it also takes away valuable time from learning basic subjects. Explain why you agree or disagree on these points.

8. To what extent are sex education programs a medium to foster population control?

9. Review the sex education courses available in your school district and report your findings to the class.

10. Analyze and evaluate selected sex education textbooks.

11. Organize a classroom debate on the need of sex education programs in public schools and the content of such programs.

SUGGESTED READINGS

Alexander, Sharon J. "Improving Sex Education Programs for young Adolescents: Parents' Views." *Family Relations* 33 (April 1984): 251–257.

Brown, L., ed. *Sex Education in the Eighties: The Challenge of Healthy Sex Education,* New York: Plenum, 1981.

Dorio, Joseph A. "Contraception, Copulation Domination, and the Theoretical Barrenness of Sex Education Literature." *Educational Theory* 35 (Summer 1985):239–254.

Freud, Sigmund. *The Basic Writings of Sigmund Freud* ed. and trans. A. A. Brill. New York: Random House, 1938.

Gordon, S. "Moral Sex Education in the Schools." *Education Digest* 47 (September 1981):5–7.

Kinsey, A. C.; Pomeroy, W. B.; & Martin, C. E. *Sexual Behavior in the Human Male.* Philadelphia: Saunders, 1948.

Kinsey, A. C.; Pomeroy, W. B.; Martin, C. E.; & Gebhard, D. *Sexual Behavior in the Human Female.* Philadelphia: Saunders, 1953.

Kirby, Douglas, "Sexuality Education: A More Realistic View of Its Effects." *Journal of School Health* 55 (December 1985):421–424.

Kirby, Douglas; Alter, Judith; and Scales, Peter. *An Analysis of U. S. Sex Education Programs and Evaluation Methods.* Atlanta: Bureau of Health Education, Centers for Disease Control, Department of Health, Education, and Welfare, 1979.

Masters, W. H., & Johnson, V. *Human Sexual Inadequacy,* Boston: Little, Brown, 1970.

————. *Human Sexual Response.* Boston: Little, Brown, 1965.

Masters, W. H.; Johnson, V. E.; & Kolodmy, R. C. *Masters and Johnson on Sex and Human Loving.* Boston: Little, Brown, 1986.

Metzger, L. A. "Our Schools Have Enough of a Job Teaching Reading and Writing without Teaching Values about Sex." *Seventeen* 43 (September 1984):56ff.

Pollis, Carol A. "Value Judgments and World Views in Sexuality Education." *Family Relations* 34 (April 1985):285–290.

Ravitch, Diane. "The New Sex Education." *New Leader* 65 (December 13, 1982): 17–19.

Rienzo, B. A. "Status of Sex Education: An Overview and Recommendations." *Phi Delta Kappan* 63 (November 1981):192–193.

Scales, P. "Arguments against Sex Education: Facts versus Fiction." *Children Today* 10 (September/October 1981):22–25.

Schiller, P. *Creative Approach to Sex Education and Counseling.* New York: Association Press, 1973.

Schulz, E. D., and Williams, S. R. *Family Life and Sex Education: Curriculum and Instruction.* New York: Harcourt, Brace, and World, 1968.

Vance, Paul C. "Love and Sex: Can We Talk about That in School?" *Childhood Education* 61 (March-April 1985):272–276.

Further Thoughts on Innovations and Alternatives

Those who develop an innovation may use various thought processes and procedures. Participants in school settings may have a sense of uneasiness, a feeling of frustration, or a disequilibrium that signals something is amiss. They may then formulate the problem, set up hypotheses, test the hypotheses, and then either accept or reject them. But if the innovative process is examined from the point of view of the school system, the following changes are likely: (1) establishing goals and priorities (2) determining where changes need to be made (3) developing a model for an innovative program or practice (4) testing the model in a pilot program (5) modifying the innovation in the light of testing (6) introducing the innovation in appropriate settings and continuing to determine what further changes may be needed; and (7) once the innovation has proven successful, disseminating it to other interested parties and educational systems.

Take the case of merit raises. Dissatisfied school board members, abetted by the complaints of influential citizens, explore the reasons for low student achievement test scores. They then define the problem more precisely as how to bring about improved achievement, and they form two hypotheses: (1) if greater incentives and rewards are given to teachers, improved teaching will result and will lead to greater student achievement; and (2) a merit pay plan is likely to be the best way to bring about such changes. The next step is to state the goals and priorities more precisely. A pilot program may be initiated that involves selected schools or grade levels within the school district and, in light of the findings, a decision is made whether the innovation should be continued in its present form, altered significantly, or discontinued altogether.

TYPES OF INNOVATIONS

The innovations presented in Part II fall into different categories. Merit pay follows a measurement model borrowed from business and industry. It is assumed that there is a product that can be measured, and that performance can be observed and accurately tested. Moreover, material incentives will induce teachers to perform at a higher level; and those whose performance proves unacceptable will not be rewarded and may be discharged unless they develop requisite skills and abilities. Such a system, it is held, is more cost-effective because the incompetent are eliminated and rewards are distributed based on observable standards.

Bilingual education and mainstreaming stress individual differences and a compensatory model. Certain groups of students, it is believed, have previously been neglected or the education provided has been inadequate; therefore, new provisions should be offered to them in a more integrated setting.

Cognitive moral development and values clarification use a secular rational approach, in contrast to a religious approach based on faith or the authority of the church or sacred scriptures, or a secular approach that employs indoctrination. Cognitive moral development uses a developmental model of moral reasoning and a moral hierarchy, whereas values clarification employs exercises to choose values, prize them, and to act on them.

The excellence movement, though not of one unified voice, seems generally to be undergirded by a belief in essentialism. Many of the movement's proponents advocate a certain body of knowledge deemed necessary for all students to study, higher standards, a longer school day and school year, strengthening graduation requirements, and higher teacher preparation requirements. Emphasis is placed primarily on the student's intellectual development, not the total person.

ASSESSING INNOVATIONS

It is important to determine the significance of an innovation, its appropriate use, and its likelihood of success. Several factors should be considered in making a full assessment of an innovation.

1. Initiator of the innovation. Was the innovation introduced by an individual, group or organization? For instance, is a national, regional, or local organization sponsoring the innovation and how influential is the organization within the school systems in which the innovation will be introduced? As for groups, are the groups involved central or marginal to the educational system, and how open and effective are their lines of communications? If an individual, is the person part of the establishment or outside of it? For instance, look at the reformers in Part I. How would you classify them in relation to the establishment? Would it be more difficult to get their reform proposals accepted if they were not part of the establishment? But whether one is within or outside the establishment is only one factor; some of the others include the incisiveness of one's argument in favor of the innovation or alternative, one's speaking ability, access to and effectiveness in using the media, and backing by powerful public and private organizations.

2. Scope of the innovation. How many people are directly affected by the innovation? Does it affect part or all of an educational system? Does the innovation affect only local schools or schools throughout the nation?

3. Necessity of retraining. The greater amount of retraining needed before an innovation can be used effectively, the less likelihood the innovation will be successful (other things being equal). Some may resist an innovation from fear of change or lack of confidence in their ability to acquire the newly demanded skills or serious doubts whether the innovation will actually mark an improvement over present practice. Innovations that demand little or no retraining and are easy to understand, use, and evaluate are more likely to prove successful. This is true not only for teaching but business and industry as well.

4. Testing of the innovation. The innovation needs first to be tried out to determine its likelihood of success when adapted to a wider educational setting. Some innovations may not prove viable and will have to be discontinued or modified considerably before they can be broadly accepted. A Rand Corporation study of federal education programs found that a school district's accepting funding for a project did not mean that the project would be implemented the way the federal government intended. Many projects were not implemented and the few that were did not continue the innovations after the funding ended. Moreover, innovations were not usually disseminated to other school districts. Obviously greater supervision by the Department of Education and cooperation with local districts are needed to ameliorate these conditions.

5. Support. Both adequate financial support and support from influential organizations and key individuals are needed for innovations to have the greatest likelihood of success. Some earlier innovations, such as computer-assisted instruction in the early 1970s, were quite costly; other innovations, such as programmed materials, were much less expensive. Large scale funding, alone, however, cannot assure the success of innovations, as was found in the case of certain compensatory education programs of the 1960s and the curriculum reform movement that led to the new science and mathematics. Thus adequate funding is a necessary condition but not a necessary and sufficient condition.

Organizational support may be needed before an innovation may be widely accepted. In the United States, for instance, the backing of the National Education Association may mean the difference between success and failure for an innovation. Also to have an innovation supported by an influential educator provides a boost for the innovation's chances of acceptance. A boost was given to such innovations as programmed materials (from B. F. Skinner), the discovery method (Jerome S. Bruner), innovations in teacher education programs

(James B. Conant), and career education (Sidney Marland).

6. Likelihood of long-term success. Education leaders are reluctant to invest funds, time, and energy in an innovation without considerable probability of success. There is no sure-fire way to ascertain the chances of long-term success; however, the factors enumerated above may prove helpful in doing so. Thus before adopting an innovation the following factors should be considered: the initiator of the innovation, the scope of the innovation, the need for retraining, the testing of the innovation, and the support available.

Appendix

SOURCES FOR RESEARCH PAPERS

Encyclopedias and Research Summaries

American Educators' Encyclopedia. Edited by Edward L. Dejnozka and David E. Kapel. Westport, Conn.: Greenwood Press, 1982. Features nearly 2,000 entries pertaining to all levels of education; each entry averages 100–200 words, followed by a short list of references. An appendix lists federal legislation, award winners, education association presidents, and other data.

Encyclopedia of Educational Research. 5th ed., 4 vols. New York: Macmillan, 1982. This considerably expanded edition features 256 signed entries and 317 contributors. Intended for professional educators and interested nonprofessionals, the entries are classified under eighteen broad headings beginning with Agencies and Institutions and ending with Teachers and Teaching. Each article is followed by extensive research references.

Handbook of Research on Teaching. 3rd ed. Edited by Merlin C. Wittrock. Chicago: Rand McNally, 1986. Includes thirty-five chapters on such areas as theories and methods of research on teaching, research on teachers and teaching, social and institutional context, differences among learners, and teaching of subjects and grade levels.

The International Encyclopedia of Education. 6 vols. T. Husen and T. N. Postelthwaite, editors-in-chief. New York: Pergamon, 1983. International in scope, representing many different perspectives on education.

The International Encyclopedia of Higher Education. 10 vols. San Francisco: Jossey-Bass, 1977. Includes individual articles on educational systems in 198 countries and territories, 282 articles on contemporary topics in higher education, entries about 142 fields of study, information about education associations, acronyms, and a glossary.

Dictionaries

The Concise Dictionary of Education. Gene R. Hawes and Lynne Salop Hawes. New York: Van Nostrand Reinhold, 1982. In one continuous alphabetical listing, this source not only provides concise definitions for such pedagogical terms as *behavioral objectives* and *individual differences,* but it also gives biographical sketches of educational pioneers (e.g., Clark Kerr, Abraham Maslow) and identifies key programs and issues throughout the history of education (e.g., Outward Bound, *Bakke* decision).

A Dictionary of Education. P. J. Hills. London: Routledge & Kegan Paul, 1982. This is actually two books in one: an introductory text to the different areas of education and an alphabetical arrangement of terms. Part One provides an excellent overview of the various fields of education with short bibliographies for additional reading. Part Two, the dictionary portion, gives considerable detail, where necessary, and also frequently suggests further readings. Note that this is a British reference source, and the selection of terms has a definite British bias.

Dictionary of Educational Acronyms, Abbreviations, and Initialisms. 2nd ed. James C. Palmes. Phoenix, Ariz.: Oryx Press, 1985. This book, prepared by Palmes under the aegis of the ERIC Clearinghouse for Junior Colleges, identifies over 4,000 acronyms that have appeared in ERIC's *Resources in Education* and 150 professional journals in education and related fields of study. The dictionary is divided into two sections: Part I, the acronyms, abbreviations, and initialisms; Part II, a reverse list, with the full name of the term or educational agency arranged alphabetically and their corresponding acronyms.

International Dictionary of Education. Compiled by G. Terry Page and J. B. Thomas. London: Kogan Page, 1977. International in scope, the 10,000-plus entries range from the fine points of curriculum development and educational research to the colloquialisms of the classroom.

Abstracts and Indexes

Current Index to Journals in Education (CIJE). New York: Macmillan, v. 1–, 1969–. A publication in the ERIC system to cover periodical literature. It selectively indexes over 700 journals and provides separate subject and author indexes that refer readers to the annotated main entry section.

Education Index. New York: Wilson, v. 1–, 1929–. A monthly subject/author index in the English language that indexes over 200 journals, as well as yearbooks, proceedings, bulletins, and government documents. Its uneven coverage lists no author index from 1961–1969.

Resources in Education, (RIE). Washington, D.C.: Educational Resources Information Center, v. 1–, 1966–. RIE, which is part of the ERIC system and a companion volume to CIJE, covers unpublished or limited distribution literature. It includes books, documents, reports, proceedings, papers, and curriculum material by subject, author and sponsoring institution, and it includes abstracts of all articles listed. Many of the articles are available on microfiche.

Historical Sources

Biographical Dictionary of American Educators. 3 vols. Edited by John F. Ohles. Westport, Conn.: Greenwood Press, 1978. Provides biographical information about those who have shaped American education from colonial times to 1976. Included are over 680 biographical sketches of eminent educators who had reached the age of sixty, retired, or died by January 1, 1975.

Education in the United States: A Documentary History. 5 vols. Edited by Sol Cohen. New York; Random House, 1974. Brings together significant documents extending from the sixteenth and seventeenth century European background to the earliest colonial beginnings to the present. Each volume is prefaced with an historical overview.

Statistical Sources

Digest of Educational Statistics. Washington, D.C.: U.S. Government Printing Office, 1962–. A compendium of statistics on all levels of education. It has a subject index and lists successive years of data to give historical perspective.

Standard Education Almanac. Chicago: Marquis Academic Media, 1968–. An annual almanac that provides statistical data and essays on all levels of education. It features personnel, geographic, and subject indexes and is arranged topically.

U.S. National Center for Educational Statistics. *The Condition of Education: A Statistical Report on the Condition of Education in the United States.* Washington, D.C.: U.S. Government Printing Office, 1975–. An annual compilation of text and statistics on education in relation to political, social, and demographic factors in the United States.

World Survey of Education Policy, Legislation, and Administration. Paris: UNESCO, 1971. Provides basic information about the educational systems of most UNESCO member countries in terms of aims and policies, administration, and the legal basis of the educational system.

Book Reviews

Book Review Index. Gale Research Co., 1965–. Indexes 422 periodicals in quarterly and annual cumulative editions. Periodicals indexed are primarily in social sciences and the humanities, with some in education.

Education Index. New York: Wilson, v. 1–, 1929–. Book reviews drawn from over 200 journals are listed alphabetically by author in the back of each volume.

Index